MAJOR ACTS OF CONGRESS

EDITORIAL BOARD

MAJOR ACTS OF CONGRESS

VOLUME 1:
A-E

BRIAN K. LANDSBERG
Editor in Chief

**MACMILLAN
REFERENCE
USA**™

THOMSON
™
GALE

New York • Detroit • San Diego • San Francisco • Cleveland • New Haven, Conn. • Waterville, Maine • London • Munich

Major Acts of Congress
Brian K. Landsberg, Editor in Chief

LIBRARY OF CONGRESS CATALOGING-IN-PUBLICATION DATA

Major acts of Congress / Brian K. Landsberg, editor in chief.
   p. cm.
Includes bibliographical references and index.
   ISBN 0-02-865749-7 (set hardcover : alk. paper) — ISBN 0-02-865750-0
(v. 1 : alk. paper) — ISBN 0-02-865751-9 (v. 2 : alk. paper) — ISBN
0-02-865752-7 (v. 3 : alk. paper)
   1. Law—United States—Encyclopedias. I. Landsberg, Brian K.
KF154.M35 2004
348.73'22—dc22   200301874

This title is also available as an e-book.
ISBN 0-02-865909-0 (set)
Contact your Gale sales representative for ordering information.

Printed in the United States of America
10 9 8 7 6 5

EDITORIAL AND PRODUCTION STAFF

Jeff Galas, *Project Editor*

Erin Bealmear, Joann Cerrito, Stephen Cusack, Mark Drouillard, Miranda Ferrara, Kristin Hart, Melissa Hill, Margaret Mazurkiewicz, Jennifer Wisinski, *Editorial Assistants*

Leitha Etheridge-Sims, Lezlie Light, Michael Logusz, Kelly Quin, *Imaging*

GGS Information Services (York, Pennsylvania), *Tables*

Taryn Benbow-Pfalzgraf, Laurie Di Mauro, Jessica Hornik Evans, Anne Janette Johnson, William L. Peper, *Copyeditors*

Deanna Raso, *Photo Researcher*

Douglas Funk, *Caption Writer*

Paula Kepos, *Sidebar Writer, unless otherwise specified*

Taryn Benbow-Pfalzgraf, Nicolet Elert, Elizabeth Henry, *Proofreaders*

Wendy Allex, *Indexer*

Pamela A. E. Galbreath, *Art Director*

Graphix Group (Fenton, Michigan), *Compositor*

Margaret A. Chamberlain, *Permissions*

Mary Beth Trimper, *Manager, Composition*

Evi Seoud, *Assistant Manager, Composition*

Rhonda Williams, *Manufacturing*

MACMILLAN REFERENCE USA

Jill Lectka, *Director, Publishing Operations*

Hélène Potter, *Director, New Product Development*

Frank Menchaca, *Vice President and Publisher*

CONTENTS

VOLUME 2

TOPIC OUTLINE

CIVIL RIGHTS

Americans With Disabilities Act (1990)
Civil Rights Act of 1866
Civil Rights Act of 1875
Civil Rights Act of 1957
Civil Rights Act of 1964
Equal Pay Act of 1963
Fair Housing Act of 1968
Force Act of 1871
Freedmen's Bureau Acts (1865, 1868)
Indian Civil Rights Act (1968)
Ku Klux Klan Act (1871)
Pregnancy Discrimination Act (1978)
Title IX, Education Amendments (1972)
Violence Against Women Act of 1994
Voting Rights Act of 1965

COMMUNICATIONS

Children's Online Privacy Protection Act (1998)
Communications Act of 1934
Communications Decency Act (1996)
Counterfeit Access Device and Computer Fraud and Abuse Act of 1984
Computer Security Act of 1987
Electronic Communications Privacy Act of 1986
Electronic Signatures in Global and National Commerce Act (2000)
Public Broadcasting Act of 1967

CONSUMER PROTECTION

Bankruptcy Act of 1841

Consumer Credit Protection Act (1969)
Federal Cigarette Labeling and Advertising Act of 1965
Federal Food, Drug, and Cosmetic Act (1938)
Pure Food and Drug Act (1906)

CRIMINAL LAW

Anti-Drug Abuse Act (1986)
Brady Handgun Violence Prevention Act (1993)
Bribery Act (1962)
Communications Decency Act (1996)
Communist Control Act of 1954
Comstock Act (1873)
Controlled Substances Act (1970)
Espionage Act (1917) and Sedition Act (1918)
Federal Blackmail Statute (1994)
Flag Protection Act of 1989
Foreign Corrupt Practices Act (1977)
Gun Control Act of 1968
Hobbs Anti-Racketeering Act (1946)
Juvenile Justice and Deliquency Prevention Act of 1974
Mail Fraud and False Representation Statutes
Mann Act (1910)
Narcotics Act (1914)
National Prohibition Act (1919)
Omnibus Crime Control and Safe Streets Act of 1968
Organized Crime Control Act of 1970
Sentencing Reform Act (1984)
Violent Crime Control Act and Law Enforcement Act of 1994

ECONOMIC DEVELOPMENT/TRADE

Bank of the United States (1791)

Community Development Banking and Financial Institutions Act of 1994

Community Reinvestment Act (1977)

Copyright Act of 1790

Copyright Act of 1976

Economic Cooperation Act of 1948 (Marshall Plan)

Economic Opportunity Act of 1964

Electronic Signatures in Global and National Commerce Act (2000)

Export-Import Bank Act of 1945

Federal Power Acts

Freedmen's Bureau Acts (1865, 1868)

Hill-Burton Act (1946)

Homestead Act (1862)

Housing and Urban Development Act of 1965

Internal Improvements Acts

Merchant Marine Act of 1920

National Industrial Recovery Act (1933)

North American Free Trade Agreement Implementation Act (1993)

Patent Acts

Tennessee Valley Authority Act (1933)

Trade Act of 1974

Trading with the Enemy Act (1917)

ECONOMIC AND FINANCIAL REGULATION

Agricultural Adjustment Act (1933)

Bank of the United States (1791)

Bankruptcy Act of 1841

Bankruptcy Act of 1978

Civil Service Acts

Clayton Act (1914)

Coinage Act of 1792

Coinage Acts

Commodity Exchange Act (1936)

Community Development Banking and Financial Institutions Act of 1994

Community Reinvestment Act (1977)

Consumer Credit Protection Act (1969)

Contract Disputes Act (1978)

Farm Credit Act of 1933

Farmers Home Administration Act (1946)

Federal Deposit Insurance Acts

Federal Employers' Liability Act (1908)

Federal Home Loan Bank Act (1932)

Federal National Mortgage Association Charter Act (1954)

Federal Reserve Act (1913)

Federal Trade Commission Act (1914)

Glass-Steagall Act (1933)

Gold Reserve Act of 1934

Gold Standard Act of 1900

Interstate Commerce Act of 1887

National Bank Act (1864)

Public Utility Holding Company Act of 1935

Pure Food and Drug Act (1906)

Securities Act of 1933

Securities Exchange Act of 1934

Sherman Antitrust Act (1890)

Small Business Act (1953)

Truth in Lending Act (1969)

Walsh-Healey Act (1936)

EDUCATION

Civil Rights Act of 1964

Elementary and Secondary Education Act of 1965

Higher Education Act of 1965

Individuals with Disabilities Education Act (1975)

Morrill Land Grant Act of 1862

No Child Left Behind (2001)

Richard B. Russell National School Lunch Act (1946)

Title IX, Education Amendments (1972)

Vocational Education Act of 1917

ENERGY

Atomic Energy Acts

Department of Energy Organization Act (1977)

Federal Power Acts

National Energy Conservation Policy Act (1978)

Natural Gas Act (1938)

Nuclear Waste Policy Act (1982)

Oil Pollution Acts

Rural Electrification Act (1936)

Tennessee Valley Authority Act (1933)

ENVIRONMENT

Clean Air Act (1963)

Comprehensive Environmental Response, Compensation, and Liability Act (1980)

Emergency Planning and Community Right-To-Know Act (1986)

Endangered Species Act (1973)

Federal Water Pollution Control Act (1948)

Fish and Wildlife Conservation Act of 1980

Food Quality Protection Act of 1996

Hazardous and Solid Waste Amendments of 1984

Highway Beautification Act (1965)

Homestead Act (1862)

Marine Mammal Protection Act (1972)

Migratory Bird Conservation Act of 1929

Mineral Leasing Act (1920)

National Emissions Standards Act (1965)

National Environmental Policy Act (1969)

National Historic Preservation Act (1966)

National Wildlife Refuge System Administration Act (1966)

Nuclear Waste Policy Act (1982)

Oil Pollution Acts

Outer Continental Shelf Lands Act (1953)

Plant Variety Protection Act (1970)

Safe Drinking Water Act (1974)

Solid Waste Disposal Act (1965)

Surface Mining Control and Reclamation Act (1977)

Toxic Substances Control Act (1976)

FOREIGN AFFAIRS/ INTERNATIONAL RELATIONS

Communist Control Act of 1954

Economic Cooperation Act of 1948 (Marshall Plan)

Espionage Act (1917) and Sedition Act (1918)

National Reclamation Act of 1902
National Wildlife Refuge System
    Administration Act (1966)
Northwest Ordinance (1787)
Soil Conservation and Domestic
    Allotment Act (1935)
Southwest Ordinance (1790)
Tennessee Valley Authority Act (1933)
Yellowstone National Park Act (1872)

SLAVERY

Compromise of 1850
Freedmen's Bureau Acts (1865,
    1868)
Fugitive Slave Acts (1793, 1850)
Kansas Nebraska Act of 1854
Missouri Compromise (1820)
Prohibition of the Slave Trade (1807)
Reconstruction Acts

**SOCIAL PROGRAMS/SOCIAL
WELFARE**

Agricultural Adjustment Act (1933)
Aid to Dependent Children (1935)
Alcoholic and Narcotic
    Rehabilitation Act (1968)
Antiquities Act of 1906
Bonus Bill (1924)
Born-Alive Infants Protection Act of
    2002
Civil War Pensions
Defense of Marriage Act (1996)

Domestic Volunteer Service Act of
    1973 (VISTA)
Drug Abuse Prevention, Treatment,
    and Rehabilitation Act (1980)
Family and Medical Leave Act of
    1993
Food Stamp Act of 1964
Freedom of Access to Clinic
    Entrances Act (1994)
Housing and Urban Development
    Act of 1965
McKinney-Vento Act (1988)
Medicaid Act (1965)
Medicare Act (1965)
National Housing Act (1955)
Occupational Safety and Health Act
    of 1970
Peace Corps Act (1961)
Personal Responsibility and Work
    Opportunity Reconciliation Act
    (1996)
Social Security Act of 1935
Truth in Lending Act (1969)
Violence Against Women Act of 1994

TAXES

Anti-Injunction Act (1793)
Bland-Allison Act (1878)
Corporate Income Tax Act of 1909
1894 Income Tax and the Wilson-
    Gorman Tariff Act
Employee Retirement Income
    Security Act of 1974

Estate and Gift Taxation
Federal Income Tax Act of 1913
Federal Unemployment Tax Act
    (1939)
Internal Revenue Act of 1954
Medicaid Act (1965)
Medicare Act (1965)
Smoot-Hawley Tariff Act (1930)
Social Security Act of 1935
Tariff Act of 1789
Tax Reform Act of 1986
Taxpayer Bill of Rights III (1998)

TRANSPORTATION

Civil Aeronautics Act (1938)
Federal Aviation Act (1958)
Hazardous Materials Transportation
    Act (1975)
Highway Act of 1956
Highway Beautification Act
    of 1965
Highway Safety Act of 1966
Motor Carrier Act (1935)
Mutual Security Act (1951)
National Aeronautics and Space Act
    (1958)
National Traffic and Motor Vehicle
    Safety Act of 1966
Rail Passenger Service Act (1970)
Shipping Acts
Staggers Rail Act of 1980
Urban Mass Transportation Acts

PREFACE

In the fall of 2001, Hélène Potter, director of development at Macmillan Reference, asked me to serve as editor in chief of an encyclopedia of major acts of Congress. I found the offer enormously exciting, because the world of reference books had seemingly neglected this area that is so central to American law, government, and history. Moreover, I helped to write, interpret, and enforce laws while at the U.S. Department of Justice Civil Rights Division, and I had taught and written about civil rights legislation. These experiences led me to appreciate how useful a clear and authoritative description of major American legislation could be. My duties as associate dean at the University of Pacific, McGeorge School of Law, initially precluded my undertaking this project. However, the publishing schedule for the encyclopedia changed, and in March of 2002 I enthusiastically signed up.

By the spring of 2002 an outstanding board of editors had agreed to join the project, and we were well underway. Each of the associate editors brings a rich understanding of legislation to the project, but each also contributes a different perspective. Professor Al Brophy of the University of Alabama School of Law is an accomplished and well-recognized legal historian. Professor Thomas Sargentich of American University's Washington College of Law has written extensively about the legal issues of the separation of powers; he serves as codirector of his law school's program on law and government. Professor Nancy Staudt of the Washington University School of Law (St. Louis) teaches and writes on tax law and social programs and has become known for her critical analyses of both tax and social policy.

Courses in American government typically teach students about the roles of the three branches established by the Constitution. Students learn that the Congress makes laws, the executive branch executes laws, and the courts apply laws. Often, however, that lesson may seem abstract. Students may fail to see the connection between these principles and their lives, the lives of their families and friends, or the history of the nation. *Major Acts of Congress* helps make concrete the law-making function of Congress and also casts light on the role of the other two branches in enforcing and applying law. It brings together for the first time, in one work, a selection from the product of the one hundred and seven Congresses which preceded this encyclopedia, as well as the current Congress.

In its first year, 1789, Congress enacted twenty-seven laws. The acts from its first ten years occupy 755 pages, in one volume of the *U.S Statutes At*

Large. By 2002, in the second and last year of the 107th Congress, we find 260 acts, occupying 3115 pages of volume 116 of the *U.S. Statutes*. The laws of the First Congress were mainly devoted to setting up the national government, which must have seemed quite distant to most Americans. By contrast, the 107th Congress enacted laws covering such subjects as agriculture (the names of fourteen laws begin with that word), education, the environment, foreign relations, intelligence, immigration, defense, crime, voter registration, radiation, securities, employment, social security, and so on. Today few aspects of our lives are untouched by federal law.

The acts described in this work demonstrate the range of congressional legislation, from the very first Congress's adoption of the Judiciary Act to the 108th Congress's enactment of legislation regulating so-called partial birth abortions. Described in more detail than one finds in most history books are landmarks of American history, such as the Fugitive Slave Act, the various civil rights acts, legislation from the New Deal and the Great Society, as well as acts that respond to such contemporary issues as terrorism and the rise of electronic technology.

Major Acts of Congress contains entries on 262 acts selected by the editorial board based on such criteria as historical significance, contemporary impact, and contribution to the understanding of American government. Hundreds of other laws are discussed in the entries and can be found through use of the comprehensive index. The entries vary in length from 2500 words down to 300 words. Entries describe the law, but they do much more than that. They typically explain the circumstances that led Congress to consider the law and the issues Congress discussed during its consideration of the law. They also provide information about the subsequent history of the law, including amendments or repeal, enforcement, and court cases.

As the list of contributors reflects, the 159 authors include legal scholars, historians, political scientists, economists, and lawyers from public and private practice. Some played a significant role in the adoption or enforcement of the act they wrote about. Others have literally written the book on the act or area of law.

The essays have been written to make accessible to students and lay persons the frequently complex, technical, arcane concepts and language of legislation. We have included brief excerpts from acts in those entries where a direct quotation would give a flavor of the law. Accessibility is enhanced by the use of sidebars to explain terms and historical allusions, as well as illustrations that help demonstrate the political and human dimension of these laws. Same-page definitions of terms and a glossary in the back matter further enhance access. Entries typically end with a short bibliography of books, articles, and Web sites, for those who wish to delve more deeply. To place the entries in perspective, *Major Acts* begins with an introduction that explains the role of the Congress and other branches. It also contains an in-depth time line in the back matter, showing who was president, the composition of each Congress, and what major events were taking place during the time when each law was enacted.

Major Acts has been a true team effort. The editorial board has worked closely with the publisher. Hélène Potter has skillfully guided the project. Jeff Galas, assistant editor at Macmillan Reference, has been invaluable in helping recruit authors and organize the work. And Kristin Hart has ably supervised the copyediting and the selection of illustrations.

Brian K. Landsberg
September, 2003
Sacramento, California

INTRODUCTION

In a democracy like the United States, congressional action reflects the will of the people. The impetus for acts comes from members of the House of Representatives who stand for election every two years and senators who—after 1916—have stood for election every six years. (Before 1916, they were selected by their state legislature.) The acts discussed in this encyclopedia illustrate the concerns of Americans, from the early national period, through the antebellum period, the Civil War, Reconstruction, the Gilded Age, the Progressive Era, the Great Depression, World War II, and the civil rights eras, right up to the administrations of Presidents Nixon, Ford, and Carter in the 1970s, and Presidents Reagan and Bush in the 1980s, and Presidents Clinton and Bush in the 1990s and 2000s.

At times, the nation is concerned with certain issues—like civil rights—and takes action. That happened in the wake of the Civil War, when Congress proposed and the states ratified three Constitutional amendments, including the Fifteenth Amendment to guarantee all adult males the right to vote, regardless of race. Congress also passed numerous acts to ensure the newly freed slaves had civil rights. Yet, after 1877 those acts lay largely dormant, until the civil rights era of the 1950s.

Examination of the Voting Rights Act of 1965 illustrates how the nation, awakened to the cause of civil rights, again turned to Congress to seek a national solution. Each law described in this encyclopedia went through the process that American students study in increasing detail as they advance through elementary and secondary school, college, and graduate school. The process is established by Article I of the U. S. Constitution. It is not easy to pass legislation, because many actors, representing a range of interests and ideologies, must reach agreement. Rather than simply providing another abstract description of the process in this introduction, we seek to bring the process to life by describing the course of one bill from initial concept to final adoption and enforcement and subsequent amendment. You will find an entry on this law, the Voting Rights Act of 1965, in volume three of this encyclopedia.

Although the Fifteenth Amendment had been added to the Constitution in 1870 in order to forbid official actions abridging the right to vote based on race, by the middle of the twentieth century most Southern states had placed a variety of obstacles in the way of African-American voter registration. The result was that by 1952 only about 20 percent of African Americans of voting age in the Deep South were registered to vote. Congress's first effort to address this problem came in the Civil Rights Act of 1957, the first modern federal civil rights law. It had been brilliantly steered through the United States Senate by Majority Leader Lyndon B. Johnson. It was, however, a bill with few teeth, principally the bare authorization for the Department of Justice to bring suits to remedy discrimination in official voting practices and race-based intimidation against potential voters. Johnson knew that it was not a strong bill, but regarded it as a start. "[I]t's only the first. We know we can do it now." As predicted, the 1957 act did not effectively end racial discrimination in voter registration. Congress tried again, in the Civil Rights Act of 1960, but again it was not politically possible to pass a strong bill. This time, Lyndon Johnson made the pragmatic argument that the legislation was "reasonable" and "the best that the able chairman of the House Judiciary Committee could get." After passage, Thurgood Marshall, the leading black lawyer in the country, said the 1960 act "isn't worth the paper it's written on." Congress made further very minor improvements in voting rights law in the Civil Rights Act of 1964, but that law primarily addressed other matters.

The weaknesses of the 1957 and 1960 acts stemmed largely from the political influence of Southern Democrats, who in those days regularly opposed all civil rights legislation. Though they were a minority in Congress, the availability of the filibuster in the Senate gave them added strength. To pass a bill over their objection required unusual consensus between Northern Democrats and the Republicans. You will see in the descriptions of many of the acts in this encyclopedia that compromises often are necessary in order to win passage and presidential approval of a bill.

Proponents of stronger legislation needed to find a way to convince Congress to abandon the approach of the prior acts. Civil rights groups believed that it would take very strong medicine indeed to effectively insure black voting rights. As you will see in Professor William Araiza's entry on the Voting Rights Act, the act interferes with state voter qualification laws, provides for federal officials to take over the registration process in some counties, and requires some changes in state law to be pre-approved by federal courts or officials before they may be implemented. Not since Reconstruction had such federal intervention into state law occurred.

Civil rights organizations mounted voter registration drives in Alabama, Mississippi, and Louisiana. The Department of Justice brought voter discrimination suits in federal court as Southern registrars turned away thousands of prospective voters. By early 1965, national newspapers and television networks began to report on events in such places as Selma, Alabama. In February 1965 during a civil rights demonstration in Marion, Alabama, Alabama State Troopers shot and killed an African American, Jimmie Lee Jackson, who had unsuccessfully tried in prior months to register to vote. To protest the killing and to dramatize the deprivations of the right to vote, civil rights organizations—the Student Nonviolent Coordinating Committee and Dr. Martin Luther King Jr.'s Southern Christian Leadership Conference—decided to march from Selma to the state capital, Montgomery. As the marchers left Selma and crossed the Edmund Pettus Bridge over the Alabama River, they were set upon by state troopers and sheriff's deputies, many of them mounted on horses. Many were beaten, all were tear-gassed, and they were pursued back to Selma by mounted men swinging billy clubs. The assault on the

Edmund Pettus Bridge in Selma occurred in broad daylight and was broadcast to an outraged nation. The following week President Lyndon Johnson gave a nationwide address in which he announced the outlines of the voting rights bill he was sending to Congress. In the flowery language of presidential addresses, he said that "the cries of pain and the hymns and protests of oppressed people have summoned into convocation all the majesty of this great Government—the Government of the greatest Nation on earth."

President Johnson's speech in the wake of the Bloody Sunday confrontation at the Edmund Pettus Bridge promised the country an effective voting rights act. The administration's interest in a new voting law predated Bloody Sunday by several months. The Department of Justice had begun drafting such a law in November of 1964, at the direction of President Johnson. The attorney general had sent the president a memorandum outlining three possible proposals by the end of December, and the president's State of the Union message on January 4, 1965, had already proposed that "we eliminate every remaining obstacle to the right and the opportunity to vote." However, Johnson had planned to delay the voting rights proposal until his Great Society social bills had passed. The events on Bloody Sunday changed all that.

In the above events we can see four important aspects of the legislative process. First, legislation normally responds to some felt need. It is necessary to mobilize public opinion and demonstrate that the nation faces a problem and that the problem requires legislation. Second, it is not enough to simply place a bill on a president's or a party's legislative agenda. The president and Congress face a myriad of problems that need solving, and they cannot solve them all. So they establish priorities. Unless a bill is given high priority, it is unlikely that Congress will enact it even if it has merit. Third, Congress is not the only player. The president plays an important role in setting the legislative agenda. Even the initial drafting of some laws may be done by executive agencies rather than Congress. Finally, Congress often addresses issues incrementally, with small starts, such as the 1957 and 1960 Civil Rights Acts, later leading to more ambitious legislation.

Within two days of President Johnson's speech, the administration proposal had been introduced in both the House and Senate. Each chamber referred the bill to its judiciary committee. The Committee on the Judiciary of the House of Representatives in turn referred the bill to a subcommittee chaired by Emanuel Celler of New York, with six other Democrats and four Republicans as members. The subcommittee began hearings the following day. It considered 122 bills dealing with voting rights, holding thirteen sessions, including four evening sessions. It then met in executive session for four days and substantially rewrote the administration bill and sent it to the full committee of twenty-four Democrats and eleven Republicans. The committee further rewrote the bill and then sent it to the House of Representatives, with a report and a recommendation that the House pass the bill in its amended form.

Meanwhile, the Senate faced a problem that flowed from the seniority system. The chair of the Senate Judiciary Committee was Senator James Eastland of Mississippi, a strong opponent of all civil rights legislation. And the committee's senior Democrats were also from the Deep South. The Senate responded by sending the bill to the committee with the mandate to report back to the Senate no later than April 9. The full Senate Judiciary Committee held hearings for nine days. It met the April 9 deadline and recommended that the Senate pass the bill, but instead of submitting a committee report submitted sets of "individual views" of the proponents and opponents.

The hearings before both the House and Senate committees began with testimony by Attorney General Nicholas Katzenbach, who presented voluminous exhibits, including the history of the fifty-one suits against voting discrimination and seventeen suits challenging intimidation against black voter registration that the Department of Justice had brought since adoption of the 1957 act. He argued that the litigation approach under these laws had not worked. He noted that the earlier laws "depended, as almost all our legislation does, on the fact that it is going to be accepted as the law of the land and is then going to be fairly administered in all of the areas to which it applies, by States officials who are just as bound as you and I by the Constitution of the United States and by Federal laws." The attorney general continued:

> I think, in some areas, it has become the theory that a voting registrar is not really required to do anything except what he has been doing until his records have been examined and he has been hauled into court and, at public expense, his case has been defended by the State, and all the delaying devices possible have been used, and then it has been taken on appeal, then appealed again with as much delay as possible. Then, when a decree is finally entered, that decree can be construed as narrowly as possible and he can do as little as he can get away with under that decree. Then that decree—what it means—can be questioned again in court, new evidence can be introduced, and meanwhile, election after election is going by.

After delivering his statement, Katzenbach was grilled for a day and half by the House committee and for three days by the Senate committee. Southern senators challenged him at every turn—on the need for legislation, the content of the legislation, and the constitutional basis of the legislation. Civil rights leaders, including the heads of the National Association for the Advancement of Colored People and the Congress for Racial Equality, testified in favor of the bill, as did religious leaders and other federal officials. Southern attorneys general and other public officials testified against the bill.

The hearings, in short, raised issues common to most legislation. First, does Congress have the authority under the Constitution to legislate on this issue? Here, the authority came from section 2 of the Fifteenth Amendment. In most cases Congress' authority is found in Article I, section 8, which contains a laundry list of areas on which Congress may pass laws. Second, why is legislation needed? For example, why isn't existing law sufficient to deal with the problem the bill addresses? Third, what should be the content of the new legislation? It is one thing to say that we need to solve a problem and quite another to agree on what are the appropriate means. For example, the act contains detailed criteria for determining which states will be subject to some of its provisions. One criterion is whether fewer than 50 percent of persons of voting age voted in the 1964 presidential general election. Why 50 percent, as opposed to 40 or 60 percent? Why the general election? These details must be worked out, usually at the committee level.

The Senate was the first chamber to debate the bill. The minority leader, Senator Everett Dirksen, Republican of Illinois, and the majority leader, Senator Mike Mansfield, Democrat of Montana, began the debate by describing the bill and supporting it. Each party had appointed other senators to lead the floor debate, Democrat Philip Hart of Michigan and Republican Jacob Javits of New

York. They spoke at length about the evidence of need. Southern opponents spoke at great length. In addition, Senator Edward Kennedy of Massachusetts proposed an amendment that would outlaw the poll tax, and Senators Robert F. Kennedy and Jacob Javits of New York proposed an amendment designed to protect the right of Puerto Ricans in New York to vote. The poll tax amendment was defeated; the Puerto Rico amendment passed. After over a month of debate, the Senate voted to impose cloture, thus preventing a full filibuster, and on May 26 the Senate adopted the bill with a vote of 79 to 18.

The House considered the bill for three days. It adopted an amendment outlawing the poll tax, and passed the bill on July 9, 328 to 74. Thus, at this point, overwhelming majorities in both chambers supported a voting rights bill, as did the president. However, the two chambers had passed different bills. Therefore the House and Senate appointed a conference committee, charged with the task of reconciling the two bills and agreeing on a final version. For example, what should be done about the poll tax? The conference committee decided that the bill would not outlaw the poll tax but would direct the attorney general to bring litigation challenging this barrier to voting. After almost a month of work, the conference committee reported on its work on August 2, 1965. As Representative Celler told the House of Representatives the next day, "The differences were many, wide, and deep. Mutual concession was essential otherwise there would have been ... no bill." The House adopted the conference bill on August 3, and the Senate did so on August 4. President Johnson signed it on August 6.

President Johnson had presented the legislation as having the highest urgency. Congress did act quickly, but the need for hearings and debates and conference committee meant that the legislative process occupied an enormous amount of the time of the members of Congress during the five months from introduction to passage. We see that, as is often the case, the House and Senate agreed on the general objective but not on the details of the bill. We also see the importance of bipartisan coalition building where, as here, a small group of senators opposes the general objective. And we see once again that compromise is often necessary in order to enact legislation.

This is the end of the story, right? Wrong! The story goes on. The attorney general had to enforce the law. The Southern states challenged its constitutionality, so the Supreme Court had to review the law's validity. Some provisions of the law were to expire after five years. Disputes arose as to the meaning of other provisions. For example, the law was silent as to whether private parties could bring suit to enforce the provision requiring preclearance of changes in voting practices. The Supreme Court therefore had to resolve that question, by trying to determine Congress's intent. Courts have interpreted and applied the act numerous times, while other provisions have been clarified by subsequent legislation, in which Congress has revisited and amended the law several times.

The history of the Voting Rights Act demonstrates that although Congress plays the primary role in enacting legislation, the president and the courts play important roles as well. The president may propose legislation and his signature is normally needed for a bill to become law. The courts may lay a legal and constitutional framework that guides the drafting of legislation, and they apply, interpret, and determine the validity of legislation once it has been enacted.

BIBLIOGRAPHY

"Article I." In *The Constitution and Its Amendments*, ed. Roger K. Newman. New York: Macmillan Reference USA, 1999.

Berman, Daniel M. *A Bill Becomes a Law: The Civil Rights Act of 1960.* New York: Macmillan, 1962.

Hawk, Barry E., and John J. Kirby. "Federal Protection of Negro Voting Rights." *Virginia Law Review* 51 (1965): 1051.

Marshall, Burke. "The Right to Vote." In *The Constitution and Its Amendments*, ed. Roger K. Newman. New York: Macmillan Reference USA, 1999.

Schwartz, Bernard, ed. *Civil Rights.* Statutory History of the United States. New York: Chelsea House, 1970.

Brian K. Landsberg

LIST OF CONTRIBUTORS

Melanie B. Abbott
Quinnipiac University School of Law
Civil Rights Act of 1964
McKinney-Vento Act (1988)

Norman Abrams
University of California, Los Angeles Law School
Violent Crime Control and Law Enforcement Act of 1994

Craig J. Albert
Reitler Brown LLC, New York
Highway Beautification Act (1965)

Ellen P. Aprill
Loyola Law School
Federal Unemployment Tax Act (1939)

William D. Araiza
Loyola Law School
North American Free Trade Agreement Implementation Act (1993)
Voting Rights Act of 1965

Carl Auerbach
University of San Diego School of Law and Northwest University School of Law
Communist Control Act of 1954

Reuven S. Avi-Yonah
University of Michigan Law School
Corporate Income Tax Act of 1909

Steven A. Bank
University of California, Los Angeles School of Law
Federal Income Tax of 1913
Internal Revenue Act of 1954

William Banks
Syracuse University College of Law
Foreign Intelligence Surveillance Act (1978)

Felice Batlan
New York University
Aid to Dependent Children (1935)

Jonathan S. Berck
University of Alabama, School of Law
Foreign Corrupt Practices Act (1977)

Richard K. Berg
Arlington, Virginia
Government in the Sunshine Act (1976)

Neil N. Bernstein
Washington University School of Law
Norris-LaGuardia Act (1932)

Christopher A. Bracey
Washington University School of Law
Civil Rights Act of 1866

Alfred L. Brophy
University of Alabama School of Law
National Historic Preservation Act (1966)

Darryl K. Brown
Washington and Lee University School of Law
Anti-Drug Abuse Act (1986)

Tomiko Brown-Nagin
Washington University School of Law
Elementary and Secondary Education Act of 1965

Alan Brownstein
Davis, California
Religious Freedom Restoration Act (1993)

Richard Buel, Jr.
Wesleyan University
Nonintercourse Act (1809)

Jennifer S. Byram
Orangevale, CA
Central Intelligence Agency Act of
1949
Electronic Communications Privacy
Act of 1986
Immigration Reform and Control
Act of 1986

Daniel P. Carpenter
Harvard University
Pure Food and Drug Act (1906)

Gilbert Paul Carrasco
Willamette University College of Law
Civil Rights Act of 1957

Federico Cheever
University of Denver College of Law
Endangered Species Act (1973)

Jim Chen
University of Minnesota Law School
Agricultural Adjustment Act (1933)

Gabriel J. Chin
University of Cincinnati
Chinese Exclusion Acts

Ruth Colker
*Ohio State University, Michael E.
Moritz College of Law*
Americans with Disabilities Act
(1990)
Individuals with Disabilities
Education Act (1975)
Pregnancy Discrimination Act
(1978)

Mikal Condon
*Electronic Privacy Information
Center, Washington, D.C.*
Communications Decency Act
(1996)

Bo Cooper
*Paul, Hastings, Janofsky, and
Walter, Washington, D.C.*
Immigration and Nationality Act
(1952)

Julie Davies
*University of the Pacific, McGeorge
School of Law*
Ku Klux Klan Act (1871)
Title IX, Education Amendments
(1972)

Derrek M. Davis
Austin Community College
Computer Security Act of 1987

Charles E. Daye
*University of North Carolina School
of Law*
Housing and Urban Development
Act of 1965
United States Housing Act of 1937

David G. Delaney
Brandeis University
Bonus Bill (1924)
Federal Civil Defense Act of 1950
Neutrality Acts

Corey Ditslear
University of North Texas
Public Broadcasting Act of 1967

Charles M. Dobbs
Iowa State University
Economic Cooperation Act of 1948
(Marshall Plan)

Keith Rollins Eakins
The University of Central Oklahoma
Brady Handgun Violence
Prevention Act (1993)
Gun Control Act of 1968

Liann Y. Ebesugawa
*University of Hawaii, Richardson
School of Law*
Civil Liberties Act (1988)

Gary J. Edles
*American University, Washington
College of Law and University of
Hull Law School*
Government in the Sunshine Act
(1976)
Motor Carrier Act (1935)

Jonathan L. Entin
Case Western Reserve University
Balanced Budget and Emergency
Deficit Control Act (1985)

Yonatan Eyal
Harvard University
Bank of the United States (1791)

Richard Finkmoore
California Western School of Law
National Wildlife Refuge System
Administration Act (1966)

Lucinda Finley
*State University of New York at
Buffalo, School of Law*
Freedom of Access to Clinic
Entrances Act (1994)

Louis Fisher
Library of Congress
Congressional Budget and
Impoundment Control Act (1974)

Employment Act of 1946
War Powers Resolution (1973)

Justin Florence
Harvard University
Alien and Sedition Acts of 1798

John P. Forren
Miami University, Ohio
Occupational Safety and Health Act
of 1970

Julia Patterson Forrester
*Southern Methodist University
Dedman School of Law*
Federal National Mortgage
Association Charter Act (1954)

James W. Fox, Jr.
Stetson University College of Law
Naturalization Act (1790)

William Funk
Lewis and Clark Law School
Federal Advisory Committee Act
(1972)

Fred Galves
*University of the Pacific, McGeorge
School of Law*
Community Reinvestment Act
(1977)

James P. George
*Texas Wesleyan University School of
Law*
Anti-Injunction Act (1793)

Richard Gershon
*Texas Wesleyan University School of
Law*
Estate and Gift Taxation
Taxpayer Bill of Rights III (1998)

Shubha Ghosh
*State University of New York at
Buffalo, School of Law*
Copyright Act of 1790
Copyright Act of 1976
Patent Acts

Michele Estrin Gilman
*University of Baltimore School of
Law*
Personal Responsibility and Work
Opportunity Reconciliation Act
(1996)

Mark Glaze
*Campaign Legal Center,
Washington, D.C.*
Federal Election Campaign Act (1971)

Linda Gordon
New York University
Aid to Dependent Children (1935)

Brian E. Gray
University of California, Hastings College of the Law
Federal Power Acts
Mineral Leasing Act (1920)
National Park Service Act (1916)
Yellowstone National Park Act (1872)

Pamela L. Gray
Purdue University
Vocational Education Act of 1917

Stuart P. Green
Louisiana State University Law Center
Bribery Act (1962)
Federal Blackmail Statute (1994)

Steven J. Gunn
Yale University Law School
Alaska Native Claims Settlement Act (1971)
Fair Housing Act of 1968
Indian Gaming Regulatory Act (1988)
Indian General Allotment Act (1887)

Daniel W. Hamilton
New York University Law School
Enrollment Act (1863) (The Conscription Act)
First and Second Confiscation Acts (1861, 1862)
Militia Act (1862)
Morrill Land Grant Act of 1862
Reconstruction Acts

Douglas B. Harris
Loyola College in Maryland
Civil Aeronautics Act (1938)
Federal Aviation Act (1958)
National Aeronautics and Space Act (1958)

Philip J. Harter
Vermont Law School
Negotiated Rulemaking Act (1990)

Neil S. Helfand
Washington, D.C.
Department of Homeland Security Act (2002)
Mutual Security Act (1951)
National Security Act of 1947
USA Patriot Act (2001)

James E. Hickey, Jr.
Hofstra University School of Law
Public Utility Holding Company Act of 1935

Thomas M. Hilbink
University of Massachusetts

Omnibus Crime Control and Safe Streets Act of 1968

Arthur Holst
Philadelphia, Pennsylvania
Hazardous Materials Transportation Act (1975)
Oil Pollution Acts

Wythe W. Holt, Jr.
University of Alabama School of Law
Judiciary Act of 1789

Herbert Hovenkamp
University of Iowa
Clayton Act (1914)
Federal Trade Commission Act (1914)
Sherman Antitrust Act (1890)

James L. Huston
Oklahoma State University
Compromise of 1850
Homestead Act (1862)
Kansas Nebraska Act of 1854
Missouri Compromise (1820)

Mark D. Janis
University of Iowa College of Law
Plant Variety Protection Act (1970)

Barry L. Johnson
Oklahoma City University
Hobbs Anti-Racketeering Act (1946)
Mail Fraud and False Representation Statutes
Sentencing Reform Act (1984)

Warren F. Kimball
Rutgers University
Lend-Lease Act (1941)

Andrew R. Klein
Indiana University School of Law— Indianapolis
Rural Electrification Act (1936)

Stephen H. Klitzman
Bethesda, Maryland
Government in the Sunshine Act (1976)

Michael H. Koby
Washington University in St. Louis School of Law
Children's Online Privacy Protection Act (1998)

Thomas C. Kohler
Boston College Law School
National Labor Relations Act (1935)

David A. Koplow
Georgetown University Law Center

Arms Control and Disarmament Act (1961) and Amendments
Nuclear Non-Proliferation Act (1978)
Weapons of Mass Destruction Control Act (1992)

Andrew Koppelman
Northwestern University School of Law
Defense of Marriage Act (1996)

David E. Kyvig
Northern University Illinois
National Prohibition Act (1919)

Julia Lamber
Indiana University School of Law
Age Discrimination in Employment Act (1967)

David J. Langum
Samford University, Cumberland School of Law
Mann Act (1910)

Marc A. Le Forestier
Department of Justice, State of California
Migratory Bird Conservation Act of 1929

Arthur G. LeFrancois
Oklahoma City University School of Law
Fugitive Slave Acts (1793, 1850)
Organized Crime Control Act of 1970

Andreas Lehnert
Washington, D.C.
Federal Reserve Act (1913)

Jennifer Rebecca Levison
Independent Scholar
Narcotics Act (1914)

Alberto B. Lopez
Northern Kentucky University, Salmon P. Chase College of Law
Born-Alive Infants Protection Act of 2002

Kyle A. Loring
Boston College
National Reclamation Act of 1902
Safe Drinking Water Act (1974)
Soil Conservation and Domestic Allotment Act (1935)
Tennessee Valley Authority Act (1933)

Jeffrey S. Lubbers
American University, Washington College of Law

Administrative Procedure Act (1946)
Paperwork Reduction Act (1980)
Regulatory Flexibility Act (1980)

William V. Luneburg
*University of Pittsburgh School of
Law*
Civil Service Acts (1883)
Federal Land Policy and
  Management Act (1976)
Federal Tort Claims Act (1946)
Hatch Act (1939)
National Environmental Policy Act
  (1969)
National Forest Management Act
  (1976)
Toxic Substances Control Act (1976)

Hether C. Macfarlane
*University of the Pacific, McGeorge
School of Law*
Walsh-Healey Public Contracts Act
  of 1936

Shahla F. Maghzi
*University of California, Berkeley
Boalt Hall School of Law*
Foreign Service Act of 1946
United States Information and
  Educational Exchange Act (1948)

Michael P. Malloy
*University of the Pacific, McGeorge
School of Law*
Community Development Banking
  and Financial Institutions Act of
  1994
Glass-Steagall Act (1933)
International Emergency Economic
  Powers Act (1977)
National Banking Act (1864)
Tariff Act of 1789
Trading with the Enemy Act (1917)
United Nations Participation Act
  (1945)

Jerry W. Markham
*University of North Carolina School
of Law*
Commodities Exchange Act (1936)
Gold Standard Act of 1900
Social Security Act of 1935

Edward J. McCaffery
*University of Southern California
Law School*
Public Debt Acts

Michael D. McClintock
Mcafee & Taft, Oklahoma City
Merchant Marine Act of 1920

Travis McDade
*Ohio State University, Michael E.
Moritz College of Law*
Administrative Dispute Resolution
  Act (1990)
Legal Services Corporation Act
  (1974)

W. Eric McElwain
*University of the Pacific, McGeorge
School of Law*
Trade Act of 1974

Robert H. McLaughlin
University of Chicago
Antiquities Act of 1906

Eric J. Miller
Harvard University Law School
Juvenile Justice and Deliquency
  Prevention Act of 1974

Chandra Miller Manning
Pacific Lutheran University
Internal Improvements Acts

Kelly A. Moore
Washington University School of Law
Federal Cigarette Labeling and
  Advertising Act of 1965

William S. Morrow, Jr.
*Washington Metropolitan Area
Transit Commission*
Urban Mass Transportation Acts

Mary-Beth Moylan
*University of the Pacific, McGeorge
School of Law*
Highway Act of 1956

Roger K. Newman
*Columbia University Graduate
School of Journalism*
Fair Labor Standards Act (1938)
Hill-Burton Act (1946)

Lawrence H. Officer
University of Illinois at Chicago
Bland-Allison Act (1878)
Coinage Act of 1792
Coinage Acts
Gold Reserve Act of 1934

Todd Olmstead
*Yale University School of Public
Health*
Highway Safety Act of 1966
National Traffic and Motor Vehicle
  Safety Act of 1966

Craig Oren
*Rutgers, The State University of New
Jersey, School of Law, Camden*
Clean Air Act (1963)

Kevin Outterson
*West Virginia University College
of Law*
Medicare Act (1965)
Prohibition of the Slave Trade (1807)

Thomas Panebianco
*Shepherd College; former General
Counsel, Federal Maritime
Commission*
Shipping Acts

Sara M. Patterson
Claremont Graduate University
Indian Removal Act (1830)

Antonio F. Perez
*The Catholic University of America
School of Law*
Foreign Assistance Act

Twila L. Perry
*Rutgers, The State University of New
Jersey, Center for Law and Justice*
Family and Medical Leave Act of
  1993

Adam P. Plant
Montgomery, Alabama
Selective Service Act of 1917
Smoot-Hawley Tariff Act (1930)

Ellen S. Podgor
*Georgia State University, College of
Law*
Counterfeit Access Device and
  Computer Fraud and Abuse Act
  of 1984

Steve Pollak
*Shea and Gardner, Washington,
D.C.*
Economic Opportunity Act of 1964

James G. Pope
Rutgers University School of Law
National Industrial Recovery Act
  (1933)

Eric A. Posner
University of Chicago Law School
Bankruptcy Act of 1978

Trevor Potter
*Campaign Legal Center,
Washington, D.C.*
Federal Election Campaign Act (1971)

L.A. Powe, Jr.
University of Texas School of Law
Judiciary Act of 1801

Ann Powers
Pace University School of Law
Federal Water Pollution Control Act
  (1948)

Steven Puro
St. Louis University
Electronic Signatures in Global and
    National Commerce Act (2000)
Food Stamp Act of 1964

Steven Ramirez
Washburn University School of Law
Federal Deposit Insurance Acts
Federal Home Loan Bank Act
    (1932)
Securities Act of 1933
Securities Exchange Act of 1934

Holly A. Reese
*Washington University School of
Law*
Taft-Hartley Act (1947)

Elizabeth Regosin
St. Lawrence University
Freedmen's Bureau Acts (1865,
    1868)

Sandra Rierson
Thomas Jefferson School of Law
Comstock Act (1873)

Eugene H. Robinson, Jr.
United States Marine Corps
Hazardous and Solid Waste
    Amendments of 1984
Solid Waste Disposal Act (1965)

Melissa Rogers
*Pew Forum on Religion and Public
Life, Washington, D.C.*
Religious Freedom Restoration Act
    (1993)

Stephen C. Rogers
Washington, D.C.
Rail Passenger Service Act (1970)

Sara Rosenbaum
George Washington University
Medicaid Act (1965)

Ross Rosenfeld
Brooklyn, New York
Atomic Energy Acts
Farm Credit Act of 1933
Farmers Home Administration Act
    (1946)
Force Act of 1871
Interstate Commerce Act of 1887
National Housing Act (1955)
Small Business Act (1953)

Seth Rosenfeld
Atomic Energy Acts
Small Business Act (1953)

William G. Ross
*Samford University, Cumberland
School of Law*
Keating-Owen Act of 1916

Theodore W. Ruger
*Washington University in St. Louis
School of Law*
Federal Food, Drug, and Cosmetic
    Act (1938)

Steve Russell
Indiana University
Indian Civil Rights Act (1968)

Lawrence Schlam
*Northern Illinois University College
of Law*
Domestic Volunteer Services Act of
    1973 (VISTA)
Equal Pay Act of 1963
Higher Education Act of 1965
Indian Reorganization Act of 1934
Peace Corps Act of 1961

Elizabeth M. Schneider
Brooklyn Law School
Violence Against Women Act of
    1994

Steven L. Schooner
*George Washington University Law
School*
Contract Disputes Act (1978)

John Cary Sims
*University of the Pacific, McGeorge
School of Law*
Emergency Planning and
    Community Right-To-Know Act
    (1986)
Privacy Act of 1974

David A. Skeel, Jr.
*University of Pennsylvania Law
School*
Bankruptcy Act of 1841

Richard Slottee
Lewis & Clark College Law School
Consumer Credit Protection Act
    (1969)
Truth in Lending Act (1969)

Charles Anthony Smith
University of California, San Diego
Outer Continental Shelf Lands Act
    (1953)

Donald F. Spak
Chicago-Kent College of Law
National Guard Acts
Posse Comitatus Act (1878)

Michael I. Spak
Chicago-Kent College of Law
National Guard Acts
Posse Comitatus Act (1878)

Andrew C. Spiropoulos
*Oklahoma City University School of
Law*
Flag Protection Act of 1989

Norman Stein
*University of Alabama School of
Law*
Civil War Pensions
1894 Income Tax and Wilson-
    Gorman Tariff Act

John P. Stimson
United States Marine Corps
Veterans' Preference Act of 1944

Robert N. Strassfeld
*Case Western University School of
Law*
Espionage Act (1917) and Sedition
    Act (1918)

Thomas Susman
Ropes & Gray, Washington, D.C.
Lobbying Disclosure Act (1995)

Matthew M. Taylor
Georgetown University
Panama Canal Purchase Act (1902)

Joseph P. Tomain
*University of Cincinnati College of
Law*
Department of Energy Organization
    Act (1977)
National Energy Conservation
    Policy Act (1978)
Natural Gas Act (1938)
Nuclear Waste Policy Act (1982)
Surface Mining Control and
    Reclamation Act (1977)

Mark Tushnet
Georgetown University Law Center
Antiterrorism and Effective Death
    Penalty Act (1996)
Civil Rights Act of 1875

James F. Van Orden
Duke University
Fish and Wildlife Conservation Act
    of 1980
National Emissions Standards Act
    (1965)

Robert W. Van Sickel
Indiana State University
Communications Act of 1934

Lynda D. Vargha
Skidmore College
Export-Import Bank Act of 1945

Robert G. Vaughn
American University, Washington College of Law
Civil Service Reform Act (1978)
Ethics in Government Act (1978)
Freedom of Information Act (1966)
Whistleblower Protection Laws (1989)

Wendy Wagner
University of Texas School of Law
Marine Mammal Protection Act (1972)

James Walker
Wright State University
Richard B. Russell National School Lunch Act (1946)

Valerie Watnick
Law Department, Baruch College, Zicklin School of Business
Food Quality Protection Act of 1996

Gregory S. Weber
University of the Pacific, McGeorge School of Law

Comprehensive Environmental Response, Compensation, and Liability Act (1980)

Richard Westin
University of Kentucky College of Law
Tax Reform Act of 1986

Daniel C. Wewers
Harvard University
Northwest Ordinance (1787)
Southwest Ordinance (1790)

Steven Harmon Wilson
Prairie View A&M University
Alcoholic and Narcotic Rehabilitation Act (1968)
Controlled Substances Act (1970)
Drug Abuse Prevention, Treatment, and Rehabilitation Act (1980)

John Fabian Witt
Columbia Law School
Federal Employers' Liability Act (1908)

Kelly A. Woestman
Pittsburg State University
No Child Left Behind (2001)

James A. Wooten
State University of New York at Buffalo, School of Law
Employee Retirement Income Security Act of 1974

Eric Yamamoto
University of Hawaii, Richardson School of Law
Civil Liberties Act (1988)

Diana H. Yoon
New York, New York
Chinese Exclusion Acts

Jeff Zavatsky
New York, New York
Farm Credit Act of 1933
National Housing Act (1955)

Christopher Zorn
Emory University
Staggers Rail Act of 1980

Lynne K. Zusman
Lynne Zusman & Associates, Washington, D.C.
Department of Homeland Security Act (2002)
Mutual Security Act (1951)
National Security Act of 1947
USA Patriot Act (2001)

A

ADMINISTRATIVE DISPUTE RESOLUTION ACT (1990)

Travis McDade

Excerpt from the Administrative Dispute Resolution Act

The Congress finds that—

(2) administrative proceedings have become increasingly formal, costly, and lengthy resulting in unnecessary expenditures of time and in a decreased likelihood of achieving consensual resolution of disputes;

(3) alternative means of dispute resolution have been used in the private sector for many years and, in appropriate circumstances, have yielded decisions that are faster, less expensive, and less contentious;

(4) such alternative means can lead to more creative, efficient, and sensible outcomes;

(5) such alternative means may be used advantageously in a wide variety of administrative programs;

(6) explicit authorization of the use of well-tested dispute resolution techniques will eliminate ambiguity of agency authority under existing law...

I n 1989, an estimated 220,000 civil cases were filed in the United States, with the federal government being a party in more than 55,000 of them. The cost of this **litigation** was almost incalculable. Aside from the money and time expended, the uncertainty and delay caused by pending court decisions as well as the legal work that could otherwise have been done by attorneys was immense. In light of this expense, prior to 1990 the private sector increasingly sought alternative methods of resolving disputes. Some of these alternatives included relying on neutral mediators to solve small disagreements or by **arbitration** where parties give a neutral evaluator the power to conclude disputes in a more formal way. Private companies had started turning to **alternative dispute resolution** (ADR) as early as 1925 after Congress passed the Federal Arbitration Act.

But the General Accounting Office had decided not to let decisions on disputes involving monetary claims with federal agencies take place outside

litigation: a lawsuit

arbitrate: to resolve disagreements whereby parties choose a person or group of people familiar with the issues in question to hear and settle their dispute

alternative dispute resolution: any means of settling disputes outside of the courtroom, typically including arbitration, mediation, early neutral evaluation, and conciliation

On October 19, 1996, President Clinton signed the ADR Act of 1996. The law made permanent the original ADR and Negotiated Rulemaking Acts of 1990.

appoint: to select someone to fill an office or position

judicial: having to do with judgments in courts of law or with the administration of justice

the courts without federal statutory authority. Although some government agencies, including the Environmental Protection Agency and the Army Corps of Engineers, had been authorized to use alternative methods such as mediation and minitrials for years, the government had no uniform requirement or guidelines on when to employ ADR techniques.

The Administrative Dispute Resolution Act of 1990 (ADRA) (P.L. 101-552, 104 Stat. 2736) changed this. The ADRA required federal government entities to consider alternative means of resolving conflicts in hopes of realizing some of the same benefits as private companies. The ADRA required that agencies **appoint** a specific person for training personnel in the use of ADR techniques and assessing all programs with ADR potential. This served the dual purpose of both normalizing ADR within the agencies, as well as establishing specific contexts in which the new tools could be used effectively.

The act provided that voluntary, binding arbitration would be authorized when all parties consented, subject to the safeguards of **judicial** and agency review. Perhaps most importantly, the act established a framework of confidentiality in ADR proceedings. Since the federal government is subject to the Freedom of Information Act (FOIA), it was important that the ADRA strike the right balance between maintaining an open and transparent process and protecting the parties' confidentiality. In passing the ADRA, Congress mandated that the act expire in October 1995, so that it could review the ADRA's impact before making it a permanent fixture in government agencies.

By 1996 it was apparent that the main flaw of ADRA was the lack of emphasis on confidentiality. When Congress renewed the act in 1996, the ADRA significantly enhanced the confidentiality protections. The new act created a specific FOIA exemption for ADR communications; it also broadened the scope of communications that could not be disclosed by parties to a dispute. The 1996 Act also made the ADRA permanent, tacitly acknowledging the effectiveness of alternative dispute resolution techniques.

See also: NEGOTIATED RULEMAKING ACT.

BIBLIOGRAPHY

Phillips, Barbara Ashley. *The Mediation Field Guide*. San Francisco, CA: Jossey-Bass, 2001.

Ware, Stephen. *Alternative Dispute Resolution*. St. Paul, MN: West, 2001.

INTERNET RESOURCE

Interagency Alternative Dispute Resolution Working Group. <http://www.usdoj.gov/adr>.

ADMINISTRATIVE PROCEDURE ACT (1946)

Jeffrey S. Lubbers

Excerpt from the Administrative Procedure Act

After notice required by this section, the agency shall give interested persons an opportunity to participate in the rule making through submission of written data, views, or arguments with or without opportunity for oral presentation. After consideration of the relevant matter presented, the agency shall incorporate in the rules adopted a concise general statement of their basis and purpose. When rules are required by statute to be made on the record after opportunity for an agency hearing, sections 556 and 557 [the formal hearing provisions] of this title apply instead of this subsection.

The Administrative Procedure Act (APA) (60 Stat. 237), enacted in 1946 and recodified in 1966, is the procedural roadmap for the federal executive branch. Unless another **statute** provides otherwise, every executive branch department and agency must follow the APA's minimum procedures for **adjudication** and rule making. It also establishes general ground rules for the judicial review of agency actions. Although it has been supplemented by several other laws discussed in this volume (e.g., the Freedom of Information Act, Regulatory Flexibility Act, and Administrative Dispute Resolution Act), it has been amended remarkably little since 1946, and its provisions have served as models for many other administrative procedure laws in the fifty states and countries around the world.

statute: a law enacted by the legislative branch of government

adjudication: the act of settling something judicially

GENERAL STRUCTURE OF THE ACT

The APA has two major subdivisions: sections 551 through 559 deal in general with agency procedures, and sections 701 through 706 deal in general with judicial review. The latter sections restate the principles of judicial review contained in many statutes and judicial decisions, but leave the details regarding judicial review to be governed by other statutes or court decisions. In addition, several sections dealing with administrative law judges—special hearing officers with special independence—are scattered through title 5 of the United States Code.

> *Rule making is essentially a legislative action because, like the making of laws, the making of rules is an action that becomes applicable in the future.*

RULE MAKING AND ADJUDICATION

The structure of the APA reflects the distinction between rule making and adjudication, with different sets of procedural requirements prescribed for each. Government agencies formulate and issue rules, statements designed to implement, interpret, or prescribe law or policy. Through rule making, government agencies can regulate the future conduct of persons. Rule making is essentially a legislative action because, like the making of laws, the making of rules is an action that becomes applicable in the future. In contrast to rule making, adjudication is a process of determining past and present rights and **liabilities**. The result of an adjudicative proceeding is the issuance of an order (rather than a rule).

liability: an obligation, responsibility, or duty that one is bound by law or justice to perform

The line separating the two types of agency action is not always clear, partly because of the sheer abundance and variety of an agency's actions. Most agencies use rule making to formulate future policy. However, adjudicative orders can also announce policies. Agencies normally use a combination of rule making and adjudication to carry out their programs.

FORMAL AND INFORMAL PROCEEDINGS

The APA subdivides the categories of rule making and adjudication into formal and informal proceedings. A rule-making or adjudication proceeding is considered formal when the proceeding is required by another statute to be "on the record after opportunity for an agency hearing." The APA prescribes complex procedures for hearings by administrative law judges in both formal rule making (a rarely used procedure) and formal adjudication. It requires relatively minimal procedures for informal rule making. The APA prescribes very few procedures for the remaining category of informal adjudication, which is by far the most common form of governmental action.

Section 553 sets forth the basic requirements for informal rule making, which is the most common form of rule making: An agency must place a notice of proposed rule making in the *Federal Register*, followed by an opportunity for written comment by interested persons. The rule must then be published, in most instances at least thirty days before it becomes effective. This process is often referred to as notice-and-comment rule making.

Section 701 states that judicial review of agency action is available unless a statute prevents such review or the action is committed by law to agency discretion. Preliminary or intermediate actions are ordinarily reviewable only on review of the final agency action. Section 702 deals with the issue of who has standing (i.e., the legal right to sue) to challenge agency action. It states that a person who suffers a legal wrong or who is negatively affected or **aggrieved** by agency action is entitled to judicial review of that action. Section 703 deals with the form of the judicial review proceeding and in which court it should be brought. Section 704 provides that judicial review is available only for final agency action. Section 705 authorizes a reviewing court to postpone the date on which an agency action will take effect or preserve the status or rights affected by an agency's order until completion of judicial review proceedings. Section 706 sets forth the scope of judicial review of agency actions. In general, the scope of review depends on the nature of the agency action under challenge. For example, that action may be a question of law, an exercise of discretion, or a determination of fact.

CIRCUMSTANCES LEADING TO THE ADOPTION OF THE ACT

Attempts to regularize federal administrative procedures go back at least to the 1930s. In 1932 the Supreme Court ruled that it was constitutional for Congress to assign the adjudication of so-called "public rights" cases to administrative agencies (*Crowell v. Benson*). This ruling confirmed the use of administrative adjudication. Early in 1939, at the suggestion of the attorney general, President Franklin D. Roosevelt requested the formation of the Attorney General's Committee on Administrative Procedure to study existing administrative procedures and to formulate recommendations. The committee produced a series of

Attempts to regularize federal administrative procedures go back at least to the 1930s.

Federal Register: A newspaper published daily by the National Archives and Records Administration to notify the public of federal agency regulations, proposed rules and notices, executive orders, and other executive branch documents

aggrieved: suffering physical injury or a loss of one's property interest, monetary interest, or personal rights

monographs on agency functions and submitted its final report to the president and Congress in 1941. These materials, plus extensive hearings held before a subcommittee of the Senate Committee on the Judiciary in 1941, are the primary historical sources for the Administrative Procedure Act.

Most legislative debate concerned the appropriateness of assigning adjudicative responsibilities to the many new agencies that had been created by the **New Deal**. The Attorney General Committee's study showed that the procedures used by agencies to decide cases and to make rules lacked basic uniformity. The study also showed that some agency hearing officers were not sufficiently independent of the investigators or prosecutors. The committee designed a compromise that would create trial-type procedures, establish quasi-independent "hearing examiners" to preside over and make initial decisions in such cases, and authorize judicial review in the regular federal courts. The rule-making procedures provoked little controversy during the debates, although decades later, as rule-making became much more common, other laws were passed that added more formality to the process. These include the Occupational Safety and Health Act and the Clean Air Act, and government-wide statutes such as the Regulatory Flexibility Act, Paperwork Reduction Act, and Unfunded Mandates Reform Act.

After President Truman signed the APA into law in June 1946, the Department of Justice compiled a manual of advice and interpretation of its various provisions. The *Attorney General's Manual on the Administrative Procedure Act,* published in 1947, remains the principal guide to the structure and intent of the APA. The *Manual* states that the purposes of the act were to: (1) require agencies to keep the public currently informed of their organization, procedures, and rules; (2) provide for public participation in the rule-making process; (3) prescribe uniform standards for the conduct of rule making and adjudicative proceedings; and (4) restate the law of judicial review.

New Deal: the legislative and administrative program of President Franklin D. Roosevelt designed to promote economic recovery and social reform during the 1930s

EXPERIENCE UNDER THE ACT

In the years following enactment of the APA, the Supreme Court issued several decisions that promoted the applicability of the act, including decisions validating the act's due process protections (*Wong Yang Sung v. McGrath,* 1950), judicial review provisions (*Universal Camera Corp. v. NLRB,* 1951), and hearing examiner program (*Ramspeck v. Federal Trial Examiners Conference,* 1953).

The APA has been widely accepted ever since. The courts have enforced its provisions by making quite clear that the agencies must follow the APA's procedures when it is applicable. Significantly, the Supreme Court has also made the APA a "safe harbor" by ruling that lower courts may not require agencies to use procedures beyond those required by procedural provisions of the APA or other statutes (*Vermont Yankee Nuclear Power Co. v. Natural Resources Defense Council, Inc.,* 1978). Congress regularly incorporates references to the APA in other legislation. Although commentators have noted some flaws, notably its lack of guidance on informal adjudication, many observers have praised its innovations, such as notice-and-comment rule making and administrative law judges. For example, the leading administrative scholar, Kenneth Culp Davis, called notice-and-comment procedures "one of the greatest inventions of modern government."

Most states have enacted state APAs that prescribe procedures for their agencies.

Only a few major amendments have been added to the APA. In 1966 the Freedom of Information Act was added to the provisions in section 552 that already called for the publication of certain government information. In 1976, as part of the Government in the Sunshine Act, a ban was added on **ex parte** communications to decision makers in formal proceedings. Also in that year, some technical amendments made it easier for challengers to sue the government. In 1978 the term "administrative law judge" was substituted for "hearing examiner." And in 1990 a few provisions were added by the Administrative Dispute Resolution Act.

ex parte: (Latin) on one side only; brought for the benefit of one party without notice to or challenge by an adverse party

RELATIONSHIP WITH OTHER LAWS

The APA is broadly related to numerous laws because many of its provisions must be triggered by another statute. The act is more directly related to such openness laws as the Freedom of Information Act, the Government in the Sunshine Act, the Federal Advisory Committee Act, and the Privacy Act. Its adjudication procedures have been supplemented by the Administrative Dispute Resolution Act. Its rule-making provisions have been supplemented by the Regulatory Flexibility Act and the Paperwork Reduction Act.

accountability: to hold one answerable or responsible for the outcome of an action or project

The APA has proved to be a durable and important force in regularizing the procedures of the federal bureaucracy. Its emphasis on transparency, fairness, and access to the courts has increased the **accountability**, fairness, efficiency, and acceptability of a wide range of government decision making.

See also: ADMINISTRATIVE DISPUTE RESOLUTION ACT; FEDERAL TORT CLAIMS ACT; FREEDOM OF INFORMATION ACT; NEGOTIATED RULEMAKING ACT; PAPERWORK REDUCTION ACT; REGULATORY FLEXIBILITY ACT.

BIBLIOGRAPHY

Asimow, Michael, ed. *A Guide to Federal Agency Adjudication.* Chicago, IL: American Bar Association Publishing, 2003.

Davis, Kenneth Culp. *Administrative Law Treatise,* Supp. vol. 1, sec. 6.15. St. Paul, MN: West, 1970.

Lubbers, Jeffrey S. *A Guide to Federal Agency Rulemaking.* Chicago, IL: American Bar Association Publishing, 1998.

Shepherd, George B. "The Administrative Procedure Act Emerges from New Deal Politics." *Northwestern Law Review* 90 (1996): 1557-1683.

AGE DISCRIMINATION IN EMPLOYMENT ACT (1967)

Julia Lamber

Excerpt from the Age Discrimination in Employment Act

(a) It shall be unlawful for an employer—

(1) to fail or refuse to hire or to discharge any individual with respect to his compensation, terms, condition, or privileges of employment, because of such individual's age;

(2) to limit, segregate, or classify his employees in any way which would deprive or tend to deprive any individual of employment opportunities or otherwise adversely affect his status an as employee, because of such individual's age; or

(3) to reduce the wage rate of any employee in order to comply with this chapter.

The Age Discrimination in Employment Act (ADEA) (P.L. 90-202, 81 Stat. 602) forbids public and private employers to engage in discrimination in employment on the basis of age against persons over the age of forty. Employers cannot refuse to hire people over the age of forty, fire employees simply because they are too old, or make distinctions among employees on the basis of age. Moreover, the act prohibits retaliation against people who assert their rights under the statute. The act also covers unions and employment agencies but is rarely applied to them. The ADEA is enforced by the Equal Employment Opportunity Commission (EEOC). The act allows both the EEOC or a private person to sue for damages as well as **injunctive relief**.

injunctive relief: a court order that requires a person to refrain from doing something and that guards against future damages rather than remedies past damages

BACKGROUND

The ADEA grew out of the congressional debate on Title VII of the Civil Rights Act of 1964, which prohibits discrimination in employment on the basis of race, color, religion, sex, or national origin. Instead of including age as one of the categories in the 1964 Civil Rights Act, Congress directed the secretary of labor to study the issues and then to submit specific proposals for prohibiting age discrimination. President Lyndon Johnson delivered a special message to Congress concerning older Americans.

The ADEA protects persons between the ages of forty and sixty-five from discrimination in employment. Three years earlier, Congress had voted against an amendment to Title VII of the Civil Rights Act of 1964 that would have included age discrimination as an unlawful employment practice.

Congress found that older workers were disadvantaged in their efforts to regain employment when displaced from jobs, that arbitrary age limits were commonplace, and that unemployment adversely affected the skill, morale, and employer acceptability of older workers. It also found, however, that age discrimination was rarely based on the sort of hostility behind other forms of discrimination, such as race or gender. Instead, it was based on stereotypes about older workers that were often unsupported by objective facts. In response, Congress passed the ADEA in 1967 to promote the employment of older workers and to prohibit arbitrary age policies in employment. The United States Supreme Court has held that the ADEA is a valid exercise of congressional power under the **commerce clause** of the U.S. Constitution but not under section 5 of the Fourteenth Amendment, which empowers Congress to enforce the nondiscrimination provisions of the Constitution.

commerce clause: the provision of the U.S. Constitution (Article I, section 8, clause 3) that gives Congress exclusive powers over interstate commerce—the buying, selling, or exchanging of goods or products between states

EXCEPTIONS

There are several exceptions to the statute's nondiscrimination provisions. First, employers may use age as an employment criterion if they can justify its use. In other words, they must prove that "age is a bona fide occupational qualification reasonably necessary to the normal operation of the particular business." Under this exception, employers must show that age is a reasonable measure of a job qualification that is important to the employer's business. The courts have interpreted this as a very narrow exception to the general prohibition of age discrimination contained in the ADEA.

The second exception applies to employee benefit plans, such as health insurance and pension plans. Providing such fringe benefits to older workers costs employers more than providing them to younger workers (who, for example, tend to have fewer health problems). The application of the ADEA to pension plans and other fringe benefits is incredibly technical and complicated. It has been the subject of much litigation and congressional activity. Currently, the statute allows fringe benefit plans that provide unequal benefits for different age groups if the differences are justified by different employer costs or are part of a voluntary early retirement plan. For example, an employer can provide each employee with $1000 of health-care insurance even though that $1000 buys less protection for older employees.

Under the third exception, the act does not define elected officials and political appointees responsible for policy making as employees. And, although the statute was amended to expressly prohibit mandatory retirement, it does allow mandatory retirement (at age 65) of executives or other employees in high, policy-making positions. For the sake of public safety, a specific amendment also allows for maximum age and mandatory retirement (at age 55) of publicly employed firefighters and law enforcement officers.

EXPERIENCE UNDER THE ACT

The main question under the ADEA is when age distinctions are justified. Should the protection against age discrimination be taken broadly, that is, striking down most distinctions, or narrowly, allowing many distinctions? In general, the courts have interpreted the protections of the statute broadly but they have imposed fairly rigorous standards of proof.

Because the ADEA is modeled on Title VII of the Civil Rights Act, this statute expands our notion of civil rights beyond the traditional categories of race and gender.

Because the ADEA is modeled on Title VII of the Civil Rights Act, this statute expands our notion of civil rights beyond the traditional categories of race and gender. It has virtually eliminated mandatory retirement for most jobs and has changed the view of both employers and the public as to who is a qualified worker. It has dramatically increased employment among older workers.

RELATED ACT

The Age Discrimination Act of 1975 prohibits discrimination based on age in programs or activities that receive federal financial assistance. This statute is enforced primarily by the Office for Civil Rights in the Department of Education and does not cover employment discrimination. The 1975 act includes many exemptions. For example, it exempts age-based statutes enacted by elected bodies such as the minimum age to enroll in school. Because of the number of exceptions written into the statute, it has had limited impact.

See also: AMERICANS WITH DISABILITIES ACT; CIVIL RIGHTS ACT OF 1964; TITLE IX EDUCATION AMENDMENTS.

BIBLIOGRAPHY

Dobrich, Wanda, Steven Dranoff, and Gerald Maatman. *The Manager's Guide to Preventing Hostile Work Environment: How to Avoid Legal and Financial Risks by Protecting Your Workforce From Harassment on the Basis of Sex, Race, Disability, Religion, and Age.* New York: McGraw-Hill, 2002.

Matthews, Joseph L. *Social Security, Medicare, and Pensions: The Sourcebook for Older Americans.* Berkley, CA: Nolo Press, 1996.

INTERNET RESOURCES

U.S. Equal Employment Opportunity Commission. <http://www.eeoc.gov>.

AGRICULTURAL ADJUSTMENT ACT (1933)

Jim Chen

Excerpt from the Agricultural Adjustment Act

It is declared to be the policy of Congress—To establish and maintain such balance between the production and consumption of agricultural commodities, and such marketing conditions therefor, as will reestablish prices to farmers at a level that will give agricultural commodities a purchasing power with respect to articles that farmers buy, equivalent to the purchasing power of agricultural commodities in the base period.

The **Great Depression** hit American farmers especially hard. With prices of **commodities** and farmers' income at historic lows, the **Dust Bowl** destroyed what little productivity was left in many farms. White farmers from Oklahoma joined the exodus that black farmers from the Mississippi Delta had already begun during the 1920s. The agricultural crisis profoundly affected the 1932 presidential campaign. During his successful run for the presidency, Franklin D. Roosevelt promised comprehensive agricultural relief.

NEW DEAL LEGISLATION

Roosevelt's plan to revive the American economy was called the **New Deal**. During the first hundred days of Roosevelt's administration, Congress passed fifteen major pieces of legislation designed to reduce unemployment. The Agricultural Adjustment Act of 1933 (48 Stat. 31), took its place alongside the National Industrial Recovery Act as a leading component of this relief package. The Agricultural Adjustment Act (AAA) pledged to restore the purchasing power enjoyed by farmers in the years immediately preceding World War I. This concept, called "parity," became a rallying point for farmers throughout the New Deal and would dominate agricultural policy after World War II. The AAA was designed to restore parity prices for "basic agricultural commodities"—initially defined as wheat, cotton, corn, hogs, rice, tobacco, and milk—by reducing supplies. Benefit payments would compensate participating farmers who agreed to curb acreage or kill excess livestock.

Great Depression: the largest and most severe economic depression in American history (1929–1939); its effects were felt throughout the world

commodity: an article of trade or commerce that can be transported; especially an agricultural or mining product

Dust Bowl: a semiarid region in the south-central United States where the topsoil was lost by wind erosion in the mid-1930s

New Deal: the legislative and administrative program of President Franklin D. Roosevelt designed to promote economic recovery and social reform (1933–1939)

During the first hundred days of Roosevelt's administration, Congress passed fifteen major pieces of legislation designed to reduce unemployment.

The AAA levied a tax on processors of agricultural commodities. Cotton gin operators, for instance, would be taxed for the benefit of cotton farmers who had agreed to reduce their acreage. The Department of Agriculture characterized this tax as "the heart of the law," because the proceeds from this tax would simultaneously enhance farmers' purchasing power and increase commodity prices by reducing supplies.

To undertake the taxing of processors and to make benefit payments to participating farmers, the AAA relied on Article I, section 8, clause 1 of the Constitution, which empowers Congress "to lay and collect Taxes, Duties, Imposts and Excises, to pay the Debts and provide for the common Defence and general Welfare of the United States." Older decisions such as *United States v. E.C. Knight Co.* (1895) had established that Con-

The Agricultural Adjustment Act of 1933 (AAA) was passed to assist American farmers who suffered the twin tragedies of both the Great Depression and the Dust Bowl. The goal of this relief package was to restore the purchasing power of farmers to their pre-World War I levels. In U.S. v. Butler (1936), the act was found unconstitutional by the Supreme Court, which ruled that it "invade(d) the reserved rights of the states to regulate and control agricultural production." In 1938, another AAA was passed by Congress and upheld by the Supreme Court in Mulford v. Smith *(1939).* (FRANKLIN D. ROOSEVELT LIBRARY)

gress's power under Article I, section 8, clause 3 "to regulate **Commerce** with foreign Nations, and among the several States, and with the Indian Tribes" did not extend to productive activities such as manufacturing, agriculture, and mining. In other words, the Constitution drew a distinction between regulating commerce and regulating production. When the Supreme Court invalidated the National Industrial Recovery Act in *A.L.A. Schechter Poultry Corp. v. United States* (1935), it not only endorsed that old distinction but also held that retailing likewise lay beyond Congress's power to regulate **interstate commerce**.

commerce: the large-scale exchange of goods, involving transportation from one place to another

interstate commerce: traffic, commercial trading, or the transportation of persons or property between or among the several states of the Union, or from or between points in one state and points in another state

JUDICIAL REVIEW

In *United States v. Butler* (1936), the Supreme Court invalidated the Agricultural Adjustment Act of 1933. Justice Owen Roberts, writing for himself and five other justices, held that the AAA "invade[d] the reserved rights of the states" by endeavoring "to regulate and control agricultural production, a matter beyond the powers delegated to the federal government." Specifically, the Court held that the AAA violated the Tenth Amendment to the Constitution, which declares: "The powers not delegated to the United States by the Constitution, nor prohibited by it to the States, are reserved to the States respectively, or to the people." Assuming that Congress could not directly compel farmers to reduce acreage or cull livestock, the Court held that Congress "may not indirectly accomplish those ends by taxing and spending to purchase **compliance**."

By a vote of 6 to 3 in United States v. Butler *(1936), the Supreme Court declared the act unconstitutional.*

comply: to act in accordance to a wish, request, demand, rule, order, or statute

The constitutional views expressed in *Schechter Poultry* and *Butler* would not last beyond 1937. Two Supreme Court decisions rendered that year greatly expanded Congress's ability to regulate commerce and to attach conditions to federal expenditures. *NLRB v. Jones & Laughlin Steel Corp.* (1937) upheld the National Labor Relations Act as a proper exercise of Congress's commerce clause powers, and *Steward Machine Co. v. Davis* (1937) upheld the Social Security Act (despite objections similar to those raised in *Butler*.) Meanwhile, minor agricultural statutes were surviving Supreme Court review. In *Wright v. Vinton Branch of the Mountain Trust Bank* (1937), the Court upheld the Farm Bankruptcy Act of 1935. In 1939 the Court upheld both the Agricultural Marketing Agreement Act (*United States v. Rock-Royal Cooperative, Inc.*) and the Tobacco Inspection Act (*Currin v. Wallace*).

FURTHER LEGISLATIVE ACTION

Emboldened by the apparent change in the Supreme Court's attitude toward the constitutionality of the New Deal, Congress passed a second Agricultural Adjustment Act, designated as the Agricultural Adjustment Act of 1938. Rather than using the proceeds from taxes on processors to motivate farmers to lower production in exchange for benefit payments, the 1938 act applied marketing quotas and overproduction penalties directly. For example, the tobacco program established by the 1938 act triggered a national marketing quota whenever the secretary of agriculture determined that supplies would exceed a threshold called the "reserve supply level." The secretary would **apportion** the quota among tobacco farms nationwide, and penalties would be assessed against auction warehouses marketing tobacco from a farm that had exceeded its quota.

apportion: to divide and assign according to a plan

In *Mulford v. Smith* (1939), the Supreme Court upheld the 1938 act with little fanfare. Even though the marketing quotas imposed by the 1938 act intruded far more aggressively into the agricultural economy than the processing taxes at issue in the 1933 act, *Mulford* found no fault in the 1938 act. Just three years earlier the 1933 act had been condemned as an unconstitutional stratagem by the federal government to interfere in agricultural markets. Yet the ruling in *Mulford* blessed the 1938 act as a program "intended to foster, protect and conserve [interstate] commerce."

Three years later, in *Wickard v. Filburn* (1942), the Supreme Court revisited the Agricultural Adjustment Act of 1938. Whereas the tobacco in *Mulford* was specifically destined for interstate sale at an auction, *Filburn* involved an Ohio farmer who fed his excess wheat to livestock on his own farm. In *Filburn* the Court held that the act could apply even to a seemingly trivial amount of excess production that never crosses state lines or otherwise affects interstate traffic in wheat, as long as any regulated farmer's "contribution, taken together with that of many others similarly situated, is far from trivial."

Wickard v. Filburn laid to rest any remaining doubt about the constitutionality of federal statutes regulating agricultural production, prices, and incomes. Together with the Agricultural Act of 1949, the Agricultural Adjustment Act of 1938 now constitutes the major part of so-called "permanent legislation" that provides federal support for commodity prices and farm incomes. Periodic "farm bills," such as the Food Security Act of 1985 and

Workers in 1937 pick cotton, which, along with wheat, corn, hogs, rice, tobacco, and milk, was a commodity covered by the Agricultural Adjustment Act of 1933. (US NATIONAL ARCHIVES AND RECORDS ADMINISTRATION)

the Federal Agriculture Improvement and Reform Act of 1996, make temporary changes in support levels and program design by amending the "permanent legislation" for a specified period, typically five or six years. The programs authorized by permanent agricultural legislation and by periodic farm bills are diverse and complex. They include production flexibility **contract** programs, nonrecourse loans for marketing assistance, marketing quotas, marketing agreements, crop insurance, and the Conservation Reserve Program.

contract: a formal agreement, usually in writing, between two or more parties that can be legally enforced

See also: FARM CREDIT ACT OF 1933; NATIONAL INDUSTRIAL RECOVERY ACT.

BIBLIOGRAPHY

Breimyer, Harold F. "Agricultural Philosophies and Policies in the New Deal." *Minnesota Law Review* 68 (1983): 333-353.

Fite, Gilbert Courtland. *American Farmers: The New Minority.* Bloomington: Indiana University Press, 1981.

Irons, Peter H. *The New Deal Lawyers.* Princeton, NJ: Princeton University Press, 1982.

Rasmussen, Wayne D. "New Deal Agricultural Policies after 50 Years." *Minnesota Law Review* 68 (1983): 353–377.

Saloutos, Theodore. *The American Farmer and the New Deal.* Ames: Iowa State University Press, 1982.

AID TO DEPENDENT CHILDREN (1935)

Felice Batlan and Linda Gordon

Aid to Dependent Children or ADC (later renamed Aid to Families with Dependent Children, or AFDC) (P.L. 74-271, 49 Stat. 620), was Title IV of the Social Security Act of 1935. At first it functioned mainly to provide federal grants to help the states maintain their mothers' aid laws which had been passed in forty states between 1910 and 1920. With the federal government providing one-third of costs, the program offered aid to poor parents, assumed at that time to be always women caring for children alone.

The ADC plan was written by Grace Abbott and Katherine Lenroot, at that time the previous and current directors of the U.S. Children's Bureau in the Department of Labor. They **lobbied** hard to get this program added to the Social Security bill. That bill, which was written by the Committee on Economic Security (CES) was aimed at male breadwinners, reflecting the masculinist assumptions and composition of the Committee. The Children's Bureau's goal was to provide aid to all children whose mothers lacked the support of a breadwinner, no matter how they had got to that position. Moreover, Abbott and Lenroot designed the legislation to operate with the highest social-work standards, offering personal casework services to lone mothers as well as cash **stipends**. They sought casework both because they wanted to remove ADC recipients from the stigma of receiving public assistance, and because they believed that mother-headed families were problematic and needed support and guidance.

lobby: to try to persuade the legislature to pass laws and regulations that are favorable to one's interests and to defeat laws that are unfavorable to those interests

stipend: a fixed or regular payment, such as a salary for services rendered or an allowance

With the federal government providing one-third of costs, the program offered aid to poor parents, assumed at that time to be always women caring for children alone.

appropriate: to set aside for or assign to a particular purpose or group

After the bill was introduced, the CES and then Congress revised Abbott and Lenroot's draft. The revisions frustrated their objectives considerably:

(1) Participation by the states was made voluntary and in 1939 eight states had no ADC program.

(2) A provision that required the programs to pay a "reasonable subsistence compatible with decency and health" was removed.

(3) Most of the federal oversight, which would have promised equal treatment to applicants regardless of race or marital status, was removed.

(4) Administration of the program was transferred from the Children's Bureau to the Social Security Administration, which lacked the Children's Bureau's commitment to poor children and their mothers.

(5) The initial **appropriation** for the program was reduced from $120 to $25 million.

Ironically, the casework provisions for supervision created an effect virtually opposite to the intention of the designers. In the program's first three decades, a provision in the law that authorized ADC assistance only to "suitable homes" reduced drastically the number of eligible children. (In 1960

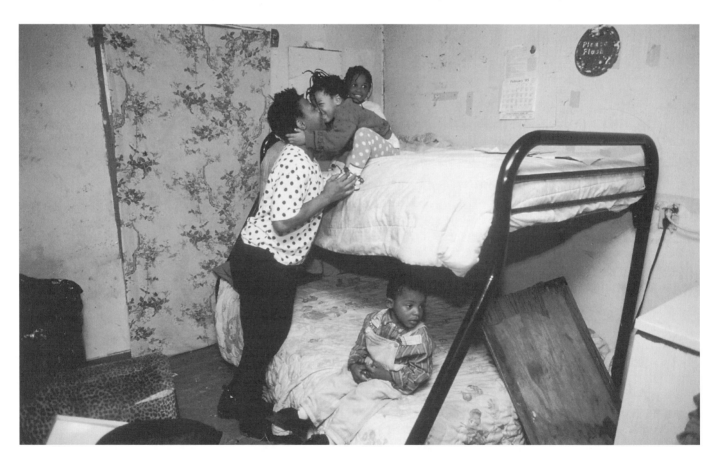

Low-income mothers and children benefit from the Aid to Families with Dependent Children AFDC. The original purpose of AFDC was to allow mothers to stay home with their children, but starting in the 1960s the system was reconfigured, and by the 1990s states required recipients to find "suitable" employment or attend school in order continue to receive benefits. AFDC was repealed in 1996.
(©Shepard Sherbell/Corbis SABA)

when 79 of every 1000 children were in need, only 30 received assistance.) This provision particularly inhibited coverage of "illegitimate" children and children of color. Local ADC policy frequently discontinued coverage during seasons of shortages in low-wage labor in fields or homes, thus forcing poor mothers into such labor.

Ironically, the casework provisions for supervision created an effect virtually opposite to the intention of the designers.

For its first three decades, ADC operated much like a private charity, with its caseworkers given discretion to investigate clients, cut off benefits to those determined to be unsuitable, and reduce benefits to those found in violation of any of ADC's many regulations. Starting in the mid-1960s the National Welfare Rights Organization, which was built primarily by African-American women and was functionally a part of the **Civil Rights movement**, began organizing to defend welfare recipients' rights. Working together with lawyers in community legal-aid offices, recipients filed hundreds of court cases challenging the administration of ADC. Such **litigation** had radical goals, which included creating a uniform federal standard for ADC administration and eliminating the most degrading eligibility provisions. The overarching objective entailed establishing a federal constitutional right to a minimum adequate income.

Civil Rights movement: the movement to win political, economic, and social equality for African Americans

litigation: a lawsuit

JUDICIAL OPINIONS AFFECTING THE PROGRAM

One of the first ADC (the program was renamed Aid to Families with Dependent Children [AFDC] after two-parent families with an unemployed parent became eligible) cases to reach the U.S. Supreme Court, *King v. Smith* (1968), challenged an Alabama regulation allowing for AFDC termination if a recipient "cohabitated" with a man. Numerous states defined "cohabitation" to include even casual relationships. (In Alabama this resulted in 16,000 children being dropped from AFDC.) The Court struck down the provision as inconsistent with federal statutory definitions of "parent," **opining** that the provision punished a woman for engaging in sexual relations and was unrelated to Congress's intent to provide aid to needy children. Notably, the Court's decision rested on statutory rather than constitutional grounds.

opining: to hold or state as an opinion

In *Shapiro v. Thompson* (1969), the Court found unconstitutional state regulations that required families to live in state for a certain time period before becoming eligible for AFDC. The Court ruled that such regulations infringed on the constitutional right to travel and that the state's interest in discouraging indigent families' **migration** did not defeat this right. *King, Shapiro,* and other cases that followed reduced the ability of states to restrict AFDC eligibility and provided some ground for the argument that AFDC was not charity but a protected entitlement.

migrate: to move from one place to another

Goldberg v. Kelley (1970) challenged a state's ability to terminate AFDC benefits prior to a hearing. The objectives of the litigation included the belief that the cost of providing such hearings would drastically curtail benefit termination, and that hearings would allow recipients to engage in active resistance. *Goldberg* also raised the significant issue of whether AFDC constituted a constitutionally protected property right. The Court found that terminations prior to a hearing violated the Due Process Clause, and strongly suggested that AFDC was a protected property right. *Goldberg* came as close as the Court ever would to finding a constitutional right to a minimum adequate income.

In *Dandridge v. Williams* (1970), the Court upheld a Maryland regulation, capping AFDC aid at $250 regardless of family size. The decision has been understood as denying the existence of a constitutional right to an adequate minimum income. Furthermore, the Court, in *Wyman v. James* (1971), refused to find unconstitutional social workers' compulsory visits and inspections of AFDC recipients' homes, arguing that such "visits" did not constitute a government search. Thus *Wyman* refused to extend additional fundamental rights into the AFDC context. The dissenting opinions argued that AFDC constituted a property right that could not be conditioned on a recipient' consent to an invasion of her fundamental right to privacy and dignity.

Although numerous court challenges failed, by the mid-1970s the Court had broken new ground by striking down, on both statutory and constitutional grounds, some of the severest state provisions regulating AFDC. Moreover, in the first thirty years of the program, some legislative changes improved conditions for recipients. For example, eligibility was extended in several ways, including to 1) children living with two parents of whom one was unemployed, 2) extending the age of eligible children to 18 if they attended school, and 3) extending eligibility to foster children and their custodians. In 1965 the federal government increased its share of costs to 50 percent. In 1969, the Nixon administration proposed a Family Assistance Plan to guarantee a minimum yearly income to all AFDC families whether employed or not. The proposal failed because it alienated both conservatives and liberals; liberals feared that the low level of support guaranteed would create a ceiling over rather than a floor under welfare benefits.

AFDC payments were federally funded income based on need and, in most cases, were counted as income. Payments were made to a family rather than an individual and were frequently referred to as "grants."

Yet despite these improvements, the bulk of the changes to AFDC during its sixty-year life worsened conditions for recipients. In principle, states had been expected to pay recipients the amount of their "need," as determined by the states, but this rarely happened. (In 1994 average "need" was $688 per month while average payment was $420 per month.) In 1981 Congress required states to count the income of "step-parents," including mothers' boyfriends, against AFDC eligibility.

AFDC'S IMPACT ON OTHER BENEFIT PROGRAMS

Understanding the actual impact of AFDC legislation requires taking note of the interaction of other benefit programs with AFDC. Additions to the Social Security and federal unemployment laws gradually took in more lone mothers and children; this removed many of the less needy from AFDC, rendering AFDC the program of last resort. Food assistance programs, expanded in 1961 and again in 1974, supplemented AFDC income, but AFDC income counted against Food Stamp eligibility—for example, for every dollar of AFDC income, food stamps were reduced by 30 cents. Several legislative efforts to increase collection of child-support payments in order to reduce AFDC expenditures have required recipients to cooperate with the state in establishing paternity of children born outside marriage and in obtaining support payments. The most important addition to the welfare system was Medicaid, providing medical insurance for welfare recipients. Ironically, this program locked many recipients into the welfare system because, typically, the jobs they were able to find offered no health-insurance benefits.

The original purpose of ADC was to allow mothers to stay home with their children, but starting in the 1960s the system was reconfigured in various ways to push mothers into the labor force. Further amendments provided tax incentives for taking jobs and cut off aid to children whose mothers refused offers of "suitable" employment. A variety of "workfare" programs, in which parents had to earn benefits through unpaid labor, were attempted at both state and federal levels. For some time many states allowed adult welfare recipients to attend school as a form of work, because education tends to reduce welfare dependence over time, but this provision was gradually squeezed out. In general, workfare was unsuccessful because the wages that most welfare recipients could earn were not adequate to raise children in safety and health.

But as politicians and poverty scholars began evaluating success in terms of declining welfare caseloads instead of declining child poverty, these welfare-to-work programs led to **repeal** of the entire AFDC program in 1996.

repeal: to revoke or cancel

See also: FEDERAL UNEMPLOYMENT TAX ACT; FOOD STAMP ACT OF 1964; PERSONAL RESPONSIBILITY AND WORK OPPORTUNITY RECONCILIATION ACT; SOCIAL SECURITY ACT OF 1935.

BIBLIOGRAPHY

Bell, Winifred. *Aid to Dependent Children*. New York: Columbia University Press, 1965.

Davis, Martha F. *Brutal Need: Lawyers and the Welfare Rights Movement, 1960-1973.* New Haven, CT: Yale University Press, 1993.

Forbath, William. "The Constitution and the Obligations of Government to Secure the Material Preconditions for a Good Society." *Fordham Law Review* 69 (2001): 1821.

Gordon, Linda. *Pitied But Not Entitled: Single Mothers and the History of Welfare*. New York: The Free Press, 1994.

Katz, Michael B. *The Undeserving Poor: From the War on Poverty to the War on Welfare*. New York: Pantheon, 1989.

Michaelman, Frank I. "The Supreme Court 1968 Term Foreword: On Protecting the Poor Through the Fourteenth Amendment." *Harvard Law Review* 83 (1969): 7.

Michaelman, Frank I. "In Pursuit of Constitutional Welfare Rights; One View of Rawl's Theory of Justice." *University of Pennsylvania Law Review* 121 (1973): 962.

Mink, Gwendolyn. *Welfare's End*. Ithaca, NY: Cornell University Press, 1998.

Reich, Charles A. "The New Property." *Yale Law Journal* 73 (1964): 733.

West, Guida. *The National Welfare Rights Movement: The Social Protest of Poor Women*. New York: Praeger, 1981.

ALASKA NATIVE CLAIMS SETTLEMENT ACT (1971)

Steven J. Gunn

Congress designed the Alaska Native Claims Settlement Act of 1971 (P.L. 92-203, 85 Stat. 688) to resolve the land claims of Alaska's Native inhabitants. Alaska Natives, including Indians, Eskimos, and Aleuts, occupied Alaska for centuries before the **Treaty** of Cession from Russia of 1867 when

treaty: a binding international agreement

the United States purchased Alaska. However, neither the Treaty of Cession nor any subsequent act (including the Organic Act of 1884, in which the United States made Alaska a "district" and allowed for the creation of a local government and the enforcement of local laws, and the Alaska Statehood Act of 1958, in which the U.S. made Alaska the forty-ninth state) clarified the nature or extent of Alaska Native land rights. These rights were based on the Natives' historic or aboriginal use and occupancy of Alaska lands, not on treaties between Alaska Natives and the United States.

By the time the United States made Alaska a state in 1958, it had formally recognized the land rights of only a handful of the state's Native villages. For example, in 1891 Congress established the Annette Island Reserve for the Metlakalta Indian Community and after 1891 a number of presidential orders created other reservations. But many Native inhabitants continued to make claims for land that government officials did not formally recognize.

The Alaska Statehood Act set in motion a conflict between the state of Alaska and its Native inhabitants that eventually led to the adoption of the Alaska Native Claims Settlement Act. Through the Statehood Act, Alaska disclaimed all rights to any lands belonging to Alaska Natives. However, the Act

The Brooks Range in Alaska towers over Dalton highway, which runs parallel to the Alaskan pipeline. The discovery of oil created pressure for the government to settle claims by the Alaskan Natives for most of the land in the newly established state. Natives received 44 million acres of land and $962.5 million in return for relinquishing their claims to the rest of Alaska. (©PAUL A. SOUDERS/CORBIS)

also authorized Alaska to select more than 102.5 million acres from so-called "vacant, unappropriated, and unreserved" public lands within the state for its own use. Because Alaska Natives had asserted claims to most of the state's public lands, the State was unable, without protest and controversy, to select such lands under the Statehood Act. In 1969 the U.S. secretary of the interior imposed a **moratorium** on approval of the State's applications for public lands, pending settlement of Native land claims. Meanwhile, the discovery of vast oil reserves on the North Slope of Alaska, and the desire among non-Native commercial enterprises to make use of those reserves created additional pressures for settlement of the Native claims.

moratorium: a legally required suspension of activity

SETTLEMENT OF NATIVE LAND CLAIMS

The Alaska Native Claims Settlement Act gave Alaska Natives legal title to approximately forty-four million acres of Alaskan land. The Act also established an Alaska Native Fund of $962.5 million to compensate the Natives for the lands and rights taken from them. The Act extinguished "[a]ll aboriginal titles, if any, and claims of aboriginal title in Alaska based on use and occupancy." The Act revoked all reservations in the state, except the Annette Island Reserve.

In the Act, Congress stated its desire to settle the Native land claims "without creating a reservation system" like that found in the continental United States. The Act established a landholding system different in two fundamental respects from that in the lower forty-eight states. First, Alaska Native lands were owned not by tribes or by the United States as trustee for the tribes, but rather by newly established regional and village corporations. The Settlement Act authorized the creation of thirteen regional corporations and over 200 smaller village corporations to own and manage the forty-four million acres selected by the Natives and paid them the $962.5 million settlement. All Natives were eligible to be shareholders in one or more of these corporations, which were **chartered** under Alaska state law. Second, Native lands were owned by the regional and village corporations as "fee simple," which meant there were no restrictions on the ability of the corporations to use or sell the lands as they saw fit. In contrast, nearly all Native lands in the continental United States are owned by the federal government, held in trust for the tribes, and cannot be used or sold without the consent of the United States.

charter: document that creates a public or private corporation and outlines the principles, functions and organization of the corporate body

ARE ALASKA NATIVE LANDS INDIAN COUNTRY?

The corporate ownership of Native lands and the ability of Native corporations to freely sell their lands distinguish Alaska Native landholdings from most, if not all, Indian landholdings in the continental United States. In view of these distinctions, the U.S. Supreme Court ruled in the case of *Alaska v. Native Village of Venetie* (1998) that Alaska Native lands (other than the Annette Island Reserve) do not qualify as "Indian country," a category of lands under United States law that includes Indian reservations, allotments made under the General Allotment Act, and other lands set apart and administered by the United States for Indians. Because Native lands are not Indian country, Alaska Natives cannot exercise full governmental powers over them. For example, Natives cannot regulate or tax the activities of nonmembers who live, work, travel, or conduct business on Native lands.

These activities are governed instead by state and federal law. Native tribes, however, do have the power to regulate many activities occurring inside Native country.

The Alaska Native Claims Settlement Act extinguished the aboriginal hunting and fishing rights of Alaska Natives. After the Act, Natives were required to comply with state laws when hunting and fishing anywhere in the state. Many of these state laws prevented Natives from engaging in their traditional subsistence ways of life. In 1980 Congress remedied this problem by enacting the Alaska National Interest Lands Conservation Act. This act allowed Alaska Natives and other rural residents to engage in subsistence hunting and fishing on public lands.

See also: INDIAN GENERAL ALLOTMENT ACT (DAWES ACT).

BIBLIOGRAPHY

Arnold, Robert D. *Alaska Native Land Claims.* Anchorage: Alaska Native Foundation, 1976.

Prucha, Francis Paul M. *The Great Father: The United States Government and the American Indians.* Lincoln: University of Nebraska Press, 1984.

ALCOHOLIC AND NARCOTIC ADDICT REHABILITATION ACT (1968)

Steven Harmon Wilson

Excerpt from the Alcoholic and Narcotic Addict Rehabilitation Act:

The handling of chronic alcoholics within the system of criminal justice perpetuates and aggravates the broad problem of alcoholism whereas treating it as a health problem permits early detection and prevention of alcoholism and effective treatment and rehabilitation, relieves police and other law enforcement of an inappropriate burden that impedes their important work, and better serves the interests of the public.... It is the purpose of this part to help prevent and control alcoholism through authorization of Federal aid in the construction and staffing of facilities for the prevention and treatment of alcoholism.

pursuant: to execute or carry out in accordance with or by reason of something

enumerated: legal term equivalent to "expressly named and granted" as in the powers specifically granted by the Constitution to the government

commerce clause: the provision of the U.S. Constitution (Article I, section 8, clause 3) which gives Congress exclusive powers over interstate commerce—the buying, selling, or exchanging of goods or products between states

Congress regulates activities, including alcohol or drug use, **pursuant** to the "police powers" **enumerated** in the Constitution, which include the power to promote health, safety, welfare, and morals. Moreover, because a major portion of the traffic in both legal and illegal drugs flows through either interstate or foreign commerce, the **commerce clause** authorizes Congress to regulate drugs. On these bases, Congress has regulated drugs since the early 1900s. For example, possession of narcotics without a prescription was illegal under the 1914 Harrison Act, and alcohol use was illegal under the 1919 Volstead Act. Although Prohibition ended in 1933, Congress nevertheless continues to regulate the use of drugs.

THE MEDICAL VIEW OF ADDICTION

The Alcoholic and Narcotic Addict Rehabilitation Act (P.L. 90-574, 82 Stat. 1006) was an amendment of the Community Mental Health Centers Act of 1963 as well as an indirect complement to the Narcotic Addict Rehabilitation Act of 1966. These statutes reflected the idea that addiction is a form of illness, and therefore addicts could benefit more from medical treatment than from criminal punishment.

The proponents of a medical response to addiction have often competed with the proponents of a punitive, or punishment, model of law enforcement. During the 1920s medical doctors opened clinics to provide morphine and heroin addicts with regulated "maintenance" doses of the drugs that would enable the addicts to function in society and wean themselves from drugs rather than turn to crime. But the federal government argued, and the U.S. Supreme Court held in various cases, that the Harrison Act made it illegal for doctors to prescribe any narcotic to addicts. Several thousand doctors were jailed for dispensing narcotics, and private attempts at such treatment were abandoned. Nevertheless, congressional interest in rehabilitating addicts emerged even as federal penalties for narcotics trafficking increased. Congress created a Narcotics Division (soon renamed the Division of Mental Hygiene) within the U.S. Public Health Service in the Porter Act in 1929. The Porter Act also established two "narcotic farms" for the separate confinement and treatment of addicts serving time in the federal prison system. These were built at Lexington, Kentucky (1935), and Fort Worth, Texas (1938). They continued to operate until the early 1970s.

The view that addiction was an illness, and specifically a mental illness, revived in the 1960s. The federal Community Mental Health Centers Act and its amendments provided grants for assistance in constructing and staffing facilities that emphasized preventive, community-based, outpatient care for persons with mental illness as an alternative to institutionalization in state mental hospitals. The movement to improve treatment for the mentally ill soon converged with efforts to treat drug addiction as a public health problem. In 1965, with the Drug Abuse Control Amendments, Congress established a Bureau of Drug Abuse Control within the Department of Health, Education, and Welfare (HEW, later Health and Human Services).

Some states began to experiment with programs to divert addicts charged with crimes into a civil process of treatment and rehabilitation. U.S. Senators Jacob Javits and Robert Kennedy of New York sought similar federal legislation, and on November 8, 1966, Congress passed the Narcotic Addict Rehabilitation Act (NARA). NARA provided that judges could offer addicted **defendants** in federal court civil commitment for an unspecified period up to several years, plus a probationary period, as an alternative to criminal **prosecution**. If the **offender** returned to drugs during the period of treatment and probation, the government could reinstate criminal prosecution. Like the Community Mental Health Centers Act, NARA authorized grants for the development of narcotic addict rehabilitation and treatment programs.

> *These statutes reflected the idea that addiction is a form of illness, and therefore addicts could benefit more from medical treatment than from criminal punishment.*

> *The movement to improve treatment for the mentally ill soon converged with efforts to treat drug addiction as a public health problem.*

defendant: one against whom a legal action is brought

prosecute: to begin and carry on a lawsuit; to bring legal action against

offender: one who breaks a rule or law

SUBSEQUENT LEGISLATION

Although NARA did not address alcohol abuse, federal lawmakers regarded this as another major public health problem. On October 15, 1968, in the

The Twelve-Step Program

The Twelve Steps of Alcoholics Anonymous (AA) is a program of recovery suggested by AA based on the group's sixty years of experience in helping alcoholics overcome their addictions. Based in spirituality, the program directs alcoholics to admit that they have become "powerless over alcohol," turn their lives over to a power greater than themselves, make "a searching and fearless inventory" of themselves, compile a list of everyone they have harmed, and try to "make amends to them all." The Twelve-Step Program has helped tens of thousands of recovering alcoholics and has been adapted for use with other addictions, including narcotics. Proponents of the program maintain that it is the best method of treating addiction, particularly when combined with counseling or therapy.

Alcoholic and Narcotic Addict Rehabilitation Amendments to the 1963 Community Mental Health Centers Act, Congress specifically provided federal support to establish facilities for the prevention of alcoholism and the treatment and rehabilitation of alcoholics. Two years later, Congress amended the statute again, to give priority to those seeking grants for programs operating in areas suffering from high rates of poverty. At that time, Title I of the Comprehensive Drug Abuse Prevention and Control Act dealt with education, treatment, and rehabilitation, and opened federally funded community treatment centers to non-narcotic drug abusers as well as narcotic addicts (Title II of the Comprehensive Act was the Controlled Substances Act). Finally, the Comprehensive Alcohol Abuse and Alcoholism Prevention, Treatment and Rehabilitation Act established the National Institute of Alcohol Abuse and Alcoholism within the National Institute of Mental Health.

See also: ANTI-DRUG ABUSE ACT; DRUG ABUSE PREVENTION, TREATMENT, AND REHABILITATION ACT; NARCOTIC ADDICT REHABILITATION ACT.

BIBLIOGRAPHY

Inciardi, James A. *The War on Drugs II: The Continuing Epic of Heroin, Cocaine, Crack, Crime, AIDS, and Public Policy*. Mountainview, CA: Mayfield Publishing, 1992.

Jonnes, Jill. *Hep-Cats, Narcs, and Pipe Dreams: A History of America's Romance with Illegal Drugs*. New York: Scribner, 1996.

Marion, Nancy E. *A History of Federal Crime Control Initiatives, 1960–1993*. Westport, CT: Praeger, 1994.

Musto, David F. *The American Disease: Origins of Narcotic Control*, 3rd ed. New York: Oxford University Press, 1999.

Rachal, Patricia. *Federal Narcotics Enforcement: Reorganization and Reform*. Boston, MA: Auburn House, 1982.

Sharp, Elaine B. *The Dilemma of Drug Policy in the United States*. New York: HarperCollins, 1994.

Walker, William O. *Drug Control in the Americas*. Albuquerque: University of New Mexico Press, 1981.

ALIEN AND SEDITION ACTS OF 1798

Justin Florence

In the summer of 1798 the young United States was on the brink of war with France, one of the mightiest powers in the world. Some worried America faced not only a powerful enemy abroad, but also a threatening undercurrent of opposition at home. Hoping to strengthen the nation during war, and at the same time crush their political rivals, the Federalist party in power passed a series of four laws collectively termed the Alien and Sedition Acts. Alexander Hamilton, a leading Federalist, believed as a result of the new laws "there will shortly be national unanimity."

Hamilton, like most other Americans in the eighteenth century, maintained that political **factions** or parties threatened the stability of the new

faction: a party or group united by a common cause

nation. Yet hardly had the first Congress convened before proto-parties began to form. An array of congressmen known as Republicans joined Thomas Jefferson and James Madison in opposing Hamilton's economic plans. Newly founded political newspapers helped congressmen and party leaders attract the support of ordinary voters. Newspaper editors in the 1790s actively aligned themselves with national figures and parties, while launching fierce attacks against political rivals.

Hamilton, like most other Americans in the eighteenth century, maintained that political factions or parties threatened the stability of the new nation.

By the middle of the 1790s foreign policy disagreements highlighted the distinction between the proto-parties. As France and England battled for European supremacy against the backdrop of the French Revolution, the American parties sought opposite alliances with the European rivals. In 1794 Federalist concerns about the anarchy of the French Revolution led President George Washington to dispatch John Jay to negotiate a treaty linking American commercial and diplomatic interests with England. Republicans, who saw France as America's natural ally because of the republican values of the Revolution, harshly criticized the Jay Treaty. By 1796 the wartime naval practices of impressment and privateering led the United States into a "Quasi War" naval and diplomatic crisis, with France. Hoping to avoid war, President John Adams sent representatives to negotiate a peace settlement with the French. The French demanded a bribe to avoid war, outraging Americans in what became known as the "X,Y,Z Affair."

The Alien and Sedition Acts of June and July 1798 were the result of the highly polarized political atmosphere of the 1790s.

Seeking to capitalize on the anti-French and anti-Republican sentiment arising from the X,Y,Z Affair and the Quasi War, Federalists in Congress proposed the four Alien and Sedition Acts in June and July of 1798. Three dealt with **aliens**—**immigrants** who had yet to become naturalized American citizens. Federalists knew these European immigrants overwhelmingly voted Republican, and took advantage of public fears that they might aid France during a war. The "Act Concerning Aliens" and the "Alien Enemies Act" established a registration and **surveillance** system for foreign nationals living in the United States. The laws allowed the president (at the time, Adams, a Federalist) to arrest and deport aliens who might endanger the nation's security. President Adams, however, never used the Alien Acts. The "**Naturalization** Act" increased the period of residence required to become a naturalized citizen and to vote, from five to fourteen years.

alien: a citizen of another country

immigrant: one who comes to a country to take up permanent residence

surveillance: the close observation of a person, place, or process

naturalize: to grant the privileges and rights of citizenship

The Sedition Act awakened even more controversy because it stifled the possibility of opposition politics. The act prohibited "any false, scandalous and malicious" writing or speaking against the U.S. government, the president, or either house of Congress. The language of the act specifically cited those who brought the government "into contempt or disrepute," anyone who might "excite … the hatred of the good people of the United States," stir up "sedition," or "excite any unlawful combinations … for opposing or resisting any law of the United States." Further, the act applied to anyone who might "aid, encourage or **abet** any hostile designs of any foreign nation." Violators of the Sedition Act were to be tried in federal court and could be punished by fines of up to $2,000 and imprisonment for up to two years.

abet: to actively, knowingly, and intentionally assist another in the committing (or attempt) of a crime

common law: system of laws developed in England, and later applied in the U.S., based on judicial precedent rather than statutory laws passed by a legislative body

seditious: urging resistance to or overthrow of the government

libel: the publication of statements that wrongfully damage another's reputation

Even before 1798, Federalists had prosecuted Republican editors in state courts under the **common law** of **seditious libel**. State judges and juries, however, leaned Republican, while the federal judiciary was overwhelmingly Feder-

resolution: a formal statement of opinion, intent, or will voted by an official body

null and void: having no legal force; invalid

secede: to depart or withdraw from an organization

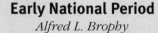

Early National Period
Alfred L. Brophy

In the first years of the United States, Congress's major legislation was concerned with establishing the federal government. It provided for a federal judiciary through the Judiciary Act of 1789 and established a census bureau, to calculate the population of each state for purposes of determining representation in Congress. Congress also set about promoting the economy, through the Copyright and Patent Acts and tariffs. Moreover, it laid the groundwork for new states through the Northwest Ordinance and provided for limited social programs by supplying Revolutionary War veterans with pensions. Political disputes between Federalists—those who wanted a strong central government—and their opponents appeared in much of the legislation. The Federalists won many of those contests. Their views prevailed with the Judiciary Act of 1789, as well as the Alien and Sedition Acts. By the early 1800s, Congress passed a Prohibition of the Slave Trade, as the North and South became increasingly divided over slavery, and as the United States headed into a second war with Great Britain.

alist. Under a fiercely partisan application of the Sedition Act, Federalist judges indicted fourteen Republican editors, with ten convicted and imprisoned. The United States had only about fifty Republican-leaning newspapers at the time, so this constituted a substantial portion of the Republican press. Major Republican journalists placed on trial for sedition included John Burk, James Callender, Thomas Cooper, and William Duane. The first and most unusual prosecution under the Sedition Act was of Matthew Lyon, a Congressman from Vermont, who became a martyr for Republicans after being fined $1,000 and sentenced to four months in jail.

The Federalist enforcement of the already unpopular Sedition Act made it even more despised. Jefferson decided that the states themselves offered the best means to protect basic rights and Republican values from the Federalists whom he believed were subverting the Constitution. Jefferson and Madison authored **resolutions** in the state legislatures of Kentucky and Virginia respectively in the late summer of 1798 to stop the new laws. The Virginia and Kentucky Resolutions introduced the doctrine of state interposition, arguing that the national government was a "compact" among the states and that the states could decide to declare **null and void** the new federal laws they believed to be unconstitutional. Republicans in Virginia went so far as to call for the state to prepare to defend itself militarily against the Federalist-controlled government.

The Federalist designs with the Alien and Sedition Acts backfired. As the crisis with France calmed, public support for the acts quickly dissipated. Popular outrage against the laws not only helped unify the Republicans, but provided a powerful platform for their campaign in 1800. The election of 1800 saw Thomas Jefferson defeat John Adams in the presidential contest, and Republicans regained a majority in the Congress. The Republican Congress repealed the Naturalization Act in 1802. The two Alien Acts and the Sedition Act contained provisions to expire automatically in the first years of the new century.

Many of the issues raised by the controversy over the Alien and Sedition Acts remained prominent. During the War of 1812 Republicans sought to destroy the Federalists for their support of a foreign enemy. The arguments that the Virginia and Kentucky Resolutions advanced on behalf of state rights would reappear in controversies over **secession** in the nineteenth century. Most fundamentally, the delicate challenge of preserving civil liberties in the face of wartime concerns over national security continued into the twenty-first century.

See also: NATURALIZATION ACT; ESPIONAGE ACT (1917) AND SEDITION ACT (1918).

BIBLIOGRAPHY

McKitrick, Stanley, and Eric McKitrick. *The Age of Federalism: The Early American Republic, 1788–1800.* London: Oxford University Press, 1993.

Schudson, Michael. *The Good Citizen: A History of American Civic Life.* Cambridge, MA: Harvard University Press, 1998.

Sharpe, James Rogers. *American Politics in the Early Republic: The New Nation in Crisis.* New Haven, CT: Yale University Press, 1993.

Smith, James Morton. *Freedom's Fetters: The Alien and Sedition Laws and American Civil Liberties.* Ithaca, NY: Cornell University Press, 1956.

AMERICANS WITH DISABILITIES ACT (1990)

Ruth Colker

ADA Title I provides that: No covered entity shall discriminate against a qualified individual with a disability because of the disability of such individual in regard to job application procedures, the hiring, advancement, or discharge of employees, employee compensation, job training, and other terms, conditions, and privileges of employment.

ADA Title II provides that: [N]o qualified individual with a disability shall, by reason of such disability, be excluded from participation in or be denied the benefits of the services, programs, or activities of a public entity, or be subjected to discrimination by any such entity.

ADA Title III provides that: No individual shall be discriminated against on the basis of disability in the full and equal enjoyment of the goods, services, facilities, privileges, advantages, or accommodations of any place of public accommodation by any person who owns, leases (or leases to), or operates a place of public accommodation.

The term disability is defined as: (a) a physical or mental impairment that substantially limits one or more of the major life activities of such individual; (b) a record of such an impairment; or (c) being regarded as having such an impairment.

The Americans with Disabilities Act (ADA) (P.L. 108-23), enacted by Congress in 1990, forbids discrimination against individuals with disabilities. The act consists of three major provisions, called "titles": Title I prohibits discrimination in public or private employment; Title II prohibits discrimination at public entities (like public universities or hospitals); and Title III prohibits discrimination at places of public accommodation (like hotels and restaurants). The ADA extended existing prohibitions against discrimination entities that receive federal financial assistance, like public parks, to private entities like privately owned recreational facilities.

In general, the statute prohibits discrimination against qualified individuals with disabilities. In order to be qualified, an individual must be able to engage in the activity in question with "reasonable accommodation." A reasonable accommodation might be a modification in a rule or procedure, or the provision of an auxiliary aid. Whether an accommodation is "reasonable" will rest, in part, on whether it is unduly expensive. Which accommodations are reasonable varies throughout the statute, depending on whether one is suing under Titles I, II, or III. Not all individuals with disabilities, however, require accommodations to engage in programs or activities. Often, they simply need an entity to provide nondiscriminatory treatment by, for example, ending their ban on participation by individuals with disabilities.

The statute also provides various "defenses," or grounds on which a person or entity can legally discriminate against an individual with a disability. One of the most important defenses is the "direct threat" defense. An employer can refrain from hiring an individual not merely because the individual might cause harm to others but because the individual may cause harm to him- or herself through the employment in question. For example, in 2002 the Supreme Court ruled in *Chevron v. Echabazal* that the employer could refrain from employing a person out of concern that working conditions would exacerbate his liver disease.

Sections 501 and 504 of the Rehabilitation Act of 1973
Ruth Colker

Section 504 of the Rehabilitation Act creates protection against disability discrimination in programs receiving "federal financial assistance" and prohibits federal contractors from discriminating on the basis of disability. Section 501 prohibits federal agencies and the U.S. Postal Service from discriminating on the basis of disability.

In an effort to forbid discrimination against persons with disabilities, Congress in 1990 enacted the American with Disabilities Act (ADA). The ADA expanded on the Rehabilitation Act of 1973 and extended existing prohibitions against discrimination from public entities to private entities. With the Jefferson Memorial as a backdrop, President George H.W. Bush signs the act. Also at the signing are Reverend Harold Wilke, rear left; Evan Kemp, chairman of the Equal Opportunity Employment Commission, left; Sandra Parrino, chairman of the National Council on Disability; and Justin Dart, chairman of the President's Council on Disabilities. (© AP/WIDE WORLD PHOTOS)

commerce clause: the provision of the U.S. Constitution (Article I, section 8, clause 3) which gives Congress exclusive powers over interstate commerce—the buying, selling or exchanging of goods or products between states

equal protection: Constitutional guarantee that prevents states from denying a person or class of persons the same protection under the law as those enjoyed by other persons or classes of persons

remedy: the means to compensate a person whose rights have been violated which usually takes the form of money damages

CONSTITUTIONAL BASIS FOR THE ACT

The constitutional basis for the ADA is the **commerce clause** authority given to Congress, as well as its authority under section 5 of the Fourteenth Amendment. Under section 5, Congress has the authority to enact legislation to enforce the Fourteenth Amendment's **equal protection** or due process clause. However, Supreme Court rulings in the years after ADA was enacted challenged the act's constitutionality under both the commerce clause and section 5. In 2001 the Supreme Court ruled in *Board of Trustees v. Garrett* that Congress could not constitutionally create a private right of action for monetary damages against the state involving employment discrimination under ADA Title I. In other words, a private individual could not bring an employment discrimination action in federal court for back pay or damages due to disability discrimination by the state. Numerous lower courts have extended that holding to ADA Title II, ruling more broadly that Congress does not have the authority to create a private right of action against the states to **remedy** disability discrimination in the nonemployment context. It is expected that the Supreme Court will ultimately resolve this issue.

Even if the Supreme Court eventually rules that Congress does not have the constitutional authority to create a private right of action against the states to remedy disability discrimination, the United States Department of Justice can still enforce the ADA against the states. **Sovereign immunity** principles protect the state from suit by private individuals. However, these principles do not apply when the federal government sues the state on behalf of an aggrieved individual (an individual with a claim of discrimination). Moreover, private rights of action may still be maintained against private defendants and against local governments.

sovereign immunity: a doctrine that prevents bringing a lawsuit against the government without the government's consent

LEGISLATIVE DEBATE AND COMPROMISE

The ADA grew out of different roots from those of the Civil Rights Act of 1964. The National Council on the Handicapped, a panel of thirteen people **appointed** by President Ronald Reagan, proposed the first version of the ADA in 1988. This version, which offered more protections for people with disabilities than the enacted version, was largely ignored when Senator Lowell Weicker, a Republican from Connecticut, introduced it in the closing days of the 100th Congress.

appoint: to select someone to fill an office or position

In the early days of the George H. W. Bush administration, the bill was cut back to make it more acceptable to the business community. Senator Tom Harkin, a Democrat from Iowa, and Representative Tony Coelho, a Democrat from California, were the chief sponsors of the new version of the ADA, which had been worked out through compromise between the act's supporters and detractors. Some disabilities rights advocates worried that proponents of the ADA gave away too much during compromise **negotiations**. The bill contained the following revisions:

negotiate: to deal or bargain with another as in the preparation of a treaty or contract

- It required modifications of existing structures to accommodate people with disabilities only if these changes could be easily achieved at reasonable expense.
- It eliminated damages for cases involving public accommodations; private individuals could only seek injunctive relief when they were excluded from public accommodations due to barrier access problems.
- It did not require television broadcasters to make their programs accessible to persons with **impaired** hearing.

impair: to lessen or reduce

- The original bill included an "undue hardship" exception to the requirement that reasonable accommodations or auxiliary aids or services be provided for persons with disabilities. This version of the bill made it easier to claim this undue hardship exception.

The compromise bill eventually became law in the summer of 1990 in an overwhelming **bipartisan** vote in both the House and Senate.

bipartisan: Involving members of two parties, especially the two major political parties

One reason for the bill's strong support was that many members of Congress had personal or family reasons for being concerned about disability issues. Other key figures in passage of the act were Attorney General Richard Thornburgh; Senator Robert Dole, a Republican from Kansas; and Senator Ted Kennedy, a Democrat from Massachusetts. The major public interest advocates for the ADA were the Disability Rights Defense and Education Fund and the American Civil Liberties Union.

THE ACT'S PRECURSORS

The historical roots of the ADA lie in section 504 of the Rehabilitation Act of 1973, which creates protection against disability discrimination in programs

The historical roots of the ADA lie in section 504 of the Rehabilitation Act of 1973, which creates protection against disability discrimination in programs receiving "federal financial assistance."

private sector: the part of the economy that is not controlled by the government

The ADA is different from most other civil rights laws in that a person must belong to a protected category to receive legal protection from it.

plaintiff: one who brings legal action against another

cause of action: reason or ground for initiating a proceeding in court

receiving "federal financial assistance." The ADA is modeled on the basic framework used in section 504, including its definition of an individual with a disability. Congress held extensive hearings before enacting the ADA, and key committees wrote extensive reports on the act before it was adopted. The Supreme Court has not relied on that background material in interpreting the act. However, it has sought to interpret the ADA consistently with previous cases argued under section 504.

Another important precursor of the ADA was the Fair Housing Act Amendments of 1988. These amendments extended some of section 504's protections to the **private sector** by prohibiting discrimination in housing on the basis of disability. It was not until the passage of the ADA in 1990, however, that the private sector began to be broadly covered under federal law by a requirement of nondiscrimination in housing as well as employment.

EXPERIENCE UNDER THE ACT

In the first decade of enforcement of the ADA, many legal cases focused on the definition of an "individual with a disability." The ADA is different from most other civil rights laws in that a person must belong to a protected category to receive legal protection from it. Under the Civil Rights Act of 1964, by contrast, both males and females can bring claims of sex discrimination, just as both whites and blacks can bring claims of race discrimination. Under the ADA, only individuals who qualify as "individuals with a disability" can bring claims of discrimination. An important defense strategy has been to argue that the **plaintiff** is not "disabled" according to the ADA's definition, and therefore does not have a **cause of action**. When that strategy is successful, the court does not even reach the question of whether unlawful discrimination occurred.

Sutton v. United Air Lines. In the 1999 case *Sutton v. United Air Lines*, the Supreme Court interpreted the definition of disability narrowly. The plaintiffs in *Sutton* sued under Title I, arguing that they had been the victims of unlawful employment discrimination when they failed the vision test required by United Air Lines to work as a commercial pilot. The Court did not come to the question of whether the discrimination they faced was unlawful (or permitted by one of the statute's defenses). Instead, it found that the plaintiffs could not bring an ADA lawsuit because they were not individuals with a disability as defined by the act.

The plaintiffs' uncorrected visual acuity (in other words, sharpness of vision without corrective lenses) was 20/200 or worse in one eye and 20/400 or worse in the other eye. With corrective lenses, their vision was 20/20 or better. The legal question in the case was whether a court should determine the disability status of individuals in their corrected or uncorrected state. The Supreme Court held that "disability under the Act is to be determined with reference to corrective measures." In simpler terms, when wearing glasses or contact lenses the individuals were not disabled. Therefore the plaintiffs had not stated a claim that they were disabled even though United Air Lines had required them to take the vision test without the use of corrective lenses. This interpretation of the ADA has prevented individuals from obtaining protection under the statute if they have an impairment that can be corrected, in part, through some means. Individuals with hearing impairments, diabetes, high blood pressure, and psychological impairments have been found not to be disabled under this narrow standard.

The Importance of Voluntary Compliance. In ADA litigation, particularly in employment discrimination cases, the winners have overwhelmingly been the defendants. Nonetheless, a glance at many public accommodations like hotels, restaurants, and recreational facilities suggests that the ADA has been effective in heightening public awareness of disability issues and encouraging voluntary compliance. Curb cuts, areas where sidewalks dip down to be level with the street to allow easy passage for wheelchairs, or other mechanisms that aid the disabled were virtually unheard of a decade ago and are now seen in most major cities. The most important factor in the act's success in its first decade seems to be voluntary compliance rather than litigation.

> *A glance at many public accommodations like hotels, restaurants, and recreational facilities suggests that the ADA has been effective in heightening public awareness of disability issues and encouraging voluntary compliance.*

RELATIONSHIP WITH OTHER LAWS

The ADA is not the only federal statute to prohibit disability discrimination. Until passage of the ADA, the strongest legislation to protect people with disabilities was probably the Individuals with Disabilities Education Act (IDEA) (formerly known as the Education of All Handicapped Children Act). This civil rights statute guarantees that each child with a disability can have an "individualized education plan" so that he or she can receive a "free appropriate public education."

Other statutes preceding the ADA include the Developmental Disabilities Bill of Rights Act of 1975, the Air Carrier Access Act of 1986, the Voting Accessibility for the Elderly and Handicapped Act of 1984, sections 501 and 503 of the Rehabilitation Act of 1973, and the Fair Housing Act Amendments of 1988.

See also: CIVIL RIGHTS ACT OF 1964; FAIR HOUSING ACT OF 1968; INDIVIDUALS WITH DISABILITIES EDUCATION ACT.

BIBLIOGRAPHY

Colker, Ruth. "The Americans with Disabilities Act: A Windfall for Defendants." *Harvard Civil Rights–Civil Liberties Law Review* 99 (1999).

Colker, Ruth, and Bonnie Poitras Tucker. *The Law of Disability Discrimination,* 3d ed. Cincinnati, OH: Anderson Publishing, 2000.

O'Brien, Ruth. *Crippled Justice: The History of Modern Disability Policy in the Workplace.* Chicago: University of Chicago Press, 2001.

ANTI-DRUG ABUSE ACT (1986)

Darryl K. Brown

Drug abuse and drug-related crime have been recurrent problems on the American political and social agenda since the early twentieth century. The federal government was relatively quiet on drug issues in the 1950s and 1960s, but in the early 1970s President Nixon declared a "war on drugs." Most presidents after Nixon continued to wage some form of that war. The high point of this period of legislative reform on national drug policy was the 1980s, and the most important set of statutes on the drug problem during that period was the Anti-Drug Abuse Act of 1986 (P.L. 99-570, 100 Stat. 3207).

FEATURES OF THE ACT

import: merchandise brought in from another country as part of a commercial business

offender: one who breaks a rule or law

The Anti-Drug Abuse Act strengthened federal efforts against drugs in many ways. One provision allows the president to increase tariffs (taxes on **imports**) on products from countries that do not cooperate with the U.S. efforts to stop drug imports into the United States. Another provision makes seizure of drug **offenders**' assets (houses, boats, cars, and money) easier.

The act also created the first laws against money laundering, or moving illegally obtained money (such as drug sale proceeds) into or out of bank accounts. In 1995 a congressional study estimated that $40 billion to $80 billion in drug profits are generated annually in the United States. Placing that money in the banking system exposes drug sellers to criminal sentences as well as **forfeiture**.

forfeiture: the loss of property or money as a result of a broken legal obligation or criminal activity

The part of the act with the most far-reaching impact, however, reinstated mandatory prison sentences for drug possession. Until 1986 the federal government had virtually no mandatory minimum sentences for drugs. The first federal mandatory drug sentences were passed in 1951 and imposed a two-year minimum sentence for first-time possession and a five-year sentence for trafficking. But those mandatory minimums were largely repealed in the Drug Abuse Prevention and Control Act of 1970.

The act attacked drug trafficking and abuse at just about every stage, e.g. authorizing increased efforts in drug-producing countries, proscribing money laundering, and creating the Department of Education's Drug-Free Schools and Communities Program.

In the 1986 act, Congress reinstated mandatory prison terms by defining the amounts of various drugs that it believed would be in the hands of drug "kingpins," or high-level dealers. Those amounts include 1,000 grams of heroin or 5,000 grams of powder cocaine. Offenders possessing, with intent to distribute, these "kingpin" amounts face a minimum ten-year prison sentence. Offenders possessing smaller amounts that would generally be possessed by "mid-level dealers"—such as 100 grams of heroin or 500 grams of powder cocaine—face a minimum five-year sentence.

DISTINCTIONS IN MINIMUM SENTENCING

More significantly, the Anti-Drug Abuse Act created distinctions in minimum sentencing between offenders who possess powder cocaine and those who possess crack cocaine. For crack cocaine, Congress departed from its "kingpin" and "mid-level dealer" categories and simply divided the amounts necessary for powder-cocaine sentences by 100. Thus 50 grams of crack, instead of 5,000 grams of powder cocaine, merit a ten-year minimum sentence, and 5 grams of crack, rather than 500 grams of powder, trigger a five-year sentence. Trafficking in 50 grams of powder cocaine carries no mandatory sentence.

Congress justified this 100-to-1 sentencing disparity by stressing the serious social harms with which crack use was associated. Although crack and powder cocaine are the same chemical substance, crack sells more cheaply on the street and can be smoked, which induces a briefer, more intense intoxicating effect. It came into widespread use only in the mid-1980s and was associated with violent street crime. In the summer and fall of 1986, press reports sparked growing popular and congressional concern about a crack "epidemic."

In an effort to respond to this concern before the November congressional elections, legislators introduced a number of bills to toughen penalties for crack dealing. Less than two months before the election, President Ronald Reagan introduced a proposal with a 20-to-1 powder/crack ratio. House Democrats then proposed a 50-to-1 ratio, and Senate Democrats followed with a proposal that prevailed, a 100-to-1 ratio between the amounts of powder and crack cocaine required for mandatory minimum sentences.

The Anti-Drug Abuse Act of 1986 was aimed at combating the large increase in drug-related crime. It allowed tariffs on imports of drug producing countries, imposed mandatory prison terms on those dealing drugs, allowed forfeiture of property, and made it illegal to move illegally obtained money into or out of bank accounts (money laundering). Additionally, persons contracting with or receiving services under government grants must certify that their workplace is drug free. These rules also apply to public housing, something this woman finds out as she is being evicted because her grandson, the co-lessee on her home, has been accused of drug possession. (© AP/WIDE WORLD PHOTOS)

The sentencing distinction between crack and powder cocaine has been controversial because of its disparate racial impact.

RACIAL ISSUES

The sentencing distinction between crack and powder cocaine has been controversial because of its disparate racial impact. Most offenders sentenced under the crack cocaine provisions are African-American, whereas white offenders make up a much higher portion of those convicted for powder cocaine offenses. Courts have rejected arguments that the different penalties are unconstitutional because minorities typically receive harsher sentences under the statute. Congress has rejected a recommendation by the U.S. Sentencing Commission to reduce the disparity between powder and crack cocaine sentences.

Although many media reports and images at the time of the act emphasized the spread of crack cocaine among inner-city minority communities, it is not clear that Congress foresaw the disparate racial impact these sentencing changes would have. Fully half of the African-American representatives in Congress voted for the act, many of them emphasizing the harm that crack use was causing to black communities. Regardless of Congress's original intent, years of evidence showing that minorities receive much harsher sentences than whites for cocaine offenses because of the powder/crack distinction has led to no serious effort to change the law. Mandatory minimum sentences appear to be a fixture of American drug policy for the foreseeable future.

See also: ALCOHOLIC AND NARCOTIC ADDICT REHABILITATION ACT; ANTI-DRUG ABUSE ACT; DRUG ABUSE PREVENTION, TREATMENT, AND REHABILITATION ACT; SENTENCING REFORM ACT.

BIBLIOGRAPHY

Kennedy, Randall. *Race, Crime, and the Law.* New York: Pantheon Books, 1997.

Massing, Michael. *The Fix.* New York: Simon & Schuster, 1998.

Musto, David F. *The American Disease: Origins of Narcotics Control,* 3d ed. New York: Oxford University Press, 1999.

ANTI-INJUNCTION ACT (1793)

James P. George

The Anti-Injunction Act limits federal courts' interference with lawsuits pending in state courts. Understanding the act requires a knowledge of injunctions, writs, and stays:

- A *writ* is an order from a judge or government official relaying a command or an instruction. English common law used writs extensively for everything from notifying defendants of a lawsuit to giving instructions to lower government departments and officers.
- An *injunction* is a type of writ ordering (enjoining) a person either to do something or refrain from it. Examples include ordering a defendant not to dispose of assets during a lawsuit, or, pertinent here, ordering a party to stop litigating a case in another court.

• A *stay* is the temporary or permanent stopping of litigation. Thus, an injunction that stays a case orders a party to stop litigating, temporarily or permanently.

Understanding Federalism is also essential to this act. Because federal courts may appear to be more powerful than state courts, people have occasionally sought federal injunctions to stop state litigation. But the doctrine of federalism—the delicate constitutional balance between our state and federal governments—dictates a careful approach to federal interference with state activities. Although the Constitution does not specifically authorize it, the Anti-Injunction Act helps maintain that balance. Apart from federalism, the act reflects a general rule in the United States and other countries that courts should not interfere with one another except in rare and important cases.

THE ORIGINAL ACT

The Anti-Injunction Act is almost as old as the federal court system. In 1789 the first Congress created federal courts, and in 1793 the second Congress enacted the original Anti-Injunction Act (1 Stat. 334). It was less than a full sentence, merely part of a larger law giving individual Supreme Court justices the power to grant the writs of *ne exeat* (incarcerating fleeing **debtors**) and injunctions. The original act provided that "writs of ne exeat and of injunction may be granted by any judge of the supreme court ... *nor shall a writ of injunction be granted to stay proceedings in any court of a state;...*" The italicized clause is the original Anti-Injunction Act in its entirety.

> *The Anti-Injunction Act is almost as old as the federal court system.*

debtor: one who owes payment or other performance on an obligation; anyone liable on a claim

Common Law
James P. George

The *common law* is a system of rights and procedures that developed in English courts in the twelfth century, forming the basis of much American law today. Although drawn partly from its predecessors—English tribal custom, Roman law, and feudal law—the common law's true beginning was in the reign of King Henry II, who formalized a system of courts whose judges would create the common law over the next several centuries. Westminster was the site for the central court, but common law judges also rode circuit in courts throughout England.

Unlike other legal systems, common law is made by judges rather than centralized authorities such as presidents or legislatures. Judges apply common law rules on a case-by-case basis, shaping the outcome to the particular facts of each case. Decisions become *precedents* which should be followed in future cases. But when facts differ—for example, when a defendant has a good excuse for not paying for goods—the judge might find an exception. As times and technology change, outdated precedents are overruled. Over time, the common law has grown into a significant body of law with well-structured rules and numerous exceptions.

The courts in America's English colonies applied England's common law, along with English statutes and their own colonial laws. After the American Revolution, and in spite of the new Americans' dislike of English rule, the new American states adopted English common law as their own, either in their new state constitutions or in statutes issued from the states' legislatures. In spite of many changes in the United States since 1775, much of our American law is derived from English common law.

Friedman, Lawrence M. *A History of American Law*, 2d ed. New York: Touchstone, 1985; Plucknett, Theodore F.T. *A Concise History of the Common Law*, 2d ed. Rochester: Lawyers Co-op, 1936.

appellate: a court having jurisdiction to review the findings of lower courts

Supreme Court justices are not all-powerful. With a mostly **appellate** role, the Supreme Court hears appeals from lower courts and then acts as an entire court rather than through its individual judges. For this reason, Supreme Court justices neither need nor have the same powers as trial court judges. In 1793, however, the United States was new and unsettled. Supreme Court justices were required to ride circuit, that is, to hold court with lower federal circuit judges who heard both trials and appeals in several locations, traveling by buggy or on horseback from one court to another. At times, quick action by one judge or justice was important, and the 1793 act ensured that the circuit-riding Supreme Court justices were legally equipped. It is interesting that the 1793 act referred to Supreme Court justices as *judges,* perhaps because they were required to act as lower federal court judges, but more likely because Congress deemed *justice* and *judge* as equivalents.

Without legislative history, and there is none for the 1793 act, we can only guess Congress's purpose. As noted in a Supreme Court case discussing the original act: "The precise origins of the [Anti-Injunction Act] are shrouded in obscurity..." but "the consistent understanding has been that its basic purpose is to prevent 'needless friction between state and federal courts'" (*Mitchum v. Foster* [1972]). Preventing needless friction is the heart of federalism, and the Anti-Injunction Act is one of federalism's best examples.

Preventing needless friction is the heart of federalism, and the Anti-Injunction Act is one of federalism's best examples.

It appears from the 1793 act's placement—as a clause in a paragraph limited to Supreme Court justices—that the original Anti-Injunction Act was simply a limit on Supreme Court justices' power to grant injunctions. Judges in lower federal courts already had injunctive power and, from adopted English common law, were similarly limited in applying injunctions against state court lawsuits. Congress may have believed that a new statute giving Supreme Court justices the unusual power to grant individual injunctions should clarify the limits on this power. In any event, the 1793 statute gave each circuit-riding Supreme Court justice the individual power to grant injunctions, but made clear that this did not include the power to issue injunctions against, or *enjoin,* state court lawsuits.

In spite of this apparently narrow purpose, by 1807 courts were applying the 1793 act as a limit on all federal courts issuing injunctions against state court lawsuits. *Diggs v. Wolcott* (1807) is the first reported application, involving a federal court in Connecticut enjoining Diggs from his debt-collection lawsuit against Wolcott in a Connecticut state court. Applying the 1793 act, the Supreme Court reversed the lower federal court and dissolved the injunction against Wolcott's state litigation. This use of the 1793 act was appropriate only if the injunction was issued individually by a Supreme Court justice temporarily assigned to the lower court, a fact not recorded in the opinion. The decision was nevertheless correct because it also relied on common law that barred courts generally from enjoining related litigation in other courts.

Later nineteenth-century cases continued to apply the 1793 act to all federal courts, with or without a temporarily assigned Supreme Court justice. Perhaps the most interesting came in 1872 in *Watson v. Jones,* a dispute in a Louisville, Kentucky, church over which **faction** of the congregation—anti-slavery or pro-slavery—was truly representative of the congregation as a whole. The controversy began in 1864 when the Presbyterian General Assembly adopted an anti-slavery, or **abolitionist**, policy. Although four-fifths of the

faction: a party or group united by a common cause

abolitionist: one favoring principles or measures fostering the end of slavery

Louisville congregation favored abolition, three pro-slavery trustees claimed title to the church. A Kentucky state trial court ruled for the abolitionists but was reversed by a state appellate court. At the abolitionists' request, a federal court enjoined the state lawsuit only to be reversed by the Supreme Court's application of the Anti-Injunction Act. The Supreme Court went on, however, to rule for the abolitionists because the state appellate court had improperly infringed on the Presbyterian General Assembly's decision.

AMENDMENTS AND JUDICIAL TINKERING

The 1793 act's broad application to all federal courts was such an accepted practice that it became part of the statute in 1874, when Congress amended the Anti-Injunction Act and changed it from a simple clause to a separate statute. It now read: "The writ of injunction shall not be granted by any court of the United States to stay proceedings in any court of a State, except in cases where such injunction may be authorized by any law relating to proceedings in bankruptcy" (18 Stat. 137). Thus, in 1874 the Anti-Injunction Act was expressly directed to all federal courts, but with a built-in exception allowing injunctions to stop state litigation against someone who filed for bankruptcy in a federal court.

In the same period, federal judges were creating two other exceptions, that is, two other grounds for enjoining state court litigation. The first was to protect property claims filed first in federal court, and the second was to protect final federal court judgments from further state court litigation. These changes led, by the early twentieth century, to three routinely recognized exceptions that allowed injunctions: those expressly authorized by Congress (such as the bankruptcy exception), those involving property claims, and those protecting federal court judgments from state court interference.

Although not endorsed by Congress, these judge-made exceptions were generally unquestioned until 1941, when the Supreme Court turned a critical eye toward them in *Toucey v. New York Life Insurance Co.* In that case, an insurance company had won a federal lawsuit and was having to relitigate the claim in state court. The Supreme Court found the first two exceptions were valid, but struck down the third exception protecting parties from state court relitigation of a claim already decided in federal court. Congress disagreed and amended the act in 1948 to include all three exceptions. This legislatively overruled the Supreme Court's *Toucey* opinion and provided the Anti-Injunction Act's current language: "A court of the United States may not grant an injunction to stay proceedings in a State court except as expressly authorized by Act of Congress, or where necessary in aid of its **jurisdiction**, or to protect or effectuate its judgments." (62 Stat. 968). The current act, then, continues to restrict federal courts from enjoining state court litigation, but incorporates all three exceptions.

jurisdiction: the territory or area within which authority may be exercised

THREE EXCEPTIONS ALLOWING INJUNCTIONS

The first exception is for injunctions "expressly authorized by Congress." Federal courts may enjoin state court litigation if Congress enacts a statute that expressly allows for an injunction, such as the bankruptcy statute. For these cases, Congress has decided that certain disputes ought to be litigated in federal court and that injunctions can be issued to stop parties from filing related claims in state courts.

The Anti-Injunction Act's current language: "A court of the United States may not grant an injunction to stay proceedings in a State court except as expressly authorized by Act of Congress, or where necessary in aid of its jurisdiction, or to protect or effectuate its judgments."

Interestingly, *expressly authorized* does not mean that the statute has to include language authorizing injunctions. The Supreme Court held in *Mitchum v. Foster* (1972) that Congress's intent to authorize injunctions can be inferred. In *Mitchum,* a Florida prosecutor filed a state court action to close Mitchum's bookstore as a public nuisance. Mitchum sued in federal court, claiming violations of free speech and seeking an injunction against the state court action. Mitchum's suit was filed under a federal civil rights statute that did not mention injunctions. The lower federal court denied his request for an injunction, but the Supreme Court reversed, concluding that the civil rights law would be meaningless in some cases if injunctions were not available. Thus, where Congress creates a federal right, in this case Mitchum's free speech rights, and where that right can be protected only by stopping the state court action, Congress is deemed to have "expressly" included injunctive relief against the state court action.

The second exception is where the injunction is "necessary in aid of [the federal court's] jurisdiction." This exception applies to a limited category of cases involving property claims (including everything from land to Internet domain names) and cases where the federal court has ongoing jurisdiction over a process (such as reapportionment or the enforcement of an arbitration agreement). Once a federal court has asserted its jurisdiction over the property or process, it may enjoin parties from pursuing related claims in state court.

The third exception is "to protect or effectuate [federal] judgments." Also known as the "relitigation exception," it is tied to the Full Faith and Credit Act, which requires both state and federal courts to recognize each other's final judgments. Under this exception, the Anti-Injunction Act allows a federal court to enjoin state court lawsuits that will interfere with the federal court's final judgment. Unlike the second exception, which applies only to a narrow category of property and related cases, the relitigation exception applies to all final federal judgments. In *Exxon Corp. v. Chick Kam Choo* (1988), the Supreme Court explained that this exception is limited to final judgments on fully **adjudicated** issues actually decided by the federal court, and not to matters the court could decide later.

adjudicated: a matter or controversy that has already been decided through judicial procedure

OTHER IMPORTANT POINTS

The Anti-Injunction Act protects only pending state court actions and does not apply to injunctions issued before the state lawsuit was filed. It applies only to state judicial proceedings, and not other functions a state court may perform (such as approving the conveyance of restricted Native American land or attorney disbarment proceedings, in which an attorney may lose the privilege to practice law). For judicial proceedings, the act protects all functions by the state court and its officers, from beginning to end. The act does not apply when the United States government seeks an injunction against state court action. Where one of its three exceptions applies, the Anti-Injunction Act does not authorize injunctions but merely permits them. Federal injunctive authority comes from the All Writs Act and from equity rules stated in *Younger v. Harris* (1971).

TWO RELATED ACTS

Two other federal statutes restrict federal court injunctions against state proceedings that, under these statutes, are not necessarily in a state court but may instead be in a state government agency. The first is the Johnson Act, prohibiting federal injunctions against "any order affecting rates chargeable by a public utility," but limited to cases not involving federal rights. The second is the Tax Injunction Act, which prohibits federal injunctions against the "assessment, levy, or collection of any state tax where a plain, speedy and efficient state court remedy is available."

See also: JUDICIARY ACT OF 1789; JUDICIARY ACT OF 1801.

BIBLIOGRAPHY

Bailyn, Bernard, ed. *Debate on the Constitution.* 2 vols. New York: Library of America, 1993.

Berger, Raoul. *Federalism: The Founder's Design.* Norman: University of Oklahoma Press, 1987.

George, James P. *The Federal Courthouse Door.* Durham, NC: Carolina Academic Press, 2001.

Hamilton, Alexander, James Madison, and John Jay. *The Federalist Papers,* 2d ed. Ed. Roy P. Fairfield. Baltimore: Johns Hopkins University Press, 1981.

Wright, Charles A. *The Law of Federal Courts,* 5th ed. Minneapolis: West Publishing, 1994.

Wright, Charles A., Arthur R. Miller, and Edward R. Cooper. *Federal Practice and Procedure,* Vol. 17 §§ 4221–26. Minneapolis: West Publishing, 1978.

ANTIQUITIES ACT OF 1906

Robert H. McLaughlin

Signed into law by President Theodore Roosevelt, the Antiquities Act of 1906 (P.L. 59-209, 34 Stat. 225) became the first major federal legislation to govern archaeology in the United States. The act prohibits the removal of antiquities from federal lands without first obtaining a permit for scientific investigation. It authorizes federal courts to impose a fine of up to $500 and imprisonment of up to ninety days against any person convicted of violating the criminal provision of the act.

The act prohibits the removal of antiquities from federal lands without first obtaining a permit for scientific investigation.

The act also established a regulatory process through which the federal government could identify sites on its lands, administer permits for archaeological fieldwork and excavations, record findings, establish collections of artifacts, and designate archaeological sites as national monuments. The Antiquities Act authorizes the president to declare historic landmarks, historic and prehistoric structures, and other objects of historic or scientific interest located on federal lands as national monuments. Under the act, permits may be "granted by the Secretaries of the Interior, Agriculture, and Army to institutions which they may deem properly qualified to conduct such examination, excavation, or gathering, subject to such rules and regulations as they may prescribe."

The Departments of the Interior and Agriculture and the Army jointly adopted regulations delegating review of permit applications to the Smithsonian Institution. The Smithsonian would review permit applications for recom-

ANTIQUITIES ACT OF 1906

The Native American Graves Protection and Repatriation Act of 1990

Adopted in 1990, the Native American Graves Protection and Repatriation Act required museums to conduct an inventory of their holdings to identify Native American remains and culturally sensitive objects. When possible, the items were to be returned to their tribes. As a result of this legislation, Native American communities were allowed to rebury the remains of their ancestors in a manner appropriate to their cultures. When artifacts were discovered in new excavations, archaeologists were allowed a brief period to analyze the materials before they had to be returned. Some archaeological groups, including the American Committee for the Preservation of Archaeological Collections, opposed the legislation, arguing that with each item repatriated, critical scientific data was lost.

Excavations performed with Antiquities Act permits led to the discovery of data that demonstrated, contrary to popular belief at the turn of the twentieth century, that the archaeological sites and material culture of North American prehistory are not the ruins of "lost civilizations."

mendation and become a repository for duplicate copies of all field reports, photographs, and catalogues of collections made during each season of archaeological fieldwork. Between 1906 and 1981, the Smithsonian did indeed review applications to conduct scientific investigations on federal lands, maintaining an archive in the Bureau of American Ethnology, now reorganized as the National Anthropological Archives.

BACKGROUND

The Antiquities Act of 1906 resulted from a combination of interests. Politicians wanted to preserve prehistory as a form of national heritage; anthropologists and archaeologists were interested in Native American societies, past and present; and cultural institutions sought to gather material collections of interest and value to the public. Politicians recognized an international trend toward the preservation of archaeological sites, in particular Britain's Ancient Monuments Act (1882) and Mexico's Law of Archaeological Monuments (1897). However, they struggled with the issue of enforcement over the vast federal land holdings in western states. Anthropologists debated the regulatory process, discussing whether the Smithsonian or, as the anthropologist Franz Boas proposed, a rotating group of recognized experts should be in charge. Meanwhile, popular interest in archaeology fueled an international antiquities market in which demand far exceeded the supplies of art and curio dealers, traders, tourists, museums, and thieves.

EXPERIENCE UNDER THE ACT

Although the regulatory components of the Antiquities Act took shape quickly, the criminal provision remained untested for decades. Illegal trafficking in antiquities continued and even escalated. Finally, the government brought charges and won a conviction against a man for the illegal removal and trafficking of face masks found in a cave located in the San Carlos Indian Reservation. On appeal, however, the United States Court of Appeals for the Ninth Circuit reversed the district court conviction. In *United States v. Diaz* (1974), the appeals court noted that the face masks were of recent crafting and found the definition of the term "antiquities" unconstitutionally vague in the statute. Although a subsequent case heard before the Tenth Circuit (*United States v. Symer* [1979]) resulted in a criminal conviction being upheld, the Supreme Court declined to hear a further appeal of that case. Thus, the validity of the criminal provision of the Antiquities Act has remained uncertain.

The Antiquities Act did, however, contribute to a major shift in knowledge and popular thinking. Excavations performed with Antiquities Act permits led to the discovery of data that demonstrated, contrary to popular belief at the turn of the twentieth century, that the archaeological sites and material culture of North American prehistory are not the ruins of "lost civilizations." Rather, these excavations, often performed under the supervision of the Bureau of American Ethnology, show that a great many sites and their contents relate historically and culturally to contemporary Native American peoples. This knowledge provides no excuse for the absence of Native American voices in the legislative record on which Congress passed the Antiquities Act of 1906. However, it pro-

MAJOR ACTS OF CONGRESS

vides the foundation for subsequent federal laws and regulations that build on and supercede the Antiquities Act.

For example, the regulatory process prescribed in the Archaeological Resource Protection Act of 1979 (ARPA) to issue permits for scientific investigations incorporates Native American interests among its criteria. The Native American Graves Protection and Repatriation Act of 1990 (NAGPRA) similarly calls for collaboration and consultation among federally recognized tribes and museums in the identification of sacred objects, cultural patrimony (heritage), and human remains. Where a cultural affiliation is determined, the objects and human remains may be subject to return or **repatriation** to the Native American tribe. Antiquities Act permits and records often prove instrumental to Native American repatriation claims. Finally, many states have also adopted preservation, sacred sites, and antiquities trafficking laws that range from **tax credits** for the conservation of archaeological sites on private lands to criminal provisions similar to those of the Antiquities Act and that apply to state lands.

repatriate: to return to the country of one's birth or citizenship

tax credit: a reduction in the amount an individual or corporation owes in taxes

BIBLIOGRAPHY

Lee, Robert F. *The Antiquities Act of 1906.* Washington, DC: Office of History and Historic Architecture, National Park Service, 1970.

McLaughlin, Robert H. "The Antiquities Act of 1906: Framing an American Anthropology and Archaeology," *Oaklahoma City Law Review* 23 (1998): 61–91.

The National Park Service. "Links to the Past." <http://www.cr.nps.gov>.

ANTITERRORISM AND EFFECTIVE DEATH PENALTY ACT (1996)

Mark Tushnet

The Antiterrorism and Effective Death Penalty Act (AEDPA) (P.L. 104-132, 110 Stat. 1214) creates the current version of the traditional writ of habeas corpus. Traditionally, habeas corpus, which literally means "you should have the body," is a protection against illegal imprisonment. Under habeas corpus, a person detained by executive officials—military officers, jailers, and prison wardens—can ask a court to determine whether his or her detention is authorized by law. The person can file a petition for the writ, and the court requires the executive official to respond in what is known as the "return" on the writ. If the court finds that the detention violates the law, it issues the writ of habeas corpus.

Habeas corpus has traditionally been a way of getting a judge to decide whether a person's detention was legally justified. Because of that function, for centuries the executive official would prevail simply by showing that a person was being detained under a judgment issued by a judge. That judgment was usually a criminal conviction, if the court had jurisdiction over the criminal case. Releasing a person through a procedure designed to determine whether a detention was legally justified was unnecessary when there was a criminal conviction, because the judge who entered the judgment of conviction had already considered whether the detention was justified.

Traditionally, habeas corpus, which literally means "you should have the body," is a protection against illegal imprisonment.

HABEAS CORPUS IN AMERICAN LAW

The Constitution provides, "The privilege of the Writ of Habeas Corpus shall not be suspended, unless when in Cases of Rebellion or Invasion the public Safety may require it" (Article I, section 9, clause 2). The Judiciary Act of

The passage of the Antiterrorism and Effective Death Penalty Act of 1996 was stimulated in part by the bombing of the Alfred P. Murrah Federal Building in Oklahoma City on April 19, 1995, which killed 160 people. The act places restrictions on habeas corpus procedures and addresses terrorism-related issues. (© AP/WIDE WORLD PHOTOS)

1791, built on this constitutional foundation, authorizes federal judges to issue writs of habeas corpus to determine whether officials of the national government had the right to **detain** the person seeking release through the procedure. International conflicts produced minor expansions of the writ's function in the 1830s and 1840s, allowing federal judges to issue writs directed at state officials under very limited circumstances, again with the purpose of allowing the federal judge to determine whether the state official was acting with legal authority in detaining the applicant for the writ.

detain: to keep in custody or temporary confinement

Important Supreme Court cases involved writs of habeas corpus challenging the detention of civilians during the Civil War. During the **Reconstruction** era that followed, Congress enacted a major expansion of the writ, allowing it to be issued whenever a person held by state officials challenged the lawfulness of the detention. People convicted of crimes in state courts could thereafter challenge their convictions in a trial-level federal court, rather than attempting to get the United States Supreme Court to use its limited resources of time to consider their claims. (Habeas corpus is less important for people convicted in federal court, because the federal trial court will have considered and rejected their claims at trial, and they can raise them on appeal to the federal appeals court.)

Reconstruction: the political and economic reorganization and reestablishment of the South after the Civil War

The Supreme Court transformed the writ into something nearly the same as an appeal of a criminal conviction, but in the federal courts instead of the state courts. By the 1940s Supreme Court rulings allowed people who had been convicted to obtain release through the writ of habeas corpus by showing that their convictions were unlawful in the sense that the Constitution (or, under the 1948 version of the habeas corpus statute, some particularly important statutes) had been violated in the proceedings leading to the conviction.

Habeas corpus matters as well when a criminal defendant's lawyer fails to present a constitutional claim at the trial. This may occur because of the lawyer's incompetence, or because the lawyer simply made an understandable mistake, or because the courts developed a new rule of constitutional law after the trial concluded. Usually a defendant cannot raise claims on appeal that were not raised at trial, but habeas corpus might provide a way for some court to consider such claims.

Ordinarily convicted defendants raise challenges to the lawfulness of their detention by appealing their convictions. Expanding the scope of the writ of habeas corpus put the writ in conflict with ordinary appeals. The Supreme Court accommodated the two paths in its decision in *Ex parte Royall* (1886), holding that a prisoner could not obtain the writ until he or she had "exhausted" the ordinary appeals process by appealing in the state courts (known as the exhaustion requirement). Without such a requirement a person could move immediately from the state court in which he or she was convicted to the nearby federal court, thereby completely cutting the state courts out of the ordinary process of reviewing criminal convictions.

During the 1960s the Supreme Court made it easier for defendants to obtain habeas corpus. It allowed them to present the same claim several times, and sometimes, when the law changed, the courts would grant the second or later petition. It prevented defendants from presenting claims on habeas corpus that they had not presented at trial only if they had made a deliberate decision to withhold the claims, a rare occurrence (*Fay v. Noia* [1963]).

Guantanamo Bay Detainees of the Afghan War

At the close of the war in Afghanistan, the U.S. Department of Defense held nearly 700 prisoners of 42 different nationalities at a naval base in Guantanamo Bay, Cuba. Because the prisoners were declared "unlawful combatants" rather than prisoners of war, they were denied the protections of the Geneva Convention, which provides guidelines for the humane treatment of prisoners of war. The captives had no access to lawyers or communication with their families while they were being held. They were interrogated in secret, and, depending on the results, were either released or subject to military trials. There was no limit on the length of time they could be held. In July 2003, most were still in prison, more than a year and a half after their arrest, with no idea of what was to happen to them.

Members of Congress concerned with law and order, and newly appointed judges and justices, believed that habeas corpus in the early 1970s undermined state criminal justice systems. The Supreme Court itself retrenched in the 1970s and 1980s, holding that claims that had not been presented at trial could not be presented on habeas corpus unless the state had somehow blocked the defendant's lawyer from presenting the claim (*Wainwright v. Sykes* [1977], *Coleman v. Thompson* [1991]), and that habeas corpus could not be granted when the defendant relied on a "new rule" of constitutional law (*Teague v. Lane* [1989]).

AEDPA

With AEDPA, Congress tightened habeas corpus procedures. The act was a response to general dissatisfaction with the law of habeas corpus. Its adoption was speeded, and the act was given its name after the bombing of the federal building in Oklahoma City. The act created a new one-year statute of limitations for filing habeas corpus proceedings, measured from the time when state court consideration of the case ended. The act made it even more difficult to present claims that had not been presented to the state courts because of an attorney's error.

Probably most important, the act provided a limited standard for the federal courts to use when assessing claims that had been presented to the state courts.

Probably most important, the act provided a limited standard for the federal courts to use when assessing claims that had been presented to the state courts. (The exhaustion requirement and the rules about claims not presented because of attorney error mean that habeas corpus is very difficult to obtain in connection with claims that were not so presented.) AEDPA provides that the federal courts should not grant the writ unless the state court's action "resulted in a decision that was contrary to, or involved an unreasonable application of, clearly established Federal law, as determined by the Supreme Court of the United States."

The writ of habeas corpus has evolved over the centuries, from a remedy for violations of law in a quite limited set of cases, to a much more general remedy for criminal convictions obtained by violating the Constitution. AEDPA, yet another stage in that evolution, is a relatively new statute. Under AEDPA, a criminal defendant with a decent lawyer still can get almost all of his or her substantial constitutional claims considered on habeas corpus. Defendants with less than fully competent lawyers are more seriously affected. As courts interpret its provisions, they will move habeas corpus to another new stage, perhaps even more restrictive than today or possibly more like the relatively expansive remedy that existed in the 1960s and 1970s.

See also: FOREIGN INTELLIGENCE SURVEILLANCE ACT; USA PATRIOT ACT.

BIBLIOGRAPHY

Freedman, Eric M. *Habeas Corpus: Rethinking the Great Writ of Liberty*. New York: New York University Press, 2001.

Hertz, Randy, and James S. Liebman. *Federal Habeas Corpus Practice and Procedure*, 4th ed. Charlottesville, VA: LexisNexis, 2001.

ARMS CONTROL AND DISARMAMENT ACT (1961) AND AMENDMENTS

David A. Koplow

The Arms Control and Disarmament Act (P.L. 87-297, 75 Stat. 631) was landmark legislation designed to entrench arms control as a key component of United States national security policy during and after the Cold War. With this act, Congress achieved three main tasks: (1) it set ambitious goals and purposes for coordinating disarmament with other defense strategies; (2) it created the U.S. Arms Control and Disarmament Agency (ACDA), a body that would make the country's commitment to arms control a part of its governing institutions; and (3) it established standards and procedures for integrating all aspects of security policy.

HISTORY OF THE ARMS CONTROL ISSUE

Arms control emerged as a highly controversial issue after World War II. The two superpowers, the United States and the Soviet Union, exchanged a series of ambitious proposals, with each government criticizing the other's as one-sided. Virtually no progress was made in achieving actual arms reductions. The issue became central to American politics, with intense controversy between the legislative and executive branches over who should exercise how much control over the direction of U.S. diplomatic moves. Arms control was also a hot issue in presidential election campaigns. Senators Hubert H. Humphrey, Democrat of Minnesota, and John F. Kennedy, Democrat of Massachusetts, championed the idea of creating a new governmental organization devoted solely to arms control matters. After his election in 1960, President Kennedy submitted exactly such a proposal. It swept through Congress with large majorities and became law on September 26, 1961.

> *Arms control emerged as a highly controversial issue after World War II.*

ARMS CONTROL LEGISLATION

Congress grandly declared that an "ultimate goal of the United States is a world which is free from the scourge of war and the dangers and burdens of armaments; in which the use of force has been subordinated to the rule of law; and in which international adjustments to a changing world are achieved peacefully." Accordingly, it created "a new agency of peace" to pursue those objectives. ACDA was intended to be permanent (not depending on international and domestic politics); focused (not carrying a broad set of substantive responsibilities that would detract attention from its core missions); independent (not dominated by the Department of State or other existing government agencies, each of which had its own institutional objectives and limitations); and small (not costing a great deal of money).

The new agency was to have four principal tasks:

(1) To conduct, support, and coordinate federal research on arms control issues
(2) To prepare for and manage U.S. participation in international arms control negotiations
(3) To inform the American public about arms control

Nuclear Weapons in the 21st Century

In 2003 there were an estimated 17,500 operational nuclear weapons in the world. The vast majority of nuclear weapons have been built by either the United States (55 percent) or Russia (43 percent). Since 1945 the United States has spent more than $5 trillion in preparations to fight a nuclear war.

(4) To prepare for and operate or direct "control systems" that might be useful in monitoring and enforcing compliance with international arms control agreements

Not surprisingly, the small ACDA (usually staffed by only 200 to 300 personnel) was unable fully to carry out those ambitious objectives. Still, it often exerted a disproportionate degree of leadership in each area.

The act also contained several other notable features. It made the agency's director "the principal adviser to the Secretary of State and the President on arms control and disarmament matters." This double responsibility—reporting to both the president and the secretary—was often referred to as a "dual hat" mechanism. The director, under this mechanism, would express an "independent voice," ensuring the forceful articulation of an arms control perspective in the most senior-level national security debates, while not straying too far from the Secretary of State's leadership in international diplomacy.

In practice, the personal relationships among the director, the secretary, and the president fluctuated over the years. The more closely the director was tied to the top national leadership, the greater the agency's influence.

The act, as amended, required ACDA to compile and submit to Congress a variety of reports that sometimes influenced national policy.

The act, as amended, required ACDA to compile and submit to Congress a variety of reports that sometimes influenced national policy. Under section 37, ACDA was to evaluate "verifiability"—in other words, how well the United States could monitor compliance with arms control treaties and major proposals for treaties under **negotiation**. For many years the agency was also given the task of leading an interagency process to draft "arms control impact statements" to study and publicize the effect that major U.S. weapons development and acquisition programs have on international arms races.

negotiate: to deal or bargain with another as in the preparation of a treaty or contract

mandate: an order or requirement

Many members of Congress were skeptical about ACDA, and section 33 of the act reflected their suspicions. First, it specified that the **mandate** for pursuing international arms control did not encompass domestic gun control; nothing in the act would permit the agency to "interfere with, restrict, or prohibit the acquisition, possession, or use of firearms by an individual for the lawful purpose of personal defense, sport, recreation, education, or training." Second, section 33 provided that no action could be taken to disarm or to reduce or limit the armed forces or armaments of the United States "except pursuant to the treaty making power of the President under the Constitution or unless authorized by further affirmative legislation." In this way, Congress sought to disallow arms control accords that might be fashioned as "executive agreements" concluded on the sole authority of the president without congressional affirmation.

EFFECTIVENESS

In many respects, the act was a tremendous success. It led to an impressive array of legally binding arms control treaties, with ACDA in the lead role. The 1963 Limited Test Ban Treaty (prohibiting atmospheric nuclear weapons tests), the 1967 Outer Space Treaty (establishing the "rules of the road" for peaceful operations in space), the 1968 Non-Proliferation Treaty (restricting the spread of nuclear weapons capabilities), and the 1972 Biological Weapons Convention (banning the development and production of

A United States atomic experiment, 1962. A nuclear device is exploded in the atmosphere, as seen from Christmas Island, Australia. Such tests were later banned by the 1963 Limited Test Ban Treaty. (© AP/WIDE WORLD PHOTOS)

germ weapons) were hallmark early successes, approved by large majorities in the U.S. Senate, and still in force today. The series of bilateral SALT (Strategic Arms Limitation Treaty) and START (Strategic Arms Reduction Talks) negotiations on nuclear arms limitation and reduction would not have been possible without ACDA, and all participants acknowledge the agency's leadership role on other such diverse subjects as chemical weapons and conventional forces.

More generally, the act made arms control a legitimate tool of U.S. policy. The concept of seeking enhanced security through negotiation, rather than solely through arms procurement, became an accepted feature of the political landscape, and even national leaders who were not inclined to value diplomatic approaches were frequently nudged in that direction by the arguments and information provided by ACDA.

TERMINATION

The agency was unable, however, to escape controversy. Its popularity, influence, and resources fluctuated wildly under different presidents and congressional leaders. Opponents charged that ACDA was too willing to secure an agreement "at any price," insufficiently vigorous in enforcing existing treaty obligations, and, especially after 1990, unnecessary when the end of the Cold War had so radically altered international security relationships. The agency's supporters, on the other hand, argued that the real reason for the objections was resentment of the agency's sheer effectiveness, saying that those who continued to reject the whole concept of arms control wanted to eliminate ACDA, its most successful **proponent**. At various

proponent: an advocate

The Cold War

Cold War is the term used to describe the hostility between the United States and the Soviet Union and their respective allies from the end of World War II until the collapse of the Soviet Union in 1991. During the Cold War standoff of more than forty years, actual warfare occurred not between the two superpowers but between their proxies in regional conflicts. The superpowers battled directly with propaganda, espionage, and economic pressures. This restraint was due in large part to "mutually assured destruction," the principle that an attack by one of the countries would result in its annihilation by the other's nuclear weapons.

The Cold War began at the end of the World War II, when the Soviet Union drew the countries of Eastern Europe into a group of Soviet-dominated satellites and sought to spread Communism elsewhere around the globe. The United States developed a policy of "containment" to limit Soviet power, supporting anti-Communist efforts in countries destabilized by the war or by Soviet pressures. Global politics became polarized as the two countries sought to increase their influence worldwide, and the United States used the CIA to overthrow governments that seemed to be turning pro-Communist—in the process coming to support ruthless regimes whose policies were no more democratic than those of the Soviets. During the 1980s, President Ronald Reagan made opposition to Communism a central tenet of his presidency, and ballooning military spending brought crushing levels of debt to both countries. The Soviet economy began to collapse, in part due to the strain of its military spending, and Soviet premier Mikhail Gorbachev began to scale back the country's military, dismantle nuclear weapons, and institute internal reforms to democratize the Soviet system. In 1989 Communist regimes were suddenly overthrown in the Soviet satellites of Poland, Hungary, Czechoslovakia, Romania, and East Germany. The Soviet system collapsed completely in 1991, and with it the bipolar structure that had defined international politics since World War II.

times, numerous initiatives were undertaken to abolish or shrink the agency or restrict its influence. For several years ACDA limped along with minimal funding and without U.S. Senate confirmation of its key presidential appointees. Finally, a reorganization of the foreign affairs bureaucracy merged ACDA into the State Department on April 1, 1999. The agency was abolished by statute, and its core functions and personnel were absorbed by State.

See also: ATOMIC ENERGY ACTS; NUCLEAR NON-PROLIFERATION ACT; WEAPONS OF MASS DESTRUCTION CONTROL ACT.

BIBLIOGRAPHY

Clarke, Duncan L. *Politics of Arms Control: The Role and Effectiveness of the U.S. Arms Control and Disarmament Agency.* New York: Free Press, 1979.

Krepon, Michael, Amy E. Smithson, and James A. Schear. "The U.S. Arms Control and Disarmament Agency: Restructuring for the Post-Cold War Era." (Pamphlet) Washington, DC: Henry L. Stimson Center, 1993.

ATOMIC ENERGY ACTS

Ross Rosenfeld and Seth Rosenfeld

The Atomic Energy Act of 1946 (The McMahon Act) established the Atomic Energy Commission (AEC) to safeguard and aid in regulating atomic resources, and created a five-person committee to oversee the activities of the AEC. The president, with the advice of the Senate, appoints each committee member.

The 1946 act reflected the desire of U.S. officials to maintain a nuclear weapons monopoly. The Cold War had just begun, and the emphasis at the time was on secrecy and discovery. In Congress, a joint committee on Atomic Energy was established. This joint committee no longer exists; there are now separate committees in the House and Senate for nuclear energy.

In 1946 experts did not view evolving nuclear technology as a public safety threat. It was believed that scientists could control the energy through good engineering. Standards for nuclear plants were left to a regulatory commission consisting of lawyers and administrators, not scientists. There was a general advisory committee, comprised of scientists, but the commissioners did not have to adhere to its opinions. The few procedural safeguards in the 1946 act were due to congressional fears that fissionable material produced in government plants could be diverted. Congress demanded that the commission license all fissionable materials and their transfer, though Congress retained final authority. Congress wanted the commission to protect the public by controlling the distribution of fissionable material and by licensing equipment using fissionable material after Congress had had ninety days to review the economic and safety implications of introducing the equipment.

> *The 1946 act reflected the desire of U.S. officials to maintain a nuclear weapons monopoly.*

By 1954 the political climate had changed. In 1946 U.S.-created materials were the major concern. But in August of 1953 the Soviet Union successfully tested a thermonuclear device; the United States no longer had a monopoly on atomic power, and the need for extreme secrecy became obsolete, replaced by a need for allies and atomic control.

Republicans, the majority of the joint committee, had always supported private ownership and development of nuclear facilities. They started drafting amendments to the 1946 act as early as 1950, but did not receive support from the AEC. The inauguration of President Dwight D. Eisenhower, a Republican, bolstered these efforts. By 1954 the president of the United States, the AEC, and the scientific and industrial communities all believed the 1946 legislation should be amended to advance commercial development.

Despite the reservations of congressional Democrats, who maintained that only the government should run nuclear power plants, President Eisenhower signed the Atomic Energy Act of 1954. Eisenhower had introduced his "Atoms for Peace Initiative" to the United Nations in December 1953. The initiative called for international cooperation in developing peaceful applica-

The public was excited by the discovery of atomic energy and its possibilities. This 1951 cartoon shows an atomic car with one drawback—ten to twenty tons of shielding would be needed to protect the driver from radiation. The Atomic Energy Act placed further development of nuclear technology under civilian rather than military control. The act said atomic energy should be directed "toward improving public welfare, increasing the standard of living, strengthening free competition among private enterprises ... and cementing world peace." The act prohibited private companies or individuals from owning nuclear materials and patenting inventions related to atomic energy. (©Bettmann/Corbis)

tions of nuclear energy. Eisenhower believed that certain fissionable materials, readily used for non-military purposes, and technological information could be shared with friendly nations. Eisenhower also wanted the AEC to encourage U.S. industry to develop nuclear power.

While the 1946 act had stated that "the effect of ... atomic energy for civilian purposes ... cannot now be determined," the 1954 act took a different view.

> Atomic Energy is capable of application for peaceful as well as military purposes. It is ... to be the policy of the United States that ... the development, use, and control of atomic energy shall be directed so as to make the maximum contribution to the general welfare subject at all times to the paramount objective of making the maximum contribution to the common defense and security; and ... the development, use, and control of atomic energy shall be directed so as to promote world peace, improve the general welfare, increase the standard of living, and strengthen free competition in private enterprise.

Private ownership of nuclear facilities was now permitted. The AEC was to develop initiatives to introduce atomic energy to the public. The 1954 act also liberalized patent rights and industrial access to technological information.

The AEC was to develop initiatives to introduce atomic energy to the public.

Yet public safety issues were not addressed for the most part. The act specified that nuclear plants must have adequate protection and should not be permitted to initiate any program that might pose an undue risk to the public. However, these terms were scarcely defined. The AEC was left to establish public safety regulations and charged with licensing all facilities and operators producing or using radioactive materials. For a nuclear power station, the party requesting permission from the AEC needed a construction license and an operating license, with such approval based on strict AEC guidelines.

Under the act, if a license is denied, any party with a stake in the decision may request a hearing. A judicial review provision is included to allow **redress** and protect applicants from abuse of power or dereliction of duty by agency officials. The U.S. Supreme Court affirmed this portion of the act in *Florida Power & Light Co. v. Lorion* (1985).

redress: to make right what is wrong

The act does not inhibit the rights of states to regulate nuclear energy matters under the Tenth Amendment—the reserved powers provision of the Constitution—unless a state law directly contradicts the act. In *Silkwood v. Kerr-McGee* (1984) the U.S. Supreme Court ruled that a state could award punitive damages to a victim of plutonium contamination caused by a federally licensed nuclear facility, so long as they do not conflict with the aims of the act. The act also provided for limited **liability** and set aside funds for victims of accidents.

liability: an obligation, responsibility, or duty that one is bound by law or justice to perform

Some challenged the legitimacy of some of the AEC's decisions during the 1970s, questioning the apparent conflict of interest in having the same organization that developed nuclear power protecting the public from nuclear danger. Congress confronted these issues with the Energy Reorganization Act of 1974, splitting the AEC into the Nuclear Regulatory Commission (NRC) and the Energy Research and Development Administration (ERDA), later the Department of Energy. Congress believed that this change would also aid in coordinating nuclear research during a crisis situation.

These organizations cannot decide what can be classified as "atomic matter" without the written consent of the president and the Congress, respec-

Some challenged the legitimacy of some of the AEC's decisions during the 1970s, questioning the apparent conflict of interest in having the same organization that developed nuclear power protecting the public from nuclear danger.

tively. When documents are to be declassified, approval must come from the Department of Defense and the president. The secretary of energy, the NRC, the Defense Department, and the State Department are all charged with keeping the atomic energy committees in the House and Senate informed.

The Department of Energy can only distribute nuclear or source material by license, and only with the concurrence of the State Department, the Department of Defense, and the NRC. No atomic exporting license can be granted without executive approval.

Any party divulging classified information in this area can be jailed for life or a fixed period, and/or be fined less than one hundred thousand dollars. If a party willfully causes interruption to a nuclear facility, that party can be fined more than ten thousand dollars and/or jailed for up to twenty years.

See also: DEPARTMENT OF ENERGY REORGANIZATION ACT

BIBLIOGRAPHY

Allardice, Corbin, and Edward R.Trapnell. *The Atomic Energy Commission.* New York: Praeger Publishers, 1974.

Campbell, John L. *Collapse of an Industry: Nuclear Power and the Contradictions of U.S. Policy.* Ithaca, NY: Cornell University Press, 1988.

Rolph, Elizabeth S. *Nuclear Power and the Public Safety.* Washington, DC: Lexington Books, 1979.

Stever, Donald W., Jr. *Seabrook and the Nuclear Regulatory Commission: The Licensing of a Nuclear Power Plant.* Hanover, NH: University Press of New England, 1980

B

BALANCED BUDGET AND
EMERGENCY DEFICIT CONTROL ACT (1985)

Jonathan L. Entin

The Balanced Budget and Emergency Deficit Control Act (P.L. 99-177, 99 Stat. 1038) is popularly known as the Gramm-Rudman-Hollings Act after the names of its principal sponsors, and was designed to reduce the federal budget deficit. The law did so primarily by setting seemingly rigid deficit limits and authorizing mandatory, across-the-board spending reductions to reach them. Although the Supreme Court ruled that a key part of this mechanism was unconstitutional, the basic concepts embodied in the statute have continued to influence the process for adopting the federal budget.

BACKGROUND AND MAJOR PROVISIONS

Although the Constitution does not mandate a balanced budget, it does require Congress to approve all federal expenditures (Article I, section 9, clause 7), and it empowers the federal government to raise revenue through taxes, tariffs, and other measures (Article I, section 8, clause 1). The latter provision also authorizes the government to incur and pay debts. Congress has passed legislation establishing procedures for adopting the federal budget (e.g., the Congressional Budget and Impoundment Control Act) and for handling the national debt (e.g., the Public Debt Act).

The government regularly ran a budget deficit in the years following World War II, but the situation became especially serious in the early 1980s. Between 1981 and 1985 the annual budget deficit nearly quadrupled, and it threatened to remain at high levels indefinitely. Further, if nothing were done, the total national debt would have more than doubled between 1985 and 1990. The Balanced Budget and Emergency Deficit Control Act was adopted in the fall of 1985 in connection with a measure that raised the national debt ceiling.

The law's most important feature was a schedule for reducing the federal budget deficit to zero by 1991. It fixed a maximum allowable deficit for each

> *The primary objective of the act was to balance the federal budget by the early 1990s. The act promised long-term lower deficits and a balanced budget, goals that have proven overly optimistic.*

fiscal year: the term used for a business's accounting year; the period is usually twelve months which can begin during any month of the calendar year

fiscal year. If Congress and the president failed to adopt a budget that met the target, the law called for across-the-board spending reductions in most federal programs. Responsibility for determining whether the budget satisfied this requirement was given to the comptroller general, who is the head of the General Accounting Office (an agency that does research and investigations at the behest of Congress). The comptroller also had the authority to order the across-the-board spending cuts needed to lower the deficit to the required level.

LEGAL CHALLENGE

Opponents of this law immediately challenged its constitutionality. In *Bowsher v. Synar* (1986), the Supreme Court ruled that the comptroller general could not exercise the authority given to that official under the act. This decision left the rest of the statute intact.

Opponents of this law immediately challenged its constitutionality.

The Court explained that the task of implementing a law passed by Congress is an executive function, and that the Constitution (Article II, section 1, clause 1) gives the executive power to the president. Of course, the president cannot personally execute all the laws passed by the legislative branch. Therefore, the chief executive must have the assistance of agents who are subject to presidential supervision and dismissal to assure their loyalty and efficiency. The comptroller general, in the Court's view, was not accountable to the president. Instead, this official was legally subservient to Congress. Allowing an official who is accountable to the legislature rather than to the president to execute the law violated the **separation of powers** embodied in the Constitution.

separation of powers: the division of the government into three branches: legislative, executive, and judicial, each with distinct powers. This separation supports a system of checks and balances

What made the comptroller general subservient to Congress? It was, the Court explained, the procedure for firing that official. The president could not dismiss the comptroller for any reason. Congress alone was in charge of the process for removing the comptroller. It could initiate removal proceedings and could even dismiss the comptroller over the president's objection.

The ability to discharge executive agents has long been regarded as a crucial component of presidential power. This issue lay at the heart of the controversy over the discredited Tenure of Office Act (1867), which required the president to obtain the Senate's approval to discharge a cabinet member. (President Andrew Johnson's defiance of that law was the primary basis for his **impeachment**.)

impeach: to set up a formal hearing on charges of high crimes and misdemeanors which could result in removal from office

The comptroller was subservient to Congress, the Court reasoned, even though the legislative branch had never threatened to remove anyone from that office for any reason. All that mattered was that the comptroller had no reason to fear the president but every reason to fear Congress in order to stay out of trouble and remain on the job. The comptroller could continue to perform other duties on behalf of Congress but could not play any role in executing or enforcing federal statutes.

AFTERMATH

The Supreme Court's ruling did not address two other problems with the statute. First, the law addressed only the projected deficit at the beginning of each fiscal year, not the actual deficit at the end of the year. Second, the law did not require that the projected deficit be based on realistic assumptions about **inflation** and economic growth or on standard accounting principles.

inflation: an increase in the volume of money and credit relative to available goods and services resulting in a continuing rise in the general price level

In response to the Court's decision, Congress amended the statute to give primary responsibility for implementation to the Office of Management and Budget, an executive branch agency, with advisory input from the Congressional Budget Office. In 1987 Congress revised the deficit targets, extended the deadline for eliminating the budget deficit, and changed the procedures for enacting the federal budget. Subsequent laws have altered the focus from the overall deficit to spending caps and other mechanisms designed to limit the growth of discretionary expenditures.

Meanwhile, Congress and the president have managed to avoid the across-the-board spending cuts authorized by the original Balanced Budget and Emergency Deficit Control Act. Only in late 1990 were such cuts ordered, but they were repealed in early 1991 after Congress and President George H.W. Bush reached agreement on a budget that complied with the deficit limit for that year. At the same time, the federal budget deficit was eliminated during the second administration of President William J. Clinton. That happened because of improvements in the national economy, however, not because of the threat of automatic spending cuts. The deficit's elimination was short-lived, as it recurred as a result of spending and tax policies during the administration of President George W. Bush.

> *After the enactment of Gramm-Rudman-Hollings in 1985 and its revision in 1987, the deficit never met the limits required by law.*

See also: CONGRESSIONAL BUDGET AND IMPOUNDMENT CONTROL ACT; PUBLIC DEBT ACTS.

BIBLIOGRAPHY

McKitrick, Eric L. *Andrew Johnson and Reconstruction.* Chicago: University of Chicago Press, 1964.

White, Joseph, and Aaron B. Wildavsky. *The Deficit and the Public Interest: The Search for Responsible Budgeting in the 1980s.* Berkeley: University of California Press, 1989.

Wildavsky, Aaron B. *The Politics of the Budgetary Process,* 4th ed. Boston: Little, Brown, 1984.

BANK OF THE UNITED STATES (1791)

Yonatan Eyal

Excerpt from the Acts to Charter the Bank of the United States

The establishment of a Bank for the United States ... will be very conducive to the successful conducting of the national finances; will tend to give facility to the obtaining of loans, for the use of the Government, in sudden emergencies; and will be productive of considerable advantage to trade and industry in general....

Alexander Hamilton, secretary of the treasury during the 1790s, had observed the instability of his fledgling republic during the 1780s, when

Articles of Confederation: first constitution of the United States (in effect 1781–1789); it established a union between the thirteen states, but with a weak central government

Shortly after the government established by the U.S. Constitution began working in 1789, Hamilton devised an economic plan intended to bring stability and prosperity to America's finances.

it still operated under the **Articles of Confederation**. The new nation's finances and politics then seemed in disarray. Shortly after the government established by the U.S. Constitution began working in 1789, Hamilton devised an economic plan intended to bring stability and prosperity to America's finances.

The Bank of the United States became a central feature of Hamilton's scheme. He expected that a national financial institution such as the Bank would centralize and manage the nation's currency and credit. The Bank would hold government monies and issue notes that could be used to pay debts to the state. It would also extend loans to stimulate manufacturing and economic growth. Additionally, Hamilton hoped that government could forge an alliance with the country's wealthy elite, and indeed the Bank's early subscribers were virtually all speculators and businessmen. The Bank played a vital role in the flourishing, commercialized society that Hamilton and the Federalist Party envisioned, and in 1791 Congress officially chartered it for a period of twenty years (1 Stat. 191).

POLITICAL DISAGREEMENTS

Members of the opposition Republican Party, led by Thomas Jefferson and James Madison, disagreed with Hamilton's philosophy. They thought that chartering a Bank exceeded Congress's constitutional authority and would lead to the unhealthy dominance of a wealthy upper class—exactly what Hamilton desired. The national Bank, they feared, would create a privileged group of nonproducers, people who got rich by handling paper money rather than through hard work. It might encourage corruption, as businessmen cultivated unsavory partnerships with the government. Finally, the Bank flew in the face of the founding republican ideology of the American Revolution, which led Jeffersonians to suspect powerful conspiracies against their liberties.

As president, Jefferson nevertheless allowed the Bank to run its course until Hamilton's charter expired in 1811. Following the War of 1812, a new generation of Jeffersonian Republicans, led by Congressman Henry Clay, rechartered the Bank for another twenty years. As was true in 1791, the Second Bank's charter of 1816 (3 Stat. 266) became part of a grand design for economic growth, now called the "American System." Clay's proposal, like Hamilton's, supplemented the Bank with protective tariffs that raised prices on imported goods in order to benefit native manufacturers. And it authorized federal funding for internal improvement projects such as canals and turnpikes.

In this postwar period the Bank fed an investment boom funded by paper currency, only to see it collapse abruptly in 1819. During that year the Bank called in its loans and contracted the currency, leading to widespread economic depression, joblessness, and bankruptcy. Many victims of these tough economic times—among them future President Andrew Jackson—blamed the Bank for their misfortunes. The resentments nursed by this "Panic of 1819" had much to do with the anti-Bank fervor of succeeding years.

LEGAL AND POLITICAL CHALLENGES

Another challenge to the Second Bank came legally, when the U.S. Supreme Court considered the constitutionality of its existence. Chief Justice John Marshall, in the case of *McCulloch v. Maryland* (1819), argued that Congress acted legitimately when creating the Bank. He emphasized the **"necessary and proper,"** or elastic, clause of the Constitution, which said that Congress could do whatever it thought essential to fulfill its obligations. In the realm of inter-state commerce, over which Congress exercised control, this included the authority to create a national bank. Marshall's ruling allowed the Bank to continue to function. But the most serious test of its survival came from Andrew Jackson and his new Democratic Party.

Under its director, Nicholas Biddle, the Bank applied for Congressional re-charter in 1832, four years before its current charter was due to expire. President Jackson, already wary of the concentration of power represented by the Bank, revitalized old Jeffersonian arguments against its continuation. The "Monster Bank," as he called it, gave too much influence to a select

necessary and proper clause: U.S. Constitution, Article I, section 8, clause 18, empowers congress to make all laws which shall be "necessary and proper" for carrying into execution the enumerated powers of Congress

The Bank of the United States as it appeared in 1799. The idea of a national bank and centralized currency to bring stability to the economy of the fledgling republic was championed by Alexander Hamilton and began its twenty-year charter in 1791. Thomas Jefferson and James Madison, who feared the bank would create a non-producing elite class of money handlers and would encourage corruption, led a strong opposition. Future presidents continued to question the wisdom of the bank and its further existence was uncertain until the onset of the Civil War when need for the institution achieved general acceptance. (LIBRARY OF CONGRESS, PRINTS AND PHOTOGRAPHS DIVISION)

group of wealthy financiers. Lost in the path of its destruction lay the down-trodden farmers and planters whom the Bank victimized by calling in loans and foreclosing on property. Jackson regarded himself as the spokesman for America's virtuous independent farmers, threatened by an impersonal institution with undue control over their daily lives.

veto: when the president returns a bill to Congress with a statement of objections

Jackson **vetoed** the Bank's re-charter in 1832, and then won a decisive presidential victory over Henry Clay in a campaign largely focused on the Bank. But Jackson thought his veto insufficient, so in mid-1833 he began withdrawing government deposits from the Bank and placing them in various state banks loyal to the Democratic Party. Biddle, in response, called in loans and tightened the currency as a way of demonstrating his power and putting pressure on the chief executive. Despite Biddle's best efforts, the Second Bank went out of existence as its charter expired in 1836.

Anti-Bank Democrats, now led by President Martin Van Buren, did propose an alternative to the "Monster" they killed. Named the "Independent Treasury," or "Sub-Treasury," Van Buren's idea was to create a government depository forbidden from issuing notes and loans and thus lacking the regulatory mecha-

The Origins of U.S. Political Parties

The first two political parties in the United States were the Federalists and the Democrats. "Federalist" originally described supporters of the Constitution (though the Democrats supported the Constitution as well). The Federalist party emerged during the 1790s as a proponent of close relations with Britain and a strong national government. The Federalists were elitists, and the party's leaders were not in favor of universal suffrage. In 1796 the Federalist John Adams was elected president, but the party was unable to organize effectively after the turn of the century, and during the 1820s the Federalists dissolved.

The Democratic party, originally known as the Democratic-Republican party, also had its roots in the 1790s, when a group of Thomas Jefferson's supporters called themselves "Democratic Republicans" or "Jeffersonian Republicans" to highlight their opposition to monarchy and belief in populist government. The party built its early identity around a popular challenge to ruling elites. It took its present name during the 1830s, when it held prominence under President Andrew Jackson. During the 1860s, the party's Southern Democrats refused to renounce slavery, so antislavery Democrats broke off to form the new Republican party, which dominated U.S. politics for the next seventy years. The Democrats returned to power during the Great Depression in the 1930s, under the presidency of Franklin Delano Roosevelt, who championed the working class. During the twentieth century the Democrats promoted liberal values

and the interests of working people. The party was known as a coalition of laborers, farmers, immigrants, urban liberals, and minorities.

The Whig party was named after a British political group that opposed the monarchy. It was formed in 1834 primarily to oppose the policies of President Jackson (who the Whigs referred to as "King Andrew"), and its members were an eclectic group with diverse principles. The Whigs elected two presidents, William H. Harrison in 1840 and Zachary Taylor in 1848. Thereafter the party began to fracture along pro- and anti-slavery lines, and in 1854 the Whig party dissolved when most Northern Whigs joined the new Republican party.

The Republican party was formed during the 1850s to oppose slavery. It soon became the dominant party in the North, and Abraham Lincoln was elected president on the Republican ticket in 1860. After the Civil War the Republican's strongest constituent groups were business interests and farmers in the North and Midwest, creating a lasting divide between the party's "Wall Street" and "Main Street" factions. From 1860 to 1932 the Republicans dominated American politics, winning fourteen out of eighteen presidential elections until the Democrats' support for the working class brought Roosevelt into office during the Great Depression. In the twentieth century the Republicans promoted conservative values and a favorable business climate. Their key issues included opposition to Communism, lower taxes, less government regulation, and a conservative social agenda.

nisms of the First and Second Banks. The Independent Treasury formed part of Van Buren's response to the devastating industrial depression afflicting the nation from 1837 to 1843. During the early 1840s members of the Whig Party in Congress dismantled it, although Democrats under President James K. Polk reinstated it in 1846. Two Whig attempts to revive a national bank failed in the early 1840s, when their renegade president John Tyler vetoed the proposed charters. However, a national monetary system came into existence yet again with the onset of the Civil War. Congress, now under Republican control, established a network of national banks that could issue bonds and thus perform the same managerial functions as the First and Second Banks.

During the first century of the American republic, the Bank of the United States remained the primary means by which statesmen who embraced Hamilton's views (that is, Federalists, National Republicans, Whigs, and then Republicans) sought to administer the nation's economic life. The federal reserve system instituted in 1913 replaced the Bank and its functions and created the modern economic regulatory structure we know today.

See also: BLAND-ALLISON ACT; COINAGE ACT OF 1792; FEDERAL RESERVE ACT.

BIBLIOGRAPHY

Hammond, Bray. *Banks and Politics in America, From the Revolution to the Civil War.* Princeton, NJ: Princeton University Press, 1957.

McFaul, John M. *The Politics of Jacksonian Finance.* Ithaca, NY: Cornell University Press, 1972.

Remini, Robert. *Andrew Jackson and the Bank War.* New York: Norton, 1967.

> *The federal reserve system instituted in 1913 replaced the Bank and its functions and created the modern economic regulatory structure we know today.*

BANKRUPTCY ACT OF 1841

David A. Skeel, Jr.

Excerpt from the Bankruptcy Act of 1841

All persons whatsoever, residing in any State, District or Territory of the United States, owing debts, which shall not have been created in consequence of a defalcation as a public officer ... who shall, by petition, setting forth to the best of his knowledge and belief, a list of his or their creditors, their respective places of residence, and the amount due to each, together with an accurate inventory of his or their property, rights, and credits...verified by oath, or, if conscientiously scrupulous of taking an oath, by solemn affirmation, apply to the proper court ... for the benefit of this act, and therein declare themselves unable to meet their debts and engagements, shall be deemed bankrupts within the purview of this act.

Enacted by Congress as a result of an unsavory round of logrolling (trading votes for promises of support for pet projects), the Bankruptcy Act of

Section 4 of the act (the discharge):

[E]very bankrupt, who shall bona fide surrender all his property, and rights of property, with the exception before mentioned [i.e., certain exempt property], for the benefit of his creditors, and shall fully comply with and obey all the orders and directions which may from time to time be passed by the proper court, ... shall (unless a majority in number and value of his creditors who have proved their debts, shall file their written dissent thereto) be entitled to a full discharge from all his debts.

The 1841 act was the first law to provide for voluntary as well as involuntary bankruptcy, and it covered all individual debtors, not just merchants and traders.

1841 (5 Stat. 440) was repealed only two years later. Nevertheless, the act introduced several innovations that have served as cornerstones for every federal bankruptcy law that followed. These innovations made the 1841 act the first modern American bankruptcy law.

The 1841 act was the second of four federal bankruptcy laws Congress enacted during the nineteenth century (the others were enacted in 1800, 1867, and 1898), and it followed the same general pattern. The two main forces leading to federal bankruptcy legislation were the onset of a major economic depression and political control by the conservative party (the Republicans or their predecessors, the Whigs and Federalists). The strongest support for federal bankruptcy legislation came from conservatives in the Northeast, who viewed such legislation as essential to establishing a commercial society. The most vigorous opponents were liberal lawmakers from the South and Midwest. They worried that federal bankruptcy legislation would threaten the stability of farming interests by, among other things, enabling Northern creditors (those to whom a debt is owed) to foreclose on farms during a temporary downturn.

The lightning rod for the 1841 act was the 1837 Panic, which devastated the American economy. Many demanded a federal bankruptcy law to address the effects of the crisis. The Whigs made bankruptcy legislation a central issue in the 1840 presidential campaign, which put the Whig candidate William Henry Harrison in the White House and gave the Whigs control of Congress. But this alone was not enough to ensure passage of the act. Almost every Democrat opposed the proposed legislation, as did a small but potentially decisive group of Whigs. The Whig leadership finally secured passage of the act by agreeing to support a land distribution bill in return for votes for the 1841 act. Almost as soon as it came together, the coalition that voted for the 1841 act started to unravel. When a small group of Southern and Midwestern Whigs defected, the 1841 Bankruptcy Act was doomed. John Tyler, who became president when Harrison died shortly after his inauguration, was much less enthusiastic about the legislation than his predecessor. Popular opinion had turned against the law, and Tyler signed the repeal legislation in 1843.

In addition to discharging (eliminating) the debts of thousands of debtors during its short life, the Bankruptcy Act of 1841 introduced two crucial innovations to American bankruptcy law. The 1800 act had provided only for involuntary bankruptcy—that is, creditors but not debtors (those who owe a debt) could file a bankruptcy petition—and it covered only merchants and traders. The 1841 act was the first law to provide for voluntary as well as involuntary bankruptcy, and it covered all individual debtors, not just merchants and traders.

The debates over federal bankruptcy law continued, and it was not until 1898 that Congress finally enacted a bankruptcy law that lasted. At the heart of this law, as with the Bankruptcy Act of 1978 that eventually replaced it, were the themes of voluntary bankruptcy and universal scope—where the law applied to everyone, not only merchants and traders—that Congress first introduced in 1841.

See also: BANK OF THE UNITED STATES; BANKRUPTCY ACT OF 1978.

BIBLIOGRAPHY

Balleisen, Edward J. *Navigating Failure: Bankruptcy and Commercial Society in Antebellum America*. Chapel Hill: University of North Carolina Press, 2001.

Skeel, David A., Jr. "Bankruptcy Lawyers and the Shape of American Bankruptcy Law."*Fordham Law Review* 67 (1998): 497–522.

Skeel, David A., Jr. *Debt's Dominion: A History of Bankruptcy Law in America*. Princeton, NJ: Princeton University Press, 2001.

Warren, Charles. *Bankruptcy in United States History*. Cambridge, MA: Harvard University Press, 1935.

BANKRUPTCY ACT OF 1978

Eric A. Posner

The Bankruptcy Reform Act of 1978 (P.L. 103-394, 107 Stat. 4106), as amended, governs the relationship between creditors and debtors when debtors can no longer pay their debts. Ordinarily, people and businesses have a legal obligation to pay their debts. If they **default** on a loan, their creditors can sue them and obtain some or all of their money or property, up to the value of the debt. When the **debtor** is a person, creditors can force a sale of the debtor's house, take away household goods, and even obtain the debtor's future wages, although in all cases federal and state law limit how much the creditor can take. When the debtor is a corporation, the creditor can seize assets even when doing so forces the shutdown of factories and the interruption of business. Bankruptcy law limits these standard legal remedies in several ways.

When the debtor files for bankruptcy, creditors must stop legal proceedings to seize the debtor's assets, and all the interested parties must come to a special bankruptcy court. The bankruptcy judge and other officials determine the extent of the debtor's debts and assets. Most of the assets will be sold and the proceeds from the sale are distributed to the creditors according to the size and legal priority of their claims. One of the main functions of bankruptcy law is to ensure the orderly sale and distribution of property, so that the maximum amount of money is raised, and to ensure that the money is distributed fairly to creditors in accordance with their legal rights.

Bankruptcy law also gives important rights to debtors. If the debtor is a person, the bankruptcy will usually result in the discharge of all of his or her debts, even though he or she does not have money to pay them. The debtor will usually be permitted to keep some assets, including furniture, clothes, sometimes his or her house, some money, and so forth. Most important, the debtor will have the right to keep future income free from the earlier claims of creditors. In this way, the debtor is given a "fresh start": he or she can begin life anew with the slate wiped clean.

If the debtor is a corporation, the bankruptcy will result either in the liquidation of the corporation or its reorganization. When a corporation is liquidat-

default: the omission or failure to perform a legal or contractual duty

debtor: one who owes payment or other performance on an obligation; anyone liable on a claim

When the debtor files for bankruptcy, creditors must stop legal proceedings to seize the debtor's assets, and all the interested parties must come to a special bankruptcy court.

ed, all of its assets (which might include whole divisions or subsidiaries) are sold off, and the money that is obtained is distributed to the creditors, with nothing to the shareholders. When a corporation is reorganized, its capital structure is rearranged. For example, the original creditors become shareholders in the reorganized firm, and the original shareholders are deprived of their shares. In principle, a firm after reorganization performs the same business as it did prior to bankruptcy. Factories are kept open and workers keep their jobs. In practice, the reorganization might involve the shutting down of inefficient factories, or the reorganized firm will shed assets and workers in order to become profitable.

CONGRESSIONAL POWER

Congress has authority to issue "uniform Laws on the subject of Bankruptcies" under Article I, section 8, clause 4, of the United States Constitution. People have always understood this authority to permit Congress to regulate the creditor side of bankruptcy, that is, to create a system through which creditors' claims against a defaulting debtor are processed and liquidated. There was some controversy in the nineteenth century over whether the Constitution also authorized Congress to determine the rights and obligations of the debtor. Traditionally, the area of law governing the rights of defaulting debtors was called "insolvency law," with "bankruptcy law" used to refer only to the creditor side. Because the Constitution authorizes Congress to regulate bankruptcy but says nothing about insolvency (the inability to pay debts), some people argued that Congress had no authority to create a right to a discharge, or to regulate corporate liquidations and reorganizations. However, this view was ultimately rejected by the courts, and today it is settled that the bankruptcy clause is the constitutional basis of all aspects of modern bankruptcy law.

There was some controversy in the nineteenth century over whether the Constitution also authorized Congress to determine the rights and obligations of the debtor.

Congress tried several times in the nineteenth century to create a bankruptcy law, but the first lasting bankruptcy law was not enacted until 1898, with an important amendment in 1938. These earlier laws included the main elements of the modern bankruptcy system: the procedure for collectively resolving claims; the discharge for the debtor; and provisions for reorganizing or liquidating insolvent corporations.

The bankruptcy filing rate was low and relatively flat for the first half of the twentieth century, averaging in the low thousands per year. But with the expansion of the credit market, the number of bankruptcies increased, and by the late 1960s there were about 200,000 bankruptcy filings per year. These figures alarmed observers, who associated bankruptcy with moral or economic failure. Observers were also unhappy with the existing laws governing corporate reorganization, which seemed to be unnecessarily complex and to generate unnecessary litigation. In 1968 Congress created a bankruptcy reform commission and asked it to propose amendments to the bankruptcy law. The commission issued its report in 1973, but **Watergate** interrupted legislative deliberations for several years.

Watergate: the scandal following the break-in at the Democratic National Committee headquarters located in the Watergate apartment and office complex in Washington, D.C., in 1972

POLICY

By the time Congress turned its full attention to bankruptcy reform, people were no longer so worried about high bankruptcy filing rates. The consumer protection movement had intervened, and people had become more skeptical about the methods of creditors than about the motives of debtors.

Three other issues dominated discussion. First, most backers of bankruptcy reform wanted to replace the existing system of state exemptions with a uniform system of federal exemptions. State exemptions are laws that allow defaulting debtors to keep some of their property even though they do not pay off the full debt. State homestead exemptions, for example, permit debtors to keep their house (usually but not always up to a dollar ceiling). The generosity of state exemptions varied greatly, and critics of the exemption system argued that it was not fair that the residents of one state could keep their houses while the residents of another state might be able to keep no more than some clothes and furniture. Defenders of the system believed that the exemption level was properly left to the states under the principles of **federalism**. The complex compromise in the act created a new federal system of exemptions but gave the states the right to "opt out" and force residents to use the state exemptions laws, and about two-thirds of the states subsequently exercised this right.

federalism: a system of political organization; a union formed of separate states or groups that are ruled by a central authority on some matters but are otherwise permitted to govern themselves independently

Second, reformers wanted to streamline the old corporate reorganization system, which included separate procedures for large public corporations and for smaller closely held businesses. Though the rhetoric was about simplifying a complex area of the law, beneath the surface the debate focused on the amount of protection to be given creditors of large corporations. History suggested to reformers that when a large corporation is reorganized, the "insiders"—managers, large shareholders, large creditors—will give themselves large stakes in the reorganized firms, while outsiders such as small creditors and workers will be given little or nothing. A variety of mechanisms, including oversight by the Securities and Exchange Commission, had been devised to protect the small stakeholders. The act weakened these protections to some extent, but not significantly.

Consumer protection advocates argue that bankruptcy should be more generous than it is. Others fear that the high filing rate threatens a collapse in the credit market.

Third, many backers of bankruptcy reform wanted to elevate the status of bankruptcy judges and lawyers, to make bankruptcy a more respectable and normal legal proceeding than it had been in the past. One source of the low prestige of the bankruptcy bar was the suspicion that bankruptcy judges were patronage appointments enjoyed by the federal judiciary (in other words, appointments made for the political advantage of judges). Reformers sought to make bankruptcy judges as much like ordinary federal judges as possible, with appointment by the president, life tenure, and so forth. Federal judges, however, objected to what they saw as a dilution of their own status. The complex compromise subsequently ran into constitutional difficulties, which were ultimately resolved through additional legislation in 1984.

EXPERIENCE UNDER THE ACT

Experience with the Bankruptcy Reform Act has been mixed. Individual bankruptcy filings increased rapidly after passage of the act, for complex reasons. The filing rate might have increased because of the generosity of the new federal exemptions, but they probably also increased simply because consumer debt has become much more common than it was in the 1970s and before.

Enron Retirement Plans

In December 2001, the Enron energy corporation filed for bankruptcy amid one of the biggest scandals in the history of U.S. business. Government investigators charged that an accounting cover-up had hidden debt and overstated the company's earnings, falsely boosting its stock price to provide billions in unearned profits. Enron executives were indicted for fraud, and the company's accounting firm, Arthur Andersen, was convicted of obstructing justice and collapsed. Among the victims of the debacle were approximately 15,000 Enron employees whose retirement plans were heavily invested in Enron stock. During the weeks before the company filed for bankruptcy, Enron prohibited rank-and-file employees from selling their stock, but executives faced no such restriction. As a result, as the stock price plunged from $26 per share to complete collapse, employees lost approximately $1.2 billion of the money they had saved for retirement. In 2003 the Justice Department was expected to charge twenty executives of Enron and its retirement plan with breach of fiduciary duty.

Enron employee Meredith Stewart (sitting) gets first hand experience of the effects of corporate bankruptcy. Under the Bankruptcy Act of 1978 both individuals and corporations are allowed to have their debts discharged and get a "fresh start." The act allows a person to keep certain necessities while a judge determines which assets are to be sold to pay the creditors. In the case of a corporation, the judge can liquidate the businesses assets and subsidiaries to pay creditors, not shareholders. Unfortunately, most Enron employees had substantial shareholder investment in the company.
(©REUTERS NEWMEDIA INC./CORBIS)

More people borrow, so more people fail to pay their debts and file for bankruptcy. Consumer protection advocates argue that bankruptcy should be more generous than it is. Others fear that the high filing rate threatens a collapse in the credit market. These warring forces left their mark on bankruptcy amendments in 1984 and 1994, and agitation for reform has been continuing.

Corporate reorganization has also become more frequent, but again it is not clear whether the act is the cause. Major changes in the economy occurred in the 1980s, resulting in a wave of transactions in which firms borrowed money in order to finance their acquisition by investors. As corporations took on debt, they became more likely to default on loans, and bankruptcy became an increasingly attractive option.

Some critics of the act argue that it has contributed to a kind of moral decline. The act did try to destigmatize bankruptcy, and it might have succeeded. And, as noted, it might have contributed to the rise of bankruptcy filings. In the view of critics, the act has thus made people feel less responsible about paying their debts. Defenders of the act argue that most people file for bankruptcy only because of devastating and unanticipated events, such as the death of a wage-earning spouse or a divorce, severe medical problems, or loss of employment during a **recession**. Bankruptcy is not a cause of, or symptom of, moral decline, but an effect of larger social forces, such as the breakup of families, economic dislocation, and the decline of communities.

recession: a period of reduced economic activity, but less severe than a depression

These debates, however, obscure what is really at stake in bankruptcy law. A generous personal bankruptcy law that shields assets and future income has both beneficial and harmful effects. On the one hand, the law reduces the hardship experienced by individuals when circumstances prevent them from paying their debts. On the other hand, the law increases the cost of credit by making it harder for creditors to collect their debts. Bankruptcy law is like an involuntary insurance policy that protects people against the financial consequences of bad events, but also costs them money in the form of a higher interest rate than they would otherwise pay.

On the one hand, the law reduces the hardship experienced by individuals when circumstances prevent them from paying their debts. On the other hand, the law increases the cost of credit by making it harder for creditors to collect their debts.

Corporate reorganization policy also involves tradeoffs. If the law is flexible, and makes it easy to reorganize firms, then insiders and large creditors might use corporate reorganization as an opportunity to improve their financial position at the expense of smaller creditors, workers, and other stakeholders. If the law makes it hard to reorganize firms, then sometimes a firm that has a good business plan but cannot pay its debts will be liquidated, which causes real harm. Good corporate bankruptcy law gives managers, creditors, and other stakeholders some flexibility to change the firm's capital structure, but not too much.

THE LANGUAGE OF BANKRUPTCY LAW

Bankruptcy law uses a lot of technical language, but it is not very difficult, as a few examples will show. When a person or business files for bankruptcy, the person or business is labeled the *debtor* (not the *bankrupt,* which was the term under prior law). The debtor must provide a list of *assets* to the court: these are any items of value, such as furniture, money, and machines. These assets are then put in the bankruptcy *estate,* which is a legal fiction (rather than an actual estate) that refers to the assets that will be sold off so that creditors can be paid. In the case of individuals, assets that are covered by state or federal *exemptions* are not included in the estate. The debtor also provides a list of *debts,* and the *creditors* are informed of the bankruptcy. Each creditor has a *claim* against the estate; the value of the claim is the same as the value of the original unpaid debt. An official named the *trustee* will, with the bankruptcy judge's approval, sell the assets in the estate, and distribute the proceeds of the sale to the creditors, with each creditor getting a pro rata share (its claim divided by the sum of all claims). The debtor than obtains a *discharge,* which wipes out all debts that existed prior to bankruptcy.

See also: BANKRUPTCY ACT OF 1841; CONSUMER CREDIT PROTECTION ACT.

BIBLIOGRAPHY

Jackson, Thomas H. *The Logic and Limits of Bankruptcy.* Cambridge, MA: Harvard University Press, 1986.

Posner, Eric A. "The Political Economy of the Bankruptcy Reform Act of 1978." *Michigan Law Review* 96 (1997): 47–126.

Skeel, David A., Jr. *Debt's Dominion: A History of Bankruptcy Law in America.* Princeton: Princeton University Press, 2001.

Sullivan, Theresa, Elizabeth Warren, and Jay L. Westbrook. *As We Forgive Our Debtors: Bankruptcy and Consumer Credit in America.* Cambridge, MA: Harvard University Press, 1989.

Warren, Charles. *Bankruptcy in United States History.* Cambridge, MA: Harvard University Press, 1935.

BLAND-ALLISON ACT (1878)

Lawrence H. Officer

After the Coinage Act of 1873 discontinued coinage of the U.S. silver dollar, the world market price of silver fell drastically. Demand decreased as the United States demonetization of silver (ceasing to use it as a monetary standard) combined with a shift in European countries from a silver to a **gold standard** (establishing gold as the standard for the basic unit of currency). Supply increased as large silver deposits were discovered in the American West, but silver-mining companies suffered with no orders coming from U.S. mints. The Coinage Act also hurt **debtors**, especially farmers. Prices in general were falling, and output (of agricultural and other products) was increasing at a faster rate than gold production. Farmers and other debtors in the South and West combined to advocate "free silver," meaning unlimited coinage of the standard U.S. silver dollar specified in the Coinage Act of 1837, with unlimited power as **legal tender**.

Some congressmen and senators supported the use of free silver, partly because of regional concerns, and partly because they believed that free silver would result in inflation and/or bimetallism (the use of both gold and sil-

gold standard: a monetary standard in which the basic unit of currency is equal in value to and exchangeable for a specified amount of gold

debtor: one who owes payment or other performance on an obligation; anyone liable on a claim

legal tender: an offer of money in the form of coin, paper money, or another circulating medium that the law compels a creditor to accept in payment of a debt

ver as monetary standards). The "silverites" saw both outcomes as desirable. Business and financial interests (especially in the Northeast), and their supporters in Congress, opposed the use of free silver. These "monometallists" believed in preservation of the gold standard and wanted a conservative monetary regime.

A VICTORY FOR SILVERITES

The Bland-Allison Act of 1878 (P.L. 45-20, 20 Stat. 25) was the first victory of the silverites, although the act was a compromise. Congressman Richard P. Bland included free coinage in his bill, but the provision was removed by Senator William B. Allison. The bill restored the standard silver dollar's full legal-tender quality. Instead of free coinage, the secretary of the treasury was directed to purchase silver bullion (the metal in its uncoined state) at the market price, in the amount of 2 to 4 million dollars monthly, and to coin the bullion into standard silver dollars. The low price of silver meant that the silver dollar became, in effect, a subsidiary coin: its face-value was greater than its metallic value. This decidedly was not a characteristic of minted gold coins.

UNWANTED CONSEQUENCES AND FURTHER LEGISLATION

The outcome of the act was unsatisfactory to everyone. The Treasury Department, never in favor of the legislation, purchased silver in minimum amounts. Thus the increase in the money supply consisting of silver coinage was limited. Silver-mining companies received a market for their product, but the price of silver continued to fall. To meet the legal dollar minimum, the Treasury had to buy an increasing volume of bullion, which meant a higher expense for coining and storage. The pressure on Congress for new legislation was universal. The outcome was the Sherman Silver Purchase Act of 1890, which directed the Treasury to purchase silver bullion in the physical amount of 4.5 million ounces monthly and to pay for it with legal-tender Treasury notes, a new kind of paper money. Now a fixed maximum weight of bullion would be purchased. Ironically, Senator John Sherman, who gave the act its name, voted for the bill only to avoid free coinage.

The price of silver continued to decline, even though the act increased Treasury purchases. An acute lack of confidence in U.S. maintenance of the gold standard followed, both at home and abroad. The cause of this lack of confidence was not monetary inflation directly. Rather, it was distrust in the gold value of the dollar, partly because of "silver agitation" in Congress, as bills for free coinage continued to be presented. A financial panic occurred in 1893, and many blamed the Sherman Act. President Grover Cleveland convened a **special session** of Congress and demanded that the act be repealed. The silver-purchase and note-issuance provisions of the Sherman Act were in fact repealed in 1893, although the legal-tender status of silver coin and Treasury notes remained.

The silver-induced monetary inflation of the Bland-Allison and Sherman Acts came to an end. Yet the threat to the U.S. gold standard increased, especially because of continuing silver agitation in Congress. The defeat of William Jennings Bryan, a prominent Democratic silverite, in the presidential election of 1896 finally put an end to silver as a political issue, along with the threat this issue posed to the gold standard.

Representative Richard P. Bland, above, sponsored the Bland-Allison Act of 1878. The act as adopted required the U.S. Treasury to purchase between $2 million and $4 million worth of silver bullion each month at market prices; this was to be coined into silver dollars, which were made legal tender for all debts. (PUBLIC DOMAIN)

The low price of silver meant that the silver dollar became, in effect, a subsidiary coin: its face-value was greater than its metallic value.

special session: an extraordinary or special session is called to meet in the interval between regular sessions

See also: BANK OF THE UNITED STATES; COINAGE ACT OF 1792; COINAGE ACTS; FEDERAL RESERVE ACT; GOLD STANDARD ACT OF 1900.

BIBLIOGRAPHY

Friedman, Milton, and Anna Jacobson Schwartz. *A Monetary History of the United States, 1867–1960.* Princeton, NJ: Princeton University Press, 1963.

Nugent, Walter T. K. *Money and American Society, 1865–1880.* New York: Free Press, 1968.

Nussbaum, Arthur. *A History of the Dollar.* New York: Columbia University Press, 1957.

Watson, David K. *History of American Coinage.* New York: G. P. Putnam, 1899.

BONUS BILL (1924)

David G. Delaney

The World War Adjusted Compensation Act (43 Stat. 121), known as the Bonus Bill, created a benefit plan for World War I veterans as additional compensation for their military service. It credited servicemembers with "adjusted service certificates" equal to $1.00 per day served in the United States and $1.25 per day served overseas, up to specified limits. The certificates, popularly known as "bonuses" because they supplemented the pay and benefits that servicemembers had received during the war, earned interest and became payable to the veteran in 1945 or to a veteran's family if he died before then. Although many saw the Bonus Bill as a worthwhile program, its $4 billion cost led fiscal conservatives to question the wisdom and necessity of paying servicemembers additional benefits for past military service.

Prior to the Bonus Bill, veterans' benefits, like the Civil War Pensions, consisted almost exclusively of pensions to surviving veterans. The only exception was a 1917 law under which the government paid enlisted personnel and their families monthly allotments during the war and maintained life insurance policies for officers and enlisted servicemembers even after the war ended. The allotment program ended with World War I in 1921, leaving numerous groups anxious to continue some form of additional benefits to returning servicemembers.

Veterans, with strong support from the newly formed American Legion, led that movement, but Democratic and Republican political progressives also supported it. What became the Bonus Bill originated in the 1920 Fordney Bill (named for Representative Joseph W. Fordney), a broader benefits program that would have let veterans choose between a cash bonus, education grants, or payments toward buying a home or farm. Many supported the plan to increase employment, promote spending, and develop rural areas of the United States. Yet the $5 billion cost proved politically unpalatable, and the Senate rejected the Fordney Bill. In 1922, however, Congress shed the education and home purchase options and passed a bonus-only bill of approximately $4 billion. Still too expensive, President Warren G. Harding promptly vetoed it for being fiscally irresponsible.

The G.I. Bill of Rights

American veterans of military service have been given grants or benefits as far back as the Revolutionary War, when veterans of the Continental Army were awarded $80 bonuses and grants of land totaling two million acres. In 1944, Congress enacted the Servicemen's Readjustment Act, also known as the G.I. Bill of Rights, to help sixteen million veterans make the transition to the civilian economy after the war. The act provided unemployment compensation, education and job training, and guaranteed housing and business loans. Nine million veterans received nearly $4 billion in "readjustment allowances," 10 million veterans took advantage of the educational benefits, and five million veterans received loans totaling more than $50 billion. Historians agree that the G.I. Bill was one of the most important pieces of economic and social legislation in American history, helping World War II veterans to become one of the most educated and prosperous generations of Americans. The benefits provided in the G.I. Bill were later extended to veterans of the Korean and Vietnam wars.

By 1924 most Americans, including some well-known business leaders like William Randolph Hearst, favored some form of additional benefits. Most fiscal conservatives, however, thought additional benefits too costly and the specific proposals unlikely to strengthen the economy. Secretary of the Treasury Andrew W. Mellon typified this group, preferring instead to lower taxes rather than burden the government with additional spending. Nevertheless, Congress reconsidered a version similar to the failed 1922 bill and passed it over President Calvin Coolidge's veto.

In 1932 most veterans were still thirteen years away from receiving their bonuses. Suffering the economic effects of the Great Depression, they

The Bonus Bill credited servicemembers with "adjusted service certificates" equal to $1.00 per day served in the United States and $1.25 per day served overseas, up to specified limits.

The Bonus Bill of 1924, or, more formally, the World War Adjusted Compensation Act allowed for World War I veterans to receive additional money based on the time of their service. The monies were to be paid in 1945 and, unlike earlier bills, the benefits were paid to the soldier's family if he was deceased. With the onset of the Great Depression, the veterans above marched on Washington to lobby Congress to make payments earlier. These marchers would have to wait another four years for Congress to authorize early payments. (U.S. SENATE HISTORICAL OFFICE)

marched on Washington and were dubbed the "Bonus Expeditionary Force" as they lobbied Congress, unsuccessfully, to receive their payments early. Forced to leave Washington by the military, the marchers would have to wait another four years for Congress to authorize the early payments, again over a presidential veto, this time from Franklin D. Roosevelt.

Although the Bonus Bill provided only one modest benefit, the political debate that preceded it introduced others that would become the mainstays of future veterans legislation. The education benefits that failed in 1920 and 1922 became the hallmark of the G.I. Bill after World War II, and the payments toward home or farm purchases became low-interest loans available to most servicemembers even without serving during a time of war. In the Bonus Bill, Congress laid a foundation for these and other successes by balancing a servicemember benefits plan desired by Americans with the economic **constraints** that the country required.

constraint: a restriction

See also: CIVIL WAR PENSIONS; VETERAN'S PREFERENCE ACT OF 1944.

BIBLIOGRAPHY

Daniels, Roger. *The Bonus March: An Episode of the Great Depression.* Westport, CT: Greenwood Publishing, 1971.

BORN-ALIVE INFANTS PROTECTION ACT OF 2002

Alberto B. Lopez

Abortion and its regulation has long sparked heated debate in the United States. During the nineteenth century, many states authored laws making the performance of abortions illegal, but state governments enforced those laws only sporadically. By the mid-twentieth century, however, states began to enforce their anti-abortion laws more rigorously, which led some women to seek abortions outside the medical profession to avoid detection. Because of the dangers associated with illegal abortions, public demand for safe abortions increased during the 1960s; therefore many states responded by legalizing abortion under certain circumstances—such as where a threat to the mother's health existed or when the unborn child faced physical or mental impairment. Nonetheless, abortion regulations remained on the books and largely eliminated the procedure from the consideration of a pregnant woman whose own health or that of her unborn child was not at risk. As a result, society continued to be passionately divided between abortion prohibitions that protected an unborn child's life and permitting a woman's choice to have an abortion.

Abortion and its regulation has long sparked heated debate in the United States.

The Supreme Court examined the impact of abortion regulations on a woman's right to choose to have an abortion in its landmark decision of *Roe v. Wade* (1973). In *Roe,* the Court deemed a Texas statute that criminalized abortion unless necessary to save the life of the mother to be an unconstitutional **infringement** on a woman's right to privacy. Although the Court deter-

infringe: to exceed the limits of; to violate

mined that a woman had a right to terminate her pregnancy rooted in her right to privacy, the Court balanced this right against the need to protect both the mother's health and the life of the unborn child. Implementing a trimester framework to guide states in their regulation of abortion, the Court ruled that the state is barred from prohibiting abortion during the first three months of pregnancy, but it may regulate abortions to the extent necessary to protect the health of the mother during the second trimester. During the final three months of pregnancy, the Court decided that the fetus could live independently of the mother and deserved constitutional protection at that point. As a result, the Court ruled that the state may ban abortions during the third trimester unless the life or health of the mother is threatened.

Controversial decisions, such as Farmer, *brought another issue to the forefront of the abortion debate—the need for the legal protection of infants who survive abortion procedures and are born alive.*

Despite the court's decision in *Roe,* the battle over abortion and its regulation continued in subsequent cases. In *Planned Parenthood of Southeastern Pennsylvania v. Casey* (1992), the court upheld Pennsylvania's ability to enact certain abortion regulations, such as a parental consent requirement for minors seeking abortions. However, the court reiterated that the state may not only prohibit abortions after viability of the fetus unless the mother's life or health is in jeopardy. Later, the Court struck down a Nebraska law in *Stenberg v. Carhart* (2000) that criminalized partial-birth abortions, a late term abortion technique involving the live delivery of an infant, while the head of that infant remains inside the woman's womb. Following *Carhart,* the United States Court of Appeals for the Third Circuit overruled New Jersey's partial-birth abortion ban in *Planned Parenthood of New Jersey v. Farmer* (2000) and held that an infant's legal rights depended upon the intention of the mother regardless of the physical position of the infant. If a mother intended to abort her pregnancy and the child survived the abortion attempt, then the *Farmer* decision suggested that the child had no right to medical care because the mother was not seeking to give birth in the first place. As a result, these controversial decisions brought another issue to the forefront of the abortion debate—the need for the legal protection of infants who survive abortion procedures and are born alive.

BORN-ALIVE INFANTS

Congress placed the rights of infants who survive attempted abortions on its legislative agenda in the form of the Born-Alive Infants Protection Act of 2000, which sought to extend the protection of federal law to all born-alive infants. During legislative hearings, witnesses confirmed the implication of the *Farmer* decision by presenting evidence that infants born alive after failed abortions went without medical care and subsequently died. Nevertheless, opponents of the legislation questioned whether it interfered with a woman's right to choose in contravention of *Roe* and the jurisprudence arising from that decision. Although the proposal passed out of the House of Representatives, the bill failed to gain sufficient support in the Senate. However, the proposal made its way back to Congress one year later in the form of the Born-Alive Infants Protection Act of 2001. Citing the Necessary and Proper Clause of the Constitution as the legal basis to enact the statute, the House of Representatives

The stated goal of this statute is to extend legal rights to infants who are born alive; therefore, the law does not create new legal rights, but rather specifies to whom those legal rights attach.

The tenuous balance between a woman's right to make choices in private and the right to life of an unborn child will be weighed and reweighed as medicine advances and as society changes.

amend: to alter or change

passed the bill by voice vote and the Senate unanimously agreed in mid-2002. President George W. Bush signed the Born-Alive Infants Protection Act (P.L. 107-207, 116 Stat. 926) into law on August 5, 2002.

The stated goal of this statute is to extend legal rights to infants who are born alive; therefore, the law does not create new legal rights, but rather specifies to whom those legal rights attach. To that end, the primary effect of the law is to redefine words like "person, human being, child, or individual" in the United States Code to include "every infant member of the species homo sapiens who is born alive at any stage of development." As defined by the statute, the phrase "born alive" means "the complete expulsion or extraction (of an infant) from his or her mother ... at any stage of development, who after such expulsion or extraction breathes or has a beating heart, pulsation of the umbilical cord, or definite movement of voluntary muscles, regardless of whether the umbilical cord has been cut, and regardless of whether the expulsion or extraction occurs as a result of natural or induced labor, cesarean section, or induced abortion."

According to the Congressional Budget Office, the practical effect of this legislation is to **amend** approximately 15,000 provisions of the United States Code and some 57,000 provisions of the Code of Federal Regulations. Given its definitional purpose, the lack of controversy surrounding its enactment, and its similarity to existing provisions in thirty states, the Born-Alive Infants Protection Act of 2002 has yet to spur a flurry of litigation and its impact is largely symbolic. Moreover, the statute has done nothing to quell the deep-seated disagreement in society over abortion despite the support for its enactment. Indeed, history itself counsels that the tenuous balance between a woman's right to make choices in private and the right to life of an unborn child will be weighed and reweighed as medicine advances and as society changes.

BIBLIOGRAPHY

Arkes, Hadley. *Natural Rights and the Right to Choose.* Cambridge, MA: Cambridge University Press, 2002.

Friedman, Lawrence M. *American Law in the 20th Century.* New Haven, CT: Yale University Press, 2002.

House Report No. 835. Born-Alive Infants Protection Act of 2000: Hearings on H.R. 4292 Before the Committee of the Judiciary of the House of Representatives, 106th Cong., 2d Sess. (2000). <ftp://ftp.loc.gov/pub/thomas/cp106/hr835.txt>

National Right to Life Committee. "Born-Alive Infants Protection Act." <http://www.nrlc.org>

White House Press Release. "President Signs Born-Alive Infants Protection Act." <http://www.whitehouse.gov/news/releases/2002/08/20020805-6.html>.

BRADY HANDGUN VIOLENCE PREVENTION ACT (1993)

Keith Rollins Eakins

On March 30, 1981, twenty-five-year-old John W. Hinckley, Jr., lurked in a crowd of people clustering around a Washington, D.C., hotel waiting for President Ronald Reagan to finish delivering a speech. As President Reagan emerged from the hotel waving to the crowd and heading for his limousine, Hinckley took aim with a .22 caliber Rohm RG-14 revolver and fired off six rounds. The president was hit in his lung, and three others accompanying him were wounded. His press secretary, James S. Brady, sustained a wound to his forehead that disabled him permanently.

In response to the tragedy, Sarah Brady, James Brady's wife, became highly active in the gun control movement. In 1989 she became the chairperson of Handgun Control, Inc. (HCI), the most prominent interest group **lobbying** for legislative regulation of firearms. Two years later Ms. Brady became chairperson of the Center to Prevent Handgun Violence, HCI's sister organization, seeking to reduce gun violence through education, research, and legal advocacy. Sarah Brady and gun control proponents believed handguns were being acquired too easily in violation of the law. The Gun Control Act of 1968 made it illegal to sell handguns to felons, drug addicts, those who were **adjudicated** "mental defectives" or committed to mental institutions, those under court orders restraining them from stalking or harassing, and those convicted of misdemeanor crimes of domestic violence. Yet in reality, criminals and others who were ineligible to buy firearms could easily purchase guns by lying about their background. Brady and other gun control advocates worked to pass a law mandating background checks and a waiting period on purchases of guns.

In 1987 the Brady Handgun Violence Prevention Act was introduced into Congress, but the backers of the bill faced a full frontal assault waged by the National Rifle Association (NRA). This powerful lobbying group was joined by prominent politicians such as Presidents Reagan and Bush and Speaker of the House Tom Foley, Democrat of Washington, in opposing the bill. Through aggressive lobbying tactics and the introduction of a substitute bill by NRA-backed Democrat Bill McCollum of Florida, the NRA successfully torpedoed the Brady bill.

Despite losing initial battles, the proponents of the Brady Act continued their efforts to push through the labyrinth of congressional politics. The fortunes of the Brady Act improved greatly in 1992 with the election of President William Jefferson Clinton, who announced his full support for the bill. Meanwhile, the influence of the formidable NRA was waning. The gun lobby's traditional tactic was to oppose vociferously even minimal gun regulation on the grounds that it was a slippery slope to a full-scale ban on guns. But the American public perceived this no-holds-barred approach to be extreme. Polls indicated that most people believed a short waiting period and background check were reasonable restrictions. Moreover, any threat of a veto, a certainty during the presidencies of Reagan and Bush, and needing a two-thirds congressional vote to **override**, was gone. President Clinton not only expressed public support for the bill, but also worked to secure its passage in the Senate. Eventually, both the House and Senate approved the measure, yet the NRA succeeded in getting a provision abolishing the five-day waiting

lobby: to try to persuade the legislature to pass laws and regulations that are favorable to one's interests and to defeat laws that are unfavorable to those interests

adjudicated: a matter or controversy that has already been decided through judicial procedure

override: if the President vetoes a bill passed by Congress, the bill can still become law if two-thirds of each House of Congress votes to override the veto

period after five years because a National Instant Check System (NICS) was supposed to be in place by then. On November 30, 1993, six years after its introduction, the Brady Act became law (P.L. 103-159, 107 Stat. 1536).

The NRA then moved its attack on the Brady Act to the federal courts by financing a lawsuit challenging the constitutionality of the law. In June 1997 the NRA won a minor victory when the U.S. Supreme Court struck down as unconstitutional the portion of the bill requiring state officials to conduct background checks. In *Printz v. United States* (1997) the Court held that the statute, by requiring state officials to conduct background checks on would-be gun purchasers, violated the constitutional principles of **federalism** underlying the Tenth Amendment. In reality, the effect of the decision on gun control efforts was minimal. The provisions invalidated by the Court were, by law, to be phased out by November 1998 when the NICS was to be in place. Moreover, the vast majority of law enforcement agencies continued the background checks on a voluntary basis. Yet debate about handgun control continues. For instance, HCI and other gun control groups would like to establish a five-day waiting period because they believe that it would reduce crimes of passion by allowing a "cooling off" period prior to gun purchases. Additionally, they contend that more

federalism: a system of political organization; a union formed of separate states or groups that are ruled by a central authority on some matters but are otherwise permitted to govern themselves independently

President Bill Clinton signs the Brady Handgun Violence Protection Act, with James Brady seated to his right. Brady, for whom the bill was named, was shot in the head and permanently injured during an assassination attempt on President Ronald Reagan in 1981. Sarah Brady (middle of those standing), James Brady's wife, became a prominent and influential advocate for stricter gun control. (© AP/WIDE WORLD PHOTOS)

time is needed to conduct background checks because many state records are not accessed by the NICS, and thus it is less effective than state background check systems.

See also: GUN CONTROL ACT OF 1968.

BIBLIOGRAPHY

Patterson, Samuel C., and Keith R. Eakins. "Congress and Gun Control." In *The Changing Politics of Gun Control,* ed. by John M. Bruce and Clyde Wilcox. Lanham, MD: Rowman & Littlefield, 1998.

Spitzer, Robert J. *The Politics of Gun Control.* Chatham, NJ: Chatham House, 1995.

Sugarmann, Josh. *National Rifle Association: Money, Firepower and Fear.* Washington. DC: National Press Books, 1992.

Brady Campaign. "Waiting Periods and Background Checks." <http://www.brady campaign.com/facts/index.asp>.

BRIBERY ACT (1962)

Stuart P. Green

The act of bribery is the payment of something of value to a person in a position of power or trust in order to influence that person's behavior. Bribery has been subject to legal prohibitions of one sort or another since the beginning of recorded legal history. Today, despite significant variations in the level of enforcement, bribery is recognized as a criminal offense in nearly every country in the world. Indeed, it is hard to imagine a modern political or legal system that does not at least claim to condemn such practices.

In the United States, prohibitions on bribery date to the earliest days of the Republic. Bribery is one of two crimes (the other being **treason**) for which the United States Constitution (Article 2, section 4) specifically prescribes impeachment of public officeholders. Under earlier law, separate provisions applied to various categories of officeholder, such as members of Congress, judges, and administrative agency employees. In 1962 these provisions were consolidated into a single statute, the Bribery Act (P.L. 87-849, 76 Stat. 1119.

Bribery has been subject to legal prohibitions of one sort or another since the beginning of recorded legal history.

treason: the offense of attempting to overthrow the government of one's own state or country

FEATURES OF THE ACT

Section 201 of the act makes it a crime to commit (1) an act of bribery (punishable by up to fifteen years in prison) and (2) the less serious offense of payment or receipt of an official gratuity, or a tip for some kind of service (punishable by up to two years in prison and a fine). Both offenses require proof that something of value was requested, offered, or given to a federal public official. Unlike the offence of giving a gratuity, the offence of bribery requires that something of value be given "in return for" influence over an official act and that such thing be given or received with "corrupt" intent. The

The statute does not apply to state and local officials or to employees of private firms, though such persons are subject to a range of related federal and state corruption provisions.

offence of giving a gratuity requires merely that something be given "for or because of" an official act.

The Bribery Act is aimed primarily at corruption among officials of the federal government. It applies to a broad range of officials who work in the judicial, executive, and legislative branches, as well as to private citizens who work for organizations that receive funds from the federal government, to witnesses in various kinds of federal proceedings, and to federal jurors. The statute does not apply to state and local officials or to employees of private firms, though such persons are subject to a range of related federal and state corruption provisions.

Despite widespread agreement about the need for antibribery laws, there remains a great deal of confusion about exactly what conduct Section 201 does, or should, make criminal. Read literally, a twenty-dollar tip to the mailman at Christmas would violate the gratuities provision, as would various run-of-the-mill political endorsements, agreements not to run for office, and instances of "logrolling" (when legislators trade votes to benefit each other's pet projects).

JUDICIAL REVIEW

Two cases illustrate the difficulty of distinguishing between illegal bribery and related forms of (presumably) legal conduct in the political and legal process. The first, a federal appeals court decision from Kansas, *United States v. Singleton* (1998), involved the common practice by which federal prosecutors promise a witness leniency (and, in some cases, even money) in return for the witness's agreeing to testify in a criminal case on behalf of the government. Under a literal reading of the statute, such practices surely do constitute an illegal gratuity. The court in *Singleton* initially reached precisely this conclusion. But federal prosecutors throughout the country argued that the effects of such a decision would be extremely troublesome. Their ability to **prosecute** would be seriously handicapped if they were no longer permitted to obtain testimony by promising witnesses leniency and other "things of value." As a result, and despite the literal reading of the statute, the initial

prosecute: to begin and carry on a lawsuit; to bring legal action against

The Teapot Dome Scandal

The Teapot Dome affair was the most famous case of corruption in the scandal-plagued administration of President Warren G. Harding. In 1921, Secretary of the Interior Albert B. Fall persuaded the secretary of the navy, Edwin Denby, to transfer the naval oil reserves at Teapot Dome, Wyoming, and Elk Hills, California, from the Department of the Navy to the Department of the Interior. Shortly thereafter, Fall leased the Elk Hills fields to his friend Edward L. Doheny of Pan-American Petroleum and the Teapot Dome fields to Harry F. Sinclair of Mammoth Oil. After Harding died in August 1923, an investigation revealed that Fall had accepted $400,000 in "loans" from the two oil companies. The Senate hearings into the matter, held in early 1924, caused a sensation in the media, and the Democrats took every opportunity to spread the blame to as many Republicans as possible. Doheny, Sinclair, and Fall were acquitted of conspiracy to defraud the government, but Sinclair was jailed for contempt of Congress and jury tampering, and Fall was convicted of bribery, becoming the first cabinet member in U.S. history to serve a prison sentence. Denby and Attorney General Harry Daugherty were acquitted of charges but forced to resign. Harding had once commented to a journalist that his enemies were not a problem, "but my damned friends.... they're the ones that keep me walking the floor nights!"

decision in *Singleton* was quickly overruled. Prosecutors could continue to make promises of leniency in return for witness testimony.

The Supreme Court case *United States v. Sun-Diamond Growers of California* (1999) illustrates a similar problem of a law casting too wide a net. Sun-Diamond Growers of California was a trade association that **lobbied** various federal agencies and officials on behalf of its members. Like many lobbying groups, this association engaged in the common practice of "wining and dining" the officials it hoped would look favorably on its members' interests. Secretary of Agriculture Mike Espy was the recipient of some of the trade association's generosity, which included tickets to a tennis tournament and several expensive meals. At trial, the association was convicted of giving illegal gratuities. On appeal, it argued that gifts given to an official merely to build up a reservoir of good will, and not to influence any particular matter before the official, should not be regarded as an illegal gratuity. The Supreme Court agreed, reversing the conviction, and drawing an extremely fine line between cases in which a gift is given to an official simply because he is a public official, and cases in which a gift is given to an official who is actually considering, or has recently considered, some specific matter of business that is of concern to the gift-giver. The Court decided that only the latter circumstances would properly give rise to a prosecution for illegal gratuities. In so doing, the Court sought to avoid a ruling that would have criminalized "token gifts to the President based on his position and not linked to any identifiable act—such as the replica jerseys given by championship sports teams each year during ceremonial White House visits," and "a high school principal's gift of a school baseball cap to the Secretary of Education, on the occasion of the latter's visit to the school."

Abscam involved six representatives and one senator. The scandal resulted in expulsion of one House member and the resignation of three. The other three escaped congressional discipline when they lost at the polls before their investigations were completed.

lobby: to try to persuade the legislature to pass laws and regulations that are favorable to one's interests and to defeat laws that are unfavorable to those interests

ENFORCEMENT

Given the potential overreaching nature of the bribery laws, it is not surprising that enforcement has tended to be somewhat less than uniform. In the 1920s, most prosecutions concerned agents enforcing **Prohibition** laws; in the 1940s, draft board members; and in the 1950s, tax officials. The **Watergate** scandal gave probably the greatest boost to anticorruption law and its enforcement. In the 1970s a whole range of new statutes, regulations, special prosecutors, and watchdog agencies were developed to fight governmental corruption of various sorts.

Perhaps the most famous bribery case in the post-Watergate era was the Abscam investigation of the late 1970s and early 1980s. FBI agents set up a fictitious company, Abdul Enterprises, to lure various public officials into accepting bribes. The agents secretly videotaped meetings between various high-ranking federal and state officials and a make-believe Arab sheik supposedly seeking various official favors. The most prominent conviction arising out of the investigation was that of Senator Harrison Williams of New Jersey, who resigned from office rather than being voted out by his colleagues. Although Abscam was successful in exposing corruption at the highest levels of the American government, it was also widely criticized for unfair entrapment techniques used to lure officials into wrongdoing.

Prohibition: period from 1919 to 1933, during which the making, transport, and sale of alcoholic beverages was illegal in the United States

Watergate: the scandal following the break-in at the Democratic National Committee headquarters located in the Watergate apartment and office complex in Washington, D.C., in 1972

See also: FEDERAL BLACKMAIL STATUTE.

BIBLIOGRAPHY

Green, Stuart P. "What's Wrong With Bribery?" In *Defining Crimes: Essays on the Criminal Law's Special Part,* edited by R.A. Duff and Stuart P. Green. Oxford: Oxford University Press, forthcoming 2005.

Noonan, John T., Jr. *Bribes: The Intellectual History of a Moral Idea.* New York: Macmillan, 1984.

Philips, Michael. "Bribery." *Ethics* 94 (1984): 621–636.

C

CAPEHART HOUSING ACT

See NATIONAL HOUSING ACT

CENTRAL INTELLIGENCE AGENCY ACT OF 1949

Jennifer S. Byram

The Central Intelligence Agency (CIA) was created by the National Security Act of 1947. The Central Intelligence Agency Act of 1949 (CIA Act) (P.L. 81-110, 63 Stat. 208) was enacted to give the CIA specific authority to carry out the duties assigned to it in 1947. Until the CIA Act, the CIA had been acting without the authorities typically given to other federal government agencies.

PROVISIONS OF THE CIA ACT

The CIA Act authorized the CIA to receive and spend money, administer overseas employees, and protect the confidential nature of CIA activities. The CIA is allowed to purchase supplies and services using procedures established in the Armed Services Procurement Act of 1947, transfer money to and from other government agencies, have employees of other agencies work for the CIA, and spend CIA funds without the same restrictions placed on other agencies. The CIA can send employees to specialized training and pay for that training; pay travel and moving expenses of employees and their families when they are assigned to work abroad, both at the time of assignment and for vacations back to the United States; and provide for medical care for employees working abroad. The Director of Central Intelligence shall protect intelligence sources and methods from unauthorized disclosure. Finally, each year the Director of Central Intelligence, with the Attorney General, may admit up to 100 immigrants and their families to the United States to help protect national security, typically granting legal residence to foreign nationals who have worked for the CIA and need to leave their homeland.

While the proponents of the CIA Act characterized it as only providing the same authorities that other agencies enjoyed, the CIA actually has significantly more freedom from legislative restrictions. For example, the CIA can have employees of other agencies temporarily transferred to the CIA, allowing people who work *at* the CIA to truthfully say they do not work *for* the CIA. The CIA is exempt from laws requiring agencies to list their organizations, functions, names, titles, salaries, and number of employees, and the Director of the Bureau of the Office of Management and Budget shall not report information about the CIA. The CIA can improve rental properties, acquire land, and construct buildings without the limits placed on other agencies.

Perhaps the most important freedoms relate to financial secrecy. The CIA may exchange funds with other agencies. This allows the CIA to spend money that has not been budgeted to it, which hides the true total the CIA spends. The CIA also can spend that money, "without regard to the provisions of law and regulations relating to the expenditure of government funds," with limited accounting for "confidential, extraordinary, or emergency" spending.

CHALLENGES TO THE ACT

Though the CIA Act passed with a strong majority, there were impassioned arguments against it. The main concerns were about the secrecy provisions and the possibility that CIA agents would work in the United States, spying on U.S. citizens. Some senators stated that the CIA Act would set up a "military gestapo" in the United States. Supporters of the act argued that information about the spending, employees, and actions of the CIA needed to be kept secret, to protect the lives of CIA agents abroad who were likely to be tortured or killed if they were suspected of being U.S. spies. The skeptical senators were told that the Senate Committee on Armed Services had seen confidential information about American intelligence that could not be shared with the full Senate, but every Senator would support the act if they had seen it. The supporters said that the attack on Pearl Harbor might have been prevented if U.S. intelligence had been given these capabilities prior to World War II. They also implied that not supporting the CIA Act was unpatriotic.

The Bay of Pigs Invasion

The Bay of Pigs invasion was an attempt by the United States to overthrow Cuban dictator Fidel Castro in 1961. Planned during the presidential administration of Dwight D. Eisenhower and managed by the CIA, the invasion involved approximately 1,500 Cuban exiles who had been trained by the CIA. The exiles were to land at the Bay of Pigs, with air and naval support from the United States, and it was assumed that their arrival would set off a popular uprising that would overthrow Castro. However, President John F. Kennedy, who had taken office three months before the invasion, refused to broaden the conflict by authorizing air strikes, and the Cuban populace stayed behind closed doors. Furthermore, counter to intelligence reports, Cuban troops were stationed nearby and moved quickly to repel the attackers. The invasion was a disaster, with 274 of the exiles killed and the rest captured. While the invasion marked the low point of the entire Kennedy administration, the president acknowledged responsibility for the disaster with such grace that his approval rating rose to more than 80 percent. Kennedy's brother, Robert Kennedy, negotiated with Castro to release the prisoners in December 1962 in exchange for $53 million in food and medical supplies.

EFFECTS OF CIA SECRECY

Continuing concern about the secret activities of the CIA has led to important amendments to the CIA Act. The amendments were designed to increase congressional oversight of the CIA. Congress created the office of the Inspector General of the CIA in 1988. The Inspector General's duties include investigating allegations of misconduct by CIA employees, performing any other investigations or audits that seem useful, and making semi-annual reports to Congress about CIA activities. Over the years, Congress has increased the Inspector General's authority to investigate and make reports several times. If an employee reports an urgent concern to the Inspector General, and is not satisfied with the response, the employee can complain directly to appropriate congressional committees.

The office of the General Counsel of the CIA was created in 1996. The General Counsel is the head lawyer for the CIA, works to ensure that the CIA operates within the law, and defends it from lawsuits. One of the duties of the General Counsel is to review proposed operations to make sure they comply with U.S. laws and treaties.

Dissatisfaction with the secrecy of the CIA has caused most of the litigation about the CIA Act. Many cases involve the interaction between the secrecy provisions of the CIA Act and the disclosure provisions of the Freedom of Information Act (FOIA). Generally, the courts have decided the CIA is exempt from the requirements of the FOIA.

The Supreme Court has decided one case, *United States v. Richardson* (1974), which challenged the constitutionality of the CIA Act. The plaintiff argued that the CIA Act's secret funding provisions violated the Statement and Account Clause of the Constitution (Article I, section 9, clause 7), which requires the government to publish an account of public expenditures. The Court held that a taxpayer does not have the right to challenge the secrecy

The Iran-Contra Affair

The Iran-Contra affair was a complicated scandal of the mid-1980s in which the administration of President Ronald Reagan secretly sold arms to Iran, an avowed enemy of the United States, for use in Iran's war with Iraq. In return, Iran used its influence to help secure the release of American hostages being held in Lebanon by pro-Iranian terrorist groups. Profits from the weapons were then secretly funneled by the CIA to the Contra rebels attempting to overthrow the leftist Sandinista government of Nicaragua. All of this was illegal. U.N. sanctions prohibited selling weapons to Iran, as did Congressional legislation. In addition, Congress had expressly forbidden covert U.S. support for the overthrow of the Nicaraguan government. In addition to the funding, the CIA provided the Contras with weapons and training in guerilla tactics (including assassination), and there is evidence that the CIA was involved in drug trafficking to raise additional funds for the Contras.

When the story first broke, Reagan repudiated it, claiming, "We did not, repeat—did not—trade weapons or anything else for hostages, nor will we." Reagan later blamed this assertion on incorrect data provided by his staff. He appointed a board called the Tower Commission, headed by former Senator John Tower, to investigate the allegations, and a joint Senate and House committee held four months of televised hearings on the affair. Neither group found the president guilty of a crime; however, both concluded that his inattentive management style had allowed his subordinates to subvert the law. No one prosecuted in the scandal was penalized with anything more than a fine. Criminal indictments against National Security Advisor John Poindexter and Oliver North of the National Security Council were dismissed, and six others who were indicted or convicted of various crimes were pardoned in 1992 by President George H.W. Bush.

provisions in court because the individual is not specifically harmed by the provisions. Because the Court will not allow any taxpayer to maintain a challenge, the secrecy provisions will not be found unconstitutional.

It is difficult to determine the exact impact the CIA Act has had on the United States because so many of the CIA's activities are not publicized. We do not hear about the CIA's successful operations, or the attacks it has prevented. We seldom hear about its failures, unless they are spectacular, like the failed Bay of Pigs invasion of Cuba, or the Iran-Contra scandal. It is certain that America must have an effective, well-regulated intelligence agency to provide us with information about hostile powers, and the CIA is that agency.

See also: DEPARTMENT OF HOMELAND SECURITY ACT; FOREIGN INTELLIGENCE SURVEILLANCE ACT; NATIONAL SECURITY ACT OF 1947; USA PATRIOT ACT.

BIBLIOGRAPHY

Central Intelligence Agency Act of 1949. P.L. 81-110, 63 Stat. 208. *Congressional Record,* 81st Congress, 1st Session, H.R. 2663 (1949).

Holt, Pat M. *Secret Intelligence and Public Policy: A Dilemma of Democracy.* Washington, DC: CQ Press, 1995.

Kessler, Ronald. *Inside the CIA.* New York: Pocket Books, 1992.

Warner, Michael, ed. *The CIA Under Harry Truman.* Washington, DC: Center for the Study of Intelligence, Central Intelligence Agency, 1994.

CHILDREN'S ONLINE PRIVACY PROTECTION ACT (1998)

Michael H. Koby

The Children's Online Privacy Protection Act of 1998 (COPPA) (P.L. 105-277, 112 Stat. 2681) protects the online privacy of children under thirteen by requiring commercial Web sites and online services to request parental consent for the collection, use, and disclosure of a child's personal information.

This legislation grew out of the fact that by 1998 roughly ten million American children had access to the Internet, and at the same time, studies indicated that children were unable to understand the potential effects of revealing their personal information online, and parents failed to monitor their children's use of the Internet. The targeting of children by marketers resulted in the release of large amounts of private information into the market and triggered the need for regulation.

In March 1998 the Federal Trade Commission (FTC) presented Congress with a report addressing the inadequate protection of children's information online. In July 1998 Senator Richard Bryan, a Democrat of New York, along with Republican Senators John McCain of Arizona and Conrad Burns of Montana, introduced the Children's Online Privacy Protection Act of 1998. The Senate Communications Committee held a hearing in September 1998, and the full Senate Commerce Committee passed an amended version of the bill by a unanimous vote on October 1. The House of Representatives incorporated portions of that bill into 105 H.R. 4328, a Department of Transportation appropriations bill enacted by Congress and signed by President Clinton on October 21, 1998. COPPA became effective on April 21, 2000.

The act applies to commercial Web sites and online services (both foreign and domestic) that are directed at children in the United States. And while the act does not apply to general audience Web sites, operators of such sites who have actual knowledge of children using their sites must comply with the act's regulations. Congress's intent in passing COPPA was to increase parental involvement in children's online activities, thereby ensuring safety during participation in such activities and protecting children's personal information.

Under COPPA it is unlawful for an operator of a commercial Web site or online service that targets children, or knowingly collects their personal information, to gather such information without:

(1) incorporating a detailed privacy policy that describes the information collected from its users;

(2) receiving verifiable parental consent;

(3) offering parents an opportunity to revoke consent and have personal information deleted;

(4) limiting collection of personal information from children participating in online games; and

(5) establishing reasonable procedures to protect the confidentiality, security, and integrity of any personal information collected from children.

Personal information covered by the act includes Social Security numbers, names, addresses (mailing and e-mail), and telephone numbers. Verifiable parental consent is defined as any reasonable effort to ensure that a parent or legal guardian of a child receives notice of and gives authorization for the operator's personal information collection, use, and disclosure practices. Operators may avoid compliance with these regulations, however, if they propose, and the FTC approves, similar self-regulatory guidelines.

An FTC survey conducted in April 2002 showed that the general trend with respect to COPPA is one of increased compliance among Web sites, although some provisions have been followed less consistently. Importantly, courts are willing to strictly interpret these provisions and grant damages or other forms of relief against Web site operators who violate the act, and this trend may contribute to the high level of compliance. Moreover, at the federal level, COPPA violations are treated like unfair or deceptive trade practices under section 5 of the Federal Trade Commission Act, for which the FTC can impose **civil penalties**. At the state level, COPPA authorizes state attorneys general to bring actions in federal district court to enforce compliance with the regulations, as well as to obtain compensation and relief.

Critics of the act have argued that it is the responsibility of the parents to control their children's online activity, and that the act draws an arbitrary line between teenagers and younger children. Furthermore, critics claim the methods outlined by the FTC for verification are insufficient and impractical, and that they **infringe** on First Amendment free speech rights.

See also: COMPUTER SECURITY ACT OF 1987; COUNTERFEIT ACCESS DEVICE AND COMPUTER FRAUD AND ABUSE ACT OF 1984.

Detective J.M. Canibano of the Dallas Police Department discusses the dramatic increase in child exploitation through the use of computers. As easy access and use of computers by children increased, often without adult supervision, laws protecting children were needed. The Children's Online Privacy Protection Act of 1998 applies to the online collection of personal information from children under the age of thirteen, such as full name, home address, email address, telephone number or any other information that would allow someone to identify or contact the child. (© AP/WIDE WORLD PHOTOS)

civil penalties: fines or money damages imposed as punishment

infringe: to exceed the limits of; to violate

BIBLIOGRAPHY

Colton, Campbell C., and John F. Stack, Jr., eds. *Congress and the Politics of Emerging Rights.* Lanham, MD: Rowman & Littlefield, 2002.

Jennings, Charles, and Lori Fena. *The Hundredth Window: Protecting Your Privacy and Security in the Age of the Internet.* New York: Free Press, 2000.

Kutais, B. G., ed. *Internet Policies and Issues.* Commack, NY: Nova Science Publishers, 1999.

Peters, Thomas A. *Computerized Monitoring and Online Privacy.* London: McFarland, 1999.

CHINESE EXCLUSION ACTS

Diana H. Yoon and Gabriel J. Chin

Excerpt from the Chinese Exclusion Act of 1882

Whereas, in the opinion of the Government of the United States the coming of Chinese laborers to this country endangers the good order of certain localities within the territory thereof: Therefore—

Be it enacted by the Senate and House of Representatives of the United States of America in Congress assembled, that ... until the expiration of ten years next after the passage of this act, the coming of Chinese laborers to the United States be, and the same is hereby, suspended; and during such suspension it shall not be lawful for any Chinese laborer to come, or, having so come, ... to remain within the United States.

immigrant: one who comes to a country to take up permanent residence

From the time they first migrated to the United States, Asians were a special concern of federal **immigration** policy. In 1862 Congress intervened in the importation of "coolie" labor, unskilled workers usually from the Far East who were paid low wages. Congress began direct regulation of immigration with the Page Law of 1875, which was designed, legislators claimed, to curtail the immigration of women from "any Oriental country" for the purpose of prostitution. That statute in fact operated to exclude most Asian women.

The demand for restriction of Asian immigration was still not fully satisfied. In 1882 Congress passed the Chinese Exclusion Act (22 Stat. 58) to prohibit the immigration of Chinese laborers for ten years. Enacted in response to a national anti-Chinese campaign, the law was the first of a series of restrictions on Chinese immigration. Because the term "laborer" was understood to include those trained to perform skilled labor, most potential immigrants were barred from entering the country. Although naturalization was already restricted to whites and those of African birth or descent, the Chinese Exclusion Act also specifically prohibited the naturalization of Chinese.

The 1882 act led to restrictions on other Asian immigrants. The policy of Asian exclusion, the only explicitly race-based

From the time they first migrated to the United States, Asians were a special concern of federal immigration policy.

This cartoon, published in Harper's Weekly *in 1871, shows the anti-Chinese sentiments of the time. Lady Liberty protects a Chinese immigrant from a mob of men; in the background is a ruined "colored orphanage" and a noose hanging from a tree, comparing the anti-Chinese discrimination to the prejudice and violence suffered by African Americans. A paper on the ground in front of the mob reads "Crimes and Drunkenness. Riots by 'Pure White' strikers," and Lady Liberty declares "Hands off gentlemen! America means fair play for all men."* (LIBRARY OF CONGRESS, PRINTS AND PHOTOGRAPHS DIVISION)

distinction in American immigration law, culminated in the Immigration Act of 1917 (39 Stat. 874), which created the "Asiatic Barred Zone" from which immigration was generally prohibited, and the Immigration Act of 1924 (43 Stat. 153), which banned immigrants of Japanese racial ancestry and other

The 1924 law also established a quota system designed to discriminate against African and southern and eastern European immigrants, although it categorized these people based on their place of birth rather than on their race, as was the case with Asians.

Asians not already prohibited. The 1924 law also established a quota system designed to discriminate against African and southern and eastern European immigrants, although it categorized these people based on their place of birth rather than on their race, as was the case with Asians.

FROM CALIFORNIA TO NATIONAL POLITICS: ECONOMICS AND RACE

Chinese immigration became a national issue by the 1860s. The strongest currents of anti-Chinese sentiment mobilized in California, where the discovery of gold and demands for labor had attracted a visible population of Chinese workers. The 1870 census reported that more than 99 percent of Chinese residing in the U.S. lived in the West. This migration had been made possible by the Burlingame Treaty of 1868 (16 Stat. 739), which established full diplomatic relations and free immigration between China and the United States.

Although historians have debated the primary cause of the exclusion laws, most point to the influence of the white labor movement in pushing for restrictive legislation. White Californians who claimed to be threatened by the "yellow peril" voiced demands to end Chinese immigration. Meanwhile, workers in the East called for an end to imported contract labor. Many viewed this type of labor as repugnant to individual freedom as well as harmful to the interests of white American workers. In response, Congress enacted labor laws aimed at preventing the importation of labor through overseas contracts, a practice blamed for the economic depression in the labor market. Hostility toward Chinese laborers intensified during periods of economic depression, with racial and cultural prejudice accompanying arguments about undesirable labor competition. No numerical limits were placed on immigration in this period, and Chinese immigrants represented a small proportion of all immigration. Nonetheless, economic depression and rising class conflict created opportunities for politicians to attack Chinese workers and push immigration restriction as a national issue in their election campaigns.

CHINESE EXCLUSION ACT OF 1882

Initial efforts to curb Chinese labor immigration faced a legal obstacle: the Burlingame Treaty's provisions for free immigration between the United States and China. This was to change in 1880. Persuaded by anti-Chinese forces, American immigration commissioners renegotiated the treaty in pursuit of the twin goals of immigration restriction and advantageous trade relations. Congress, having secured the power to regulate Chinese immigration, passed the Chinese Exclusion Act of 1882. The debates in Congress reflected blatant racism and a discriminatory prejudice not only against the Chinese but against African Americans and Indians as well. As one senator argued, "the Caucasian race has a right, considering its superiority of intellectual force and mental vigor, to look down upon every other branch of the human family ... We are the superior race today."

Under the act, Chinese laborers already residing in the U.S. were allowed to leave and return by obtaining a reentry certificate from the collector of customs. This provision was challenged in *Chew Heong v. United States* (1884), when immigration officials excluded former residents who could not obtain the required certificates because they were abroad when the act was passed.

The Supreme Court ruled that a Chinese person could reenter without a certificate if he was a lawful resident at the time of the Burlingame Treaty revisions.

Subsequent legislation effectively nullified *Chew Heong*. The 1888 Scott Act (25 Stat. 476) prohibited Chinese laborers from entering the country, including those with valid return certificates. This legislation was found constitutional in *Chae Chan Ping v. United States* (known as the Chinese Exclusion Case, 1889). Chae Chan Ping had left for a trip to China in 1887 with a valid return certificate. The Scott Act, however, was passed while he was at sea, and he was denied entry upon landing. He argued that the Scott Act violated his right to reenter the United States.

> *In* Chae, *the Supreme Court held that congressional power to restrict entry of aliens into the United States was a fundamental tenet of national sovereignty.*

The Supreme Court, however, declared that Congress, in exercising its sovereignty, could exclude noncitizens to protect the nation from dangerous foreigners. In the Court's view, exclusion of Chinese might be necessary for "the preservation of our civilization." Congress, by exercising its "plenary power" to regulate immigration, could determine whether a noncitizen could continue to live in the United States.

As a result of the Scott Act, an estimated 20,000 reentry certificates were voided and many individuals were barred from returning to their families and

Workers help to construct an anti-Chinese wall in this lithograph from Puck *magazine. The wall is built with prejudices against the Chinese, and is being held together with "congressional mortar." At the same time that America was blocking Chinese immigration, China was opening up to international trade, symbolized by the wall in the background being torn down.* (LIBRARY OF CONGRESS, PRINTS AND PHOTOGRAPHS DIVISION)

property. In subsequent years the Court's ruling had a tremendous influence on the development of American immigration law. Courts continue to give great deference to congressional determinations of who may and may not enter the United States.

Under immigration restrictions, women were defined by the status of their male spouses. As a result, spouses of laborers were categorically excluded from entering the country and women who were U.S. citizens married to Asians in the United States could lose their citizenship.

GEARY ACT

Passed in 1892 the Geary Act (27 Stat. 25) had three provisions: It (1) extended the ban on Chinese immigration for ten years; (2) created a presumption that persons of Chinese descent were residing in the United States unlawfully, thereby forcing any Chinese found in the country to prove his or her right to be here; and (3) required laborers to obtain a certificate confirming their legal status. In *Fong Yue Ting v. United States* (1893), the Court upheld the certificate requirement. Other noncitizens were not required to obtain a certificate. In 1902 and again in 1904, Congress extended these restrictions indefinitely.

CONSEQUENCES

Although most American immigrant populations increased over time the Chinese population in the U.S., as a result of the anti-Chinese laws, decreased from 100,000 in 1882 to about 85,000 in 1920. These figures also reflect the drastic imbalance in the ratio of Chinese males to females, as well as laws of various states that prevented family formation in early Chinese American communities.

The ban on Chinese immigration and naturalization was lifted in 1943, when Congress repealed the Chinese exclusion laws.

The ban on Chinese immigration and naturalization was lifted in 1943, when Congress repealed the Chinese exclusion laws. Subsequently, the laws affecting those of other Asian racial groups were gradually relaxed. Naturalization (the process by which immigrants become U.S. citizens) was made entirely race-neutral in 1952. After a century of laws designed to restrict Asian immigration, the 1965 amendments to the Immigration and Nationality Act eliminated the remaining racial classifications from the law, and since then Asians have immigrated to the United States in significant numbers.

See also: IMMIGRATION AND NATIONALITY ACT; IMMIGRATION REFORM AND CONTROL ACT OF 1986.

BIBLIOGRAPHY

Chan, Sucheng, ed. *Entry Denied: Exclusion and the Chinese Community in America, 1882–1943*. Philadelphia: Temple University Press, 1991.

Chin, Gabriel J. "The Civil Rights Revolution Comes to Immigration Law: A New Look at the Immigration and Nationality Act of 1965." *North Carolina Law Review* 75 (1996): 273–345.

Gyory, Andrew. *Closing the Gate: Race, Politics, and the Chinese Exclusion Act*. Chapel Hill: University of North Carolina Press, 1998.

Hill, Bill Ong. *Making and Remaking Asian America Through Immigration Policy, 1850–1990*. Stanford, CA: Stanford University Press, 1993.

CIVIL AERONAUTICS ACT (1938)

Douglas B. Harris

Excerpt from the Civil Aeronautics Act

[T]he [Civil Aeronautics] Authority shall consider the following ... as being in the public interest ... the encouragement and development of an air-transportation system properly adapted to the present and future needs of the foreign and domestic commerce of the United States, of the Postal Service, and of the national defense ... [and] the regulation of air commerce in such manner as to best promote its development and safety...

The Civil Aeronautics Act of 1938 (CAA) (PL 75-706, 52 Stat. 973) created a Civil Aeronautics Authority, later called the Civil Aeronautics Board (CAB), to centralize commercial and safety regulation of civil air travel. In addition to the five-member "Authority," the act created a civil aeronautics administrator and a three member Air Safety Board, all appointed by the president subject to the advice and consent of the U.S. Senate. Moreover, key provisions of the act involved the allocation of U.S. Post Office contracts to airlines to carry mail, as well as regulations covering the registration and safety of air travel. The authority to regulate air travel and the airline industry was based on Congress's power to regulate interstate commerce under Article I, section 8 of the Constitution.

> *In addition to the five-member "Authority," the act created a civil aeronautics administrator and a three member Air Safety Board, all appointed by the president subject to the advice and consent of the U. S. Senate.*

EARLY FORAYS IN FEDERAL AIRLINE REGULATION

Congress's first major legislation regulating the airline industry was the Air Commerce Act (ACA) of 1926, situating both commercial regulatory authority and safety regulation in the Department of Commerce. In the decade that followed, technological advances in air travel and the likelihood that air travel soon would develop a consumer-orientation meant that additional federal regulation was needed. Questions regarding the fairness of the U.S. Postal Service's practices of contracting with specific airlines also spelled the need for regulatory reform.

In the era prior to the regular consumer air travel, government contracts to carry mail for the U.S. Postal Service determined the commercial viability of airline companies. According to economist Richard E. Caves, in the first years of the Roosevelt administration "the Postmaster General had canceled all existing contracts with airlines to carry air mail, on the basis of charges that they had originally been parceled out" during the Hoover administration through "a collusive spoils session" rather than competitive bidding. In response to the charges of collusion, Congress passed the Air Mail Act of 1934 that reformed the procedure by which airlines would compete for postal routes. Still, according to Caves, the Mail Act left airline deregulation too decentralized. As a result, "untenable" jurisdictional disputes arose between the Post Office (which continued to control bidding for the postal contracts that determined the commercial viability of new carriers), the Interstate Commerce Commission (which determined the rate of pay for postal routes), and the Commerce Department's Bureau of Air Commerce (which governed safety regulations).

CONGRESS CONSOLIDATES FEDERAL AUTHORITY OVER AIRLINE REGULATION

Congress passed the CAA to centralize the federal government's authority over airline regulation. In 1935, the Federal Aviation Commission (FAC), a board created by Congress in 1934 to study airline regulation and recommend policy, called for the creation of a centralized and independent authority to regulate the airline industry. Responding to FAC's recommendation, the Congress considered and eventually passed the CAA. The CAA both amended the ACA and transferred power over airline regulation from the Department of Commerce to a newly constituted and independent Civil Aeronautics Authority.

In 1935, the Federal Aviation Commission (FAC), a board created by Congress in 1934 to study airline regulation and recommend policy, called for the creation of a centralized and independent authority to regulate the airline industry.

Senator Pat McCarran, Democrat from Nevada, was the primary author of the CAA. On April 14, 1938, McCarran introduced S. 3845, a bill to establish an independent civil aeronautics authority to regulate aviation-related commerce and safety. In floor debate, McCarran emphasized the likely increases in air traffic, the growing segment of the economy represented by aviation, and the reality that aviation would soon be a major source of interstate transportation in the United States. On this last point, McCarran observed, "If we are ever to have safe, regular, and economically sound air transport, it must be administered by a strictly nonpolitical body. Safety regulations are largely nullified by political influences, and, in my opinion, the time is not far distant when the air-traveling public will rise up and demand reasonably safe air transportation." Although some senators opposed the creation of yet another new federal agency and maintained that the Commerce Department was adequate to the current needs of airline travel, the bill passed the Senate by voice vote.

In the House, Representative Clarence Lea was the principle architect of the act. House members heatedly debated Lea's bill, seeking to ensure that airline companies and routes from their districts and states would not lose existing advantages or endure new disadvantages from the new regulations. Despite a procedural attempt to delay or kill the bill, the House passed the CAA bill by voice vote. The Senate disagreed with the House version of the bill and requested a conference committee.

Although there were technical differences regarding regulation and important structural differences in the CAA proposed by McCarran and Lea, the House and Senate proponents were largely in agreement. The Conference Committee reconciled differences over the size of the Civil Aviation Authority and the safety board, the role of the administrator, and whether to "grandfather in" old Post Office contracts. The House and Senate conferees split the difference on their disagreements over the structure of the authority and reached unanimous agreement on the legislation.

The disputes between the House and the Senate were minor compared to ongoing struggles with the executive branch. Jealous of their control over air travel, officials from the Post Office, Commerce Department, and Defense

Department resisted the efforts to create the CAA. Franklin Roosevelt opposed the creation of the CAA as late as the summer of 1937, believing instead that airline authority should remain with the Interstate Commerce Commission. Still, a series of fact-finding hearings convinced President Roosevelt that greater regulation was needed. In a January 1938 meeting at the White House, Roosevelt told McCarran and Lea he would support the creation of the authority. Roosevelt signed the CAA on June 23, 1938.

Franklin Roosevelt opposed the creation of the CAA as late as the summer of 1937, believing instead that airline authority should remain with the Interstate Commerce Commission.

EXPERIENCE UNDER THE CIVIL AERONAUTICS ACT

In 1940 Roosevelt's administration reorganized the Civil Aeronautics Authority and the Air Safety Board. The reorganization returned some of the functions of the original CAA to the Department of Commerce—as Roosevelt had wished prior to the act's passage—transferring the remaining powers, including economic regulation, postal contracts, and safety regulations to the newly-created Civil Aeronautics Board (CAB).

The consensus surrounding the act and the reorganized CAB forged a remarkably stable political alliance. The CAA and the CAB constituted a formidable political "subsystem," creating a mutually beneficial alliance between the CAB, the airline industry, and key congressional committees and subcommittees. The stability of this subsystem proved to be a primary impediment to the creation of the Federal Aviation Administration (FAA). Just as the opposition of turf-conscious executive departments originally slowed passage of the CAA, congressional proponents of the Federal Aviation Act in 1958 faced opposition from the CAB, as well as its defenders in the airline industry and Congress.

Despite its unique political coalition of support, the CAA's "subsystem" grew weaker after 1950. When the Federal Aviation Act was passed in 1958, the CAB was both reconstituted and restructured. In reconstituting the CAB, the Federal Aviation Act allowed for the CAB to continue regulating the commercial practices of the airline industry, regulating fares, and conducting accident investigations, but the newly created FAA assumed the CAB's function of regulating the safety of air travel. When Congress created the Department of Transportation (DOT) in 1967, the CAB's responsibility to investigate airline accidents was transferred to the National Transportation Safety Board (NTSB). This left commercial deregulation as the primary function of the CAB. Congress's Airline Deregulation Act of 1978 deregulated the commercial aspects of the airline industry, and spelled the eventual demise of the CAB. In 1985 the CAB ceased to exist under the authority of the Civil Aeronautics Boards Sunset Act of 1984.

Congress's Airline Deregulation Act of 1978 deregulated the commercial aspects of the airline industry, and spelled the eventual demise of the CAB.

See also: FEDERAL AVIATION ACT; NATIONAL AERONAUTICS AND SPACE ACT.

BIBLIOGRAPHY

Brown, Anthony E. *The Politics of Airline Deregulation.* Knoxville: University of Tennessee Press, 1987.

Caves, Richard E. *Air Transport and Its Regulators: An Industry Study.* Cambridge: Harvard University Press, 1962.

Redford, Emmette S. *Democracy in the Administrative State.* New York: Oxford University Press, 1969.

Smith, Henry Ladd. *Airways: The History of Commercial Aviation in the United States,* reprint ed. Washington, DC: Smithsonian Institution Press, 1991.

INTERNET RESOURCES

Federal Aviation Administration. <http://www.faa.gov>.

CIVIL LIBERTIES ACT (1988)

Eric K. Yamamoto and Liann Y. Ebesugawa

Excerpt from the Civil Liberties Act

With regard to individuals of Japanese ancestry. The Congress recognizes that, as described by the Commission on Wartime Relocation and Internment of Civilians, a grave injustice was done to both citizens and permanent resident aliens of Japanese ancestry by the evacuation, relocation, and internment of civilians during World War II. As the Commission documents, these actions were carried out without adequate security reasons and without any acts of espionage or sabotage documented by the Commission, and were motivated largely by racial prejudice, wartime hysteria, and a failure of political leadership. The excluded individuals of Japanese ancestry suffered enormous damages, both material and intangible, and there were incalculable losses in education and job training, all of which resulted in significant human suffering for which appropriate compensation has not been made. For these fundamental violations of the basic civil liberties and constitutional rights of these individuals of Japanese ancestry, the Congress apologizes on behalf of the Nation.

Japanese American Evacuation Claims Act of 1948

Eric K. Yamamoto and Liann Y. Ebesugawa

The Japanese American Evacuation Claims Act of 1948 provided for initial compensation to remedy damages. It fell far short, however, of the actual economic damages incurred. The act only compensated well-documented property losses, and did not even begin to measure the pain and suffering entailed. The process of making claims was slow, and because compensation was made on the basis of prewar prices, applicants received on average no more than ten cents on the dollar. The program, although well intentioned, was not designed to offer reparations for all wrongs suffered by Japanese Americans during the war. Additionally, the law was not flexible enough to cover the full range of situations and did not take into account intangible losses—the cost of human anguish and the damage to reputation, the missed opportunities, and the years of captivity lost forever.

The Civil Liberties Act of 1988 (P.L. 100-383), stands as a landmark. Through the act, Congress for the first time authorized a presidential apology to an entire group of Americans: Japanese Americans imprisoned by the United States because of their race during World War II without charges, trial, or evidence of necessity. Congress also mandated $1.2 billion in reparations (payment to compensate for damages) to these Japanese Americans and an additional amount to Aleut and Pribilof Islanders who had also been unlawfully imprisoned.

THE INTERNMENTS

Following Japan's attack on Pearl Harbor on December 7, 1941, U.S. government suspicions and public sentiment turned against Japanese Americans. Business leaders, the media, and government officials questioned the loyalty of Japanese Americans even though they were solid American citizens. Most were born, educated, and employed in the United States. Nevertheless, West Coast military commander General John DeWitt asserted that Japanese Americans were disloyal simply because of their Japanese heritage and he claimed they posed a threatened to national security, even though no Japanese American had engaged in any act of espionage or sabotage. DeWitt further stated that "a Jap is a Jap ... and [despite American birth, education, and

Japanese Americans located at an internment camp in Puyallup, Washington, line up during mealtime in this 1942 photograph. The Civil Liberties Act of 1988 authorized a presidential apology and $1.2 billion in reparations to Japanese Americans who were held in internment camps during World War II. They were held without trial, charges, or evidence of necessity. (©Seattle Post-Intelligencer Collection; Museum of History & Industry/Corbis)

citizenship] the racial strains are undiluted." With a fearful public clamoring for a scapegoat, President Roosevelt signed **Executive Order** 9066 on February 19, 1942. The order directed the military to impose a curfew and then forcibly to exclude from the western coastal areas and ultimately detain persons of Japanese ancestry, including American citizens. The order, which did not apply to persons of German or Italian ancestry, had popular support.

The government's racial exclusion and internment (imprisonment during wartime) actions undermined the Constitution. The Constitution's Fifth Amendment ensures U.S. citizens protection against the federal government's taking of life, liberty, or property without due process of law. It is also interpreted to guarantee equal protection of all citizens under the law. Without charges, hearings, or evidence of individual or racial group disloyalty, the government, with armed military standing by, removed 120,000 Japanese Americans from their homes, forcing them to abandon businesses, jobs, and belongings. They were first detained in makeshift assembly centers, with many sleeping in horse stalls at race tracks. From there, the government dispersed them to nine desolate internment prisons, encircled by barbed wire, in the western interior. Specifically, the internment prisons were located in California, Idaho, Utah, Arizona, Wyoming, Colorado, and Arkansas. The camps were located in desert areas except for the two camps in Arkansas which were located in swamplands. Japanese Americans left their homes not knowing where they were going, for how long, on what grounds, or whether they would survive. More than 1,800 people did not survive, and those who did suffered deep, lasting psychological wounds, along with financial devastation.

Executive Order: an order issued by the president that has the force of law

Without charges, hearings, or evidence of individual or racial group disloyalty, the government, with armed military standing by, removed 120,000 Japanese Americans from their homes, forcing them to abandon businesses, jobs, and belongings.

THE REPARATIONS MOVEMENT

The wounds were so deep that the Japanese American community refused to discuss the internment for many years. In the late 1960s during the heyday of the Civil Rights movement, a reparations movement emerged. Yet it was still another two decades before Japanese Americans took legal action, in two different kinds of lawsuits, to support the reparations movement.

The first type of lawsuit, in 1983, was *coram nobis* litigation, a rare legal procedure allowing the reopening of old cases of current importance. It was initiated by Fred Korematsu, Gordon Hirabayashi, and Min Yasui, who had been convicted during World War II for refusing to be interned. The Supreme Court had said at the time that the internment was constitutional because military necessity justified it. Forty years later, the *coram nobis* proceedings sought reversal of their convictions based on startling government World War II documents found in dust-covered boxes in 1981. Those documents revealed the following:

invidious: tending to arouse ill will or animosity; an offensive or discriminatory action

(1) before the internment all government intelligence services involved in the issue at the time had determined that West Coast Japanese Americans as a group posed no serious danger and that there was no basis for mass internment;

(2) the military based its internment decision on **invidious** racial stereotypes about Japanese Americans; and

(3) the military, the Department of Justice, and the Department of War concealed and destroyed key evidence, deliberately misled the Supreme Court, and fabricated the military necessity justification for the internment.

Based on this evidence the federal courts in the *coram nobis* cases found "manifest injustice," overturned the convictions of Korematsu, Hirabayashi, and Yasui, and thereby laid the legal foundation for reparations.

class action: a lawsuit brought by a representative member of a large group of people who have suffered the same injury or damages

The second suit was a **class action** damages lawsuit, *Hohri v. United States,* filed by former internees to obtain compensation for the material and psychological harms of the internment. Although the courts ultimately dismissed that case because it was filed too long after the events, the suit led to greater public awareness of and education about the real internment story.

The reparations movement gained moral force from former internees and Asian American organizations together with a wide range of groups, including civil liberties groups, the NAACP, churches, veterans and labor associations, and even local governments. This support helped Asian American members of Congress from California and Hawaii to push through legislation creating the Commission on Wartime Relocation and Internment of Civilians. The commission's 1983 report, *Personal Justice Denied,* concluded that the causes of the internment were race prejudice, wartime hysteria, and a failure of political leadership.

THE ACT

lobby: to try to persuade the legislature to pass laws and regulations that are favorable to one's interests and to defeat laws that are unfavorable to those interests

In response to a variety of reparations efforts—the lawsuits, the commission's hearings and report, extensive **lobbying** by diverse groups, and persistent media reporting—Congress passed the Civil Liberties Act of 1988, which was signed into law by President Ronald Reagan.

Most important for many Japanese Americans, the act called for a formal presidential apology. It also authorized reparations of $20,000 for each surviving internee who was a U.S. citizen or legal resident immigrant at the time of internment. A 1992 amendment to the 1988 act remedied difficult questions of eligibility (for instance, for those barred from their homes but not incarcerated) and key problems with funding (it eliminated the need for yearly appropriations of money by establishing a fund from which reparations could be drawn).

Most important for many Japanese Americans, the act called for a formal presidential apology.

IMPLEMENTATION

The Office of Redress Administration (ORA), created by the act, implemented the reparations program. The act authorized the ORA to identify, register, verify, and administer reparation payments to eligible individuals within a ten-year period. The ORA worked effectively with the National Coalition for Redress/Reparations (NCRR) and the Japanese American Citizens League (JACL) to provide information about reparations through Japanese American newspapers, community meetings, and newsletters. Former internees submitted over 60,000 reparations applications as a result of these collective efforts.

The 1988 act also established the Civil Liberties Public Education Fund to "sponsor research and public educational activities, and to publish and distribute the hearings, findings, and recommendations of the Commission." Public education became a major dimension of redress. Projects sponsored by the Education Fund produced high school, college, and law school curricula on the internment and civil liberties; documentaries on internment camp life; oral histories of survivors; and new research on the accommodation of national security and civil liberties.

The redress of wrongs committed against Japanese Americans was about much more than money. The Civil Liberties Act recognized the United States's grave injustice against its own citizens on account of their race, and it acknowledged the need to repair lasting wounds, both to Japanese Americans and to the Constitution.

BIBLIOGRAPHY

Maki, Mitchell T., Harry H. L. Kitano, and S. Megan Berthold. *Achieving the Impossible Dream: How Japanese Americans Obtained Redress.* Chicago: University of Illinois Press, 1999.

Yamamoto, Eric K. "Friend or Foe or Something Else: Social Meanings of Redress and Reparations." *Denver Journal of International Law and Policy* 223 (1992).

Yamamoto, Eric K., et al. *Race, Rights and Reparation: Law and the Japanese American Internment.* New York: Aspen Publishers, 2001.

CIVIL RIGHTS ACT OF 1866

Christopher A. Bracey

The Civil Rights Act of 1866 (14 Stat. 27) was a momentous chapter in the development of civic equality for newly emancipated blacks in the years following the Civil War. The act accomplished three primary objectives designed to integrate blacks into mainstream American society. First, the act proclaimed "that *all persons* born in the United States ... are hereby declared to be citizens of the United States." Second, the act specifically defines the rights of American citizenship:

> Such citizens, of every race and color, and without regard to any previous condition of slavery or **involuntary servitude**, ... shall have the same right in every state and territory in the United States, to make and enforce contracts, to sue, be parties, and give evidence, to inherit, purchase, lease, sell, hold, and convey real and personal property, and to full and equal benefit of all laws and proceedings for the security of person and property, as is enjoyed by white citizens, and shall be subject to like punishment, pains, and penalties, and to none other, any law, statute, ordinance, regulation, or custom to the contrary notwithstanding.

Third, the act made it unlawful to deprive a person of any of these rights of citizenship on the basis of race, color, or prior condition of slavery or involuntary servitude.

CIRCUMSTANCES LEADING TO THE ACT

The roots of the Civil Rights Act of 1866 are traceable to the Emancipation Proclamation, delivered by President Abraham Lincoln on January 1, 1863, which freed slaves held in **bondage** in the rebel states. In some ways, the proclamation appears to have been crafted to achieve certain military goals rather than advance the abolitionist movement per se. The declaration of freedom for blacks in the rebel states was intended to destabilize plantation society by encouraging slaves to challenge authority. Slaves forced into service as laborers on behalf of the Southern Army would become insubordinate. Plantations, drained of southern white men who were drawn into military service, were administered by the wives and elderly men. Not surprisingly, slaves would begin to challenge their authority in ways that served as a distraction to the war effort.

A second military goal was to secure a labor source to support the ever-expanding Union military efforts. Perhaps the most radical feature of the Emancipation Proclamation was the enrollment of free and newly emancipated blacks into military service. Black soldiers, though not considered equal to their white counterparts, nevertheless played a crucial role in constructing and holding fortified positions, and ensured the flow of goods along Union supply lines.

Although the proclamation was grounded in military necessity, however, it quickly transformed the political landscape and strengthened opposition to the institution of slavery. As President Lincoln noted in December 1863, slavery had now become a "moral impossibility" in American society. The growing antislavery sentiment was confirmed by election results in 1864, which swept into Congress a core group of Republican leaders supportive of progressive **Reconstruction** efforts and protection of the rights and interests of blacks.

Andrew Johnson's ascension to the presidency following Lincoln's assassination signaled a turning point in the postwar Reconstruction efforts. Beginning in May 1865, President Johnson instituted a policy of Presidential Reconstruction designed to reconstitute the Union as quickly and painlessly as possible. Lincoln understood that the restoration of the Southern states to

involuntary servitude: forced service to a master

bondage: a state of being involuntarily bound or subjugated to someone or something

Congress passed the act in response to the Black Codes passed by the former Confederate states.

Reconstruction: the political and economic reorganization and reestablishment of the South after the Civil War

the Union was insufficient without a reconstruction of Southern beliefs and attitudes concerning slavery and the Southern way of life. But Johnson's Reconstruction eased requirements for reentry into the Union and encouraged a defiant assertion of states' rights and resistance to black suffrage. As the historian Eric Foner wrote in 1988, Johnson's Reconstruction empowered white Southerners to "shape the transition from slavery to freedom and define blacks' civil status without Northern interference"(p. 189).

Not surprisingly, as whites regained social and governmental control from Union governors in accord with Johnson's policies, they often undertook simultaneous efforts to severely limit access by newly emancipated blacks to the ordinary rights and liberties enjoyed by whites. Former confederate states—such as South Carolina, Mississippi, and Alabama—passed and strictly enforced "Black Codes," oppressive laws that applied only to blacks. Black Codes took a variety of forms, including mandatory apprenticeship laws, oppressive labor contract laws, strict vagrancy laws, and restrictive travel laws. Black Codes often authorized more severe punishment of blacks than of whites for the identical conduct.

> *Not surprisingly, as whites regained social and governmental control from Union governors in accord with Johnson's policies, they often undertook simultaneous efforts to severely limit access by newly emancipated blacks to the ordinary rights and liberties enjoyed by whites.*

This wood engraving, printed in Harper's Weekly *in early 1867, depicts doubts about the actual freedom of blacks in the post-Civil War South. Depicted here are illustrations accompanying two newspaper clippings, one headline reading "Negroes Sold as Punishment for Crime" and the other reading "Negroes Whipped as a Punishment for Crime."* (LIBRARY OF CONGRESS, PRINTS AND PHOTOGRAPHS DIVISION)

freedman: one freed from slavery

In addition to the Black Codes, Southerners engaged in private acts of discrimination and outright violence against **freedmen**. As Foner recounts, "the pervasiveness of violence [against blacks after the Civil War] reflected whites' determination to define [freedom in their own way,] ... in matters of family, church, labor, or personal demeanor" (p. 120). Historian Randall Kennedy notes that this sometimes led to the beating or killing of blacks for such "infractions" as "failing to step off sidewalks, objecting to beatings of their children, addressing whites without deference, and attempting to vote" (1997, p. 39).

Although the Thirteenth Amendment had been ratified, and slavery constitutionally abolished, prevailing policies in the South threatened to make a mockery of the freedom granted to blacks. Under the leadership of Representative Thaddeus Stevens of Pennsylvania, the Joint Committee on Reconstruction was formed to monitor and react to racially oppressive conditions in the South. The Joint Committee, in grappling with the question of "how the liberties of the black race were to be made secure," ultimately arrived at the conclusion that additional measures needed to be adopted for the safety and elevation of newly emancipated blacks. One of those additional measures would become the Civil Rights Act of 1866.

LEGISLATIVE DEBATE

ratify: to formally approve; three-fourths of all states in the Union must approve an amendment for it become part of the Constitution

Senator Lyman Trumbull of Illinois introduced the bill that would later become the Civil Rights Act of 1866. Trumbull told the Thirty-Ninth Congress that the proposed legislation was needed to reinforce the grant of freedom to blacks secured by **ratification** of the Thirteenth Amendment: "When it comes to be understood in all parts of the United States that any person who shall deprive another of any right or subject him to any punishment in consequence of his color or race will expose himself to fine and imprisonment, I think such acts will soon cease." Trumbull declared his intention to destroy the discriminatory Black Codes. Other Republican congressmen focused on the rights of blacks "to make contracts for their own labor, the power to enforce payment of their wages, and the means of holding and enjoying the proceeds of their toil." If states could deprive blacks of these fundamental rights, as one Congressman remarked, "I demand to know, of what practical value is the amendment abolishing slavery?"

THE BILL'S LIMITED DEFINITION OF RIGHTS

Although radical for its time, it is important to understand the limits of the bill. The bill plainly sought to overrule the Black Codes by affirming the full citizenship of newly emancipated blacks and by defining citizenship in terms applicable to all persons. Under the bill, the designation as an American citizen meant that one possessed certain specific rights, such as the right to make and enforce contracts, the right to file lawsuits and participate in lawsuits as parties or witnesses, and the right to inherit, purchase, lease, sell, hold and convey real property. In defining citizenship in this manner, the act effectively overruled state-sponsored Black Codes.

The bill plainly sought to overrule the Black Codes by affirming the full citizenship of newly emancipated blacks and by defining citizenship in terms applicable to all persons.

At the same time, the act specified that these rights were "civil rights," giving the first clear indication that, in the con-

The Fourteenth Amendment promised and guaranteed equality—ideas illustrated in this lithograph. (LIBRARY OF CONGRESS, PRINTS AND PHOTOGRAPHS DIVISION)

text of race relations, there were different levels, or tiers, of rights at stake. "Civil rights" at this time were understood in terms of property rights, contract rights, and equal protection of the laws. These rights were distinct from "political rights," which involved the right to vote and hold public office, and "social rights," which related to access to public accommodations and the like. Thus the bill reflected the common view that political participation and social integration were more or less "privileges" and not basic elements of citizenship.

Political rights would later be secured by the ratification of the Fifteenth Amendment and the passage of civil rights legislation in 1870, and revisited nearly a century later in the Civil Rights Act of 1965. Congress's attempt to grant social rights to blacks in the Civil Rights Act of 1875 was struck down by the United States Supreme Court as unconstitutional in *The Civil Rights Cases* (1883). However, Congress ultimately prevailed in granting social rights to blacks with the passage of the Civil Rights Act of 1964.

PRESIDENTIAL VETO

veto: when the president returns a bill to Congress with a statement of objections

Despite these apparent limits on the scope of protections afforded under the act, President Johnson nevertheless **vetoed** the bill. Johnson's principal objection was a matter of procedure. In his veto message he argued that Congress lacked the constitutional authority to enact the bill because "eleven of the thirty-six States are unrepresented in Congress at the present time." Johnson also made clear, however, that he rejected the very idea of federal protection of civil rights for blacks, arguing that such a practice violated "all our experience as a people" and represented a disturbing move "toward centralization and the concentration of all legislative powers in the national government."

Perhaps the most striking feature of Johnson's veto message was its racism and inflammatory language. For example, Johnson objected that the act established "for the security of the colored race safeguards which go infinitely beyond any that the general government has ever provided to the white race. In fact, the distinction of race and color is by the bill made to operate in favor of the colored and against the white race." Johnson also argued that blacks were simply unprepared to become citizens, at least as compared to immigrants from abroad, because, having been slaves, they were "less informed as to the nature and character of our institutions." Johnson even mentioned the supposed threat of interracial marriage, suggesting that protection of the civil rights of newly emancipated blacks would somehow upset the established social hierarchy.

Excerpt from the Emancipation Proclamation

Whereas on the 22nd day of September, A.D. 1862, a proclamation was issued by the President of the United States, containing, among other things, the following, to wit:

"That on the 1st day of January, A.D. 1863, all persons held as slaves within any State or designated part of a State the people whereof shall then be in rebellion against the United States shall be then, thenceforward, and forever free; and the executive government of the United States, including the military and naval authority thereof, will recognize and maintain the freedom of such persons and will do no act or acts to repress such persons, or any of them, in any efforts they may make for their actual freedom....

And by virtue of the power and for the purpose aforesaid, I do order and declare that all persons held as slaves within said designated States and parts of States are, and henceforward shall be, free; and that the Executive Government of the United States, including the military and naval authorities thereof, will recognize and maintain the freedom of said persons.

And I hereby enjoin upon the people so declared to be free to abstain from all violence, unless in necessary self-defence; and I recommend to them that, in all case when allowed, they labor faithfully for reasonable wages.

And I further declare and make known that such persons of suitable condition will be received into the armed service of the United States to garrison forts, positions, stations, and other places, and to man vessels of all sorts in said service.

And upon this act, sincerely believed to be an act of justice, warranted by the Constitution upon military necessity, I invoke the considerate judgment of mankind and the gracious favor of Almighty God."

The effect of Johnson's veto was to strengthen Republican opposition to his presidential policy. Congress **overrode** the veto and enacted the Civil Rights Act of 1866. It also proposed the Fourteenth Amendment to the U.S. Constitution to remove all doubt about its power to pass this sort of protective legislation. Unlike the 1866 act, however, the Fourteenth Amendment, ratified two years later, employs general language to prohibit discrimination against citizens and to ensure equal protection under the laws. Incorporating these protections into the Constitution marked a critical moment in the development of federal power over the states when it came to protecting the rights of citizens. To emphasize this new commitment to federal power, the Civil Rights Act of 1866 was reenacted as section 18 of the Civil Rights Act of 1870. The 1870 act prohibited conspiracies of two or more persons that threatened a citizen's "enjoyment of any right or privilege granted or secured to him by the Constitution or laws of the United States." It also extended federal protection to voting rights for blacks.

override: if the President vetoes a bill passed by Congress, the bill can still become law if two-thirds of each house of Congress votes to override the veto

THE ACT'S ENDURING SPIRIT

The spirit of the Civil Rights Act of 1866 lives on in modern antidiscrimination laws. One such law (42 U.S.C., section 1981) provides, in language derived largely from section 1 of the 1866 act, that "all persons within the jurisdiction of the United States shall have the same right in every State and Territory to make and enforce contracts, to sue, be parties, give evidence, and to the full and equal benefit of all laws and proceedings for the security of persons and property as is enjoyed by white citizens." This law is often relied on by plaintiffs alleging employment discrimination or discrimination in public or private education. Another law (42 U.S.C., section 1982), which was originally a part of section 1 of the 1866 act, "bars all racial discrimination, private as well as public, in the sale or rental of property," and is frequently used in connection with housing discrimination lawsuits. A law (42 U.S.C., section 1983) granting private individuals today the right to sue for deprivation of civil rights by state officials echoes section 2 of the 1866 act as well as a subsequent act, the Civil Rights Act of 1871 (also known as the Ku Klux Klan Act), which authorized civil and criminal penalties against rights violators in response to claims of lawlessness in the South.

The spirit of the Civil Rights Act of 1866 lives on in modern antidiscrimination laws.

See also: CIVIL RIGHTS ACTS OF 1875, 1957, 1964; FAIR HOUSING ACT OF 1968; FORCE ACT; KU KLUX KLAN ACT; VOTING RIGHTS ACT OF 1965.

BIBLIOGRAPHY

Du Bois, W. E. B. *Black Reconstruction in America: 1860–1880.* New York: Harcourt, Brace and Company, 1935.

Foner, Eric. *Reconstruction: America's Unfinished Revolution 1863–1877.* New York: Harper & Row, 1988.

Hyman, Harold M., and William M. Wiecek. *Equal Justice Under Law: Constitutional Development 1835–1875.* New York: Harper & Row, 1982.

Kennedy, Randall. *Race, Crime, and the Law.* New York: Pantheon Books, 1997.

Wilson, Theodore Brantner. *The Black Codes of the South.* University: University of Alabama Press, 1965.

Woodward, C. Vann. *The Strange Career of Jim Crow,* 3d rev. ed. New York: Oxford University Press, 1974.

CIVIL RIGHTS ACT OF 1871

See KU KLUX KLAN ACT

CIVIL RIGHTS ACT OF 1875

Mark Tushnet

The Civil Rights Act of 1875 (18 Stat. 335) was the last of the civil rights statutes enacted by Republican-dominated Congresses after the Civil War. Senator Charles Sumner of Massachusetts was a leader among the so-called Radical Republicans who sought to protect the rights of the newly freed slaves as a matter of principle and to preserve the Republican Party's power in the South. Sumner proposed a civil rights act in 1870 that would have banned racial discrimination in public schools, churches, and places of public accommodation such as hotels and theaters. Eliminating segregated public schools went well beyond what the nation's **electorate** was willing to support. As a result, Congress ignored the proposal until the 1874 elections, which gave the Democrats the majority in the House of Representatives. The outgoing Republican-controlled House knew that the incoming House would not adopt *any* civil rights legislation. They therefore pushed forward with Sumner's proposal. However, after Democrats in the House used procedural maneuvers to block the passage of the original proposal, Republican leaders stripped it of the most controversial provisions dealing with schools and churches.

electorate: the body of people qualified to vote

> Sumner proposed a civil rights act in 1870 that would have banned racial discrimination in public schools, churches, and places of public accommodation such as hotels and theaters.

In February 1875 Congress passed the Civil Rights act, which President Ulysses S. Grant signed on March 1, 1875. The act provided that: "All persons ... shall be entitled to the full and equal enjoyment of accommodations, advantages, facilities, and privileges of inns, public conveyances on land or water, theaters, and other places of public amusement." The act created a damage remedy of $500 to people who were victims of discrimination, and also made discrimination a criminal offense subject to a $1,000 fine and imprisonment for up to one year. Neither President Grant nor his successor, Rutherford B. Hayes, devoted much effort to enforcing the act, and relatively few private lawsuits were brought in the years immediately following its enactment.

SUPPORTERS AND DETRACTORS

The act's supporters drew on a rule developed by judges enforcing the general law of contracts, called the "common carrier" rule. According to this rule, which developed outside the context of race discrimination, transportation companies, hotels, and other places that offered services to the general public could not discriminate against anyone who sought to use the services. The common carrier rule required services be offered on a first come, first served basis. By the 1870s some state courts had begun to apply the common carrier rule to bar race discrimination in places of public accommodation.

The Civil Rights Act of 1875 attempted to extend the common carrier rule throughout the nation, and to provide a remedy for discrimination in federal court. The constitutional basis for the act was the power given to Congress under section 5 of the Fourteenth Amendment to enact legislation to enforce section 1 of that Amendment. Section 1 provides: "No State shall make or enforce any law which shall abridge the privileges or immunities of citizens of the United States; nor shall any State deprive any person of life, liberty, or property, without due process of law; nor deny to any person within its jurisdiction the equal protection of the laws."

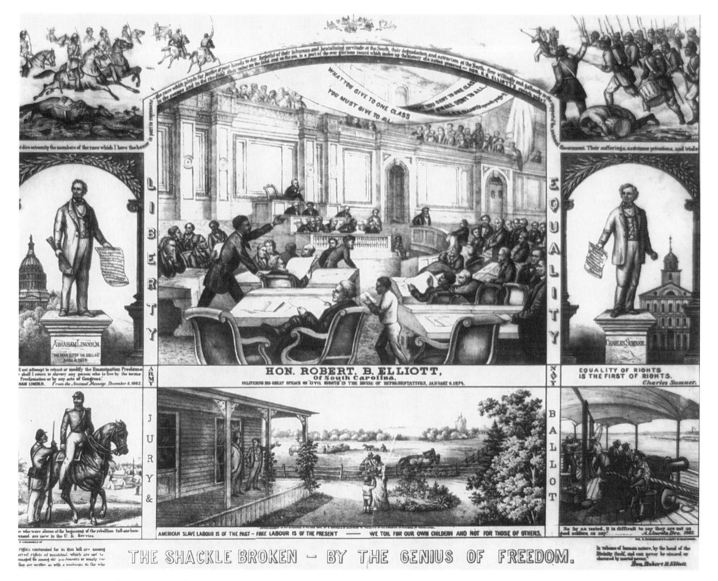

THE SHACKLE BROKEN — BY THE GENIUS OF FREEDOM.

Depicted here is a famous speech given by South Carolina representative Robert B. Elliot to the House of Representatives in favor of the Civil Rights Act, January 6, 1874. The central image shows Elliot speaking on the floor of the House. A banner with a quotation from his speech is hanging from the ceiling: "What you give to one class you must give to all. What you deny to one class you must deny to all." To the left of the center scene is Abraham Lincoln holding a bundle of arrows and the Emancipation Proclamation. To the right is Civil Rights advocate Charles Sumner, with his words "Equality of rights is the first of rights," below him. The bottom row of images makes references to black soldiers (left and right) and to a black family that owns a farm (center). (LIBRARY OF CONGRESS, PRINTS AND PHOTOGRAPHS DIVISION)

Opponents of the act raised constitutional objections. The most forceful objection was that the Fourteenth Amendment applied by its terms only to actions by states, whereas the act attempted to regulate the activities of private companies. The act's supporters responded that states could use the common carrier rule to bar race discrimination by common carriers, and that their failure to do so was an action (or at least a decision in the form of inaction) by the state's lawmakers. As Supreme Court Justice Joseph P. Bradley put it in a private letter written in 1871, the Fourteenth Amendment prohibited actions "denying" equal protection of the laws. Furthermore, "Denying includes inaction as well as action. And denying the equal protection of the laws includes the omission to protect, as well as the omission to pass laws for protection."

CONSTITUTIONAL CHALLENGES

Constitutional challenges to the Civil Rights Act of 1875 reached the Supreme Court in a group of cases all decided in 1883 under the collective name, the *Civil Rights Cases*. Justice Bradley wrote the Court's opinion finding the act unconstitutional because it regulated not state action but actions by private companies operating hotels and theaters. The act, Justice Bradley wrote, "does not profess to be corrective of any constitutional wrong committed by the states." Bradley pointed out that the Civil Rights Act allowed the federal courts to displace state enforcement of its own laws even in states that had "the justest laws respecting the personal rights of citizens," and where those laws were really enforced. According to Justice Bradley, "The wrongful act of an individual ... is simply a private wrong," and "if not sanctioned in some way by the State, or not done under State authority, [the victim's] rights remain in full force." Victims of such wrongs, he said, could sue the wrongdoers in state courts and did not need the special assistance a federal claim provided. As Justice Bradley put it, the Fourteenth Amendment did not "authorize congress to create a code of municipal law for regulation of private rights."

Justice Bradley also rejected the argument that the Thirteenth Amendment gave Congress the power to enact the Civil Rights Act. The Thirteenth Amendment abolished slavery, and the act's defenders asserted that racial discrimination in places of public accommodation was a continuing "incident" of slavery. The Court responded, "It would be running the slavery argument into the ground to make it apply to every act of discrimination which a person may see fit to make ... as to the people he will take into his coach or cab or car." For Justice Bradley, "When a man has emerged from slavery, ... there must be some stage in the progress of his elevation when he takes the rank of a mere citizen, and ceases to be the special favorite of the law." The former slaves in the United States, Justice Bradley believed, had reached that point. Only Justice John Marshall Harlan, a former slaveholder turned strong Republican, dissented, saying that the Thirteenth Amendment did give Congress the power to enact antidiscrimination laws.

MODERN APPLICATIONS OF THE *CIVIL RIGHTS CASES*

In 2000 the Supreme Court reaffirmed the *Civil Rights Cases* in a controversial decision, *United States v. Morrison*. This decision struck down a provision of the Violence Against Women Act that allowed victims of gender-based violence to sue their attackers in federal court. The Court held that, despite findings of bias against women in state court systems, Congress did not have sufficient evidence of a breakdown of the states' own enforcement processes to establish that the states had denied women the equal protection of the laws. For the Court, this case resembled the *Civil Rights Cases*. Once again, a legal claim had been made that a federal statute could apply to private conduct (in the 2000 case, violence against women) even if that conduct was not connected to a state's having denied a person equal protection under the laws.

An important result of the *Civil Rights Cases* was the creation of the so-called "state action" requirement. According to this requirement only decisions by the state, and not decisions by private parties or corporations, can violate a person's constitutional rights.

The problem, identified by Justice Bradley in 1871, is that most of what private companies do *could* be regulated by the states. In other words, how can courts decide when a private party's decision is the result of a state's failure to regulate—or, put another way, its inaction?

Congress did not attempt to enact further civil rights statutes until the Civil Rights movement of the 1950s and 1960s took hold. In the Civil Rights Act of 1964, Congress did prohibit race discrimination in public accommodations by relying on the **commerce clause** of the Constitution, which gives Congress the power to regulate interstate commerce. In *Heart of Atlanta Motel v. United States* (1964), the Supreme Court upheld the 1964 act as a valid exercise of that power.

Justice Bradley's initial thought that the government could be responsible for private acts of discrimination that it failed to prevent would have had a dramatic impact on the nation's understanding of the relation between individuals and the government. By 1883, when the Supreme Court confronted the constitutionality of the Civil Rights Act of 1875, **Reconstruction** was over and the nation's white majority was unwilling to commit itself to the kind of large-scale transformation of social relations Senator Sumner had hoped for. Although the Supreme Court overturned the act, the theory underlying the Civil Rights Act of 1875 has never been successfully refuted. The people of the United States, however, have found it easier to act against racial discrimination using more specific legal theories aimed at limited rather than wide ranging goals.

See also: CIVIL RIGHTS ACTS OF 1866, 1957, 1964; FAIR HOUSING ACT OF 1968; FORCE ACT OF 1871; VOTING RIGHTS ACT OF 1965.

> An important result of the Civil Rights Cases was the creation of the so-called "state action" requirement. According to this requirement, only decisions by the state, and not decisions by private parties or corporations, can violate a person's constitutional rights.

commerce clause: the provision of the U.S. Constitution (Article I, section 8, clause 3) which gives Congress exclusive powers over interstate commerce—the buying, selling or exchanging of goods or products between states

Reconstruction: the political and economic reorganization and reestablishment of the South after the Civil War

BIBLIOGRAPHY

Franklin, John Hope. "The Enforcement of the Civil Rights Act of 1875." In *Race and History: Selected Essays 1938–1968*. Baton Rouge: Louisiana State University Press, 1989.

Mack, Kenneth W. "Law, Society, Identity, and the Making of the Jim Crow South: Travel and Segregation on Tennessee Railroads, 1875–1905." *Law and Social Inquiry* 24, no. 2 (1999): 377–410.

Westin, Alan F. "The Case of the Prejudiced Doorkeeper." In *Quarrels That Have Shaped the Constitution,* ed. John A. Garraty. New York: Harper & Row, 1962.

Wyatt-Brown, Bertram. "The Civil Rights Act of 1875." *Western Political Quarterly* 18 (1965): 763–775.

CIVIL RIGHTS ACT OF 1957

Gilbert Paul Carrasco

The Civil Rights Act of 1957 (CRA) (P.L. 85-315, 71 Stat. 634) began a new era in civil rights legislation and enforcement after more than three-quarters of a century of congressional inaction. The act initiated a greater federal role in protecting the rights of African Americans and other minorities. The Civil Rights Act of 1957 did not create new rights, but it increased protection of voting rights and laid the foundation for federal enforcement of civil rights law by creating the Civil Rights Division in the Department of Justice, a Civil Rights Commission within the executive branch, and expanding federal enforcement authority to include civil lawsuits.

LEGAL AND SOCIAL CONDITIONS PRIOR TO THE ACT

The federal law in force at the time of the 1957 Civil Rights Act dated from the **Reconstruction** period following the Civil War. The Fourteenth and Fifteenth Amendments to the U.S. Constitution, which were ratified in 1868 and 1870 respectively, granted Congress the power to enforce civil rights with legislation, and it is this power that serves as the constitutional basis of the act.

Reconstruction: the political and economic reorganization and reestablishment of the South after the Civil War

From 1866 to 1875, Congress enacted a series of statutes intended to confer broad rights on African Americans to be free from discrimination. Many of the protections of these civil rights acts, however, were severely restricted through U.S. Supreme Court interpretation, as occurred in the *Civil Rights Cases* (1883). Among the most significant lasting effects of these laws was the establishment of federal authority to enforce criminal civil rights provisions.

Although many of the more violent forms of racial oppression had been reduced by the 1950s, in the South state law was often used to prevent African Americans from exercising their civil rights. To register to vote, for example, many states required that applicants take a voter qualification test. The questions on the test were designed so registrars could disqualify most of the African Americans attempting to register.

Although many of the more violent forms of racial oppression had been reduced by the 1950s, in the South state law was often used to prevent African Americans from exercising their civil rights.

Renewed federal efforts to enforce the criminal provisions of civil rights laws began in 1939. That year a civil rights section was created within the Criminal Division of the Department of Justice.

CIRCUMSTANCES LEADING TO ENACTMENT

The bill that became the 1957 act was introduced in Congress during the administration of President Dwight D. Eisenhower. Attorney General Herbert Brownell played a large role in shaping the bill. It was very similar to a 1956 bill which was not enacted because of the resistance of Southern senators.

The Eisenhower administration's proposed bill initially contained four parts. Part I created a Civil Rights Commission within the executive branch to investigate civil rights violations. Part II created an assistant attorney general for civil rights, which led to the elevation of the civil rights section of the Department of Justice to the Civil Rights Division (as had been recommended by President Harry Truman in 1948). In Part III, the proposed bill contained broad language that expanded the department's authority to enforce civil rights through civil and criminal proceedings. Part IV authorized the attorney general to bring civil lawsuits and obtain preventive injunctions (court orders) for the protection of voting rights. After debate, the bill passed the House of Representatives on June 18, 1957, by a vote of 286 to 126.

The biggest obstacle to civil rights legislation in 1957 was the bloc of Southern Democrats led by Senator Richard Russell of Georgia. Southern senators had blocked every piece of civil rights legislation proposed since 1875. The most vocal supporters of the bill in the Senate were Republican leader William Knowland of California and liberal Democrat Paul Douglas of Illinois. Although neither senator was a particularly strong leader, it appeared that they had public opinion and Senate votes on their side. Whereas the coalition in support of the bill was not a closely unified group, the Southern senators in opposition were. Many believed the bill would die in the Senate, despite its support, because Southern senators would **filibuster**, if necessary, to defeat the bill.

> *The biggest obstacle to civil rights legislation in 1957 was the bloc of Southern Democrats led by Senator Richard Russell of Georgia.*

filibuster: a tactic involving unlimited debate on the floor of the House and Senate designed to delay or prevent legislative action

In 1957 civil rights legislation had a highly effective, if unlikely, supporter. Senate Majority Leader Lyndon B. Johnson and many others believed that the future national success of the Democratic Party, and of Johnson's 1960 presidential hopes, depended on the enactment of civil rights legislation. A Texas Democrat, Johnson's constituents were not likely to view his leadership on civil rights favorably. In the past Johnson had not supported the civil rights bills presented to the Senate. In fact, he had embarrassed Senator Douglas while playing a role in the defeat of the 1956 civil rights bill. Nonetheless, in 1957 Johnson quietly began to use his political skill and influence to help enact the first civil rights legislation in over eighty years.

> *In 1957 Senate Majority Leader Lyndon B. Johnson quietly began to use his political skill and influence to help enact the first civil rights legislation in over eighty years.*

Senator Russell presented the South's position on July 2, 1957, in a powerful speech that drastically influenced debate on the bill. Reviving negative images of Reconstruction that haunted Southerners, Russell won sympathy from many who were cautious about forcing federal policy on the states. The speech attacked Part III of Eisenhower's bill for its broad authorizations to interfere with state law. Russell also noted that Part III contained a connection to the Civil Rights Act of 1866 that might allow the federal government to use armed forces to enforce court orders and the provisions of civil rights law. Russell also attacked Part IV because it did not provide for a jury trial in criminal contempt proceedings, which meant that those who violated civil rights would be punished by a judge (rather than an all-white jury, which might be more lenient toward defendants in such cases). These two aspects of the bill would become the key sacrifices needed for a compromise with the Southerners. Lyndon Johnson recognized that securing a compromise on those aspects of the bill and preventing a filibuster was among the only ways that the bill could pass. Yet, to many liberals, Part III was the most important part of the entire bill. The amended bill passed the Senate on August 7, 1957, by a vote of seventy-two to eighteen.

Many liberals were disappointed the bill had been so severely weakened. House and Senate leaders negotiated for two weeks, then presented a bill

Under the 1957 act, the commission was designed to terminate within two years. Half a century later, however, the U.S. Commission on Civil Rights continues to investigate civil rights violations, gather information, appraise federal law, submit reports to the president and Congress, and issue public announcements.

bipartisan: involving members of two parties, especially the two major political parties

preventive relief: relief granted to prevent a foreseen harm

much like the one passed by the Senate but with slight modifications to the jury trial amendment. This bill was passed in the House of Representatives on August 27, 1957, by a margin of 279 to 97. Passage in the Senate was not quite as easy. Senator Strom Thurmond of South Carolina began a sort of one-man filibuster on August 28. His speech of more than twenty-four hours set a record in the Senate. Following this oration, on August 29 the Senate passed the Civil Rights Act of 1957 by a margin of 60 to 15. President Eisenhower signed the bill on September 9, 1957, and the Civil Rights Act became law.

FEATURES OF THE ACT

As finally enacted, Part I of the Civil Rights Act of 1957 created a six-member **bipartisan** Commission on Civil Rights. The commission's duties included investigation of allegations that "certain citizens of the United States are being deprived of their right to vote and have that vote counted by reason of their color, race, religion, or national origin." Further, the commission was required to "study and collect information concerning legal developments constituting a denial of equal protection of the laws under the Constitution."

The commission was also given a third investigative responsibility, to "appraise the laws and policies of the Federal Government with respect to equal protection of the laws under the Constitution." For these purposes, the commission could compel testimony from witnesses through the subpoena power granted in the act, provided the hearing was held in the state where the witness was located. In the event the witnesses refused to appear, the attorney general was given power to secure an order from a federal district court that was enforceable through contempt.

Under the 1957 act, the commission was designed to terminate within two years. Half a century later, however, the U.S. Commission on Civil Rights continues to investigate civil rights violations, gather information, appraise federal law, submit reports to the president and Congress, and issue public announcements.

Part II of the act created an additional assistant attorney general. Shortly after enactment, Attorney General William Rogers ordered the creation of the Civil Rights Division within the Department of Justice. Part III amended existing civil rights law by conferring federal court jurisdiction over civil suits that could provide a wider range of remedies for civil rights violations, including infringement of the right to vote.

Part IV contains the most significant enforcement powers granted by the act. It prohibits actions by any person, including private individuals, designed to "intimidate, threaten, [or] coerce ... for the purpose of interfering with the right [of any person] to vote as he may choose." The act also expanded federal authority to enforce the ban on racially discriminatory denials of the right to vote by authorizing the attorney general to initiate civil lawsuits in the federal district courts "for **preventive relief**, including an application for a permanent or temporary injunction, restraining order, or other order."

Part V of the act was the compromise "jury trial" provision that had caused difficulty in the Senate. It limits the authority of the courts to enforce Part IV of the act through civil contempt, or criminal contempt imposing a

$1,000 fine or less and/or a prison term of six months or less. It also provides that the accused has a right to a jury trial **de novo** for any criminal contempt proceeding that imposed a fine of more than $300 or imprisonment for more than forty-five days. Despite these limitations, Part V explicitly preserved the right of the courts "by civil contempt proceedings, without a jury, to secure compliance with or to prevent obstruction of, as distinguished from punishment for violations of," any court order.

de novo: (Latin) anew, a second time; the same as if it had not been heard before

ENFORCEMENT AND JUDICIAL ACTION

Under the 1957 act, the Department of Justice's authority to enforce civil rights was limited to criminal prosecutions and civil voting rights suits. The Civil Rights Division had fifteen attorneys in 1958 and twenty-seven in 1959. It was initially organized into a General Litigation Section and a Voting and Elections Section, which reflected the emphasis on voting rights in the 1957 Act. In 1959 the Commission on Civil Rights criticized the division because it had brought only three actions under its authority to seek preventive relief.

The division's strategy changed beginning in 1960. In 1961 John F. Kennedy became president, and new people began to work in the Civil Rights Division. Robert F. Kennedy became the attorney general in his brother's administration and appointed Burke Marshall as the head of the division. Marshall, along with other attorneys in the division, went to various areas of the South to investigate voting discrimination and compiled overwhelming evidence that it existed. The division used the evidence in a county-by-county and state-by-state campaign to challenge voting discrimination in the federal courts, where it won some significant victories. The division attorneys, however, faced a pervasive state-sponsored system of discrimination that would be very difficult to stop.

The division initiated its first lawsuit against the Dallas County, Alabama, Board of Registrars in 1961. It lost in district court, but on appeal, the court of appeals ordered the district court to issue an injunction against the discriminatory use of a questionnaire and oral questioning to disqualify applicants unless complete records were kept and all questioning complied with federal law.

In *U.S. v. Atkins* the Civil Rights Division presented evidence that in 1961, 8,597 out of 14,400 whites in Dallas County and 242 out of 15,115 blacks were registered to vote, along with other significant indicators of discrimination. Despite some victories in the courts, by 1963 only 320 African Americans in Dallas County were registered to vote. After four years of federal efforts, in 1965 only 1,516 more African Americans in Dallas county were registered to vote than in 1961. In 1965 the Voting Rights Act was enacted to address many of the enforcement problems under the 1957 act. By 1966 over 10,000 African Americans were registered to vote in Dallas County. Another example of difficulties in the division's efforts to enforce voting rights under the 1957 act was its lawsuit against the State of Mississippi. John Doar, who served in the division from 1960 to 1967 (including two years as assistant attorney general), described the case against Mississippi as "a prime example" of resistance by federal judges in the Southern district courts.

In that case, *U.S. v. Mississippi* (1964), the Justice Department sought to prove that certain Mississippi state constitu-

The Congressional Commission on Civil Rights, in its 1959 report, stressed the inadequacy of existing voting rights protections. Intense legislative activity laid the foundations for the passage of the Civil Rights Bill of 1960.

The Civil Rights Act of 1960

Gilbert Paul Carrasco

The Civil Rights Act of 1960 (P.L. 86-449, 74 Stat. 86) amended the Civil Rights Act of 1957 to strengthen the voting rights of African Americans. It gives the attorney general authority to seek a court order declaring a person qualified to vote when the court finds a "pattern or practice" of discrimination based on race or color. It also empowers courts to appoint "voting referees" to take evidence and report findings of discrimination to such courts. The act further provides that a state may be sued in a case in which state officials are accused of voting discrimination. Finally, this law extends the powers of the U.S. Commission on Civil Rights.

Although the Civil Rights Division's efforts under the Civil Rights Act of 1957 did not in every case immediately protect the voting rights of African Americans, let alone other civil rights, it did begin the era of civil rights reform.

subpoena: a writ issued under authority of a court to compel the appearance of a witness at a judicial hearing

tional provisions and other state laws were designed to prevent African Americans from voting in significant numbers. Two of three district court judges viewed the case as a "frontal attack" by the federal government on the State of Mississippi. They dismissed the Justice Department's complaint by maintaining that the department lacked the authority to bring the suit for a declaration that Mississippi's voter qualification laws were unconstitutional, stating that the Civil Rights Act did not grant authority "to bring any action to destroy any state's constitution or laws." Judge Brown issued a long and powerful dissent, stating that no state or nation "can survive if, professing democratic rule of the governed, it flagrantly denies the voting right through racial or class discrimination." Judge Brown went on to discuss the long history of voting discrimination in Mississippi, which resulted in registration of less than five percent of adult African Americans.

The case eventually went before the U.S. Supreme Court, which explained that the Civil Rights Act of 1957 was constitutional under the Fifteenth Amendment (guaranteeing the right to vote) and that the Justice Department could bring suit against a state. In *U.S. v. Mississippi* (1965), the Supreme Court also stated it could "find no possible justification for" the district court's interpretation of the Civil Rights Act and it "had no doubt whatsoever" that the district court should not have dismissed the complaint.

BEGINNING AN ERA OF REFORM

Although the Civil Rights Division's efforts under the Civil Rights Act of 1957 did not in every case immediately protect the voting rights of African Americans, let alone other civil rights, it did begin the era of civil rights reform. The work of the Civil Rights Division in the early 1960s began to dismantle the discriminatory legal structure of the Southern states in significant ways by challenging discriminatory voter qualification requirements. The division's work also brought attention to the degree of discrimination in the South, having a significant impact on the enactment of other civil rights laws.

Along with the Civil Rights Division, the Civil Rights Commission was making significant progress toward awareness of civil rights problems. In 1958 state officials in Montgomery, Alabama, refused to appear at hearings held by the commission, violating a **subpoena**. This defiance drew attention from national newspapers. The subpoena was enforced by the Justice Department through a court order. In a 1960 ruling the Supreme Court upheld the commission's hearing process as constitutional and described the commission as an exclusively investigative body. Initially, the commission focused largely on voting discrimination, but it expanded its scope of investigation during the Kennedy administration. In the Civil Rights Act of 1964, the commission's mission was expanded to include serving as a national clearinghouse of information.

The work of the Civil Rights Division and the Commission on Civil Rights created a dramatic record of the systematic discrimination occurring in the Southern states. This record would play a significant role in determining the shape of the more sweeping civil rights protections guaranteed by the Civil Rights Act of 1964, the Voting Rights Act of 1965, and other subsequent civil rights legislation. The Civil Rights Act of 1957 was a historically significant enactment because it ended three-quarters of a century of congressional inaction. It has carried a lasting significance through efforts of the Civil Rights Division and Civil Rights Commission, whose actions helped to set in motion forces that have eradicated much of the institutional discrimination dominating the Southern states in 1957.

See also: CIVIL RIGHTS ACTS OF 1866, 1875, 1964; FORCE ACT OF 1871; KU KLUX KLAN ACT; VOTING RIGHTS ACT OF 1965.

BIBLIOGRAPHY

Caro, Robert A. *The Years of Lyndon Johnson,* Vol. 3: *Master of the Senate.* New York: Alfred A. Knopf, 2002.

Belknap, Michal R. *Federal Law and Southern Order: Racial Violence and Constitutional Conflict in the Post-Brown South.* Athens: University of Georgia Press, 1987.

Doar, John. "The Work of the Civil Rights Division in Enforcing Voting Rights under the Civil Rights Acts of 1957 and 1960." *Florida State University Law Review* 25, no.1 (1997): 1–17.

Frye, Jocelyn C., Robert S. Gerber, Robert H. Pees, et al. "The Rise and Fall of the United States Commission on Civil Rights." *Harvard Civil Rights—Civil Liberties Law Review* 22, no. 2 (1987): 449–505.

King, James D., and James W. Riddlesperger, Jr. "Presidential Leadership Style and Civil Rights Legislation: The Civil Rights Act of 1957 and the Voting Rights Act of 1965." In *Presidential Leadership and Civil Rights Policy,* ed. James W. Riddlesperger, Jr., and Donald W. Jackson. Westport, CT: Greenwood Press, 1995.

Landsberg, Brian K. *Enforcing Civil Rights: Race Discrimination and the Department of Justice.* Lawrence: University Press of Kansas, 1997.

Mann, Robert. *The Walls of Jericho: Lyndon Johnson, Hubert Humphrey, Richard Russell, and the Struggle for Civil Rights.* New York: Harcourt Brace, 1996.

Schwartz, Bernard, ed. *Statutory History of the United States: Civil Rights.* New York: Chelsea House, 1970.

Winters, Paul A., ed. *The Civil Rights Movement.* San Diego, CA: Greenhaven Press, 2000.

INTERNET RESOURCE

U.S. Commission on Civil Rights. <http://www.usccr.gov>.

Civil Contempt vs. Criminal Contempt

Contempt is an act of disobedience to a court order or an act of disrespect toward a court. A charge of civil contempt differs from a charge of criminal contempt in its intent: A civil contempt charge is coercive, in that it is intended to stop the misbehavior or make the person charged comply with the court order. A criminal contempt charge is punitive, or intended to punish the defendant for his or her behavior. Someone charged with civil contempt must be permitted to appear before the court to "purge" the contempt by demonstrating compliance with the order. A criminal contempt defendant does not have the same right, since the purpose is punishment for past behavior. The penalty for criminal contempt is usually a fine or prison sentence. The penalty for civil contempt may be a fine, a prison sentence, or compensation to the victim of the act committed in disregard of the court order. Part V of the Civil Rights Act of 1957 did not significantly detract from the courts' powers to ensure compliance with its orders. It only limited the power to impose punishment for past disobedience.

CIVIL RIGHTS ACT OF 1964

Melanie B. Abbott

The years following World War II in the United States brought a period of economic prosperity for many Americans. The economy was strong and workers found themselves able to use their income to pay for new homes and goods and services that had been unheard of for prior generations. Not all U.S. residents, however, shared equally in the prosperity. Throughout the 1940s and 1950s, white Americans enjoyed many benefits that were unavailable to people of color. African Americans attempting to vote in local, state,

Pressure on the federal government for additional civil rights protection increased in the years following 1960.

and federal elections faced poll taxes and rigid entry requirements, though their white neighbors had no such barriers. In parts of the United States white people had preferential seating on buses and in movie theaters; water fountains and municipal swimming pools bore signs indicating that their use was restricted by race; and drugstore soda fountains and restaurants refused to serve people of color.

In the same vein, public schools admitted students not on the basis of their residence, but rather on the basis of their race. The education provided in the schools attended by white children was different from that provided to black children. Students of color who wished to attend college had many fewer choices than white students with equal ability. Housing, too, was restricted, both by the refusal of white landlords to rent to black tenants and by the refusal of white homeowners to sell their homes to people of color. As a result, neighborhoods in many parts of the country were segregated.

During the 1950s activists like Dr. Martin Luther King, Jr. began to stage protests against widespread racial discrimination. African American leaders held marches in cities in the South, joined by many Northern supporters, both white and black. Many of these nonviolent protests were met with violent responses, including the use of police dogs, water hoses, and physical abuse of the protesters. Newspapers and magazines covered the confrontations, bringing the struggle to the attention of many Americans who had remained unaware of the extent and severity of racial discrimination.

By the time the presidential election campaign of 1960 began, a national debate on the issue of race discrimination was occurring in the media, schools, and local government chambers. Both national parties made Civil Rights a part of their campaign platforms in 1960. The 1960 Democratic platform said: "The peaceful demonstrations for first-class citizenship which have recently taken place in many parts of the country are a signal to all of us to make good at long last the guarantees of our Constitution.... The time has come to assure equal access for all Americans to all areas of community life." The Republican platform stated, "We pledge the full use of the power, resources, and leadership of the Federal Government to eliminate discrimination based on race, color, religion, or national origin."

Against this backdrop, John F. Kennedy was elected president in 1960. Progress on legislation addressing the promises made by both parties was slow. Congress considered legislation to address inequality in public accommodations, but failed to pass it. Legislators tried, but also failed, to pass a widespread Civil Rights law in 1963. Those who argued against the law's passage asserted that the remedies proposed by the law were unconstitutional, in violation of the rights of the states to govern their own affairs, and an impermissible infringement on the rights of business owners to decide for themselves with whom to do business. It was only after the assassination of President Kennedy in 1963 and the swearing-in of Lyndon Johnson in his place, that the legislative tide turned in favor of passage of Civil Rights legislation.

It was only after the assassination of President Kennedy in 1963 and the swearing-in of Lyndon Johnson in his place, that the legislative tide turned in favor of passage of Civil Rights legislation.

THE ACT'S PROVISIONS

The Civil Rights Act of 1964 (P.L. 88–352, 78 Stat. 241) addressed voting rights, desegregation of public facilities,

Even though the inequality of the treatment of blacks was clear, for Congress there were many questions of what remedies would be constitutional. Here Senate Majority Leader Mike Mansfield (D-Mont.) (left) and Senate Minority Leader Everett M. Dirksen (R-Ill.) work together to pass the Civil Rights Act of 1964. (U.S. SENATE HISTORICAL OFFICE)

desegregation of public education, and equal employment opportunity. It provided for the extension of the Commission on Civil Rights, the creation of the Equal Employment Opportunity Commission, and mandated that federally assisted programs be nondiscriminatory.

The voting rights provisions of the act stated that for federal elections, persons acting "under color of law" could not apply standards to some voters that were different from those applied to all other voters, and could not use immaterial errors in written applications to bar voters from participating in federal elections. The act also barred the use of literacy tests for some voters but not others and allowed the U.S. attorney general to sue in federal court for violations of these provisions by state officials.

Title II of the act rendered illegal barriers imposed by owners of restaurants, motels, and other public businesses against people of color, stating, "all persons shall be entitled to the full and equal enjoyment of the goods, services, facilities, privileges, advantages, and accommodations of any place of public accommodation ... without discrimination or segregation on the ground of race, color, religion, or national origin."

Title IV called for the commissioner of education to conduct a survey to determine the extent to which public schools and public colleges were providing equal educational opportunities to all without regard to race, religion, or national origin. It also authorized the attorney general to initiate lawsuits against public educational officials in response to complaints from those who believed they had been deprived of equal educational opportunity.

Title VI provided that discrimination on the basis of race, color, or national origin is illegal in "any program or activity receiving Federal financial assistance." This section applied to programs in which the federal government provided grants, loans, contracts, or other financial support to other organizations, public or private.

Title VII made it illegal for an employer "to fail or refuse to hire or to discharge any individual, or otherwise to discriminate against any individual with respect to his terms, conditions or privileges of employment, because of such individual's race, color, religion, sex, or national origin." Title VII's provisions applied to labor organizations, apprenticeship providers, and employment agencies. The act also created the Equal Employment Opportunity Commission (EEOC), a bipartisan commission, intended to be independent of control by the president or the Congress. Its role has been to investigate and attempt to remedy violations of Title VII. Cases in which the EEOC is unable to reach a satisfactory resolution go on to federal court for judicial proceedings.

IMPORTANT LEGAL EFFECTS OF THE CIVIL RIGHTS ACT

The Civil Rights Act served to unite in federal law a number of important principles. Primary among these, of course, was the clear statement that discrimination on the basis of race, color, or national origin was illegal when practiced by public officials or those providing public accommodations. The voter registration drives in the early 1960s had made clear there were substantial barriers to full participation by all Americans in the federal electoral process. By allowing suits for cases in which the attorney general could find a "pattern or practice of discrimination," the act made it possible for black voters to challenge actions by local officials that deprived them of the right to participate equally with white voters.

The Civil Rights Act served to unite in federal law a number of important principles, including the clear statement that discrimination on the basis of race, color, or national origin was illegal when practiced by public officials or those providing public accommodations.

The 1964 act strengthened earlier laws preventing racial discrimination against black voters and helped lay the groundwork for the Voting Rights Act of 1965. The Civil Rights Act's prohibition of discrimination by those providing public accommodations also made possible a giant step in racial equality, preventing most local businesses from refusing service to people of color.

The Equal Employment Opportunity provisions in Title VII have had the most wide ranging, and perhaps unexpected, effects. These provisions certainly served to open opportunities to people of color seeking jobs and training opportunities previously unavailable to them. Manufacturing companies, **labor unions**, police and fire departments, and innumerable other employers were forced or encouraged to open their doors to applicants of all races and national origins. In addition to those expected results, however, the inclusion of the word "sex" among the prohibited bases of discrimination meant that Title VII has been the focus of considerable attention and analysis long after most of the other provisions in the act have ceased to be noteworthy.

labor union: an association of workers whose main purpose is to collectively bargain on behalf of workers with employers about the terms and conditions of employment

SIGNIFICANCE OF CHANGES IN THE LAW

The Civil Rights Act is well known for the remedies it provided for those routinely discriminated against on the basis of race or national origin. It also, however, made some significant advances in the way courts considered violations of these laws. For example, Title I includes a section making it possible for the U.S. attorney general to request that a three-judge panel of federal judges hear cases brought by persons alleging discrimination against them in connection with voting. This is different from the usual practice, in which a single federal judge hears a case and makes a ruling, which can then be appealed to a three-judge panel of an appellate court. One reason for this change from the standard practice was the concern on the part of those sponsoring the law that some judges and court officials had acted to block access to the courts by people of color seeking to assert their rights. This section also required that federal courts treat voting rights cases as priorities, rather than subjecting them to the usual docketing practices of the courts.

Another significant development in the law is in the connection the act makes between interstate commerce (or state action) and barriers created by owners of public accommodations to prevent people of color from using these facilities. Previously, owners of local pools, hotels, motels, theaters, and

In the 1960s all Americans still did not share in the prosperity of the nation. Through the work of activists like Dr. Martin Luther King Jr., the inequality of the treatment of blacks became a subject of national debate. The Civil Rights Act of 1964 created a federal right that addressed voting rights, desegregation of public facilities, desegregation of public education, and equal employment opportunities. (©BETTMANN/CORBIS)

other places to which the public is admitted could claim their discriminatory decisions were individually made, motivated by their desire to please the majority of their customers. The Civil Rights Act required that businesses affecting interstate commerce be operated in a nondiscriminatory manner.

The Civil Rights Act did not explicitly make "separate but equal" education illegal; the Supreme Court had taken that step ten years earlier in *Brown v. Board of Education* (1954). Instead, the act incorporated into federal statutory law a requirement that public schools be desegregated, allowing the U.S. attorney general to sue schools that failed to provide equal opportunities for all students and making nondiscrimination a prerequisite to receiving federal financial assistance. Not until after the enactment of the 1964 act were desegregation requirements enforced throughout the country.

Not until after the enactment of the 1964 act were desegregation requirements enforced throughout the country.

Following passage of the Civil Rights Act in 1964, much of the activity surrounding efforts to integrate facilities of all types moved from the streets to the courts. Lawsuits concerning discrimination in many different settings allowed the courts to define, refine, and apply the provisions of the act. Education was a major arena in which legal action helped to effect desegregation. Though the decision in *Brown v. Board of Education* predated the Civil Rights Act, the passage of the act provided significant support for efforts of those seeking to open educational institutions to students of color.

Among the most significant post-act decisions was *Regents of University of California v. Bakke* (1978), in which a white student sued the medical school of the University of California, alleging that the school had violated his civil rights by setting aside several seats in the class for members of disadvantaged groups. The Court upheld the state court's decision that the quota system was unlawful, but also held that it was acceptable under the Equal Protection clause of the Fourteenth Amendment and under the Civil Rights Act for the school to take race into consideration as one factor in an admissions program seeking educational diversity.

In 1992 the Supreme Court held that a state's obligations under Title VI of the act were not satisfied merely by operating a race-neutral admissions system. In *United States v. Fordice* (1992), the Court ruled that a formerly segregated public university system must eliminate remnants of the dual system even if those aspects of the program had no discriminatory purpose. The Supreme Court considered race in college admissions most recently in 2003, holding that a quota system for undergraduates of color at the University of Michigan violated Title VI of the Civil Rights Act of 1964, but further ruling that race-conscious admissions to the University's Law School were acceptable in pursuit of the goal of racial diversity so long as the University made decisions on an individual basis (*Gratz v. Bollinger* and *Grutter v. Bollinger*, both 2003).

Courts have also held that the act requires states operating public recreational facilities, such as pools, parks, and playgrounds, to make those facilities equally available to persons of all races.

Courts have also held that the act requires states operating public recreational facilities, such as pools, parks, and playgrounds, to make those facilities equally available to persons of all races. In *Daniel v. Paul* (1969), the Court ruled that an amusement park in Arkansas was a "place of public accommodation" covered by the act and therefore could not limit use of its facilities to whites who had paid a twenty-five cent "membership fee." The Court rejected the operator's argument that the park's operation was entirely private, noting the park was advertised in magazines and on broadcast outlets, that it served out-of-state visitors, and that the food sold in the park's snack bar moved in interstate commerce.

Subsequent legislation has further developed and amplified the provisions of the act as they apply to many areas, especially discrimination in housing, which was largely unaddressed by the act. The provisions of Titles II and VII of the act were expanded in 1990 with the passage of the Americans with Disabilities Act (1990). The Americans with Disabilities Act (ADA) required that the Civil Rights Act's prohibitions against discrimination apply to people with physical and mental disabilities as well. Recognizing that discrimination in employment on the basis of age was a related problem, Congress supplemented Title VII of the Civil Rights Act in 1967 with the Age Discrimination in Employment Act. The Equal Pay Act of 1963, a part of the Fair Labor Standards Act, further supplemented Title VII by prohibiting employers from paying men and women different wages for the same work.

Though much progress has occurred since passage of the Civil Rights Act's passage in 1964, courts and legislatures throughout the country continue to address many difficult issues on a regular basis.

See also: AMERICANS WITH DISABILITIES ACT OF 1990; CIVIL RIGHTS ACT OF 1866, 1875, 1957; EQUAL PAY ACT OF 1963; FORCE ACT OF 1871; KU KLUX KLAN ACT; TITLE IX EDUCATION AMENDMENT; VOTING RIGHTS ACT OF 1965;

BIBLIOGRAPHY

Branch, Taylor. *Parting the Waters: America in the King Years 1954–1963*. New York: Simon & Schuster, 1989.

Carson, Clayborne, et al., eds. *The Eyes on the Prize Civil Rights Reader: Documents, Speeches, and Firsthand Accounts from the Black Freedom Struggle*. New York: Viking Penguin, 1991.

Williams, Juan, *Eyes on the Prize: America's Civil Rights Years, 1954–1965*. New York: Viking Penguin, 1987.

CIVIL SERVICE ACTS (1883)

William V. Luneburg

Since the formation of the United States under the Constitution, the government has taken various and sometimes controversial approaches to the hiring of federal and state administrative staff, or the civil service. In general, the basic choice has appeared to be between, on the one hand, an administrative staff that represents and reflects "the people" (the democratic vision) and, on the other, one that is made up of long-term professionals with the knowledge and experience necessary to carry out the complex and demanding tasks of government (the technocratic vision).

The federal government has historically faced difficulty in fully integrating the constitutional provisions relating to civil service. The Constitution places the president at the head of the executive branch but makes the civil service dependent on Congress.

HISTORICAL BACKGROUND

During the colonial years, it was not uncommon to fill public offices with those who paid for them. This experience, along with dislike of the British colonial bureaucracy, gave ample basis for the leaders of the new republic to distrust public employees. During his two terms as president, George Washington insisted on "fitness of character" as the prime qualification to hold a government job. This standard, it was hoped, would create a "patrician" civil service that would avoid what many saw as the pitfalls of democracy. Removals from office were rare.

With the rise of political parties after 1800, it was only a matter of time before newly elected chief executives would want people of their own political persuasions holding the important positions in the administrative hierarchy. It was not, however, until the election of Andrew Jackson in 1828 that appointment to and removal from public office on partisan grounds was fully embraced as the appropriate approach to staffing the public service. After this time, public service positions would be handed out according to the "spoils system"—in other words, the party victorious in an election could hand out civil service positions as a kind of plunder (spoils) to members of the party or anyone else it deemed fit to serve. This system would ensure that government was not the tool of the wealthy, powerful, and privileged but rather more democratic, with staff drawn from a more representative cross section of the electorate and therefore (presumably) more responsive to the popular will. Although the spoils system was criticized for filling offices with incompetents and creating vast incentives to corruption, those objections fell on deaf ears for over half a century.

It was not until the election of Andrew Jackson in 1828 that appointment to and removal from public office on partisan grounds was fully embraced as the appropriate approach to staffing the public service.

THE CALL FOR CIVIL SERVICE REFORM

Following the Civil War, the movement for civil service reform intensified. The public was questioning the spoils system on moral grounds. In addition, many legislators had come to believe that the increasingly complicated industrial economy required a high level of knowledge and experience among civil service employees. Such qualifications were necessary for public policy to be adequately formulated and implemented.

It took the assassination of President James Garfield in 1881 by a crazed disappointed office-seeker to make reform a matter of the highest urgency. Ironically, the vice president who became the next president, Chester A. Arthur, had himself been a firm believer in and beneficiary of the spoils system. But, to the surprise of his former political allies, Arthur, believing that his reelection would depend on reaching out to more reformist and independent elements in the electorate, threw his support behind the enactment of civil service reform.

THE PENDLETON ACT AND RELATED ACTS

The popular feeling against political patronage was running so strong that both Democrats and Republicans joined forces to enact the first Civil Service

In this 1872 cartoon published in Harper's Weekly, *a congressman is "presenting a few of his constituents" for appointment to jobs in federal offices. Before the Civil Service Reform Act (Pendleton Act) was passed in 1883, civil service appointments were given based on a patronage system; that is, those who were loyal to an individual or party were rewarded with government jobs.* (LIBRARY OF CONGRESS, PRINTS AND PHOTOGRAPHS DIVISION)

Act, known as the Pendleton Act (22 Stat. 403), in 1883. This act, largely drafted by the New York Civil Service Reform Association, created the Civil Service Commission, which was directed to create a system of competitive examinations to fill vacancies in federal service positions and to ensure that the civil service was not used for political purposes. Originally only about 10 percent of federal positions were included within what was known as the "classified" service (chosen by examination), but that percentage grew to over 70 percent by 1919.

The Pendleton Act had closed the "front door" to civil service. But the "back door," or removal from office, remained unprotected from party politics. Indeed, it was common for members of the classified service to be removed for political reasons. In 1897, however, President William McKinley issued an executive order providing that removals of classified service personnel could only be made for "just cause." Moreover, classified employees were entitled to a written explanation for the removal and the right to make a reply. In 1912 Congress passed the Lloyd-LaFollette Act (P.L. 336, 37 Stat. 539), which prevented future presidents from interfering with these rights on their own initiative and, in addition, expanded to some degree the procedural protections against removal. The Civil Service Commission created a system for administrative review of removal decisions to ensure that proper procedures had been followed.

In 1944, anticipating that a wave of World War II veterans would seek and hold jobs in the federal government, Congress enacted the Veterans Preference Act (P.L. 359, 58 Stat. 387). For veterans only, this act expanded the procedural protections beyond removals from office to other significant **adverse** personnel actions (for example, thirty-day suspensions) and provided for review by the Civil Service Commission of the appropriateness of removals and other actions.

adverse: contrary to one's interests; harmful or unfavorable

THE CIVIL SERVICE REFORM ACT

By the 1970s dissatisfaction with the operation of the civil service system had become so widespread that legislators knew they had to take action. Procedural protections for employees were viewed as inadequate. Many criticized the Civil Service Commission for failing to protect employees' rights, particularly when allegations of racial, sexual, and other types of discrimination were made in response to proposed personnel actions. As unions grew among the federal workforce, federal employees and others voiced concerns that no independent impartial agency existed to oversee the federal sector's labor management program. These critics also saw a need to strengthen the role of the system for resolving disputes that involved unionized employees and their employing agencies.

To deal with these and other concerns, in 1978 Congress enacted the Civil Service Reform Act (CSRA) (P.L. 95-454, 92 Stat. 1111), which radically restructured the civil service framework. The statute defined the principles for a merit system:

The Assassination of James Garfield

James Garfield was assassinated by Charles Guiteau, a lawyer with a long history of erratic behavior. In the 1860s Guiteau had joined the Oneida Community, a communal religious movement espousing free love, but he soon argued with the group's leaders and was asked to leave. After passing the bar in Illinois, he pretended to collect debts for clients, but kept the money for himself and maintained that it was irretrievable. Guiteau was frequently jailed for his debts. He toured the country as an evangelist (one newspaper reported that he had "fraud and imbecility plainly stamped upon his countenance"), and again later making speeches on behalf of presidential candidate Garfield. Eventually feeling that his efforts on Garfield's behalf had earned him an ambassadorship to Vienna—though later he thought Paris might be nicer—he began to besiege the White House with letters and visits. Receiving no encouragement, he became embittered and

increasingly impoverished. Guiteau blamed his plight on Secretary of State James G. Blaine, who, pushed beyond endurance, cried, "Never speak to me again on the Paris consulship as long as you live!" Increasingly unhinged, Guiteau wrote to Garfield, "Mr. Blaine is a wicked man, and you ought to demand his immediate resignation; otherwise you and the Republican Party will come to grief." On July 2, 1881, Guiteau shot President Garfield in a Washington train station. Garfield survived for three months after the shooting, finally succumbing on September 19th after a spectacular demonstration of malpractice, in which sixteen bickering doctors had managed to turn a nonfatal wound into a raging infection. Attempting to use the then-uncommon defense of medical malpractice, Guiteau said at his trial, "Your honor, I admit to the shooting of the president, but not the killing." Most historians agree with his assessment; nevertheless, he was convicted and hanged.

Recruitment should be from qualified individuals from appropriate sources in an endeavor to achieve a work force from all segments of society, and selection and advancement should be determined solely on the basis of relative ability, knowledge, and skills, after fair and open competition which assures that all receive equal opportunity.

The act also prohibited certain practices such as the preferred hiring of family members (nepotism) and established rules for removing employees for inadequate performance. It also created a new tier of civil servants, the Senior Executive Service, allowing more flexibility in administration at the top of the government.

The act also created a new executive branch agency, the Office of Personnel Management, to establish the rules governing the civil service. Under the act, federal employees of certain types (veterans and members of the classified service) can resort to an independent administrative "court" (the Merit Systems Protection Board) to determine if actions taken against them are appropriate. The Office of Special Counsel investigates and prosecutes before the board cases where employees have been the victims of prohibited practices (such as nepotism). The Equal Employment Opportunity Commission has primary jurisdiction over the implementation and enforcement of antidiscrimination law in federal employment. Finally, another new agency, the Federal Labor Relations Authority, oversees **collective bargaining** and the process for dispute resolution involving federal employees who belong to a union.

collective bargaining: negotiations between an employer and a representative of organized employees concerning wages, hours, and other conditions of employment

See also: CIVIL SERVICE REFORM ACT; HATCH ACT; VETERANS PREFERENCE ACT OF 1944.

BIBLIOGRAPHY

Ingraham, Patricia W., and Carolyn Ban., eds. *Legislating Bureaucratic Change: The Civil Service Reform Act of 1978*. Albany: State University of New York Press, 1984.

Mosher, Frederick. *Democracy and the Public Service*. New York: Oxford University Press, 1968.

Pfiffner, James P., and Douglas A. Brook, eds. *The Future of Merit: Twenty Years After the Civil Service Reform Act*. Washington, DC: Woodrow Wilson Center Press and Baltimore, MD: Johns Hopkins University Press, 2000.

Van Riper, Paul. *History of the United States Civil Service*. Westport, CT: Greenwood Press, 1958.

CIVIL SERVICE REFORM ACT (1978)

Robert G. Vaughn

The Civil Service Reform Act (P.L. 95-454, 92 Stat. 111), the first comprehensive civil service law since 1883, fulfilled the campaign promise of President Jimmy Carter to reform the federal civil service. Along with Reorganization Plan Number 2, it abolished the Civil Service Commission and created three new agencies to implement these reforms: the United States Merit Systems Protection Board, the Office of Personnel Management, and the Federal Labor Relations Authority. Of particular concern were the problems of employees with poor job performance and the protection of federal employees who "blew the whistle" on government misconduct and fraud.

The legislation, however, contains two themes that at times are inconsistent with one another.

The legislation, however, contains two themes that at times are inconsistent with one another. First, the act seeks greater accountability of federal employees for their performance. It does so by increasing the discretion and authority of federal managers. The provisions related to job performance reflected public and congressional concerns about the performance of federal agencies. Second, the act emphasizes protection of the rights of federal employees from abuses by federal managers. This aspect of the act was a response to the constitutional crisis of the **Watergate** scandals and President Richard Nixon's abuse of the civil service system.

Watergate: the scandal following the break-in at the Democratic National Committee headquarters located in the Watergate apartment and office complex in Washington, D.C., in 1972

To increase the accountability of federal employees, the act gives federal managers and politically appointed officials greater control over personnel policy. The highest-ranking civil servants become part of a Senior Executive Service over which agency officials assert greater authority in assignment and pay. The act authorizes merit pay and bonuses that give senior officials greater control over middle-level managers. Under the act, pay, job retention, and discipline depend on job performance. In addition, the act increases the ability of each government agency to create its own standards and procedures within the framework of the act.

The discretion and authority of federal managers, however, can threaten the legitimate rights of federal employees. Congress believed that these rights ensured the impartiality of the civil service and helped to guarantee the rule of law. Thus the act increases protections for federal employees. It prohibits a number of personnel practices that constitute abuses of the personnel system, such as favoritism. But the most important provision protects federal employee "whistleblowers" who disclose information that they reasonably believe provides evidence of "a violation of law, rule or regulation, gross mismanagement, a gross waste of funds, an abuse of authority, or a specific and substantial danger to public health and safety."

adjudicate: to hear and settle a case by judicial procedure

The act provided a statutory basis for protections accorded to employees whom managers seek to discipline. It also created a quasijudicial agency, the United States Merit Systems Protection Board, to **adjudicate** appeals by disciplined employees. To help enforce the prohibitions against certain personnel practices, the act established an Office of Special Counsel with broad powers to investigate, adjudicate, and remedy violations of these provisions, including disciplinary actions against federal managers who commit such practices. Finally, the act supplies a statutory basis for labor relations in the federal sector and grants federal employee unions a number of rights to collective bargaining.

See also: CIVIL SERVICE ACTS; WHISTLEBLOWER PROTECTION LAWS.

BIBLIOGRAPHY

Ingraham, Particia W., and David H. Rosenbloom, eds. *The Promise and Paradox of Civil Service Reform.* Pittsburgh: University of Pittsburgh Press, 1992.

Vaughn, Robert G. *Merit Systems Protection Board: Rights and Remedies,* rev. ed. New York: Law Journal-Seminars Press, 2003.

CIVIL WAR PENSIONS

Norman Stein

The idea of veteran pensions is an old one, such pensions having been paid at least as far back as ancient Rome. In the United States, the first military pensions were paid to some disabled soldiers who fought in the Revolutionary War. This pension program was originally paid for and administered by the states, until the creation of the new federal government in 1789 when responsibility gradually shifted to the new central government. In 1818 pensions were extended to impecunious veterans who had served at least nine months in the military during the Revolution, and in 1832 to all remaining living veterans of the War. Military pensions were also paid to disabled veterans (and the families of slain officers) of the War of 1812, the U.S. Mexican War, and the Indian wars. Ultimately, pensions based on military service alone were awarded to veterans of each of these wars.

The pension program for Union veterans of the Civil War was different, from its origins to its expansion into a massive old age support system some social scientists argue had important implications for social insurance in the twentieth century. What originally began as a limited regime of protections for soldiers, widows, and orphans, eventually morphed into a system of old age pensions for almost one third of the elderly population. The various Pension Acts for veterans of the Civil War also affected a range of social, economic, and political institutions, including the institution of marriage, the ascendancy of the Republican party as the dominant political party for half a century, the size of the peacetime federal government, and in some ways the beginnings of a modern regulatory state. The pension system also reflected national issues of race and class.

In 1861, shortly after the Civil War began, Congress, in large part to attract recruits to the military, enacted legislation providing pensions for soldiers who suffered war-related disabilities, as well as the widows and orphans of soldiers killed in action. Congress amended the law in 1862 to provide a maximum pension of $8 per month for total disability, with proportionately reduced awards for partial disability.

The same award was made for widows and orphans, although amendments to the law increased the allowance to widows by $2 per dependent child. Where a veteran left no widow or children, the law provided benefits to dependent mothers or sisters, and eventually, if there were no dependent mother or sister, dependent fathers and brothers.

The law was amended repeatedly in the 1860s, 1870s, and 1880s. The amendments increased the generosity of the program, extended the program to veterans with disabilities that developed after the war but stemmed from wartime injuries, introduced finer distinctions between grades and specific types of disabilities, and tied the amount of the pension to the severity of the disability under this expanding matrix.

In 1890 Congress enacted a new law that paid pensions to any Union veteran of the Civil War who served for at least ninety days, was honorably discharged, and suffered from a disabili-

The idea of veteran pensions is an old one, such pensions having been paid at least as far back as ancient Rome.

In 1890 Congress enacted a new law that paid pensions to any Union veteran of the Civil War who served for at least ninety days, was honorably discharged, and suffered from a disability, even if not war-related.

ty, even if not war-related. In 1904 Theodore Roosevelt ruled that old age itself was a disability, basically transforming the system into a government pension system for all Civil War veterans. Three years later, in 1907, Congress legislatively endorsed this position in the Service and Age Act. Congress, in subsequent legislation during the first quarter of the twentieth century, increased pensions and tied the amount of the pension to the period of military service.

The last Civil War pensioner, Albert Woolson, who joined the Union Army as a seventeen-year-old in 1864, was collecting a monthly pension of $135.45 at the time of his death in 1956. And perhaps more remarkably, there were still nineteen dependents of Civil War veterans receiving benefits in the last years of the twentieth century. At its peak, the Civil War pension system consumed approximately 45 percent of all federal revenue and was the largest department of the federal government (other than the armed services). In addition, state pension systems were developed in the former Confederate states to provide pension and disability benefits to Confederate veterans.

For many historians and other social scientists, the Civil War pension system represents both a mirror of social and economic features of the United States between the Civil War and the turn of the century, and a bridge between an era of limited government and the regulatory state that emerged in the last seven decades of the twentieth century.

One question debated by historians is why the Civil War pension system expanded from a system of limited disability and survivor benefits into an old age entitlement program for Civil War veterans and dependent family members.

One question debated by historians is why the Civil War pension system expanded from a system of limited disability and survivor benefits into an old age entitlement program for Civil War veterans and dependent family members. Social scientists credit a number of reasons, but two seem most important: the first, was the political organizing ability of the veterans and their families, which emerged as special interest groups who engaged in lobbying and shaping public opinion. One of the groups, the Grand Army of the Republic, was national in scope and highly effective in advocating the interests of veterans and their families. The second reason was that the political parties competed for veteran votes and the Republican Party fashioned together a successful electoral coalition of Northern business interests and veterans of the Civil War.

The Civil War pension scheme attracted criticism in its time and after. The system attracted accusations of fraud and favoritism, bureaucratic incompetence, and class and racial bias. Some criticized veterans for greed and one of the enduring critiques of the program was that it transferred tax dollars to veterans regardless of need.

Theda Skocpal, a professor of sociology and political science at Harvard University, authored an important book that argued the Civil War pension system provided a structural model for a public system of old age support and also suggested that in the nineteenth and early twentieth centuries American citizens were willing to adopt a broad social insurance policy that veered from the liberal ideal of self-reliance and limited government. But Skocpal also argues that the Civil War pension system slowed U.S. progress toward adopting a comprehensive system of social insurance. Both public reaction to the shortcomings of the Civil War system and the cost of providing generous benefits aimed at a relatively narrow group of beneficiaries put the United States behind industrialized European nations in adopting social insurance schemes (and continues to leave Americans with a less comprehensive social insurance program).

The Civil War pension laws also created a large bureaucracy, of which doctors (who had to evaluate a veteran's disability) and lawyers (who were employed by claimants to contest denied claims) played an important part. Some scholars have suggested that this administrative system was an early harbinger of the modern regulatory state.

The Civil War pension legislation and its implementation provide insights into nineteenth century attitudes about race, class, disability, and family. Although the pension legislation was racially neutral and provided an important source of income to African American veterans and, as a result, contributed to the economic stability of some Northern African American communities, the administration of the pension laws also demonstrated racial bias, with African American veterans being denied benefits at greater rates than white veterans. Similarly, research suggests that officers and others of higher social class received preferential treatment. Interestingly, legal scholar Peter Blank has found that the pension administration favored some disabilities over others, and looked with relative disfavor at nervous disorders and infectious diseases. The pension system, by providing survivor benefits for widows and orphans, also led the government into defining what constituted acceptable families and gave government support to the idea of a nuclear family and traditional marriage.

> *The Civil War pension legislation and its implementation provide insights into nineteenth century attitudes about race, class, disability, and family.*

See also: BONUS BILL; VETERANS PREFERENCE ACT OF 1944.

BIBLIOGRAPHY

Blanck, Peter David, and Michael Millender. "Before Disability Civil Rights: Civil War Pensions and the Politics of Disability in America." In *Alabama Law Review* 52, no. 1 (2000).

Cott, Nancy. *Public Vows: A History of Marriage and the Nation*. Canbridge, MA: Harvard University Press, 2000.

Frankel, Noralee. "From Slave Women to Free Women: The National Archives and Black Women's History in the Civil War Era." Government Archives (1997). <http://www.archives.gov/publications/prologue/summer_1997_slave_women.html.>

Glasson, William H. *Federal Military Pensions in the United States,* ed. David Kinley. New York: Oxford University Press.

Linares, Claudia. "The Civil War Pension Law." University of Chicago (2001). <http://www.cpe.uchicago.edu/publication/lib/pension_cpe.pdf>.

Shaffer, Donald R. "An Ambiguous Victory: Black Civil War Veterans from a National Perspective." <http://uwadmnweb.uwyo.edu/dshaffer/Hist4450Spring2000/B-Vets/blackvets.htm>.

Skocpal, Theda. *Protecting Soldiers and Mothers: The Political Origins of Social Policy in the United States*. Cambridge, MA: Belknap Press.

CLAYTON ACT (1914)

Herbert Hovenkamp

The political seed for the Clayton Act (38 Stat. 730) was sown in the 1912 presidential election, a three-way contest between William Howard Taft, the incumbent Republican; Woodrow Wilson, the Democrat challenger; and Theodore Roosevelt, running for his old job on the Progressive Party, or "Bull Moose," ticket. All three parties believed that the Supreme Court had been far too lenient to large corporations and that antitrust laws needed to be strengthened. When Wilson won the election, he instructed Congress to work on new legislation, and the Clayton Act emerged two years later in 1914.

The principal provisions of the Clayton Act, which is far more detailed than the Sherman Act, the law it was meant to supplement, include (1) a prohibition on anticompetitive price discrimination; (2) a prohibition against certain tying and exclusive dealing practices; (3) an expanded power of private parties to sue and obtain treble (triple) damages; (4) a labor exemption that permitted union organizing; and (5) a prohibition against anticompetitive mergers.

PRICE DISCRIMINATION

Section 2 of the Clayton Act states that: "It shall be unlawful ... to discriminate in price between different purchasers of commodities ... where the effect of such discrimination may be to substantially lessen competition or tend to create a monopoly." The drafters of the Clayton Act believed that large firms such as Standard Oil perpetuated their **monopolies** by engaging in selective, or discriminatory predatory pricing. For example, Standard might be charging ten cents per gallon for its fuel oil in towns where it had a monopoly. It might then cut the price to below cost in a competitive town until it drove the competitors out of business, using the high profits from the monopoly towns to finance the below-cost prices in the competitive town. Section 2 was intended to prevent this strategy by forbidding Standard from charging two different prices in the two sets of town if the result was to extend Standard's monopoly.

The provision against predatory pricing was widely used through the 1960s to condemn this type of price discrimination. However, critics increasingly argued that the provision condemned hard competition and actually forced firms to charge more than they otherwise would. In *Brooke Group Ltd. v. Brown & Williamson Tobacco Co.* (1993), the Supreme Court developed strict standards for proving that price discrimination did in fact "substantially lessen competition." Since then, it has been almost impossible for plaintiffs to win any cases.

TYING AND EXCLUSIVE DEALING

Section 3 of the Clayton Act provides that: "It shall be unlawful ... to make a sale ... of goods ... on the condition ... that the ... purchaser ... shall not use or deal in the goods ... of a competitor ... where the effect ... may be to substantially lessen competition or tend to create a monopoly...." This provision of the Clayton Act was passed in response to the Supreme Court's decision in *Henry v. A.B. Dick & Co.* (1912). The Court had found no violation when A. B. Dick required users of its mimeograph machines (an early form of copy machine) to purchase all their paper and ink from that company as well. Congress believed that firms like A.B. Dick used such "tying arrangements" to expand one monopoly into two. In this case, the company already had a

monopoly: a market structure in which one or only a few firms dominate the total sales of a product or service

By some estimates there are as many as 700 antitrust cases filed in the United States every year.

monopoly on its patented mimeograph machine. By requiring everyone who used the machine to use its paper and ink, the company could also monopolize the market for paper and ink used in those machines.

Today most economists and others interested in antitrust law believe this practice is rarely competitively harmful. In fact, A.B. Dick may have had good reasons to tie paper and ink. For example, its machine might work better when its own paper and ink are used, making consumers happier. In its 1984 decision in *Jefferson Parish Hospital v. Hyde,* the Supreme Court made unlawful tying more difficult to prove. That case approved an arrangement under which the hospital required all surgical patients to use its own approved anesthesiology firm. Competition was not harmed, the Supreme Court concluded, because the hospital admitted only 30 percent of the patients in the area, meaning there was ample room for other anesthesiologists to practice their profession.

The other practice that section 3 of the Clayton Act occasionally condemns is exclusive dealing, which occurs when a firm insists that retailers handle its brand exclusively. In *Standard Oil of California v. United States* (1949), the Supreme Court found it unlawful for Standard to require its gasoline stations to sell Standard's gasoline exclusively. In more recent years we are inclined to think decisions like this are harmful, because they limit a manufacturer's power to control the quality of its products. For example, in *Krehl v. Baskin-Robbins Ice Cream Co.* (1982), the court held that Baskin-Robbins could require its stores to sell only Baskin-Robbins ice cream. Otherwise, customers might be deceived into buying cheaper brands when they thought they were getting the real thing. Today most, but not all, exclusive dealing is legal.

PRIVATE LAWSUITS

Both the United States government and individual states have the power to enforce antitrust laws. Yet 90 percent of lawsuits are brought by private parties such as consumers or business firms. Section 4 of the Clayton Act states: "any person who shall be injured in his business or property by reason of anything forbidden in the antitrust laws may sue therefore in any district court of the United States ... and shall recover threefold the damages by him sustained, and the cost of suit, including a reasonable attorney's fee." This provision creates a major inducement to sue because it means that a private plaintiff can obtain a damage award three times as large as the actual loss. Further, if the plaintiff wins, the defendant will have to pay the plaintiff's attorneys' fees.

For example, suppose that compact disc (CD) manufacturers fix the price of music CDs, including those that you buy, at $18. Price fixing is an automatic violation of section 1 of the Sherman Act. The lawyer managing this suit would probably bring a "class action" on behalf of thousands of people who paid too much for CDs. The lawyer would also hire an expert economist who would testify about the price of CDs in a competitive market. Suppose the jury accepted this expert's testimony that if the price fixing had not occurred the price of CDs would have been $15. In that case you are the victim of an "overcharge" equal to the difference between the cartel price and the competitive price, or $3. At that point you would have to show how many CDs you purchased during the cartel period. Suppose you had purchased twelve. Your "actual" injury would then be $3 times 12, or $36. However, under the antitrust laws this number would be trebled to $108.

Progressive Party of 1912

The Progressive Party of 1912 was founded by former members of the Republican Party who opposed the Republicans' presidential nominee, William Howard Taft, who they perceived as being too conservative and promoting business interests at the expense of the worker. The Progressives rallied their supporters around issues including tariffs, income tax, and conservation. Their first presidential candidate, Theodore Roosevelt, had already served as president from 1901 to 1909, first succeeding to the office after the assassination of William McKinley. On the Progressive ticket, Roosevelt received 25 percent of the popular vote, but the Democratic candidate, Woodrow Wilson, won the election. The Progressives did not field another presidential candidate until Senator Robert M. La Follette of Wisconsin in 1924. Basing his candidacy on some of the original platform, La Follette won 17 percent of the popular vote, with much of his support coming from antiestablishment organizations. After Calvin Coolidge, a probusiness Democrat, won the election, the Progressive Party collapsed. In 1948 the name was resurrected by an unrelated group that also espoused liberal causes.

One thing that surprised many Progressives in the United States was the degree to which the Supreme Court permitted use of the antitrust laws to break labor strikes.

Damages awards in antitrust cases can be very high, sometimes as much as $1 billion. This makes antitrust litigation very attractive to lawyers and explains why so many antitrust cases are filed. By some estimates there are as many as 700 antitrust cases filed in the United States every year.

THE LABOR EXEMPTION

Section 6 of the Clayton Act provides that: "The labor of a human being is not a commodity or article of commerce. Nothing contained in the antitrust laws shall be construed to forbid the existence and operation of labor ... organizations?; nor shall such organizations, or the members thereof, be held or construed to be illegal combinations or conspiracies in restraint of trade, under the antitrust laws."

One thing that surprised many Progressives in the United States was the degree to which the Supreme Court permitted use of the antitrust laws to break labor strikes. A labor strike is an agreement among laborers that they will not work unless they get paid a certain wage. Economically, this agreement is identical to a price fixing agreement in a product such as a CD. Because section 1 of the Sherman Act did not distinguish between price fixing in goods and price fixing in labor, the Supreme Court held that labor strikes were just as unlawful as cartels. (An example can be found in *Loewe v. Lawlor* [1908], known as the Danbury Hatters case.)

Section 6 was intended to change these outcomes by immunizing labor strikes from antitrust suits. The statute had to be strengthened by other legislation passed during the New Deal and after, but the ultimate outcome was that labor unions are free to organize and agree on a wage without violating the antitrust prohibition against price fixing.

MERGERS

Probably the most often used section of the Clayton Act is the prohibition of anticompetitive mergers. A merger occurs when one company buys another and the two firms become one. For example, Chrysler Motors at one point acquired Jeep, Inc. Later, Chrysler was itself acquired by Daimler-Benz, the maker of Mercedes-Benz automobiles. As a result, Mercedes-Benz cars, Jeeps, and Chrysler cars such as Dodge and Plymouth are all manufactured today by the same very large company.

Most mergers are legal, and in general economists think they benefit the economy by enabling manufacturers to produce or distribute goods more cheaply. A few mergers are anticompetitive, however. They might create a monopoly or make price fixing much easier than it was before the merger occurred. Section 7 of the Clayton Act provides: "No person engaged in commerce ... shall acquire ... the whole or any part of ... another person engaged also in commerce ... where in any line of commerce or in ... any section of the country, the effect of such acquisition may be substantially to lessen competition, or to tend to create a monopoly." The term "person" in this provision refers to a "legal" rather than a biological person. Legally, corporations are also treated as persons. As a result, the provision applies both

Most mergers are legal, and in general economists think they benefit the economy by enabling manufacturers to produce or distribute goods more cheaply. But some are anticompetitive, presenting the risk of monopoly or price fixing.

to firms owned by a single person but also to very large corporations. Only acquisitions involving fairly large firms, however, are typically found to be unlawful.

Mergers are unlawful when they either create a monopoly or make it much easier for the remaining firms in the market to fix prices. A good example is *Federal Trade Commission v. Heinz, Inc.* (2001), which prohibited a merger between two manufacturers of baby food. Gerber, Heinz, and Beech-Nut were the three major producers of baby food in the United States. Heinz offered to purchase Beech-Nut so the two would become a single firm. Under the law, large mergers have to be reported to the Department of Justice or the Federal Trade Commission, the two federal agencies that enforce the antitrust laws. In this case the Federal Trade Commission challenged the merger. The court accepted its evidence that with three firms in the market there was a significant amount of competition in the baby food market, and this tended to keep prices low. If the merger were permitted, the market would have only two firms and these would not compete as fiercely as firms in a three-firm market. As a result of the court's decision, Heinz abandoned the merger plans and the market continued to have three major baby food producers.

See also: FEDERAL TRADE COMMISSION ACT; SHERMAN ANTITRUST ACT.

BIBLIOGRAPHY

Chamberlain, John. *The Enterprising Americans: A Business History of the United States.* New York: Harper & Row, 1974.

Faulkner, Harold U. *American Economic History.* New York: Harper, 1960.

Hovenkamp, Herbert. *Federal Antitrust Policy: The Law of Competition and Its Practice,* 2d ed. St. Paul, MN: West Group, 1999.

Sklar, Martin J. *The Corporate Reconstruction of American Capitalism, 1890–1916.* Cambridge, UK: Cambridge University Press, 1988.

Excerpt from Clayton Act Defining the Term "Person"

Title 15, Chapter 1, Section 12:

The word "person" or "persons" wherever used in this Act shall be deemed to include corporations and associations existing under or authorized by the laws of either the United States, the laws of any of the Territories, the laws of any State, or the laws of any foreign country.

CLEAN AIR ACT (1963)

Craig Oren

Excerpt from the Clean Air Act

(1) to protect and enhance the quality of the Nation's air resources so as to promote the public health and welfare and the productive capacity of its population;

(2) to initiate and accelerate a national research and development program to achieve the prevention and control of air pollution;

(3) to provide technical and financial assistance to State and local governments in connection with the development and execution of their air pollution prevention and control programs; and

(4) to encourage and assist the development and operation of regional air pollution prevention and control programs.

The Clean Air Act (P.L. 88-206 77, Stat. 401) established a program to help clean up dirty air and to maintain clean air. Congress extended its efforts to remedy and prevent air pollution in the Clean Air Act Amendments of 1970, whose provisions form the basics of today's air pollution standards. Congress amended the 1963 act out of concern that, without stricter standards, the air quality in our nation's cities would never be improved to healthful levels. At the time there was also a great deal of public concern about air pollution. Senator Edmund Muskie, a prime sponsor of the 1970 amendments, stated: "Our responsibility is to establish what the public interest requires to protect the health of persons. This may mean that people and industries will be asked to do what seems to be impossible at the present time." President Richard Nixon also pushed for improvements to the Clean Air Act. In fact, the president and Senator Muskie competed to see who could offer a stricter version of the amendments. As a result, the 1970 amendments established stringent deadlines for the achievement of air quality standards, as well as deadlines for auto manufacturers to produce cars with dramatically reduced pollutants in their emissions.

The 1970 amendments established stringent deadlines for the achievement of air quality standards, as well as deadlines for auto manufacturers to produce cars with dramatically reduced pollutants in their emissions.

FEATURES OF THE ACT

Under the act, the Environmental Protection Agency (EPA) sets "national ambient air quality standards" (NAAQS). These standards limit the allowable concentrations of pollutants in the outdoor air. There are presently standards for carbon monoxide, lead, nitrogen dioxide, ozone, particulate matter, and sulfur oxide. The EPA sets both primary and secondary ambient air quality standards; primary standards protect the public health with an adequate margin of safety, and secondary standards protect public welfare. Neither kind of standard can be based on cost considerations.

The act requires each state to submit a State Implementation Plan (SIP) showing how it will limit emissions from sources of air pollution. The state must demonstrate that its plan will result in attainment of the primary standards by a specific deadline, and of the secondary standards "as expeditiously as possible." Generally, a state may pick any mix of emission control measures that would result in attainment and maintenance on time. Each major source of air pollution receives a permit containing the measures that apply to it. States can, in general, choose to be stricter than the Clean Air Act.

Under the act, the federal government sets emission standards for categories of new motor vehicles. Congress has sometimes set these standards itself, and has sometimes directed the EPA to set them. (California has the authority to set its own standards and other states can adopt them rather than follow the federal standards.) These standards are based on the emission levels the EPA projects can be achieved by vehicle manufacturers after a period of lead time. In addition to standards for motor vehicles, the EPA sets performance standards for categories of new and modified stationary sources of pollutants, such as new power plants. These standards are based on assessments of what is technologically feasible using the best system of emissions reduction.

Each state's plan must also include a Prevention of Significant Deterioration (PSD) program to protect areas whose air quality is better than the levels of the NAAQS. A major stationary source can be constructed or modified in such an area only if the operator (a) installs the best available control technology to minimize pollutants, and (b) shows the source will not cause a violation of "increments" that limit increases in air pollution in clean air areas.

States must also impose requirements on the construction and modification of a major stationary source that would cause or contribute to a violation of the NAAQS. The new source must be subject to strict controls, and the new source's emissions must be offset by extra reductions at other sources.

Another provision of the act attempts to deal with the interstate transport of air pollution. For instance, the act requires power plants to reduce emissions of sulfates that can cause acid rain as well as reduced visibility and damage to human health. Each plant is assigned a set of allowances for sulfur dioxide. Plants that can reduce emissions at low cost can over control their emissions and sell excess allowances to plants that cannot reduce at low cost. In this way, the emission target can be met at the lowest possible cost.

Clouds of pollutants surround this United Steel Corporation coke plant even though it had been previously cited for violation of the Clean Air Act. The act dates back to 1963 but the basics of today's act were established in the Clean Air Act Amendments of 1970. Under the act, the EPA sets "national ambient air quality standards." These standards limit the allowable concentrations of pollutants in the outdoor air. Each state must submit a State Implementation Plan (SIP) showing how it will limit emissions from sources of air pollution and include a Prevention of Significant Deterioration (PSD) program to protect areas whose air quality is better than the levels of the national ambient air quality standards. (US NATIONAL ARCHIVES AND RECORDS ADMINISTRATION)

For instance, the act requires power plants to reduce emissions of sulfates that can cause acid rain, reduced visibility, and damage to human health.

The act also attempts to reduce emissions of air pollutants that may cause cancer or other life threatening diseases. The EPA sets standards that compel new and existing major sources of these pollutants to do the utmost to control their emissions. The EPA must set additional, stricter standards if a risk to public health remains.

JUDICIAL REVIEW

In *South Terminal v. EPA* (1973), the U.S. Court of Appeals held that the constitutional basis for the act is Congress's power to regulate interstate commerce, because air pollution and some of its sources (like motor vehicles) move across state borders. Several important judicial decisions have interpreted the act:

(1) In *Sierra Club v. Ruckelshaus* (1972), the federal district court in the District of Columbia held that the EPA could not approve state plans unless those plans called for the protection of existing clean air from degradation. This led to the PSD program mentioned above.

(2) In *Ethyl Corp. v. EPA* (1976), the U.S. Court of Appeals for the District of Columbia Circuit held that the EPA could regulate a substance even though it could not be proved that the substance was harmful. The court said the EPA could proceed if it could show a significant risk of harm. The ruling in this case has been incorporated in the Clean Air Act.

(3) In *Union Electric v. EPA* (1976), the U.S. Supreme Court held that states may require air pollution sources to achieve tough emission limits, even if the technology does not presently exist to achieve those limits.

(4) In *Whitman v. American Trucking Associations* (2001), the Supreme Court held that the EPA may not consider costs in setting ambient air quality standards, and that the act's command that primary standards be set to protect public health with an adequate margin of safety gives the EPA sufficient direction in setting these standards.

FURTHER AMENDMENTS

In 1977 Congress passed a lengthy series of amendments that extended the original deadlines for areas to attain air quality standards but at the same time required more intensive efforts to attain those standards. The amendments also extended the deadlines for auto manufacturers to produce cleaner vehicles, and established the PSD program.

Congress passed an even longer series of amendments in 1990. These amendments again extended deadlines to attain air quality standards in exchange for greater efforts to attain those standards. The amendments further established the act's current programs to combat acid rain and hazardous air pollutants, and tightened the standards for new motor vehicles.

If a source does not obey the emission limits set in an approved SIP, then the state, the federal government, or citizens can enforce the limit.

ENFORCEMENT

If a source does not obey the emission limits set in an approved SIP, then the state, the federal government, or citizens can enforce the limit. If a state does not establish an SIP, or refuses to carry it out, the federal government can establish and enforce its own plan for the state.

Since 1970 there have been drastic reductions in emissions of most air pollutants. These reductions are especially remarkable considering that the nation's national economic product, as well as the number of vehicle miles traveled in the nation, have doubled since that year. Although important air quality problems remain, an increasing number of areas have come into compliance with the EPA's ambient air quality standards. The EPA estimates that the monetary benefits of controlling air pollution have greatly outweighed its costs.

See also: NATIONAL EMISSIONS STANDARDS ACT; NATIONAL ENVIRONMENTAL POLICY ACT.

BIBLIOGRAPHY

Doland, Edward F. *Our Poisoned Sky.* New York: Cobblehill Books, 1991.

Gay, Kathlyn. *Air Pollution.* New York: F. Watts, 1991.

INTERNET RESOURCE

Environmental Protection Association. <http://www.epa.gov/students/air.htm>.

COINAGE ACT OF 1792

Lawrence H. Officer

The Coinage Act of 1792 (P.L. 2–16, 1 Stat. 246) was Congress's first use of its constitutional power regarding coinage and money. Congress faced four major problems. First, there was no common system of monetary accounting in the new nation. Each state, as a colony, had created its own unit of account, based on the British system of pounds, shillings, and pence, that it continued to use—doubly unacceptable to the newly constituted nation.

Second, the medium of exchange (money used in transactions) was the Spanish dollar, a silver coin. The difference between the unit of account and medium of exchange was tremendously inconvenient. Third, a variety of other coins—both gold and silver—circulated. So the monetary relationship of gold to silver needed to be established. Fourth, these coins were all foreign: A domestically-produced coinage would be a hallmark of independence.

The provisions of the Coinage Act were based on a report prepared by Alexander Hamilton, secretary of the treasury. Hamilton suggested coinage that implicitly adopted a decimal system of account: the dollar, "tenth part" of the dollar, and "hundredth part" of the dollar. The Coinage Act provided that "the money of account of the United States shall be expressed in dollars or units, dismes or tenths, cents or hundredths, and milles or thousandths." Concretely, "all accounts in the public offices and all proceedings in the courts of the United States shall be kept and had in conformity to this regulation." Thus a decimal monetary system was created—the first in history for any country! The private sector followed the official shift to a decimal system of accounting within a decade.

> The Coinage Act of 1792 was Congress's first use of its constitutional power regarding coinage and money.

Although the bimetallic standard worked initially, it lost effectiveness when the market ratio differed from the legal ratio.

Only with the Act of 1857 was the legal tender of foreign coins finally terminated.

Hamilton advocated a bimetallic standard, using both gold and silver coins. He observed that merchants valued the Spanish dollar at 24.75 grains of pure gold (a grain is 1/437.5th of the customary ounce), and he measured the average amount of silver in the Spanish dollar as approximately 371.25 grains. Following common practice in other countries, he suggested fineness of 11/12th for the coins, meaning alloy of 1/12th. The gross weight of the gold dollar would be 27 grains, and the silver dollar 405 grains. Hamilton recommended minting a $10 gold piece, called the "eagle" in the Coinage Act. The act also authorized coinage of half-eagles and quarter-eagles, as well as silver half-dollars and quarter-dollars. Hamilton's plan involved coinage of a gold dollar—wisely rejected by Congress, as this coin would have been very small.

The most ill-advised deviation of Congress from Hamilton's report was to legislate a gross weight of 416 grains for the silver dollar, implying a fineness of 1485/1664th (slightly less than 11/12th). The cumbersome fineness arose because the amount of pure silver in the Spanish dollar had been reduced below its legal standard of 11/12th, but the U.S. dollar was to be based on that coin. Hamilton's solution was a smaller coin; Congress opted for a lower fineness. The clumsy fineness led to technical problems at the mint and required correction in subsequent legislation.

The ratio of pure silver to pure gold (by weight) in the dollar was 15 to 1, recommended by Hamilton because this legal gold/silver price ratio was consistent with the relative market valuation of the two metals at the time. Although the bimetallic standard worked initially, it lost effectiveness when the market ratio differed from the legal ratio. Later legislation addressed this problem.

Consistent with bimetallism, Congress authorized "free coinage" of both gold and silver, meaning that anyone could bring either gold or silver bullion to the mint to be coined. Much later, free coinage of silver became a troublesome political issue. Also, all gold and silver coins were made full legal tender, meaning they had to be accepted in payment of a monetary obligation in any amount. The problem with this provision was that fractional coins (below a dollar) could all be lost should bimetallism be thwarted by a changed market ratio. Further Congressional action was needed to remedy this problem.

Finally, while the Coinage Act of 1792 established a U.S. mint, only foreign coins were circulating in the country. Hamilton recommended that foreign coins be permitted to circulate for just a three-year period. However, a number of subsequent Congressional acts continued the legal-tender status of foreign coins long beyond Hamilton's suggested period. Only with the Act of 1857 was the legal tender of foreign coins finally terminated.

See also: BANK OF THE UNITED STATES; BLAND-ALLISON ACT; COINAGE ACTS; FEDERAL RESERVE ACT OF 1913; GOLD STANDARD ACT OF 1900.

BIBLIOGRAPHY

Carothers, Neil. *Fractional Money*. New York: John Wiley, 1930.

Nussbaum, Arthur. *Money in the Law: National and International*. Brooklyn, NY: Foundation Press, 1950.

Nussbaum, Arthur. *A History of the Dollar.* New York: Columbia University Press, 1957.

Officer, Lawrence H. *Between the Dollar-Sterling Gold Points.* Cambridge, MA: Cambridge University Press, 1996.

COINAGE ACTS

Lawrence H. Officer

The Coinage Act of 1873 (P.L. 42-131, 17 Stat. 424) comprehensively revised and rewrote the existing laws regarding mint and coinage issues. The important sections of the act of 1873 concerned gold and silver coinage, the basis of the monetary standard of the United States at the time. The act has a legislative history that dates to the Coinage Act of 1792, and it led eventually to the enactment of the Gold Standard Act of 1900.

For a country to be considered to be on metal standard, whether gold, silver, or bimetallic—using both gold and silver—its mint must issue coins.

LEGISLATIVE HISTORY OF GOLD AND SILVER COINS

For a country to be considered to be on metallic standard, whether gold, silver, or bimetallic—using both gold and silver—the first principle is that its mint must issue coins. The Authority for Gold and Silver Coinage, 1792–1875 table details laws that authorized U.S. coins between 1792 and 1875. Two features are of note. First, the least valuable gold coin was worth one dollar, and the most valuable silver coin also was worth one dollar. As gold was (and still is) much more valuable per ounce than silver, a silver coin worth more than one dollar would have been too large for practical use, and a gold coin worth less than a dollar would have been too small. Second, the Act of 1873 eliminated three existing coins made of silver, of which the silver dollar was the most important, and created a "trade-dollar," a special silver dollar coin to be used in international trade.

Authority for Gold and Silver Coinage, 1792–1875

Authorizing Act	Silver Coins	Gold Coins
1792, P.L. 2–16, 1 Stat. 246	dollar[a], half-dollar, quarter dollar, dime, half dime[a]	eagle[b], half-eagle, quarter eagle
1849, P.L. 30–109, 9 Stat. 397		gold dollar[c,d,] double-eagle[e]
1851, P.L. 31–20, 9 Stat. 587	three cents[a]	
1853, P.L. 32–79, 10 Stat. 160		three dollars[d]
1873, P.L. 42–131, 17 Stat. 424	trade-dollar[f]	
1875, P.L. 43–143, 18 Stat. 478	twenty cents[g]	

[a]Discontinued by Coinage Act of 1873.
[b]Ten-dollar piece.
[c]Renamed one-dollar piece in Coinage Act of 1873.
[d]Discontinued by Act of 1890 (P.L. 51–945, 26 Stat. 485).
[e]Twenty-dollar piece.
[f]Intended for use only in international transactions. Discontinued by Act of 1887 (P.L. 49–396, 24 Stat. 634).
[g]Discontinued by Act of 1878 (P.L. 45–79, 20 Stat. 47).

A second important consideration is that the coins issued must be accepted and satisfy the owner's monetary obligations, whatever the amount. The

Legal-Tender Power of Gold and Silver Coin, 1792–1875 table shows that from 1792 to 1875, gold coins could satisfy unlimited financial obligation (had "unlimited legal-tender power"); whereas after 1853, silver coins other than a silver dollar could only satisfy obligations up to five dollars (possessed only "limited legal-tender power"). While The Coinage Act of 1873 essentially did not address this issue, a revised statute the next year also limited the standard silver dollar to a value of five dollars as legal tender.

Legal-Tender Power of Gold and Silver Coin, 1792–1875

Authorizing Act	Silver Coins		Gold Coins	
	Coins	Payments[a]	Coins	Payments[a]
1792, P.L. 2–16, 1 Stat. 246	all	unlimited[b]	all	unlimited[b]
1834, P.L. 23–95, 4 Stat. 699			all	unlimited[b]
1837, P.L. 24–3, 5 Stat. 136	all	unlimited	all	unlimited
1849, P.L. 30–109, 9 Stat. 397			double-eagle, gold dollar	unlimited
1851, P.L. 31–20, 9 Stat. 587	three cents	30 cents		
1853, P.L. 32–79, 10 Stat. 160	half-dollar, quarter dollar, dime, half dime	five dollars	three dollars	unlimited
1873, P.L. 42–131, 17 Stat. 424	trade-dollar[c], half-dollar, quarter-dollar, dime	five dollars	all	unlimited[d]
1874, P.L. 43–333, 18 Stat. 113[e]	all[f]	five dollars	all	unlimited[d]
1875, P.L. 43–143, 18 Stat. 478	twenty cents	five dollars		

[a]Limit, if any.
[b]Coins less that full weight at values proportional to their actual weights.
[c]Legal tender eliminated in 1876 (J.R. 44-17, 19 Stat. 215).
[d]Coins less than standard weight and limit of tolerance at valuation proportional to their actual weights.
[e]Leading to 1874, 43-3586, Rev. Stat. 708.
[f]Including dollar.

A third element of a coin standard is that there be "free coinage," meaning that any private party may bring gold or silver in large quantities to the mint to be coined, and receive the coin or money equivalent. The Freedom of Coinage, 1792–1873 table shows that free coinage for gold was always available from 1792 to 1873 (and in fact until the United States abandoned the gold standard in 1933). However, free coinage for silver coins less than a dollar ended in 1853, and the Act of 1873 ended free coinage of the standard silver dollar. It was never restored.

Freedom of Coinage, 1792–1873

Authorizing Act	Silver	Gold
1792, P.L. 2–16, 1 Stat. 246	all	all
1837, P.L. 24–3, 5 Stat. 136	all	all
1853, P.L. 32–79, 10 Stat. 160	silver dollar only	
1873, P.L. 42–131, 17 Stat. 424	trade-dollar only	all

The "fine weight" of a coin is the amount of the pure metal (either gold or silver) that it contains. The "standard fineness" is the percentage of the coin's weight consisting of the pure metal, the remainder being essentially a worthless alloy. The "standard weight" is the total weight of the coin (pure metal plus alloy). The Legal Gold and Silver Value of Dollar, 1792–1873 table lists the legislated fine and standard weights of the gold and silver dollar from 1792 to 1873. The table also shows the legal gold/silver price ratio (number of ounces of silver compared to ounces of gold in a coin), the "mint ratio." Not shown is the fineness, which is 1485/1664 and 11/12 for gold and silver coins, respectively (Act of 1792), 116/129 for gold coin (Act of 1834), and 9/10 for gold and silver coins (Acts of 1837 and 1873).

Legal Gold and Silver Value of Dollar, 1792–1873

| | Weight of Dollar (grains[a]) | | | | |
| | Silver | | Gold | | Gold/Silver |
Authorizing Act	Fine	Standard	Fine	Standard	Price Ratio[b]
1792, P.L. 2–16, 1 Stat. 246	371.25	416	24.75[c]	27[c]	15.0000
1834, P.L. 23–95, 4 Stat. 699			23.2[c]	25.8[c]	16.0022
1837, P.L. 24–3, 5 Stat. 136	371.25	412.5	23.22[c]	25.8[c]	15.9884
1873, P.L. 42–131, 17 Stat. 424	378[d]	420[d]	23.22	25.8	—

[a]Under the customary "avoirdupois" measurement system (16 ounces = 1 pound), 1 ounce = 437.5 grains.
[b]Ratio of fine-silver to fine-gold content of dollar, when both gold and silver are unlimited legal tender.
[c]Inferred as one-tenth weight of eagle ($10 gold piece).
[d]Trade-dollar, limited legal tender.

All of the coins worth less than one dollar—called fractional coins—were made of silver. Fractional coins were much more important in the nineteenth century than today, because prices were so much lower. In fact, retail transactions were conducted largely with such coins. The Fine-Silver Content of Fractional Coin, 1792–1875 table summarizes the legislated fine-metal content of such coin compared to the standard silver dollar. Until the Act of 1853, the relative value (the fine-weight to total-weight ratio) of fractional silver coins (except for the three-cent coin) was the same as the silver dollar. The Act of 1853 reduced the ratio, thus overvaluing fractional coins relative to the dollar. The Act of 1873 slightly increased this ratio for fractional coins.

> *Fractional coins, coins worth less than one dollar, were much more important in the nineteenth century than today, because retail transactions were conducted largely with such coins.*

Fine-Silver Content of Fractional Coin, 1792–1875

Authorizing Act	Coins	Divergence from Silver Dollar
1792, P.L. 2–16, 1 Stat. 246	all	zero
1837, P.L. 24–3, 5 Stat. 136	all	zero
1851, P.L. 31–20, 9 Stat. 587	three cents	−16.67 percent
1853, P.L. 32–79, 10 Stat. 160	all except three cents	−6.91 percent
1853, P.L. 32–96, 10 Stat. 181	three cents	−6.91 percent
1873, P.L. 42–131, 17 Stat. 424	all except twenty cents	−6.47 percent
1875, P.L. 43–143, 18 Stat. 478	twenty cents	−6.47 percent

EFFECTS OF COINAGE LEGISLATION

Legally, the Coinage Acts of 1792 and 1837 placed the United States on a bimetallic (gold and silver) standard, and all other amendments until 1853 were consistent with this standard. However, a bimetallic standard is inherently unstable, because the mint ratio (the ratio of value of gold to value of silver in coins set by legislation) can differ from the world market ratio (the ratio of the market value of gold to the market value of silver). Private parties melted down the undervalued coins, and sold the metal on the free market—realizing a profit they coined the "overvalued" metal at the mint and used it for domestic money. In the early 1790s the mint ratio of 15:1 (gold being worth fifteen times more per ounce than silver) was close to the market ratio; but the market ratio increased (gold becoming even more valuable relative to silver) so that by the turn of the nineteenth century, with gold undervalued at the mint, gold-coin was melted down and ceased to circulate, while silver (overvalued at the mint) was coined and circulated domestically: the United States was on an effective silver standard.

The Coinage Act of 1834 increased the mint ratio sufficiently so that the relationship between legal and market ratio was reversed. Overvalued gold drove out silver coins; but the situation did not become that bad for fractional silver coin (because of the expense in collecting and processing a given dollar value of such coins, compared to the silver dollar) until Australian and Californian gold discoveries greatly increased world gold production in the late-1840s, reducing the market ratio and enhancing the legal overvaluation of gold. It then became profitable even to ship fractional coin abroad, and retail trade suffered.

The impact of the gold dollar, authorized in the Coinage Act of 1849, was minimal, because its small size made the coin unpopular and its denomination was too high to complete most retail trades. More effective was the three-cent silver piece authorized by the Postage Act of 1851. This was the first U.S. subsidiary silver coin, meaning that its legal (denominational) value was higher than its intrinsic (metallic) value. Such overvaluation protected silver coins from being melted into bullion and/or exported, even in the face of a favorable (low) market gold/silver price ratio. The Secretary of the Treasury enhanced the overvaluation of the coin by interpreting the act as if it included essentially free coinage: the mint allowed private parties freely to exchange any U.S. gold or silver coin for the new piece (in lots of 100 coins worth $3.00). Though a temporary success, the coin was too small in size (the smallest coin ever to circulate in the United States) and too low a denomination to solve the "small-change" shortage.

The Coinage Act of 1873, in eliminating the free coinage of silver, added to the upward pressure on the price of gold emanating from other countries adopting the gold standard and a smaller increase of gold output.

The Coinage Act of 1853 provided the solution by making subsidiary all fractional silver from the half-dime to the half-dollar. Though free coinage was expressly forbidden, the act authorized the mint to purchase bullion to produce the coins and to exchange them (in lots of $100) for gold coin. The three-dollar gold coin, authorized in the same act, was an odd denomination, never popular, and only a small number were ever issued.

deflation: a general decline in prices of goods and services

The Coinage Act of 1873, in eliminating the free coinage of silver, added to the upward pressure on the price of gold emanating from other countries adopting the gold standard and a smaller increase of gold output. Nobel Laureate Milton Friedman believes that **deflation** and financial panics resulted from the adoption of the act, and that legal bimetallism, involving an alternating effective gold or silver standard, would have provided greater economic stability in subsequent decades.

RATIONALES FOR COINAGE LEGISLATION

A mint ratio of 16:1 (gold to silver) in the Coinage Act of 1834 was suddenly, at the end of the legislative process, included in the bill as a substitute for the original ratio of 15.625 (one much closer to the market rate). Several reasons for this shift have been offered: (1) to bring about an effective gold standard, desired by eastern businesses and commercial interests; (2) to enhance profits from gold production, thereby assisting gold-mining companies in southern states; (3) to help destroy the Second Bank of the United States, by substituting gold coin for its notes, in response to pressure from President Andrew Jackson and his allies.

It is thought that the gold coin's unwieldy fineness (116/129) resulted from this hurried amendment procedure. Combined with the fineness of silver coins (1485/1664) prescribed in the 1792 Coinage Act, the legislated proportion of alloy in coin was inconvenient for the mint to produce. The Act of 1837 provided a fineness of 9/10, thus correcting an arithmetic difficulty—an unusual reason for any legislation.

The one-dollar gold piece authorized by the Coinage Act of 1849 was an attempt to provide a substitute for vanishing fractional silver coins. The three-cent silver piece authorized by the Postage Act of 1851 was intended simply to make it convenient to purchase the three-cent postage stamp legislated by that act (replacing the five-cent rate). Unintentionally, the coin helped fulfill the need for a fractional coinage.

The rationale for the Coinage Act of 1853 is controversial. One interpretation is that the purpose of the act was simply to render a proper subsidiary coinage, which it indeed accomplished; and also formal bimetallism was preserved. Another view is that the reduction of fractional silver to subsidiary status with restricted legal-tender power was a move toward adoption of the gold standard. That the standard silver dollar was left unaffected by the act mitigates against the latter interpretation, although it is also possible that the silver dollar was unmentioned because it was virtually unknown (none had been coined from 1806 to 1835, and few thereafter issued compared to the half-dollar).

Because the Coinage Act of 1873 discontinued coinage of the silver dollar, it is viewed by many as the formal end of bimetallism in the United States. An alternative interpretation is that omission of the silver dollar merely modified the coinage law to reflect the reality that the coin had not been in circulation for many years. Indeed, historians have described the silver dollar as a coin unknown to most Americans at the time.

> *Because the Coinage Act of 1873 discontinued coinage of the silver dollar, it is viewed by many as the formal end of bimetallism in the United States.*

Subsequent to the 1873 act, bimetallism supporters (and silver producers, who found they could no longer have their bullion coined) argued that the act was the "Crime of 1873"—the result of a conspiracy against silver and bimetallism. Modern scholars believe that accusation to be absurd; but scholars generally agree that proponents of the bill feared that an effective silver standard would result from continuing free silver coinage in the face of an imminent decline in the market price of silver (increase in the market gold/silver price ratio). Some think that most members of Congress were ignorant of the intricacies and implications of the 1873 act; but it has been pointed out that this was probably true for all the coinage laws and all complex legislation.

The Act of 1873 left undisturbed the full legal-tender power of existing silver dollars. The general revision of all statutes adopted in 1874 implicitly included the silver dollar in the restricted legal tender of "all" silver coins (see the Legal-Tender Power of Gold and Silver Coin, 1792–1875 table). It was this 1874 revision that accomplished the true demonetization of silver and thereby placed the country on a legal gold standard. Whether the revision respected the intent of Congress manifested in the Act of 1873 depends on whether the omission of silver-dollar coinage in the act was deliberate or intentional.

See also: BLAND-ALLISON ACT; COINAGE ACT OF 1792; GOLD STANDARD ACT OF 1900

BIBLIOGRAPHY

Carothers, Neil. *Fractional Money.* New York: John Wiley, 1930.

Friedman, Milton. "The Crime of 1873." *Journal of Political Economy* 98, no. 6 (1990): 1159–1194.

Friedman, Milton, and Anna Jacobson Schwartz. *A Monetary History of the United States, 1867-1960.* Princeton, NJ: Princeton University Press, 1963.

Laughlin, J. Laurence. *The History of Bimetallism in the United States.* New York: D. Appleton, 1900.

Officer, Lawrence H. *Between the Dollar-Sterling Gold Points.* Cambridge, MA: Cambridge University Press, 1996.

Weinstein, Allen. "Was There a 'Crime of 1873'? The Case of the Demonetized Dollar." *Journal of American History* 54, no. 2 (1967): 307-326.

COMMODITY EXCHANGE ACT (1936)

Jerry W. Markham

The Commodity Exchange Act (P.L. 74-765, 49 Stat. 149) is the successor to earlier legislation that had proved ineffective in stopping the manipulation of commodity prices. Although the Commodity Exchange Act was itself later found to be a flawed mechanism for regulating the commodity markets (and was supplemented by legislation in the 1970s), it has played an important historical role.

Prior to the act's adoption in 1936, Congress had adopted the Futures Trading Act of 1921, which required all commodity futures trading to be conducted on an exchange licensed as a contract market by the federal government. This requirement was designed to allow federal scrutiny of the trading of commodity futures and to stop the so-called "bucket shops" that were essentially betting parlors for speculation in commodity prices.

After World War I, the U.S. agricultural sector experienced a recession. That economic downturn was blamed, in part, on speculative excesses occurring in the trading of commodity futures. The Futures Trading Act was the result of a massive investigation of the grain trade by the Federal Trade Commission (FTC) conducted in the wake of the recession. The FTC's massive report found that many abuses were occurring in the industry. Congress confirmed that finding in its own hearings on the Futures Trading Act.

In 1922, in *Hill v. Wallace*, the Supreme Court declared the Futures Trading Act unconstitutional because it was improperly based on the taxing powers of Congress. A manipulation in grain prices that occurred just after this Supreme Court finding spurred the reenactment of the Futures Trading Act, with a different name, under the commerce powers of Congress. The new act, called the Grain Futures Act, was held to be constitutional by the Supreme Court in *Chicago Board of Trade v. Olsen* (1923).

Commodity prices declined dramatically during the **Great Depression**, which followed the stock market crash of 1929. Newly elected President Franklin D. Roosevelt requested legislation for the regulation of securities and commodity futures as a part of his **New Deal** reforms. The commodity futures legislation, however, took a route different from that of the federal securities laws because the agriculture committees in Congress, rather than the banking committees, had jurisdiction over the exchanges that traded futures contracts. During the hearing on this legislation, Congress found numerous abuses, including what were described as speculative "orgies" and manipulations by large speculators that were thought to be driving down commodity prices.

One of the more rapacious of these speculators was Arthur Cutten, a Chicago trader who was responsible for several massive attacks on the commodity markets before moving to New York. There he became equally famous for his manipulations of the securities markets. A sensational price collapse in wheat and corn in 1933 on the Chicago Board of Trade and a dramatic drop in cotton prices in 1935 overcame industry resistance to legislative reforms, allowing the adoption of the Commodity Exchange Act in 1936.

GOALS AND FUNCTIONS OF THE ACT

The Commodity Exchange Act prohibited the manipulation of commodity futures prices and carried forward the requirement contained in the 1922 Grain Futures Act that commodity futures trading on "regulated" commodities be traded only on licensed contract markets. Fraud was prohibited and brokerage firms handling customer orders (referred to in the industry as "futures commission merchants") were required to register with the federal government. The Commodity Exchange Act was to be administered by a Commodity Exchange Commission composed of the attorney general and the secretaries of agriculture and commerce, a structure carried over from the Grain Futures Act.

Day-to-day regulatory responsibility was delegated to the Grain Futures Administration, later renamed the Commodity Exchange Authority, a bureau within the Department of Agriculture. Unlike the legislation adopted in the securities industry, no authority was given to the government to control the level of margins in the futures industry. Rather, the government was given the authority to limit the size of speculative positions by individual traders or those acting in concert with each other. The Commodity Exchange Act also sought to stop commodity options trading on regulated commodities because such instruments were viewed to be highly speculative.

The Futures Trading Act was the result of a massive investigation of the grain trade by the Federal Trade Commission (FTC) conducted in the wake of the recession.

Great Depression: the longest and most severe economic depression in American history (1929–1939); its effects were felt throughout the world

New Deal: the legislative and administrative program of President Franklin D. Roosevelt designed to promote economic recovery and social reform during the 1930s

A flaw in the act's provisions allowed the trading of options and futures on unregulated commodities, in other words, those not listed in the Commodity Exchange Act.

EXPERIENCE UNDER THE ACT

The Commodity Exchange Act did not prove to be effective in stopping either manipulations or speculative abuses. A flaw in its provisions allowed the trading of options and futures on unregulated commodities, in other words, those not listed in the Commodity Exchange Act. The act could not be amended rapidly enough to keep up with the expansion of trading in options and futures on those unregulated commodities. This led to large losses in the early 1970s, when unregulated commodity options firms collapsed, causing losses to many unsophisticated customers. A large run-up in commodity prices during that period also raised

Key Financial Terms for the Commodity Exchange Act

Jerry W. Markham

Commodity A commodity is defined under the Commodity Exchange Act of 1936 to include every item on which futures trading may be conducted, except onions (trading on onions is not permitted because of prior difficulties with that commodity). A commodity will include such things as interest rates and stock prices, as well as traditional commodities such as wheat and soybeans.

Futures A futures contract is a derivation of two more basic forms of contracts: cash and forward contracts. A cash (or "actual" transaction) is one for immediate payment and delivery. A forward contract calls for the delivery of the commodity at a future date. The forward contract is individually negotiated in all of its terms, including price, delivery date, grade of the commodity and its delivery point. The futures contract is like a forward contract except that all of its terms are standardized other than price, which is individually negotiated through an auction process on the floor of a commodity exchange.

Exchange and Contract Market A commodity exchange (also called a board of trade) is a centralized market where trading in futures contracts takes place. A contract market is a commodity exchange that is licensed by the federal government to trade commodity futures contracts.

Speculation Traders in the commodity markets may be speculators that are simply seeking a profit from price changes in a commodity by buying and selling futures contracts. This is not mere gambling because those traders provide valuable information to the market and lead to more efficient pricing of commodities.

Manipulation Manipulation is a term of art in the commodity markets that involves trading that causes commodity prices to reach an artificial level with the intent and ability to do so by the traders involved.

Federal Securities Laws The federal securities laws are a series of statutes that were enacted as a part of President Franklin Roosevelt's New Deal during the Great Depression. Among other things, those statutes created the Securities and Exchange Commission, an independent federal agency charged with regulating the securities markets. Securities sold to the public must be registered with that agency.

Brokerage Firms Brokerage firms accept and route customer orders to the marketplace for execution. In the commodity markets, such firms are called "futures commission merchants."

Options An options contract is an agreement that gives the holder of the option the right but not the obligation to purchase or sell a commodity. Options contracts are distinguishable from traditional futures contracts because the parties to a futures contract must make and accept delivery of the commodity unless offset by another futures contract.

Stock Index Futures A stock index futures contract is an agreement to deliver the change in value of a group of stocks that comprise a stock index such as the Dow Jones Industrial Average.

Over-the-Counter Derivative Instruments Over-the-counter derivatives are instruments with some elements of futures and options on the one hand and securities elements on the other. These instruments may be traded directly between dealers rather than through a central market or contract market.

Swaps A swap contract is simply an exchange of two sets of cash flows or other rights.

concerns in Congress. The result was the enactment of the Commodity Futures Trading Commission Act, which created the Commodity Futures Trading Commission (CFTC), an independent federal agency intended to function like the Securities and Exchange Commission (SEC), the forceful regulator for the securities industry.

The CFTC assumed the powers of the Commodity Exchange Commission and was given broad new powers, including the authority to impose civil penalties of up to $100,000 for each violation of the Commodity Exchange Act or CFTC rules. New classes of registrants were added, including commodity trading advisers and commodity pool operators. The latter were pools of customer funds that were traded in commodity futures.

The CFTC very quickly encountered a number of problems, including the renewed fraudulent sale of commodity options to unsophisticated customers. This problem was handled by suspending commodity options trading until the exchanges allowed options trading under regulated conditions. The CFTC was also soon clashing with the SEC, as financial innovations led to futures trading on financial instruments regulated by the SEC. Such financial instruments included stock index futures and futures on fixed income instruments such as government securities. An agreement between the agencies, enacted into law, settled this dispute by drawing a boundary between their jurisdictions. That solution, however, was not long lasting.

The SEC blamed the stock market crash of 1987 on the destabilizing effects of futures trading on stock indexes. The development of over-the-counter derivatives instruments such as swaps led to other clashes between the SEC and CFTC on how those instruments should be regulated. These clashes intensified when several large institutions suffered big losses from trading those instruments during the early 1990s. A long-running debate then arose over how those instruments should be regulated. After some vacillation, the CFTC decided to deregulate the commodity markets except where retail customers are involved. That program was enacted into law through the Commodity Futures Modernization Act. This act amended the Commodity Exchange Act to free institutional traders from regulatory restrictions in their derivative transactions, provided that their counter party was also an institution. Observers criticized the 2000 legislation, however, after the failure of the Enron Corporation in 2001. Enron had used the provisions of the 2000 act to escape regulation of its broad-based commodity trading activities.

See also: SECURITIES ACT OF 1933; SECURITIES EXCHANGE ACT OF 1934.

BIBLIOGRAPHY

Johnson, Philip McBride, and Thomas Lee Hazen. *Commodities Regulation,* 3d ed. New York: Aspen Law and Business, 1998.

Markham, Jerry W. *Commodities Regulation: Fraud Manipulation and Other Claims.* St Paul, MN: West Group, 2002.

Markham, Jerry W. *The History of Commodity Futures Trading and Its Regulation.* New York: Praeger, 1987.

COMMUNICATIONS ACT OF 1934

Robert W. Van Sickel

Excerpt from the Communications Act of 1934

For the purpose of regulating interstate and foreign commerce in communication by wire and radio so as to make available ... without discrimination on the basis of race, color, religion, national origin, or sex, a rapid, efficient ... wire and radio communication service with adequate facilities at reasonable charges, for the purpose of the national defense, for the purpose of promoting safety of life and property ... and for the purpose of securing a more effective execution of this policy by centralizing authority heretofore granted ... to several agencies and by granting additional authority with respect to interstate and foreign commerce in wire and radio communication, there is created a commission to be known as the Federal Communications Commission.

Great Depression: the longest and most severe economic depression in American history (1929–1939). Its effects were felt throughout the world

The act's major intent was to consolidate all federal regulation of electronic communication within a single independent agency.

Passed in the midst of the **Great Depression**, the Communications Act of 1934 (48 stat. 1064), which created the Federal Communications Commission (FCC), reflected a continuing effort by Congress to both encourage and regulate electronic communication in the United States. The act's major intent was to consolidate all federal regulation of such communication within a single independent agency. Although substantially amended several times since its adoption, the Communications Act continues to provide the basic institutional structure for the federal government's regulation of all forms of electronic mass communication, including radio, television, the telephone system, and perhaps eventually, aspects of the Internet. Although the public may have little knowledge of the FCC, the Commission has played a major role in determining what Americans see and hear on the airwaves. That this act has survived for seven decades during a period of intense technological and social change is itself something of an achievement.

THE STRUCTURE AND AUTHORITY OF THE FCC

The FCC is an independent regulatory agency. In general terms, the FCC is charged with regulating interstate and international communications by radio, television, wire, satellite, and cable. The FCC's jurisdiction covers the fifty states, the District of Columbia, and all U.S. possessions. It is headed by five commissioners appointed by the president, with the advice and consent of the Senate, to staggered five-year terms. No more than two commissioners (excluding the chairperson) may represent a single political party. In practice, this has meant that the Commission consists of two Democrats, two Republicans, and a chairperson representing the current president's party. Designated by the president, the FCC chairperson exercises significant control over the Commission's policy agenda, internal operations, and relations with Congress.

Although the FCC is most visible through its licensing and oversight of commercial television and radio, it is also charged with regulating interstate common carrier systems, industrial and trucking radio systems, taxi cab communication networks, doctor-hospital and marine-ship systems, aviation communication, police and fire networks, as well as more recently developed technologies such as cable television and satellite communications, including cellular telephone systems. Although the FCC is an independent agency, it should be noted that *no* federal agency is truly independent of politics. Accordingly, the FCC must contend with presidential and congressional review both in the budget process and in regard to amendments to its enabling legislation. Additionally, nearly all of the FCC's activities are subject to judicial review. And finally, the Commission, although exercising formidable regulatory powers under the **commerce clause**, must navigate the waters of state and local governments throughout the country.

The Commission supervises a staff of approximately 2,500 people, and has an annual budget of roughly $250 million. FCC personnel are organized into various *bureaus* and *offices,* although the majority of them work in Washington, D.C. Perhaps the most important of these bodies is the Mass Media Bureau, which handles such highly recognizable FCC functions as the granting and renewal of broadcast licenses, and the adoption and enforcement of technical and operational standards for broadcasters. The FCC has long been organized in terms of the various forms of communication media, such as commercial radio, commercial and public television, cable systems, common carriers, private radio systems, and so on. However, recent years have witnessed the phenomenon known as convergence, in which the former distinctions made among various media, and the utility of organizing government regulation along such lines, have been called into question.

In terms of constitutional provisions, the Communications Act, which is designed to be consistent with the First Amendment's freedom of speech and press provisions, rests on the commerce clause of Article I, section 8. The act is a direct descendent of the Radio Acts of 1912 and 1927. The Communications Act consolidates responsibility for several problems that Congress had dealt with in the two decades prior to 1934.

Although the FCC is most visible through its licensing and oversight of commercial television and radio, it is also charged with regulating interstate common carrier systems, industrial and trucking radio systems, taxi cab communication networks, doctor-hospital and marine-ship systems, aviation communication, police and fire networks, as well as more recently developed technologies such as cable television and satellite communications, including cellular telephone systems.

commerce clause: the provision of the U.S. Constitution (Article I, section 8, clause 3) which gives Congress exclusive powers over interstate commerce—the buying, selling or exchanging of goods or products between states

REGULATING ELECTRONIC MEDIA

But while all mass communications share certain similarities, the electronic media exist in a legal environment far different from that enjoyed by the traditional print media. Some of the legal principles governing print and electronic media are identical, such as the legal meaning of libel, invasion of privacy, copyright, and various access restrictions. However, the legal differences outweigh the similarities. To begin with, the electronic media require government licensing, whereas anyone who has the resources and desire may start a newspaper or magazine. There have been a number of justifications for treating electronic communications differently, many based on such concepts as *public rights of way, pervasiveness, intrusiveness,* and *scarcity.* Although these justifications are widely accepted, their validity is not self-evident.

Public rights of way are geographic spaces such as roads, telephone and power lines, tree rows, and alleys, which are considered to be public property designated for the provision of public services. Similarly, the airwaves are seen as belonging to the public, and thus should be regulated in the public

Whereas all mass communications share certain similarities, the electronic media exist in a legal environment far different from that enjoyed by the traditional print media.

interest. Pervasiveness and intrusiveness are related ideas under which it is thought that the electronic media are both ubiquitous and unavoidable, and thus different from the print press, which one presumably could ignore if one wished. The notion of scarcity, however, may be the most common justification for government control of the electromagnetic spectrum, and it served as a major impetus for passage of the Communications Act.

Scarcity refers to the ostensibly limited number of frequencies on the spectrum, a fact that, in a democracy, requires fair access and a diverse range of viewpoints. This concept was problematic from the beginning, and has arguably become even more outmoded since 1934. First, although the FCC grants licenses to utilize particular frequencies, the federal government maintains ownership and control of about fifty percent of the available frequencies, based on national security and public safety concerns. Perhaps more damaging to the idea of scarcity has been the continuous growth of electronic access through the development of cable television, satellite technology, and the Internet. While the original concern of Congress was to distribute what it saw as a very limited number of frequencies in the face of unlimited opportunities for private parties to develop newspapers, today the number of newspapers in the United States has dwindled to a fraction of the number of television and radio stations.

COMMUNICATIONS ISSUES IN THE EARLY TWENTIETH CENTURY

It cannot be overemphasized that the Communications Act was the culmination of a long series of attempts by Congress to respond, often belatedly and ineffectively, to rapid changes in communications technology. As early as the mid-nineteenth century, it became clear that traditional notions of a free press might prove inadequate as legal frameworks for emerging technologies. Indeed, as early as the 1850s Congress debated a proposal to commit public funds to the creation of a transcontinental subterranean telegraph system. The Communications Act grew out of a time when Congress was concerned with radio technology primarily as a means of achieving public safety through increased military and maritime coordination, rather than as a format for commercial news and entertainment. Indeed, the Radio Act of 1912 was a direct congressional response to the sinking of the *Titanic* that year, a disaster that was widely believed to be related to the lack of a coherent distribution of radio frequencies along the eastern seaboard, preventing the ship's distress signals from being effectively relayed to maritime safety officials. Thus, through the first Radio Act, Congress seized control of the electromagnetic spectrum for the first time.

The Communications Act was the culmination of a long series of attempts by Congress to respond, often belatedly and ineffectively, to rapid changes in communications technology.

At the same time, American business had begun to see the *commercial* potential of radio. By the mid-1920s there were hundreds of essentially unregulated (although federally licensed) stations broadcasting throughout the country. The federal government's first substantive effort to regulate broadcasting, however, came with the 1927 Radio Act, which created a Federal Radio Commission designed to regulate that medium in "the public interest, convenience, and necessity." Still, the Department of Commerce, the Interstate Commerce Commission, and the Department of Defense controlled federal regulation of communication. Within a few years, pressure to consolidate all telecommunications regulation for both wired and wireless services prompted new legislation with a wider mandate.

THE ERA OF THE COMMUNICATIONS ACT

In early 1934, President Franklin Delano Roosevelt's congressional allies introduced the bill that would become the Communications Act. Perhaps surprisingly, given the scope of the regulation involved, there was little legislative debate on the bill. Indeed, hearings in the Senate lasted barely a week, while the House of Representatives heard testimony for only a single day. Some observers did voice concerns that the legislation would allow the new FCC to undermine educational and public safety broadcasting, but the final version of the bill, which FDR signed in June 1934, left the balance of commercial and educational broadcasting to be struck by the new Commission.

Although the Communications Act has been the subject of regular litigation and judicial review, the United States Supreme Court has exercised its power to review FCC activities in a surprisingly limited number of cases. The Court has rarely struck down FCC rules. Congress, however, has amended the Communications Act many times, largely in response to changes in technology, and in rare instances by making attempts to strengthen the public interest aspects of the act. Important technological developments have included television, satellite and microwave communications, cable television, cellular telephones, digital broadcasting, and personal communications systems. These new technologies gave rise to amendments and related legislation such as the Communications Satellite Act of 1962, the Cable Act of 1992, and the Telecommunications Act of 1996. Public interest concerns led to the establishment of FM radio in 1941, to the creation of the Corporation for Public Broadcasting (PBS) in 1967 and National Public Radio (NPR) in 1972, and to the passage of the Children's Television Act in 1990.

Although the Communications Act has been the subject of regular litigation and judicial review, the United States Supreme Court has exercised its power to review FCC activities in a surprisingly limited number of cases.

Occasionally, calls for major alterations to the act, or even for the abolition of the FCC, have arisen. Two very different political perspectives drive these suggestions. The first of these perspectives holds that the federal government has already *over-regulated* the electronic media, and has thus undermined both the normal workings of the marketplace and the FCC's ability to respond quickly and effectively to complex technological and business developments. Because of the problems (or opportunities) of *convergence,* it is believed that rivalries among the broadcast, cable, telephone, Internet, and newspaper industries can only be worked out through free market competition. On the other hand, there are those who believe that the FCC has failed to protect the public interest and the democratic values of fair access and diversity of viewpoints among the media. Advocates of this perspective point to recent FCC rules that have allowed a small group of large corporations to gain control of mass media content both in particular markets and throughout the nation. To some degree, advocates of both perspectives view the 1934 act, despite its many changes, as an anachronism developed in an age before the development of modern communications systems.

IMPACT AND DEVELOPMENT OF THE FCC

It is difficult to summarize the societal impact of the Communications Act, just as it is hard to discuss briefly the broader social changes in American life since 1934. Whether the FCC has effectively pursued its responsibility to protect the

The electronic media pervade the lives of all Americans, providing virtually all entertainment and public information for a majority of citizens. Thus, the FCC and the Communications Act will continue to be of central importance in the lives of Americans.

public's "interest, convenience, and necessity" is a debated question. Perhaps inevitably, the FCC has adopted an essentially corporate model of regulation. The Commission, albeit with notable exceptions, has moved steadily toward a market-based interpretation of its mission. In recent years, the FCC has abandoned its *fairness doctrine,* which required broadcasters to present opposing viewpoints on public issues. It has weakened ownership limitations, allowing corporate media conglomerates essentially to monopolize particular markets through the acquisition of television, radio, newspaper, and cable providers. Finally, the Commission no longer seriously reviews renewal applications for broadcasting licenses, thus making such privileges virtually permanent, while following a highly amorphous requirement that broadcasters present at least some (self-defined) public interest programming.

On the other hand, one could conclude that, given the rapid technological change of the past seventy years, the FCC has benefited both consumers and producers by enthusiastically adapting its rules to emerging industries. One thing is certain: The electronic media now truly pervade the lives of all Americans, providing virtually *all* entertainment and public information for a majority of citizens. Thus, the FCC and the Communications Act will continue to be of central importance in the lives of Americans.

See also: PUBLIC BROADCASTING ACT OF 1967.

BIBLIOGRAPHY

Benjamin, Louise. *Freedom of the Air and the Public Interest: First Amendment in Broadcasting to 1935.* Carbondale: Southern Illinois University Press, 2001.

Carter, T. Barton, et al. *Mass Communications Law in a Nutshell,* 5th ed. St. Paul, MN: West Group, 2000.

"Communications Act of 1934 (47 U.S.C. 151 [1934])." Federal Communications Commission Homepage. <http://www.fcc.gov/Reports/1934new.pdf>.

Gillmor, Donald M., et al. *Fundamentals of Mass Communication Law.* St. Paul, MN: West Publishing, 1996.

Goldberg, Godles, Wiener, and Wright. "Communications Law and Regulation." *Findlaw Professionals.* <http://profs.lp.findlaw.com/communicate/index.html>.

McChesney, Robert W. *Telecommunications, Mass Media & Democracy: The Battle for Control of U.S. Broadcasting, 1928–1935.* New York: Oxford University Press, 1993.

Messere, Fritz. "Analysis of the Federal Communications Commission."*Encyclopedia of Television.* <http://www.oswego.edu/~messere/FCC1.html>.

Paglin, Max D. *A Legislative History of the Communications Act of 1934.* New York: Oxford University Press, 1989.

Ray, William B. *FCC: The Ups and Downs of Radio–TV Regulation.* Ames: Iowa State University Press, 1990.

Zelezny, John D. *Communication Law: Liberties, Restraints, and the Modern Media.* Belmont, CA: Wadsworth, 1993.

COMMUNICATIONS DECENCY ACT (1996)

Mikal Condon

The Communications Decency Act (CDA) (P.L. 104-104, 110 Stat. 133) was enacted as an amendment of the Telecommunications Act of 1996. The first version of this amendment, sponsored by Senator James Exon without hearings and with little discussion among committee members, would have made it illegal to make any indecent material available on computer networks. The House version of the amendment, sponsored by Representatives Christopher Cox and Ron Wyden, encouraged private, rather than government, solutions to the problem of indecency. The final, compromised amendment sought to protect minors from harmful material online by criminalizing Internet transmission of indecent materials to minors. The CDA prohibited posting "indecent" or "patently offensive" materials in a public forum on the Internet—including Web pages, newsgroups, chat rooms, or online discussion lists. This prohibition included materials that without doubt would enjoy the full protection of the First Amendment if published in print.

The final, compromised amendment sought to protect minors from harmful material online by criminalizing Internet transmission of indecent materials to under-age users.

President William J. Clinton signed the Telecommunications Act despite his administration's concern that the CDA, "[b]y criminalizing the transmission of material outside the scope of the legal definition of 'obscenity,' ... will be subject to First Amendment challenge." The administration also informed Congress, as the amendment was debated, that the law was unnecessary because existing laws already authorized its ongoing efforts to prosecute obscenity, child pornography, and child solicitation.

CHALLENGES TO THE ACT

A broad-based coalition of civil liberties groups, Internet companies, and Internet users challenged the CDA beginning on the day it was signed. In June 1996, a three-judge panel granted a preliminary injunction against the CDA, ruling unanimously that the CDA was an unconstitutional abridgment of rights protected by the First and Fifth Amendments.

In 1997 the Supreme Court ruled unanimously to invalidate the CDA in *Reno v. American Civil Liberties Union*. The Court held that the Internet is a "unique and wholly new medium of worldwide human communication" deserving full First Amendment protection. In applying the First Amendment to developing technologies, the Court established different sets of rules, using a medium-by-medium approach. An examination of the unique characteristics of each medium would be necessary to determine the level of First Amendment protection that should be afforded to each. The Court applied this "medium-specific" analysis to determine that the Internet does not possess any of the characteristics that, when present in other forms of communication, have led the Court to make exceptions in the level of First Amendment protection applied to the medium.

In applying the First Amendment to developing technologies, the Court established different sets of rules, using a medium-by-medium approach.

Justice John Paul Stevens held that the CDA was an unconstitutional restriction on speech because "the [Act] places an unacceptably heavy burden on protected speech." He also found that all provisions of the CDA are unconstitutional as they apply to "indecent" or "patently offensive" speech. Because

Reno recognized that the Internet is a unique medium entitled to the highest protection under the free speech protections of the First Amendment to the U.S. Constitution.

only obscenity can be regulated, the regulations would in effect reduce the constitutionally protected material available to adults "to only what is fit for children." The unique characteristics of Internet communications (its ready availability and ease of use) were an essential factor in the decision. Because it is possible to warn Internet users about indecent content (unlike radio, where warnings fail to protect all potential listeners), and because alternatives exist, at least in theory, the CDA's provisions cast a "far darker shadow over free speech which threatened to torch a larger segment of the Internet community than [any] speech restrictions previously encountered."

In a separate concurrence, Chief Justice William Rehnquist and Justice Sandra Day O'Connor agreed that the provisions of the CDA were unconstitutional except in their narrow application to "communications between an adult and one or more minors."

THE INTERNET AS A UNIQUE MEDIUM

Reno recognized that the Internet is a unique medium entitled to the highest protection under the free speech protections of the First Amendment to the U.S. Constitution. The Court acknowledged in its opinion that the nature of the Internet makes it a medium ideally suited to accomplish what Supreme Court Justice Oliver Wendell Holmes termed the "marketplace of ideas." In light of this desirable characteristic, the Court concluded that, "as a matter of constitutional tradition, in the absence of evidence to the contrary, we presume that governmental regulation of the content of speech is more likely to interfere with the free exchange of ideas than to encourage it. The interest in encouraging freedom of expression in a democratic society outweighs any theoretical but unproven benefit of censorship."

BIBLIOGRAPHY

"Administration Concerns Regarding S. 652: The Telecommunications Competition and Deregulation Act of 1995." <http://www.cdt.org/speech/cda/admin_s652_comnts.html>.

Letter from Kent Markus, Acting Assistant Attorney General, U.S. Department of Justice, to Senator Patrick Leahy. 141 *Congressional Record* S8342 (June 14, 1995).

INTERNET RESOURCE

Communications Decency Act Archive. EPIC. <http://www.epic.org/CDA>.

COMMUNIST CONTROL ACT OF 1954

Carl Auerbach

In February 1954, at a time of great public concern and anxiety about Communist subversion fed by the Cold War and Communist successes in Korea and Indochina, Senator Joseph McCarthy denounced the Democrats as the "party of communism, betrayal and treason." McCarthy's tactics in rooting out and exposing supposed Communists in the United States came to be known as "McCarthyism." These tactics were not the exclusive practice of the senator from Wisconsin. McCarthy was supported by Senator Robert A. Taft of Ohio and other conservative Republicans in Congress. President Dwight Eisenhower, who never publicly criticized McCarthy, benefited from the Republican charge that the Democrats were soft on Communism in his 1952 campaign against Adlai Stevenson.

At the time Congress began debating the Communist Control Act, significant anti-Communist legislation already existed.

Senator Hubert Humphrey of Minnesota, one of the founders of Americans for Democratic Action, a staunch liberal and anti-Communist organization, acknowledged the public's concerns about Communist subversion. He believed that liberals should take the lead in fighting Communism as well as all other **totalitarian** creeds and movements. Abandonment of the anti-Communist issue to the far Right, he feared, would damage the Democratic Party and the non-Communist Left generally. At the same time, McCarthyism was a boon to the Communists. The plight of those falsely accused by Senator McCarthy diverted attention from the actual Communists who were able to pose as innocents maligned by the Senator and as champions of the freedoms of speech and association guaranteed by the First Amendment to the United States Constitution. In 1954 Senator Humphrey and his legislative assistant Max M. Kampelman (later ambassador for human rights and arms control in the Carter and Reagan administrations) began drafting a bill called the Communist Control Act of 1954 (65 Stat. 775).

totalitarian: the political concept that the citizen should be totally subject to an absolute state authority

PRIOR ANTI-COMMUNIST LEGISLATION

At the time Congress began debating the Communist Control Act, significant anti-Communist legislation already existed. The 1940 Smith Act made it a crime to "teach, advocate, or encourage the overthrow or destruction of ... government by force or violence." Nazis and leaders of the Socialist Workers (American Trotskyist) Party and the Communist Party had been convicted of violating the Smith Act and subjected to fines and imprisonment. The Voorhis Act of 1940 required subversive organizations to register with the attorney general. In 1947 President Harry Truman issued an executive order establishing a program to rid the federal government of employees found to be disloyal or security risks.

In 1950 a Democratic Congress, over the veto of President Truman, enacted the Internal Security (McCarran) Act (ISA). The Subversive Activities Control Act (SACA), a part of ISA, required Communist-action and Communist-front organizations and members of Communist-action organizations to register with the attorney general. Members of Communist-action organizations were barred from employment by the federal government, working in a private defense facility, getting passports, or receiving classified information. People who had been members of a Communist Party at any time were prohibited from entering the United States. The other part of ISA authorized the detention of spies and saboteurs during any national emergency declared by the president.

The Supreme Court of the United States upheld the constitutionality of the Smith and ISA Acts in 1950, in *Dennis v. United States*, and in 1961, in *Communist Party of the United States v. Subversive Activities Control Board*.

labor union: an organization of workers whose main purpose is to collectively bargain with employers about the terms and conditions of employment

slander: to make a false statement that defames and damages another's reputation

self-incrimination: the giving of testimony that will likely subject one to criminal prosecution

CONGRESSIONAL DEBATE AND REVISION

The SACA relied on publicity to root out the Communists. Senator Humphrey proposed a new approach that would strike at both the Communist Party and the false accusations of McCarthyism. In August 1954 the 83rd Congress was debating a bill, introduced by Senator John M. Butler of Maryland, to combat Communist infiltration of **labor unions**. Humphrey offered his bill as a substitute for Butler's bill. The Humphrey bill subjected any person with knowledge of the objectives of the Communist Party who willfully became or remained a party member to imprisonment for not more than five years and a fine of $10,000. Any person prosecuted under the bill would have the benefit of the Bill of Rights and all other procedural safeguards accompanying any criminal proceeding, including the presumption of innocence. The prosecution would have to prove beyond a reasonable doubt that an accused individual was a knowing and willful member of the Communist Party. Anyone making false accusations against innocent individuals would face libel and **slander** actions. Humphrey believed his bill would deter McCarthyite tactics of character assassination and protect the reputations of innocent individuals.

Twenty senators co-sponsored the Humphrey bill, including liberal senators John F. Kennedy of Massachusetts, Paul Douglas of Illinois, and Wayne Morse of Oregon. The Senate voted to add the Humphrey bill as an amendment to, rather than substitute it for, the Butler bill. After modifying it in certain respects, the Senate passed the Butler-Humphrey bill by a vote of 85 to 0. The Butler provisions amended SACA by adding the category of "Communist-infiltrated organizations" to the category of "Communist organizations" required to register with the attorney general. The Butler provisions also made it illegal for any member of a Communist-action or Communist-front organization to hold office or employment with any labor organization or represent any employer in proceedings under the National Labor Relations Act. A labor union found to be a Communist-infiltrated organization was denied the benefits of the National Labor Relations Act.

Ultimately, Congress rejected the Humphrey provisions as passed by the Senate because of doubts about their constitutionality. Legislators also shared the concern expressed by Republican attorney general Herbert Brownell that the provisions would lead to the invalidation of SACA's registration requirements because the combination of provisions would compel individuals to disclose they were committing the crime of being members of the Communist Party and, therefore, violate the Fifth Amendment to the United States Constitution, which protects against **self-incrimination**. Instead, Congress confined the Communist Control Act to two objectives: (1) to outlaw the Communist Party, and (2) to subject party members to SACA's registration requirements and penalties applicable to members of a Communist-action organization. In its final form, the act passed the Senate by a vote of 79 to 0 and the House by a vote of 265 to 2. President Eisenhower signed the bill on August 24, 1954.

FEATURES OF THE ACT

The act begins by setting forth a finding of facts about the nature of the Communist Party of the United States that distinguishes it from other politi-

Pictured here, the House Un-American Activities Committee, created in 1938, investigates alleged Communists in Seattle, in 1954. The Communist Control Act of 1954 declared that the existence of the Communist Party presented a "clear and present danger to the security of the United States." Senator Hubert Humphrey had hoped to include a provision in the bill that provided for libel and slander charges against anyone making false accusations against innocent persons, which was meant to deter character assassination and other tactics associated with McCarthyism. Humphrey's provisions, however, were not included in the final form of the bill. (SEATTLE POST-INTELLIGENCER COLLECTION; MUSEUM OF HISTORY & INDUSTRY/CORBIS)

cal parties and justifies its being outlawed. Congress found that the party presents itself as a political party like any other political party but in fact "constitutes an authoritarian dictatorship within a republic, demanding for itself the rights and privileges accorded to political parties, but denying to all others the liberties guaranteed by the Constitution." It is "the agency of a hostile foreign power" controlled by the world Communist movement and an instrument of "a conspiracy to overthrow the government of the United States" by "any available means, including resort to force and violence." Therefore, the party's existence presents "a clear and present danger to the security of the United States" and "should be outlawed." These findings were confirmed by evidence in the archives of the former Soviet Union that the Communist Party was involved in Soviet espionage in the United States.

Outlawing the party was accomplished through a provision stating that the Party is not "entitled to any of the rights, privileges, and immunities attendant upon legal bodies created under the jurisdiction of the laws of the United States or any political subdivision thereof; and whatever rights, privileges, and immunities which have heretofore been granted to said party or any subsidiary organization by reason of the laws of the United

Key terms for the Communist Control Act
Carl Auerbach

Communist-action organizations Communist-action organizations were defined as organizations substantially controlled by the foreign government controlling the world Communist movement (that is, the Soviet Union), and operated primarily to advance the objectives of that movement.

Communist-front organizations Communist-front organizations were defined as organizations substantially controlled by a Communist Action organization, a Communist foreign government, or the world Communist government.

Communist-infiltrated organizations Communist-infiltrated organizations were defined as organizations substantially controlled by persons actively engaged in giving aid or support to a Communist-action organization, a Communist foreign government, the world Communist movement, or in impairing the military strength of the United States or the industrial capacity of the United States to furnish logistical or other material means of support required by the armed forces of the United States.

States or any political subdivision thereof, are hereby terminated." Beyond revealing Congress's intent to keep the Communist Party off the ballot in any national, state, or local election, the scant legislative history fails to delineate the scope of these provisions. As made clear by the rejection of the original Humphrey bill, the act as passed was not intended to make the Communist Party's very existence unlawful. A provision in the act that it shall not be construed as an amendment to SACA indicated that the obligations and disabilities imposed on the party by SACA would remain. The provision would make no sense if the act was intended to bring about the dissolution of the Communist Party because there would then be no one to discharge these obligations.

JUDICIAL AND LEGISLATIVE REVIEW

Only a few court cases interpreted the scope of the act's termination of the party's "rights, privileges and immunities." In 1954 the New Jersey Supreme Court held that, under the act, a candidate who was not a nominee of the party could not appear on the ballot in a state election under the party label (*Salwen v. Rees,*). The Supreme Court upheld the judgement of the New Jersey Superior Court in favor of the defendant-election official and adopted the Superior Court judge's oral opinion as its own. That opinion explained that the plaintiff-candidate was proclaiming that he was the candidate of the Communist Party and that a vote for him was a vote for "party enthronement." "In order to make good the outlawry of the Communist Party as such," the Superior Court judge stated, "it becomes unavoidable that individuals be prevented from carrying its banner." This "peculiar method, as chosen by the [plaintiff-candidate], is a keen way of circumventing the statute, because if it were valid for him to take the course that he has chosen, it would be valid for a complete set of candidates to do the same thing, the consequence of which, of course, would be to frustrate completely the design of federal law." In 1973 a federal district court in Arizona decided

The Hollywood Blacklist

In the late 1940s, the House Un-American Activities Committee (HUAC) held a series of hearings—widely considered witch-hunts—to determine the extent of Communist influence in the U.S. government and the arts. Hollywood in particular was targeted because of suspicions that Communists had infiltrated America's most important mass medium, where they might be planting subversive propaganda. One of the most renowned hearings was that of the Hollywood Ten, a group of screenwriters and directors who refused to answer the famous question, "Are you now or have you ever been a member of the Communist party?" Cited for contempt of Congress, the ten defendants were fined and sentenced to prison terms of six months to one year. Their names were placed on the "blacklist," which barred them from employment in the entertainment industry. In further investigations in the early 1950s, some defendants avoided the contempt charge—and thus jail—by pleading the Fifth Amendment (in other words, they weren't obligated to offer testimony that might incriminate them). But they were still blacklisted, and careers, marriages, and friendships were destroyed as financial and emotional pressures took their toll. Writers (who made up 60 percent of those blacklisted) were sometimes able to continue working under pseudonyms, but many actors and other professionals left the industry or even the country. By 1960, the blacklist had been largely broken down, but fewer than ten percent of those blacklisted were able to resume their Hollywood careers.

that the act was unconstitutional and Arizona could not keep the party off the ballot in the 1972 general election (*Blawis v. Bolin*). In 1961 the Supreme Court of the United States ruled that the act did not bar the party from participating in New York's unemployment insurance system (*Communist Party v. Catherwood*).

The Supreme Court of the United States has not ruled on the act's constitutionality, and **civil libertarians** remain divided on the issues of the constitutionality and wisdom of the act. No administration has tried to enforce it. Congress began to dismantle SACA in 1968 when it repealed the provisions relating to the registration with the attorney general of Communist-action and Communist-front organizations and of members of Communist-action organizations. In 1993 it repealed all the other provisions of SACA as they related to the party. By this time, the Soviet Union, and with it the world Communist movement, had collapsed, the Cold War had ended, and the Communist Party of the United States had dwindled into complete insignificance.

civil libertarian: one who is actively concerned with the protection of the fundamental freedoms guaranteed to the individual by the Bill of Rights

Congress began to dismantle SACA in 1968 when it repealed the provisions relating to the registration with the attorney general of Communist-action and Communist-front organizations and of members of Communist-action organizations.

THE ACT IN A POST-COMMUNIST WORLD

The provisions of the act "outlawing" the party have not been repealed. A tiny remnant of the party continued to exist into the twenty-first century under its lifetime leader, the octogenarian and unregenerate Gus Hall. It maintains a Web site. But it did not participate in any federal or gubernatorial elections in 2002. There is no evidence that it appeared in any state or local election, but there is a report that it may have been on the ballot in an election in the Bronx, New York.

Despite the irrelevance of the act here at home, the controversy over its consistency with democratic principles has important international implications. Many nations have laws outlawing totalitarian organizations. The United States may have to take a position on whether democratic principles give legitimacy to Muslim fundamentalist movements, such as those in Algeria and Pakistan, that seek political power by legal means only to crush democracy. The Communist Control Act is a precedent for not tolerating intolerant political movements.

See also: Alien Sedition Acts of 1798; Espionage Act (1917) and Sedition Act (1918).

BIBLIOGRAPHY

Hayes, John Earl, and Harvey Klehr. *Venona: Decoding Soviet Espionage in America.* New Haven, CT: Yale University Press, 1999.

Hayes, John Earl, Harvey Klehr, and Kyrill M. Anderson. *Venona: The Secret World of American Communism.* New Haven, CT: Yale University Press, 1998.

Kampelman, Max M. *Entering New Worlds: The Memoirs of a Private Man in Public Life.* New York: Harper Collins, 1991.

Morgan, Donald G. *Congress and the Constitution: A Study in Responsibility.* Cambridge, MA: Harvard University Press, 1966.

COMMUNITY DEVELOPMENT BANKING AND FINANCIAL INSTITUTIONS ACT OF 1994

Michael P. Malloy

The Community Development Banking and Financial Institutions Act of 1994 (CDBFIA) (108 Stat. 2163) constitutes an integral part of the Riegle Community Development and Regulatory Improvement Act of 1994 (Riegle Act). Enacted on September 23, 1994, the Riegle Act pursued a wide range of objectives. According to section 102(h), Congress's objective was "to create a Community Development Financial Institutions Fund to promote economic revitalization and community development through investment in and assistance to" so-called community development financial institutions (CDFIs). In part, this effort addressed an increasingly controversial issue in bank regulatory policy—to what extent should the law require banks to involve themselves in the economic well-being and development of local communities served by their operations?

The CDBFIA authorized financial incentives for depository institutions to participate voluntarily in community-development-oriented banking programs and activities. CDFIs receiving incentives are expected to focus on financial activities and transactions intended to promote community development. However, such legislative efforts are relatively specialized, and they avoid, rather than resolve, the underlying controversy: If "full-service" banking enterprises enjoy a competitive advantage in aggregating credit by taking in deposits and dispensing resources in the form of loans because of their relatively exclusive government charters, should they not be required to serve their local communities?

The CFDI program is available for banks and other depository institutions, including credit unions. Periodically, regulators announce the availability of incentive funds for the program. In 2000, the National Credit Union Administration, as federal regulator of federal credit unions and federally-insured state credit unions, published an interim final rule with respect to its Community Development Revolving Loan Program. Overall, CDFI resources seem relatively limited, and voluntary participation in community development under the CDBFIA is not pervasive among institutions.

Awarding funds for community development, however, was not the sole purpose of the Riegle Act. According to the conference report accompanying the act, a second major objective of the Riegle Act was "to reduce administrative requirements for insured depository institutions to the extent consistent with safe and sound banking practices." The Riegle Act accomplished this by requiring regulators and other depository institutions to review their rules periodically and to eliminate or modify provisions that imposed regulatory burdens on depository institutions. The task of amending federal regulations in light of this mandate is a continuing obligation for the federal bank regulatory agencies.

A third technical objective of the Riegle Act, eliminating obsolete provisions from federal banking legislation, is of related importance. Many experts viewed this effort as long overdue, and the technical amendments included in the act in this regard are extensive. Thus in February 2003 the Community Development Financial Institutions Fund revised its rules to replace semiannual reporting requirements with an annual reporting requirement. It also achieved regulatory economy and efficiency by deleting references to the

> *The CDBFIA authorized financial incentives for depository institutions to participate voluntarily in community-development-oriented banking programs and activities.*

required contents of CDFI applications, since these matters were addressed in various application forms themselves. In March 2003 the Federal Reserve Board amended its rules implementing the Equal Credit Opportunity Act to create an exception to its rules that prohibited a bank from inquiring about a loan applicant's national origin, race, age, or similar characteristics, so that a bank could collect such data for the purpose of conducting a self-text of its compliance with nondiscrimination requirements.

See also: COMMUNITY REINVESTMENT ACT.

BIBLIOGRAPHY

Malloy, Michael P. *Banking Law and Regulation.* 3 Vols. New York: Aspen Law & Business, 1994 & Cumulative Supplements.

Malloy, Michael P., ed. *Banking and Financial Services Law: Cases, Materials, and Problems.* Durham, NC: Carolina Academic Press, 1999 & 2002-2003 Supp.

Malloy, Michael P. *Bank Regulation Hornbook* 2d ed. St. Paul, MN: West Group, 2003.

COMMUNITY REINVESTMENT ACT (1977)

Fred Galves

Congress adopted the Community Reinvestment Act (CRA) (P.L. 95-128, 91 Stat. 1147) in 1977 to combat "redlining," the "systematic denial of credit to persons living within a certain area." CRA prohibited redlining by requiring regulated financial institutions to show that their depository facilities met the "convenience and needs of the communities in which they are chartered to do business."

The lack of adequate lending, coupled with the depletion of available government funds, had caused economic decay in poor neighborhoods and left the urban areas crime ridden and economically devastated. Congress hoped by codifying an affirmative obligation to meet the needs of local communities that financial lending mandated by CRA would foster neighborhood stability and revitalization.

Originally, Congress intended CRA to respond to problems associated with depository institutions transferring funds they received as savings deposits from local residents to borrowers outside the communities regardless of whether the communities were rural, urban, or suburban. Thus, at its inception, Congress's intent was to improve the banking services in poorer communities, although Congress knew the likely beneficiaries would be racial minorities. However, regulators soon discovered that CRA had little real power, and that the law was difficult to enforce because of its vague language. In its first twelve years (between 1977 to 1989), the CRA merely required banks to show a good faith effort in becoming more aware of the needs of the communities they served.

SUBSEQUENT LEGISLATION

This situation changed in 1989 when Congress amended the CRA as a part of the Financial Institutions Reform, Recovery Enforcement Act (FIRREA). FIR-

REA amended the CRA by mandating public disclosure of all CRA reviews. This was a substantial change because it allowed the American public to have access to a banking industry "report card."

FIRREA established the four-tiered grading system that is still in effect today to evaluate a bank's CRA performance. The rating system is: (1) "outstanding," (2) "satisfactory," (3) "needs to improve," or (4) "substantial noncompliance." After Congress adopted FIRREA the regulatory agencies issued a joint statement that outlined a set of twelve new assessment factors that would be used to examine the banks for CRA compliance.

Congress implemented another change to the CRA as a part of the Federal Deposit Insurance Corporation Improvement Act of 1991 (FDICIA). FDICIA required public discussion regarding the regulator's assessment of an institution's CRA performance in the public portion of the CRA evaluation. Under FDICIA, regulators must consider this record when the agency is examining an application for a deposit facility by the financial institution. The institution's performance may be a basis for denying or conditioning that application on further activities.

In response to a growing number of bank complaints regarding the intensive documentation required under CRA, President Clinton proposed changes that made the CRA less burdensome to the banking industry, while still preserving its intended purpose. The new regulations replaced the twelve assessment factors with a more quantitative system based on actual performance as measured by various tests. These new regulations emphasize performance, not process. Many experts argue that the new, revised approach to the CRA enables banks to focus more on the lending, and less on the paperwork.

CRA IMPACT ON AVAILABILITY OF LOANS

Public and administrative efforts have succeeded in getting money to individuals in poor neighborhoods. By 1993, 14 percent of the 152 banks examined in their first six months of 1993 did an "outstanding" job under the CRA. That was up from only 8 percent of those banks examined between July 1990 and December 1992, prior to the implementation of the new regulations. Moreover, the CRA has decreased the racial disparities in lending practices. Between 1991 and 1995, while conventional home-purchased loans to whites increased by two-thirds, loans to blacks tripled (from 45,000 to 138,000 a year) and loans to Hispanics more than doubled. During the same period, loans in predominantly minority neighborhoods rose by 137 percent—while loans in areas where population was almost all white grew by just 37 percent.

LITIGATION AND CONTROVERSY

The Justice Department has sought to enforce the fair lending laws, and this may also have had a positive impact on banks' willingness to invest in minority neighborhoods. The utility and fairness of the CRA, however, continues to generate substantial debate in congress and among advocacy groups. Former Senator Phil Gramm, Republican of Texas, for example, stated that "I want to get back to lending and end these kickbacks whereby you give the protesting organization money, but you don't make loans in the community." Senator Gramm was claiming the community groups were using the CRA rating as a way of unfairly taking money from banks.

However, John Taylor, president of the National Community Reinvestment Coalition questioned this criticism. In testimony to the House Committee on Banking and Financial Services, he admitted there might have been a few instances of "greenmail." However, his organization and its membership renounce this practice as counterproductive, since it creates adversity and may not produce long lasting collaborations among banks and community groups. He states that because these partnerships involve a high degree of cooperation and trust, **extortion** is simply not a part of the partnership.

The Community Reinvestment Act is good legislation for all involved. The banks make profits from loans they probably would not have made unless the government assisted the credit transfers. Consumers win because they have the much-needed resources to keep their communities economically viable. This leaves our country in a more democratic and economically fair place for all.

extortion: the obtaining of money (or other concessions) by force or intimidation

See also: COMMUNITY DEVELOPMENT AND BANKING FINANCIAL INSTITUTIONS ACT OF 1994; FAIR HOUSING ACT OF 1968.

BIBLIOGRAPHY

Baldinucci, E.L. "The Community Reinvestment Act: New Standards Provide New Hope." *Fordham Urban Law Journal* 23 (Spring 1996): 831, 846–856.

Canner, Glenn B., and Wayne Passmore. "Home Purchasing Lending in Low-Income Neighborhoods and to Low-Income Borrowers." *Federal Reserve Bulletin* 81 (February 1995): 71–103.

Garwood, M., et al. "The Community Reinvestment Act: Evolution and Current Issues." *Federal Reserve Bulletin* (1993): 251–267.

Johnson, Marcia, et al. "The Community Reinvestment Act: Expanding Access." *Kansas Journal of Law & Public Policy* 12 (2002): 89–123.

COMPREHENSIVE ENVIRONMENTAL RESPONSE, COMPENSATION, AND LIABILITY ACT (1980)

Gregory S. Weber

Excerpt from the Comprehensive Environmental Response, Compensation, and Liability Act

Whenever ... any hazardous substance is released or there is a substantial threat of such a release into the environment ... the President is authorized to act, consistent with the national contingency plan, to remove or arrange for the removal of, and provide for remedial action relating to such hazardous substance, pollutant or contaminant at any time (including its removal from any contaminated natural resource), or take any other response measure consistent with the national emergency plan which the President deems necessary to protect the public health or welfare or the environment.

The Comprehensive Environmental Response, Compensation, and Liability Act of 1980 (P.L. 96-510, 94 Stat. 2767) is known both by its acronym, CERCLA (pronounced "SIR-cluh"), and by one of its major program components, the *Superfund,* described below.

BACKGROUND

When enacted, CERCLA addressed a substantial gap in national environmental law. The Resource Conservation and Recovery Act of 1976 (RCRA) had addressed the cleanup of *active* hazardous waste sites. Yet the late-1970s saw a series of front-page stories of property contamination and human sickness associated with *abandoned* waste sites, such as at Love Canal, New York. Faced with the cleanup of thousands of such sites across the nation, congressional committees held hearings in 1979 that highlighted the potential costs and complexities of the cleanup efforts. In late 1980, with both a **lame-duck** Congress and president, the bill that became CERCLA was introduced and passed virtually overnight.

Critics have traced many problems in CERCLA's implementation to this hasty legislative process. Indeed, as originally enacted, CERCLA lacked many critical details and left limited legislative history. While these criticisms have merit, the statute's principal amendment, the Superfund Amendments and Reauthorization Act of 1986 (SARA), addressed many of the charges. SARA added many detailed provisions and provided substantial legislative history.

THREE PRINCIPAL ELEMENTS

Three key elements underlie CERCLA. These include: (1) the EPA's cleanup authority and processes; (2) cleanup liability; and (3) the *Superfund.*

EPA Cleanup Authority and Processes. CERCLA authorizes the Environmental Protection Agency (EPA) to *respond* to *releases or threatened releases* into the environment of *hazardous substances* from *vessels or facilities. Hazardous substances* are broadly defined to include just about anything that is toxic or hazardous, except petroleum-based substances. (Given this exclusion, cleanups of petroleum-based substances are best addressed under RCRA, which contains no such exclusion.) *Facility* covers just about any kind of structure, pipeline, pit, or container, except a "consumer product in consumer use." *Release* includes all accidental and intentional discharges, except for motor vehicle emissions or radioactive materials. And finally, as its *responses,* the EPA may conduct either short-term removals or long-term remedial response actions. The former apply when prompt action is needed. Examples include fencing a site. The latter apply to all other situations. Examples include pumping and treating contaminated groundwater. These long-term actions may cost millions of dollars and take decades to complete.

A complicated array of procedures details how EPA prioritizes and supervises the cleanup work. Only sites placed on a National Priority List (NPL) are proper subjects for long-term remedial actions. The EPA places sites on the NPL by assessing their relative risks to the public under a detailed Hazard Ranking System (HRS). Guiding the EPA's cleanup efforts at these sites is the National Contingency Plan (NCP). The NCP details each step of the cleanup

lame-duck: an elected officer holder who is to be succeeded by another; in the case of Congress, the time it is in session between the November elections and the convening of the new Congress the following year

process, from initial site assessment and inspection, through remedy selection, to remedy implementation. Among other matters, the NCP has substantial provisions addressing public participation in site planning.

Cleanup Liability. CERCLA casts a wide net over those *potentially responsible parties* (PRPs) who are liable for site cleanup costs. Four classes of PRPs exist: (a) present site owners or operators; (b) those who owned or operated at the time of disposal; (c) persons who arranged for disposal; and (d) transporters who selected the disposal site. Hundreds of court cases have fleshed out these categories. For example, courts have addressed the liabilities of parent corporations, successor corporations, individual shareholders, and those who have loaned money to a PRP for its use on the site. Congress eventually addressed the latter issues in the Asset Conservation, Lender Liability, and Deposit Insurance Act of 1996.

An equally large number of cases have extended liability in other ways. Under case law, liability is strict, that is, no fault needs to be proven. Liability is also joint and several, that is, any individual PRP is liable for the entire site cleanup costs, even if it only contributed a small amount of the waste. (EPA, however, generally offers small contributors special settlement terms in amounts proportionate to the amount and type of waste involved.) Finally, liability is retroactive, that is, applies to disposals that occurred prior to 1980.

The principal defense to CERCLA liability requires proof of a PRP's lack of knowledge or reason to know that hazardous substances had been released on a site. Few PRPs have succeeded in providing such proof. Because enormous financial consequences may come with even unwitting

Love Canal

Love Canal, envisioned as a route for ships to bypass Niagara Falls, was created in the nineteenth century by entrepreneur William T. Love. After only one mile of canal had been excavated, however, Love was forced to abandon his project for lack of funding, and in 1920 his land was sold and the trench became a municipal and chemical dump. During the 1940s and early 1950s the landfill was used by the Hooker Chemical Company to bury 20,000 tons of chemical waste. When the trench reached capacity, Hooker covered it with dirt and donated the land to the city of Niagara Falls for $1. Although the transfer paperwork included a warning that the property had been used to dispose of chemical waste, a neighborhood of single-family homes grew up around the land and a school was built directly on the site of the former canal. Residents frequently complained of "seepage" of chemicals into their yards and basements, and by the mid-1970s, many were suffering from serious health problems, including birth defects, miscarriages, and kidney and bladder problems. The situation was brought to public attention by Michael Brown, a reporter for the *Niagara Falls Gazette*, and Lois Gibbs, a twenty-seven-year-old mother of two who was elected president of the Love Canal Homeowners' Association. In 1978, after conducting tests, New York State Health Commissioner Robert Whalen announced that Love Canal was a "great and imminent peril to the health of the public." The state paid for pregnant women and children under the age of two to relocate out of the area; however, once the children passed the age of two, they were expected to return, despite the demonstrable health hazards. Finally, in 1980, the state agreed to buy 800 homes and relocate 1,000 families. After a protracted legal battle, in 1995 Occidental Chemical Company, which had purchased Hooker Chemical, agreed to pay $129 million for the cleanup of the site. The public health disaster at Love Canal led Congress to pass the Comprehensive Environmental Response, Compensation, and Liability Act of 1980.

ownership of a hazardous waste site, prospective property owners now must thoroughly inspect property prior to purchase. Reluctance to purchase possibly contaminated property led to what became known as *brownfields*. Brownfields are abandoned sites, largely in urban areas, with contamination issues. To encourage development of these areas, Congress has authorized the EPA to offer financial assistance to help fund their cleanup.

The *Superfund.* The *Superfund* is an EPA-administered trust that ensures the availability of cleanup funds. Supported by taxes on, among other things, crude oil and certain chemicals, the *Superfund* totals $8.5 billion. EPA can use it to pay response costs, natural resource damages, and research, development and demonstration costs.

Because even at $8.5 billion the *Superfund* is inadequate to pay the full cleanup costs of all the NPL sites, EPA hoards it carefully. As a result, EPA's favored CERCLA enforcement tool is to negotiate a settlement among a site's PRPs. Under the settlement, the PRPs will clean up the site under EPA's supervision. Any cleanup costs expended by EPA and recovered from a PRP are returned to the fund to finance future cleanups.

ACCOMPLISHMENTS AND CHALLENGES

In a report commemorating CERCLA's twentieth anniversary, EPA summarized its progress in hazardous waste cleanup. It noted that it had taken over 6,400 emergency actions; had completed construction at 757 NPL sites; had gotten PRPs to conduct cleanup work at 70 percent of all NPL sites; had secured $18 billion from PRPs to fund cleanups; and had de-listed 219 sites. Nevertheless, because new sites frequently arise or are discovered and because cleanups often require decades to complete, CERCLA-like legislation likely will be needed for the foreseeable future.

See also: HAZARDOUS AND SOLID WASTE AMENDMENTS OF 1984; TOXIC SUBSTANCES CONTROL ACT.

BIBLIOGRAPHY

"CERCLA Overview." *U.S. Environmental Protection Agency.* July 2003. <http://www.epa.gov/superfund/action/law/cercla.htm>.

Cooke, Susan M. *The Law of Hazardous Waste: Management, Cleanup, Liability, and Litigation.* New York: Matthew Bender, 1992.

Grad, Frank. *Treatise on Environmental Law.* New York: Matthew Bender, 1993.

Moya, Olga L., and Andrew L. Fono. *Federal Environmental Law: The User's Guide.* St. Paul, MN: West Group, 2001.

Rogers, William H., Jr. *Environmental Law,* 2d ed. St. Paul, MN: West Publishing Co., 1994.

Sprankling, John G., and Gregory S. Weber. *The Law of Hazardous Wastes and Toxic Substances in a Nutshell.* St. Paul, MN: West Publishing Co., 1997.

Stensvaag, John-Mark. *Hazardous Waste Law and Practice.* New York: Wiley, 1989.

COMPROMISE OF 1850

James Huston

Slavery presented innumerable problems to the United States prior to 1850, but none proved more unsolvable than those connected with westward expansion. Heated arguments arose over the Louisiana Purchase (1803), the admission of Missouri into the Union (1820–1821), and the annexation of Texas (1845). Each time politicians responded with some type of compromise that allowed the Union to continue with a slaveholding section and a free labor section. The Compromise of 1850 was the last important compromise between North and South over slavery and it did not last. By the end of 1863, in the midst of Civil War, almost all the provisions of the Compromise of 1850 had been repudiated.

The Mexican War of 1846–1848 generated the conflict that produced the Compromise of 1850. Northern Democrats, upset at Southern domination of the party, rallied behind a slogan of slavery prohibition from any territory acquired from Mexico—the Wilmot Proviso. But President James K. Polk desired to fill out the continental boundaries of the United States, and in the treaty of Guadalupe Hidalgo (1848) he obtained the area now consisting of California, New Mexico, Arizona, Colorado, and Utah. Southern politicians immediately denounced the Wilmot Proviso and insisted slavery could expand into any territory acquired by the United States. Between 1847 and the beginning of 1850, Congress was consumed by the slavery expansion issue and it burned away all other issues. The problem simply would not go away.

From 1820 to 1850, the Missouri Compromise (1820) governed the issued of slavery in the territories. Westward expansion led to a new compromise.

At the same time California was annexed to the United States as a territory, settlers found gold and within one year California had enough population to become a state. But if California became a free state, it would tip the balance of free to slave states in the nation in favor of the free states. The politics of the situation became desperate. In the 1848 election, the citizenry voted Zachary Taylor into the White House. Taylor, who was a Louisiana slaveholder, nonetheless believed the western territories would be free and so he favored the admission of both California and New Mexico as free states. This outraged Southern politicians and by December 1849 they were speaking of secession.

Henry Clay, called the "Great Compromiser" because of his previous roles in resolving sectional conflicts, was sent back to the U.S. Senate by Kentucky to forge a compromise. He fashioned legislation that he believed resolved all standing issues between the free and slave states. These issues were the admission of California as a free state; the implementation of a settler decision on slavery in the territories of Utah and New Mexico; the abolition of the slave trade in Washington, D.C.; a new fugitive slave law; a new boundary between Texas and New Mexico; and the federal government's agreement to pay the state debts of Texas. Clay placed all these matters in one bill called the "**Omnibus**." The Omnibus, however, failed to obtain the necessary majority to pass and failed on July 31, 1850. Clay soon left the Senate in disgust.

omnibus: covering many things or situations at once

What changed the situation, however, was the death of Zachary Taylor and the installation of Millard Fillmore as president. Fillmore gave signals that he would sign a compromise act if one were passed by Congress. Illinois senator Stephen A. Douglas and Georgia representative Howell Cobb

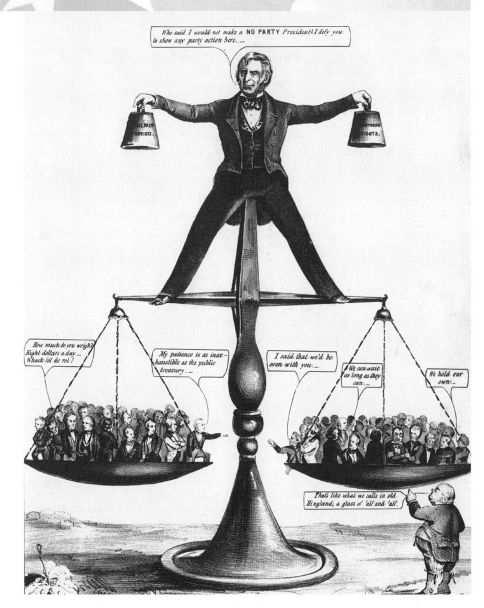

President Zachary Taylor is the subject of satire as he attempts to balance the interests of the North and the South. (LIBRARY OF CONGRESS, PRINTS AND PHOTOGRAPHS DIVISION)

What changed the situation, however, was the death of Zachary Taylor and the installation of Millard Fillmore as president.

leapt at the opportunity. They divided the Omnibus into separate bills, calculating they could win a majority for each bill even though the composition of the majority would change with every vote. And so in August and September 1850, separate bills passed the Senate and the House representing the elements of Clay's original Omnibus bill; those separate pieces of legislation were referred to as "The Compromise of 1850."

But the Compromise of 1850 was weak and destined to a short life. The Fugitive Slave Law created a furor in the North; Southerners in the Gulf states debated leaving the Union in 1850 and 1851, but retreated in the face of overwhelming support for the Union. More importantly, Stephen A. Douglas's ill-conceived legislation to start territorial government in the Kansas and Nebraska territories (the Kansas-Nebraska Act of 1854), reignited the slavery extension issue and so undid much of the good achieved by the Compromise of 1850. The unsolvable nature of the slavery issue then produced Southern secession in 1860 and 1861, which in turn led to the War for the Union from 1861–1865.

During the Civil War, the Union Congress ended the Fugitive Slave Law, emancipated slaves in the District of Columbia and then throughout the Union with the Thirteenth Amendment. So the Compromise of 1850, except for the settlement of the New Mexico-Texas boundary and the admission of California to the Union, was entirely unraveled in the space of fifteen years.

See also: FUGITIVE SLAVE ACTS; KANSAS-NEBRASKA ACT OF 1854; MISSOURI COMPROMISE

The Compromise of 1850, except for the settlement of the New Mexico-Texas boundary and the admission of California to the Union, was entirely unraveled in the space of fifteen years.

Henry Clay addresses the Senate in this 1850 drawing. Clay, a senator from Kentucky, was known as the "Great Compriser"; he engineered a single omnibus bill that formed the substance of what would become known as the Compromise of 1850. (LIBRARY OF CONGRESS, PRINTS AND PHOTOGRAPHS DIVISION)

BIBLIOGRAPHY

Brock, William R. *Parties and Political Conscience: American Dilemmas, 1840–1850.* Millwood, NY: KTO Press, 1979.

Hamilton, Holman. *Prologue to Conflict: The Crisis and Compromise of 1850.* Lexington: University Press of Kentucky, 1964.

Huston, James L. *Calculating the Value of the Union: Slavery, Property Rights, and the Economic Origins of the Civil War.* Chapel Hill: University of North Carolina Press, 2003.

Johannsen, Robert W. *Stephen A. Douglas.* New York: Oxford University Press, 1973.

Nevins, Allan. *Ordeal of the Union,* Vol. 1: *Fruits of Manifest Destiny, 1847–1852.* New York: Scribners, 1947.

Potter, David M. *The Impending Crisis, 1848–1861.* New York: Harper & Row, 1976.

Stegmaier, Mark J. *Texas, New Mexico, and the Compromise of 1850: Boundary Dispute and Sectional Crisis.* Kent, OH: Kent State University Press, 1996.

COMPUTER SECURITY ACT OF 1987

Derrek M. Davis

Personal computers (PCs) have brought about an information revolution. The PC has become a universal tool for developing, storing, and accessing information. The Internet has also grown exponentially, connecting computers together worldwide, and creating an "information superhighway" for the transmission of PC users's thoughts and ideas. This information revolution, in turn, has led to a high level of hacker activity and other abuses that disrupt the system. All of these events created concern in the federal government, one of the largest computer users in the country, over the security of its computer systems and the information housed within them. To further exacerbate the situation, federal employees lacked training in security technology, and the government had not created a central authority responsible for setting standards and policies for its computer security. This situation prompted Congress and federal agencies to address the rising concern over computer security in the federal government.

By the mid-1980s Congress passed several pieces of legislation attempting to address the issue of computer security.

By the mid-1980s Congress passed several pieces of legislation attempting to address the issue of computer security. The Computer Fraud and Abuse Act, for example, made it a federal offense to either knowingly access a computer without authorization, or to have proper authorization and use a computer for unauthorized purposes. The legislators, however, made no attempt to create a central authority in the federal government responsible for computer security.

Originally, The Office of Management and Budget was responsible for computer security policy, the National Security Agency (NSA) was responsible for securing classified information, and the Department of Commerce had responsibility for setting computer and processing standards for federal government computers, but no central authority existed to coordinate the effects of these three government agencies. Seeing this problem, in 1984 President

Ronald Reagan issued National Security Decision Directive 145, the National Policy on Telecommunications and Automated Information Systems Security, handing control for security of government computer systems to a National Telecommunications and Information Systems Security Council composed primarily of defense and intelligence agencies. This directive, however, was controversial and subject to widespread criticism. Nevertheless, the growing need for a central authority led Congress to act.

CSA sought to improve the security and privacy of sensitive information in federal computer systems and it ultimately won comprehensive approval and became law in 1987.

After numerous hearings on the subject of computer security and information privacy, Representative Dan Glickman of Kansas introduced the Computer Security and Training Act of 1985, to place the duty of computer security training and standards under the authority of the National Bureau of Standards. This bill failed and Representative Glickman introduced a second bill, the Computer Security Act of 1987 (CSA) (P.L. 100-235, 101 Stat. 1724), this time addressing four major concerns: federal government computer security, the role of the NSA, a new sensitive but unclassified information classification, and the lack of training government employees had in the use of federal computers containing sensitive information. In short, this bill sought to improve the security and privacy of sensitive information in federal computer systems and it ultimately won comprehensive approval and became law in 1987.

The passage of the Computer Security Act (CSA) did not, however, clarify the role of the government's actions in technology security and the NSA continued to seek a more active role in setting governmental security standards than Congress originally intended. In 1994 President Clinton issued Presidential Decision Directive 29, a directive that created a Security Policy Board. This Board proposed that the President consolidate all government computer security activities by placing them under the auspices of the NSA. In 2001, President George W. Bush disbanded this Board and transferred its duties to the Policy Coordination Committees, which includes the Records Access and Information Security Committee under the authority of the NSA.

These changes led Congress to reconsider the CSA in an effort to reaffirm the role of a single agency for the purposes of establishing computer security standards. Congress sought to amend the act with the Computer Security Enhancement Acts of 1997, 1999, and 2001, bills designed to address technological advancements that had occurred since 1987 and to reaffirm a single agency to lead computer security activities. Each measure passed the House and made its way through the Senate subcommittees, but none reached the Senate Floor for a vote. There have since been no new attempts to amend the Computer Security Act.

The CSA provided a clear framework for the establishment of federal government security standards. Since this time, however, it is apparent that the defense and intelligence communities, led by the executive branch and the NSA, have made attempts to change its framework. It appears the security of government computers falls into an uncertain realm where both the executive and legislative branches seek to gain authority and to control security activity. Unless these two branches of government make a

The security of government computers falls into an uncertain realm where both the executive and legislative branches seek to gain authority and to control security activity.

concerted effort to centralize the security of federal computer systems, no real coordination of efforts will occur and governmental systems could remain insecure.

See also: COUNTERFEIT ACCESS DEVICE AND COMPUTER FRAUD AND ABUSE ACT OF 1984; ELECTRONIC COMMUNICATIONS PRIVACY ACT OF 1986.

BIBLIOGRAPHY

Geewax, Marilyn. "Government Computer Security Found Lacking," *Atlanta Journal-Constitution,* November 10, 2001: F4.

Hillburg, Bill. "Fed's Computer Security Effort Gets Failing Grade." *Daily News (Los Angeles)* November 20, 2002: N16.

Mulhall, Tom. "Where Have All the Hackers Gone?: Part 4—Legislation." *Computers and Security* 16, no. 4 (1997): 298–303.

Russell, Deborah and G.T. Gangemi, Sr. *Computer Security Basics.* Sebastopol, CA: O'Reilly & Associates, 1991.

Schneider, Fred B., ed. *Trust in Cyberspace.* Washington, DC: National Academy Press, 1999.

Van Heuven, Marten, Maarten Botterman, and Stephan de Spiegeleire. *Managing New Issues: Cyber Security in an Era of Technological Change.* Santa Monica, CA: Rand, 2003.

COMSTOCK ACT (1873)

Sandra Rierson

The brainchild of a zealous and devout New England Congregationalist, Anthony Comstock, the Comstock Act (17 Stat. 599) was passed after little debate in March 1873, in the last days of Ulysses S. Grant's first term as president. The act prohibited the dissemination of any "article of an immoral nature, or any drug or medicine, or any article whatever for the prevention of contraception or procuring of abortion" through the U.S. mail or across state lines. Although the act was amended to delete references to contraceptive devices, it remains on the books today and forbids use of the mails to distribute "**obscene**" material and anything "which is advertised or described in a manner calculated to lead another to use or apply it for producing abortion...." The act's constitutionality was upheld in three cases on the grounds that the First Amendment does not protect "obscene" speech (*Smith v. United States,* 1977; *United States v. Reidel,* 1971; and *Roth v. United States,* 1957). However, the courts have not ruled on its provisions regarding abortion-related information, largely because they are not enforced.

obscene: morally offensive; designed to degrade or corrupt

BACKGROUND

Congress first contemplated censorship of the U.S. Mail while the **Abolitionist** movement was under way. In 1836 President Andrew Jackson sponsored a

abolitionist: one favoring principles or measures fostering the end of slavery

bill to prevent use of the mail to disseminate inflammatory Abolitionist tracts. The bill was rejected, largely on First Amendment grounds. Congress did not take up censorship of the mails again until 1842, when it amended the Tariff Act to ban importation of "prints" and "pictures" that were "obscene or immoral." In doing so, Congress made little progress in stemming the flow of objectionable materials in the U.S. mail.

The Tariff Act did nothing to prevent circulation of home-grown "pornography," and it soon became apparent that Civil War combatants were receiving more than just letters from home via the U.S. mail. The war had spawned a thriving business, primarily based out of New York City, in arguably "obscene" novels, pamphlets, and photographs. Congress first tackled the problem in 1865, as the war itself drew to a close. The new obscenity law made it a crime to mail any "obscene book, pamphlet, picture, [or] print." Violation of the law was a misdemeanor offense punishable by a fine of no more than $500 or imprisonment of up to one year.

Although the act was amended to delete references to contraceptive devices, it remains on the books today and forbids use of the mails to distribute "obscene" material and anything "which is advertised or described in a manner calculated to lead another to use or apply it for producing abortion...."

ANTHONY COMSTOCK'S CRUSADE

Efforts to stamp out pornography took a great leap forward in 1873, largely thanks to the efforts of Anthony Comstock (1844–1915). Comstock was a pre-eminent and, in the opinion of many, infamous social reformer of the **Reconstruction** era. Born in rural New Canaan, Connecticut, Comstock was a fire-and-brimstone devotee of the Congregationalist Church. He served in the Union Army and subsequently moved to a boarding house in New York City, where he found work as a dry-goods clerk. Comstock was appalled by the moral decay he perceived around him, evidenced by the rampant drinking, gambling, solicitation of prostitution, and consumption of "dirty books" by his fellow boarders.

Reconstruction: the political and economic reorganization and reestablishment of the South after the Civil War

Comstock began a personal crusade against the purveyors of "obscene literature," which soon became his full-time job. Sponsored by the affluent members of the Young Men's Christian Association (YMCA), and later the New York Society for the Suppression of Vice (NYSSV), Comstock persuaded merchants to sell him sexually explicit books, and then demanded that the local police arrest the merchants for violating state obscenity laws. Comstock used this technique, which today would be known as entrapment, throughout his career as a crusader against vice. Comstock took his campaign to a national level when, under the sponsorship of the NYSSV, he lobbied Congress for a tougher federal obscenity law. His efforts culminated in the Comstock Act, which was signed into law by Ulysses S. Grant on March 3, 1873.

The Comstock Act significantly broadened and toughened the 1865 obscenity law passed by Congress. It expanded the definition of obscenity to include any information "for preventing conception or producing an abortion." The penalty for a first-time offender increased to a maximum $5000 fine or five years in jail. A repeat offender could be fined up to $10,000 or spend up to ten years in prison.

The Tariff Act did nothing to prevent circulation of home-grown "pornography," and it soon became apparent that Civil War combatants were receiving more than just letters from home via the U.S. mail.

As the power of the federal government expanded, crusaders increasingly viewed Congress as the preferred vehicle for restoring moral order to the country.

Prohibition: period from 1919 to 1933, during which the making, transport, and sale of alcoholic beverages was illegal in the United States

Other works of literature that Comstock sought to censor included such classics as works by Homer, Ovid, and Boccaccio.

censor: to restrict the expression of something considered objectionable

UNSETTLED AND UNSETTLING TIMES

Although Anthony Comstock referred to the new law as "my Act," the Comstock Act was more than just the product of Comstock's personal religious fervor and dogged determination. The years following the Civil War were a time of great social upheaval in America. The twin forces of industrialization and Reconstruction, combined with record levels of immigration, shook the foundations of American society, just as it was reeling from the death and devastation wrought by the Civil War. As the power of the federal government expanded, crusaders increasingly viewed Congress as the preferred vehicle for restoring moral order to the country. With the Morrill Act of 1862, Congress ended polygamy in Utah. The Federal Lottery Act prohibited use of the mail to transport lottery tickets. The Mann Act outlawed the transportation of women across state lines for prostitution. Perhaps the most well-known of the moral reform crusades was the Temperance Movement, which ushered in the period of **Prohibition**. In 1919 Congress passed the Volstead Act and ratified the Eighteenth Amendment, banning the manufacture and sale of alcohol throughout the United States.

PROSECUTIONS

Three days after the Comstock Act was enacted, Comstock was commissioned to enforce the act as a Special Agent of the U.S. Post Office. He was given the power to arrest those who violated the act. He once bragged that he had convicted enough people to fill sixty-one passenger cars on a train, approximately 4,000 individuals. One of the most well-publicized prosecutions under the Comstock Act was that of Margaret Sanger, a leader of the birth control movement, in 1914. Sanger was arrested for publishing *The Woman Rebel,* a monthly newspaper which took a radical stand on many women's issues, including birth control, and *Family Limitation,* a pamphlet describing birth control methods. While her trial was pending, Sanger fled to Europe. She returned to the United States a year later, and ultimately the charges against her were dismissed. Her husband, William Sanger, was not so lucky. He was convicted of violating the act for distributing a copy of *Family Limitation.* In another widely publicized case, Comstock arrested Ezra Heywood in 1877 for publishing *Cupid's Yokes, or, The Binding Forces of Conjugal Life,* a book attacking the institution of marriage and the Comstock Act. Heywood was convicted but later pardoned by President Rutherford B. Hayes in 1878.

Comstock targeted not only birth control advocates as purveyors of the obscene. Comstock put the poet Walt Whitman's *Leaves of Grass* in this category, specifically the poems *To a Common Prostitute* and *A Woman Waits For Me,* due to their use of sexual imagery. Most likely because of negative publicity, the charges were dropped. Other works of literature that Comstock sought to **censor** included such classics as works by Homer, Ovid, and Boccaccio. Comstock also arrested Alfred Knoedler, a respected art dealer on New York City's Fifth Avenue, for selling reproductions of nudes by the French painter Jean-Jacques Henner. Public reaction to Knoedler's arrest was also overwhelmingly negative.

SUBSEQUENT HISTORY

In 1878 a petition signed by approximately 70,000 citizens, requesting the repeal of the Comstock Act, was presented to Congress. But Congress did not repeal it, and it remains on the books in a modified form today.

The most significant change in today's Comstock Act is the absence of any restrictions regarding contraceptive devices. Although court opinions began to undermine this aspect of the Comstock Act in the 1930s, Congress did not amend the act to delete references to contraception until 1971. Congress amended the law by striking the blanket prohibitions on the mailing of all advertisements for contraceptives in 1971, but it did not delete the particular ban on **unsolicited** advertisements. In 1983 the Supreme Court ruled that the ban on such advertisements was unconstitutional in *Bolger v. Youngs Drug Products Corp.*

Surprisingly, the act's restrictions regarding abortion-related information remain on the books, even though the restrictions are inconsistent with the Supreme Court's 1973 decision in *Roe v. Wade*. In 1994 Congress increased the maximum fine for a first-time violation of the act from $5,000 to $250,000. In 1996 Congress amended the Comstock Act to extend the ban on abortion-related information to the Internet. Although bills have been introduced in both the House and Senate to repeal the abortion-related provisions of the Comstock Act, they have not become the law. Alexander Sanger, president of Planned Parenthood of New York City, and other plaintiffs filed a lawsuit challenging the 1996 amendments to the Comstock Act, but the suit was dismissed because the government had not yet attempted to enforce the act. As long as the government chooses to ignore the Comstock Act, it is unlikely to go away.

See also: MANN ACT.

BIBLIOGRAPHY

Beisel, Nicola. *Imperiled Innocents: Anthony Comstock and Family Reproduction in Victorian America*. Princeton, NJ: Princeton University Press, 1997.

Broun, Heywood and Margaret Leech. *Anthony Comstock, Roundsman of the Lord*. New York: A & C Boni, 1927.

Chen, Constance M. *The Sex Side of Life: Mary Ware Dennett's Pioneering Battle for Birth Control and Sex Education*. New York: The New Press, 1996.

Comstock, Anthony. *Frauds Exposed; or, How the People are Deceived and Robbed, and Youth Corrupted*. 1880. Reprinted by Patterson Smith Publishing, 1969.

Comstock, Anthony. *Morals Versus Art*. New York: J. S. Ogilvie and Co., 1887.

Foster, Gaines M. *Moral Reconstruction: Christian Lobbyists and the Federal Legislation of Morality, 1865–1920*. Chapel Hill: University of North Carolina Press, 2002.

Paul, James C. N., and Murray L. Schwartz. *Federal Censorship: Obscenity in the Mail*. New York: Free Press, 1961.

Sanger, Margaret. *Comstockery in America*. 1915. Transcribed by the Margaret Sanger Papers Project, Sponsored by the Department of History at New York University (1999). <http://www.nyu.edu/projects/sanger/comstockery_in_america.htm>.

Tone, Andrea. *Devices and Desires: A History of Contraceptives in America*. New York: Hill and Wang, 2001.

unsolicited: not wanted or requested

The Comstock Act and the Internet
Sandra Rierson

In 1996, as part of the omnibus Telecommunications Decency Act (TDA), Congress amended the Comstock Act to extend the ban on abortion-related information to the Internet. Representative Henry Hyde, Republican of Illinois, was instrumental in adding this language to the Comstock Act. As amended, the act states that anyone who "knowingly uses" an "interactive computer service" to obtain anything "designed, adapted, or intended for producing abortion" or any "advertisement" or other notice indicating the means by which an abortive device may be obtained, is guilty of violating the act. The courts later found many provisions of the Telecommunications Decency Act unconstitutional.

CONGRESSIONAL BUDGET AND IMPOUNDMENT CONTROL ACT (1974)

Louis Fisher

Excerpt from the Congressional Budget and Impoundment Control Act

(1) to assure effective congressional control over the budgetary process;

(2) to provide for the congressional determination each year of the appropriate level of Federal revenues and expenditures;

(3) to provide a system of impoundment control;

(4) to establish national budget priorities; and

(5) to provide for the furnishing of information by the executive branch in a manner that will assist the Congress in discharging its duties.

In response to decades of budget conflicts between presidents and the legislative branch, in 1974 Congress passed the Congressional Budget and Impoundment Control Act (P.L. 93-344, 88 Stat. 297). The act was intended to reorganize budgetary procedures and place limits on presidents who refused to spend funds for the purposes set forth in appropriations bills. Through reforms contained in the Budget Act, Congress hoped to correct problems such as late appropriations, dependence on continuing resolutions (short-term spending measures), budget deficits, and inadequate control over entitlement programs (including Social Security and Medicaid).

However, those problems not only persisted, they grew worse. When budget deficits exploded after 1981, Congress and the executive branch agreed that the 1974 process could not handle the crisis. The two branches turned instead to new statutes, including the Gramm-Rudman-Hollings Act of 1985 (often referred to as Gramm-Rudman), the Budget Enforcement Act of 1990, and the Line Item Veto Act of 1996.

GOALS OF THE ACT

The Budget Act of 1974 assumed that lawmakers would behave more responsibly if they faced up to budget totals and voted explicitly on budget aggregates (in other words, budgets viewed as whole units). Previously, Congress voted on separate bills concerning appropriations, revenues, and authorizations. The heart of the statute consisted of new budget committees in each house of Congress that would be responsible for reporting budget resolutions. These resolutions contained five aggregates: total outlays, total budget authority, total revenues, the deficit or surplus, and the public debt. Outlays and budget authority were organized into major functional categories, such as national defense, agriculture, and transportation, to permit debate on budget priorities. Under the act, the first resolution (eventually discarded) would be passed by May 15 of each year, providing a target for the second resolution, to be acted on by September 15 of each year. The budget resolution provided a ceiling on spending and a floor on revenues. If a mis-

The Budget Act of 1974 assumed that lawmakers would behave more responsibly if they faced up to budget totals and voted explicitly on budget aggregates (in other words, budgets viewed as whole units).

match existed between the totals in the fall resolution and passage of individual bills, Congress could enact a "reconciliation bill" to direct committees to report additional savings.

The 1974 statute also established the Congressional Budget Office (CBO) to give lawmakers technical support. CBO estimates the cost of pending legislation, performs scorekeeping functions, and makes projections (forecasts) about the economy. The statute changed the fiscal year (accounting period) to begin October 1 rather than July 1. This change was meant to give Congress additional time to pass all the appropriations bills before the fiscal year began, in the hopes of avoiding reliance on continuing resolutions. However, in practice, appropriations bills are enacted later than ever, if at all. Before the Budget Act, it was rare for a fiscal year to end without Congress passing the regular appropriations bills. After 1974, it became a common practice. Moreover, deficits were larger—far larger—than they were before passage of the Budget Act. Time after time, budgets submitted by presidents and budget resolutions passed by Congress have been unreliable and deceptive, because they underestimated spending and overestimated revenues. Budget deadlines established by the statute are routinely ignored.

The purpose of the Budget Act was to restore legislative control over the purse. Under some circumstances, however, the new system vastly increases presidential power. That potential emerged in 1981 when President Ronald Reagan managed to seize control of the budget resolution, enabling him to cut back domestic programs, increase military spending, and cut taxes. The previous system was decentralized, making it difficult for any president to dictate budget results to such a degree. Under that system, action at the committee and subcommittee level served to modify presidential proposals. After 1974, however, the centralized system of budget resolutions offered presidents a new means of dominating the process.

THE PRESIDENTIAL POWER OF IMPOUNDMENT

From George Washington forward, presidents at times declined to spend all of the funds that Congress had appropriated. Political compromises and understandings between the legislative and executive branches kept those conflicts from developing into serious problems. This informal system broke down in the 1970s when President Richard Nixon began to withhold, or impound, funds in a manner—quantitatively and qualitatively—that threatened congressional power. He severely curtailed and in some instances terminated federal programs. In a series of cases, federal courts ruled against the administration's policy of impoundment.

Congress responded by passing legislation, Title X of the 1974 statute, to place new limits on the presidential power of impoundment. If the withholding was temporary (a *deferral*), either house of Congress could disapprove it at any time, and the funds would have to be released. If the withholding was to be permanent (a *rescission*), the president would have to obtain the support of both houses of Congress within forty-five days of continuous session. Otherwise, the funds would have to be released.

COURT CHALLENGES

The rule concerning deferrals was shaken in 1983 when the Supreme Court struck down the legislative veto in *INS v. Chadha*. The veto by one house of

The purpose of the Budget Act was to restore legislative control over the purse.

Line Item Veto Act of 1996

The Line Item Veto Act of 1996 allowed the president of the United States to strike individual items from spending bills approved by Congress. Previously, the president had been required either to accept an entire bill or to veto it in its entirety. The purpose of the act was to allow the president to eliminate unnecessary spending in order to help balance the budget. Proponents argued that the Line Item Veto allowed the president to target wasteful spending that Congress had approved for political reasons; critics argued, on the other hand, that it was antidemocratic and liable to be abused to subvert the will of Congress. In 1998 the Line Item Veto was declared unconstitutional by the Supreme Court on the grounds that the president was not allowed to rewrite bills approved by Congress.

Congress was now no longer available to disapprove deferrals. Initially, the Reagan administration agreed not to abuse its veto-free deferral power. But after 1985 the administration began using deferrals aggressively to meet deficit targets imposed by Gramm-Rudman. Members of Congress and private parties went to court to challenge the president's deferral authority.

In 1986 a federal district judge decided that the president's deferral authority under the 1974 law was no longer available. The judge concluded that the history of the statute demonstrated that Congress would have preferred no statute to one stripped of the one-house veto. That decision was upheld by an appellate court in *New Haven v. United States* (1987). Those decisions limited presidential deferrals to routine managerial actions, a policy that Congress in 1987 enacted into law. As federal deficits climbed in the 1980s, lawmakers were under pressure to delegate greater authority to the president to curb spending. The result was the Line Item Veto Act of 1996.

EFFECTIVENESS

Budget resolutions were initially praised as an effective method of permitting centralized, systematic, and coherent legislative action. In 1974, as now, it was difficult to defend fragmentation, splintering, and decentralization when reformers pressed eagerly for "coordination" and a "unified budget process." However, a legislative approach that examines pieces of the whole as well as the whole is a healthy check on presidential initiatives. Ironically, the centralized framework of the 1974 statute helps advance presidential goals.

See also: BALANCED BUDGET AND EMERGENCY DEFICIT CONTROL ACT; PUBLIC DEBT ACTS.

BIBLIOGRAPHY

Cogan, John F., Timothy J. Muris, and Allen Schick. *The Budget Puzzle: Understanding Federal Spending*. Stanford, CA: Stanford University Press, 1974.

Fisher, Louis. *The Politics of Shared Power*. College Station: Texas A & M University Press, 1998.

Gilmour, John B. *Reconcilable Differences? Congress, the Budget Process, and the Deficit*. Berkeley: University of California Press, 1990.

Pfiffner, James P. *The President, the Budget, and Congress: Impoundment and the 1974 Budget Act*. Boulder, CO: Westview Press, 1979.

Schick, Allen. *Congress and Money: Budgeting, Spending, and Taxing*. Washington, DC: Urban Institute Press, 1981.

Stockman, David A. *The Triumph of Politics: How the Reagan Revolution Failed*. New York: Harper and Row, 1986.

CONSUMER CREDIT PROTECTION ACT (1969)

Richard Slottee

The Consumer Credit Protection Act (CCPA) (1969, P.L. 90-321) is the compendium of federal statutes found in Title 15 of the United States Code.

Congress has amended the CCPA on several occasions by adding individual federal statutes, called subchapters, each focusing on a specific consumer issue.

SUBCHAPTERS OF CCPA

Subchapter I of CCPA is the Truth in Lending Act (TILA), becoming effective on July 1, 1969. Congress's primary purpose in adopting TILA was to ensure the meaningful disclosure of significant credit terms to consumers. The act requires those sellers, lenders, and lessors of personal property subject to the act to disclose certain credit terms with uniform **terminology**, location, and meaning in the contract, regardless of where the parties sign the agreement.

To effectuate TILA, The Federal Reserve Board adopted "Regulation Z." TILA, along with Regulation Z, contain provisions regarding the issuance of credit cards, liability for unauthorized use of credit cards, credit card billing error resolution procedures, **notice and disclosure requirements** for credit card solicitations, disclosure requirements for **high-rate mortgages** and **reverse mortgages**, and **rescission provisions** for various types of transactions in which a **security interest** is retained in a consumer's principal residence.

Subchapter II of the CCPA is the Restriction on Garnishment Act that became effective July 1, 1970. This law provides a maximum level of wage **garnishment** for any **judgment debtor** and prohibits an employer from terminating an employee based solely on the fact that the employee's wages have been garnished.

Subchapter II-A is the Credit Repair Organizations Act, enacted by Congress on September 30, 1996. This statute pertains to credit repair organizations that provide services to individuals with debts resulting from consumer credit transactions. The law prohibits certain types of deceptive practices, requires mandatory **disclosures** in any contract signed by a customer of a credit repair organization, and allows the customer three business days from the date the contract is signed to **rescind** the contract.

Subchapter III of CCPA is the Fair Credit Reporting Reform Act of 1996 (FCRA) also enacted on September 30, 1996. This law applies to consumer reporting agencies, users of consumer reports, and persons or businesses that report negative information to consumer reporting agencies. The purpose of the FCRA is to protect individual consumers from false, misleading, or obsolete credit information by requiring consumer-reporting agencies to adopt reasonable procedures with regard to the confidentiality, accuracy, relevancy, and proper utilization of such information. The FCRA also requires consumer reporting agencies and users of **consumer credit information** to make certain disclosures to consumers affected by use of that information. Administrative enforcement of the FCRA rests primarily with the Federal Trade Commission that has **promulgated** Statements of General Policy regarding the various provisions of the FCRA.

Subchapter IV of CCPA is the Equal Credit Opportunity Act (ECOA) and became effective on March 23, 1977. The purpose of the ECOA is to prohibit discrimination in credit transactions on one or more of nine bases: race, color, religion, national origin, sex, marital status, age, the fact that all or part of income derives from a public assistance program, or the fact that an applicant has in good faith exercised any right under the compendium of statutes in the Consumer Credit Protection Act.

The ECOA applies to every aspect of credit transactions, from advertising of credit availability to the termination of existing credit. The act applies

terminology: the vocabulary of technical terms and usages appropriate to a particular trade, science, or art

notice and disclosure requirements: in contracts and other transactions, the law requires that key provisions and penalties be disclosed in plain English so a consumer can make an informed decision

high-rate mortgages: a mortgage with a high interest rate because it is perceived to be a higher risk based on the purchaser's credit history

reverse mortgage: a type of home mortgage under which an elderly homeowner is allowed a long-term loan in the form of monthly payments against his or her paid-off equity as collateral, repayable when the home is eventually sold

rescission provisions: provisions in a contract that, if they occur or fail to occur, allow the contract to be rescinded

security interest: a form of interest in property which provides that the property may be sold on default in order to satisfy the obligation for which the security interest is given; a mortgage is used to grant a security interest in real property

garnish: process whereby one's property or money that is in the possession of a third party is paid to another to satisfy one's debt

judgment debtor: one who owes money as a result of a judgment in favor of a creditor

disclosure: obligation of parties to reveal material facts deemed necessary for one to make an informed decision

rescind: to declare a contract void in its inception and to put an end to it as though it never existed

consumer credit information: credit experiences, such as your bill-paying history, the number and type of accounts you have, late payments, collection actions, outstanding debt, and the age of your accounts

promulgate: to make the terms of a law known by formal public announcement

aggrieved: one who has been injured or suffered a loss to one's property interest, monetary interest, personal rights, or physical injury

whether the credit is business or consumer credit, whether the obligation involves a finance charge or installment payments, or whether the person **aggrieved** by the discrimination is an individual or a business organization. The ECOA applies to the extension of credit where the right to defer payment of an obligation is granted. To enforce, interpret, and expand the ECOA, the Federal Reserve Board promulgated "Regulation B."

Subchapter V of CCPA is the Fair Debt Collection Practices Act (FDCPA) that became effective March 20, 1978. The purpose of the FDCPA is to eliminate unethical and abusive practices by debt collectors while engaged in the collection of consumer debts. The FDCPA attempts to accomplish this goal through a series of open-ended lists of prohibited activities. The Act applies to debt collectors who collect debts on behalf of third parties, but it does not apply to the collection efforts of original creditors. Under appropriate circumstances, an attorney is considered a debt collector subject to the provisions of the act. For example, an attorney who, in the regular course of business, rep-

The Consumer Credit Protection Act of 1969 as amended provides for the recovery of damages by the aggrieved consumer, with jurisdiction in either state or federal court. The act covers the meaningful disclosure of significant credit terms, the issuance of credit cards, wage garnishments, credit repair organizations, consumer reporting agencies, and prohibits discrimination in credit transactions on one or more of nine bases: race, color, religion, national origin, sex, marital status, age, and the fact that all or part of someone's income derives from a public assistance program. The act protects the consumer above, as she pays her bills online. (©2003 KELLY A. QUIN)

resents creditors attempting to collect consumer debts would be considered a debt collector. The Federal Trade Commission issues official staff commentary that serves as official interpretations of the FDCPA.

Finally, Subchapter VI of CCPA is the Electronic Fund Transfers Act (EFTA), enacted on August 9, 1989. The purpose of the EFTA is to establish the basic rights, responsibilities, and obligations of consumers and financial institutions involved in transactions using electronic money transfer. The act provides limitations on the liability of consumers for the unauthorized use of access devices such as the codes, cards, or devices used to reach funds through an automated teller machine (ATM). It requires federal institutions to provide certain disclosures to consumers prior to issuing an access device, and sets out procedures for the investigation of the unauthorized use of an access device. To effectuate, interpret, and expand EFTA, the Federal Reserve Board adopted "Regulation E."

All of the laws in the Consumer Protection Act provide for the recovery of damages by the aggrieved consumer, and have jurisdiction in either state or federal court.

See also: TRUTH IN LENDING ACT.

BIBLIOGRAPHY

Fonseca, John R. *Consumer Credit Compliance Manual.* 2nd ed. Rochester, N.Y.: Lawyers Co-operative Publishing, 1984.

INTERNET RESOURCE

The Federal Reserve Board Consumer Handbook to Credit Protection Laws. <http://www.federalreserve.gov/pubs/consumerhdbk/>

CONTRACT DISPUTES ACT (1978)

Steven L. Schooner

The Contract Disputes Act (P.L. 95-563) allows federal government contractors to sue the United States government for monetary damages related to their contractual dealings. This act is tremendously important to the numerous contractors that provide the federal government with more than $200 billion of services, supplies, and construction each year. The act **waives** the government's **sovereign immunity**, permitting contractors to sue the government in either an administrative tribunal (a board that hears appeals) or in a court. The act establishes the procedures to be used by contractors and contracting officers (those authorized to bind the government in contract) in resolving disputes involving contracts with the federal government, specifically the executive branch.

Congress intended the act to replace the existing system for resolving government contract disputes, a system that had developed over time without good planning, and to impose order on the process. Accordingly, the act contains detailed provisions for handling contract claims by and against the government, which, ultimately, evolve into disputes. It is

waive: to give up voluntarily

sovereign immunity: a doctrine that prevents bringing a lawsuit against the government without the government's consent

This act is tremendously important to the numerous contractors that provide the federal government with more than $200 billion of services, supplies, and construction each year.

important to distinguish disputes, which arise between a contractor and the government during or after the performance of a contract, from protests, which involve an offeror, or prospective contractor, contesting the award of the contract or the conduct of the contractor selection process.

THE CLAIMS AND DISPUTES PROCESS

The disputes process begins with a claim. A claim is a written demand for a sum certain of money (but cannot be an invoice or routine request for payment). The Contract Disputes Act (CDA) requires that, prior to litigation, the parties to the contract (the contractor and the government agency) exhaust an administrative remedy, intended to facilitate negotiation and settlement. For example, the CDA requires that, if contractors' claims exceed $100,000, they must certify that: (1) the claim is made in good faith, (2) the claim's supporting data are accurate and complete to the best of their knowledge and belief, and (3) the amount requested is an accurate tally of how much the contractor believes the government is liable for.

This certification requirement has prompted staggering amounts of litigation. The requirement was added at the urging of Admiral Hyman Rickover, the father of the nuclear navy, who sought to deter contractors from artificially inflating their claims in the hope of extracting favorable negotiated settlements from the government. For that reason, the act also includes a severe penalty for contractors that improperly inflate their claims: "If a contractor is unable to support any part of his claim and it is determined that such inability is attributable to misrepresentation of fact or fraud on the part of the contractor, he shall be liable to the Government for an amount equal to such unsupported part of the claim in addition to all costs to the Government attributable to the cost of reviewing said part of his claim."

Prior to litigation, the disputed claim must be the subject of a written decision of a contracting officer, who has the authority to resolve the matter. The contracting officer's decision requires certain formalities, the most important of which is that the decision must notify the contractor of its rights to initiate further litigation. If the contracting officer fails to render a decision within a specified period, typically sixty days, the claim is considered to have been denied, and the contractor can initiate its suit.

Once the contractor receives a contracting officer's decision, the CDA provides contractors with their choice of a forum in which to litigate their claims. A contractor may appeal a contracting officer's decision to an agency board of contract appeals (BCA) or to the United States Court of Federal Claims. Regardless of which forum a contractor chooses, if the contractor is dissatisfied with the result, it may appeal the decision to the United States Court of Appeals for the Federal Circuit. If still dissatisfied, either party can petition for review in the Supreme Court.

Under the act, boards of contract appeals can grant any relief that would be available to a litigant asserting a contract claim in the United States Court of Federal Claims.

BCAs AND THE COURT

Under the act, boards of contract appeals can grant any relief that would be available to a litigant asserting a contract claim in the United States Court of Federal Claims.

The main difference between the BCAs and the Court of Federal Claims is that the court can also hear a counterclaim in fraud, whereas the BCAs lack jurisdiction over fraud matters.

Another difference has to do with the authority to settle disputes. If a contractor chooses to litigate at a board of contract appeals, the government's settlement authority rests with the agency's contracting officer. If the contractor files suit in the Court of Federal Claims, settlement authority rests with the U.S. attorney general. If a contractor decides to file separate but related claims in more than one forum, the Court of Federal Claims may order that all of the suits either be consolidated at the court, or transferred to a BCA.

The CDA formally created the boards of contract appeals and established the position of administrative judge to preside over board proceedings. Each BCA must have at least three administrative judges. In the 1990s the number of BCAs decreased. The largest of the agency boards is the Armed Services Board of Contract Appeals (ASBCA), with approximately two dozen administrative judges. The General Services Administration Board (GSBCA), with less than half as many judges, is the second largest. Most boards have attempted to maintain uniform rules.

In an effort to make resolution of claims efficient, quick, and inexpensive, the CDA provides expedited procedures for small claims (of $50,000 or less) and accelerated procedures for claims of $100,000 or less. If a contractor chooses these procedures, the BCA must render a decision within 120 or 180 days, respectively. The act also provides for the payment of interest from the time the contracting officer receives a contractor claim until payment.

HISTORICAL BACKGROUND

Prior to the CDA, a contractor's right to sue the government depended on the terms of the contract, which typically included a standard disputes clause. The pre-CDA disputes clause required contractors to exhaust their administrative remedy (in other words, litigate in the boards of contract appeals) before pursuing litigation in court. The precursor to the CDA was the Wunderlich Act of 1954. The purpose of that act was to overcome the effect of the 1951 Supreme Court decision in the case of *United States v. Wunderlich*. Under the ruling in *Wunderlich*, the decisions of government officers in relation to the disputes clause were held to be final in the absence of fraud on the part of the government officers. The Wunderlich Act ensured that contract clauses would not prevent judicial review of agency decisions on disputes. It also permitted the courts to overrule administrative decisions that were not supported by "substantial evidence."

Prior to the CDA, a contractor's right to sue the government depended on the terms of the contract, which typically included a standard disputes clause.

One of the CDA's most significant contributions was that it included claims that both *arose out of* and *related to* the contract. A claim *arising out of* the contract is a claim that can be resolved under a contract clause that offers a remedy. A claim *relating to* the contract is one for which no specific contract clause provides such relief.

AMENDMENTS

The act has been amended in attempts to resolve unanticipated jurisdictional problems. The most controversial of these problems dealt with nonmonetary claims, such as claims related to the termination of a contract for contractor **default**. In addition, the act now specifically endorses the use of **alternative dispute resolution** (ADR) procedures.

default: the omission or failure to perform a legal or contractual duty

alternative dispute resolution: any means of settling disputes outside of the courtroom, typically including arbitration, mediation, early neutral evaluation, and conciliation

See also: WALSH-HEALEY ACT (PUBLIC CONTRACTS ACT OF 1936).

BIBLIOGRAPHY

Bond, Gene Perry, et al. "The Contract Disputes Act of 1978 Twentieth Anniversary Essays." *Public Contract Law Journal* 28, no. 4 (summer 1999): 525-676.

Cibinic, John, Jr., and Ralph C. Nash, Jr. *Administration of Government Contracts,* 3d ed. Washington, DC: George Washington University Press, 1995.

Peacock, Robert T., and Peter D. Ting. *Contract Disputes Act: Annotated.* Washington, DC: Federal Publications, Inc., 1998.

CONTROLLED SUBSTANCES ACT (1970)

Steven Harmon Wilson

Excerpt from the Controlled Substances Act

... Many of the drugs included ... have a useful and legitimate medical purpose and are necessary to maintain the health and general welfare of the American people ... [yet] illegal importation, manufacture, distribution, and possession and improper use of controlled substances have a substantial and detrimental effect on the health and general welfare of the American people ....

The Controlled Substances Act (CSA) of 1970 (P.L. 91-513, 84 Stat. 1242) is the common name of Title II of the Comprehensive Drug Abuse Prevention and Control Act of 1970. The Comprehensive Act sought to clarify the overall aims of federal control of dangerous drugs by updating or replacing many disparate laws. Also in pursuit of this goal, the CSA attempted to establish logical and consistent penalties for criminal violations, principally by eliminating what many concerned observers considered to be unduly harsh mandatory sentencing.

HISTORY OF DRUG REGULATION

Congress has been regulating the importation and manufacture of drugs since the early 1900s. Criminal penalties for unauthorized possession of drugs began with the Narcotics Act of 1914 (the Harrison Act). In 1951 the Boggs Amendment instituted mandatory minimum sentences and eliminated parole or probation after the first offense. The Narcotic Control Act of 1956, known as the Daniel Act, increased the minimums.

The increase in drug use during the 1960s resulted in numerous long sentences and led the federal government to reexamine its punitive approach.

The increase in drug use during the 1960s resulted in numerous long sentences and led the federal government to reexamine its punitive approach. In 1965 Congress enacted the Drug Abuse Control Amendments (DACA). DACA established a Bureau of Drug Abuse Control (BDAC) within the Department of Health, Education, and Welfare (HEW, later

Health and Human Services). The law created misdemeanor penalties (that is, generally speaking, a penalty not more than one year in prison and/or fine) for illegal manufacture and sale of certain depressants, stimulants, hallucinogens, and other drugs that had not been covered under the Harrison Act and its amendments. The HEW thus gained responsibility for curbing the abuse of the newly prohibited "psychedelic" drug called LSD. The Federal Bureau of Narcotics (FBN, an agency of the Department of the Treasury) retained authority over many other drugs, including heroin, cocaine, and marijuana.

Many applauded the emergence of a multifaceted approach to the drug problem. But those who were committed to the criminal justice model of drug enforcement (generally, favoring the benefits to society of strict punishment over the benefits to the criminal of efforts at rehabilitation) were not satisfied. In February 1968 President Lyndon Johnson called the laws "a crazy quilt of inconsistent approaches and widely disparate criminal sanctions." He asked Congress to pass tougher laws and to create a powerful organization to

New York City deputy inspector Kenneth Cully behind by a ton of cocaine, 1000 pounds of marijuana and $5 million in cash seized in "Operation Whiteout." Since the 1900s Congress has been regulating the importation and manufacture of drugs. The goal of the Controlled Substances Act of 1970 was to have a comprehensive plan that would address the federal control of dangerous drugs and to update the laws and punishments that often resulted in excessive sentences. The act divided drugs into five different schedules and made distinctions between simple possession versus possession with intent to distribute. The act also covers education, treatment, and rehabilitation. (© AP/WIDE WORLD PHOTOS)

enforce them. On April 8, 1968, Congress abolished the FBN and the BDAC and created a new Justice Department agency, the Bureau of Narcotics and Dangerous Drugs (BNDD). Even after the creation of the BNDD, however, there remained other federal agencies involved somewhat in drug regulation.

President Richard Nixon proposed that Congress reduce the confusion over policy and the duplication of effort by federal agencies by combining disparate regulations into a single statute. Congress complied by enacting the Comprehensive Drug Abuse Prevention and Control Act of 1970. Nixon signed the bill on October 27, 1970, and it became effective on May 1, 1971. The legislation sought a balanced approach to the nation's drug problem. For example, Title I of the Comprehensive Act dealt with education, treatment, and rehabilitation.

MAJOR FEATURES OF THE ACT

Title II, of the CSA was the heart of the new statute. This established five "schedules" that ranked substances by balancing potential for abuse against medical usefulness. Drugs on Schedule One, including heroin, marijuana, and LSD, were deemed to have a high potential for abuse but no accepted medical use. Penalties were tied to the schedules, and violations were also ranked, with, for example, simple possession receiving a lesser punishment than possession with intent to distribute. Finally, Congress responded to criticism of mandatory minimum sentences for drug violations. Possession of a controlled substance for one's own use (that is, without an intent to distribute) was made a misdemeanor. Judges were given the discretion to place first-time, simple possession offenders on probation.

Title II established five "schedules" that ranked substances by balancing potential for abuse against medical usefulness.

FURTHER LEGISLATION

From time to time, amendments to the controlled substances statutes have been necessary. In the 1980s so-called "designer drugs," such as Ecstasy, became popular. These drugs produce effects and have a chemical structure similar to those of existing illegal drugs. In 1986 Congress prohibited these substances. More significant has been the revival of mandatory minimum sentencing. This began with the Sentencing Reform Act (SRA) of 1984, through which Congress abolished federal parole and compelled judges to observe sentencing guidelines.

Two years after enacting the SRA, Congress passed the Anti-Drug Abuse Act of 1986, which set mandatory minimum sentences based on the weight of the drugs involved in a crime. This was passed in the midst of public outcry over the crack-cocaine epidemic. Because of the political climate, the bill passed the House by a 392–16 vote. In 1988 Congress passed the Omnibus Anti-Drug Abuse Act, which created an even more comprehensive set of quantity-based mandatory minimum sentences. The disproportionate impact these laws have had on defendants of racial minorities has provoked much analysis and debate.

See also: ANTI-DRUG ABUSE ACT; NARCOTICS ACT; SENTENCING REFORM ACT.

BIBLIOGRAPHY

Inciardi, James A. *The War on Drugs II: The Continuing Epic of Heroin, Cocaine, Crack, Crime, AIDS, and Public Policy.* Mountainview, CA: Mayfield Publishing, 1992.

Jonnes, Jill. *Hep-Cats, Narcs, and Pipe Dreams: A History of America's Romance with Illegal Drugs.* New York: Scribner, 1996.

Marion, Nancy E. *A History of Federal Crime Control Initiatives, 1960–1993.* Westport, CN: Praeger, 1994.

Musto, David F. *The American Disease: Origins of Narcotic Control,* 3d ed. New York: Oxford University Press, 1999.

Rachal, Patricia. *Federal Narcotics Enforcement: Reorganization and Reform.* Boston, MA: Auburn House, 1982.

Sharp, Elaine B. *The Dilemma of Drug Policy in the United States.* New York: Harper-Collins, 1994.

Walker, William O. *Drug Control in the Americas.* Albuquerque: University of New Mexico Press, 1981.

COPYRIGHT ACT OF 1790

Shubha Ghosh

It is well known that freedom of speech and freedom of the press are the cornerstones of American democracy. Less well known is the connection between these twin freedoms and copyright law. Mark Twain, the humorist and an advocate of copyright reform, said: "Only one thing is impossible for God: to find any sense in any copyright law on the planet." More than 210 years after the passage of the first copyright law in the United States, copyright remains an elusive and complex subject.

HISTORICAL BACKGROUND: ENGLISH LAW

In the past, publishing one's writing was not nearly as easy as it is today, with the advantages of the word processor and the Web page. Take, for example, England in the sixteenth and seventeenth centuries. The right to publish depended on receiving a license to publish from the monarch. Only authorized printers, or stationers, could publish and distribute written materials. Requiring a license to print limited who could write and what could be written. Since all rights stemmed from the monarch, it was ultimately the monarch who determined what writings would be published.

In 1644 the English poet John Milton, author of *Paradise Lost,* voiced the concerns of authors whose ability to write and distribute their work freely was hampered by the political and economic organization of publishing. In *Areopagitica,* a speech named after the Ancient Greek council that espoused the burning of offensive books, Milton championed the rights of the author against the arbitrary grants of the license to publish. *Areopagitica* was presented as a "speech for the liberty of unlicensed printing before the Parliament of England." Milton condemned the requirement that printers be licensed, comparing the strict control over what could be written and the creation of books to homicide.

Milton's important work sparked a debate over the rights of authors that resulted in the enactment of the Statute of Anne in 1710. The statute was described as "an act for the encouragement of learning, by vesting the copies of printed books in the authors or purchasers of such copies." The first sentence of the statute clearly described the problem to be addressed: "Printers, Booksellers and other Persons have of late frequently taken the Liberty of printing, reprinting and publishing or causing to be printed, reprinted, and published Books and other Writings, without the Consent of the Authors or Proprietors of such Books and Writings to their very great detriment and too often to the ruin of them and their Families." To prevent this unauthorized printing, reprinting, and publishing, authors were given the exclusive right to publish, print, or reprint their books for a period of fourteen years, which could be extended upon renewal of the copyright for another fourteen years. The statute provided a modest set of fines for publishing, printing, or reprinting a book without the author's permission.

THE COLONIES, THE CONSTITUTION, AND COPYRIGHT

Against this background we come to the American colonies and the United States Constitution. Prior to Independence, several colonies had statutes that protected writers modeled on the Statute of Anne. After the Revolutionary War, all but Delaware had a statute protecting the copyright of authors. The drafters of the Constitution, without much formal debate, recognized the need for a single, uniform, national-level law to protect and regulate copyrights. This need was met by the inclusion of article I, section 8, clause 8 in the United States Constitution, which gave Congress the power "to promote the progress of Science and the Useful Arts by securing for limited times to Authors and Inventors the exclusive right to their respective Writings and Discoveries." One of Congress's first acts, in 1790, was to pass legislation on copyrights and patents.

One of Congress's first acts, in 1790, was to pass legislation on copyrights and patents.

The Copyright Act of 1790 (1 Stat. 124) was titled "An Act for the Encouragement of Learning, by Securing the Copies of Maps, Charts and Books to the Authors and Proprietors of Such Copies" and was modeled on the Statute of Anne. Both acts were concerned with the "encouragement of learning." Both secured the rights of authors in copies of their works. Both acts provided protection for two consecutive fourteen-year terms. The term of the 1790 act was extended in 1831 to two twenty-eight-year terms.

Fair Use

"Fair use" is the term for the set of principles under which a copyrighted work, or parts of it, can be used without permission from the creator or the payment of royalties. Unfortunately, there are no simple rules defining fair use; lawmakers have provided an ambiguous set of principles to allow for judicial interpretation. According to current copyright law, fair use takes into consideration the interaction of four factors: "1) the purpose and character of the use, including whether such use is of a commercial nature or is for nonprofit educational purposes; 2) the nature of the copyrighted work; 3) the amount and substantiality of the portion used in rela-

tion to the copyrighted work as a whole; and 4) the effect of the use upon the potential market for or value of the copyrighted work." Commercial uses are more likely to be seen as an infringement of copyright than nonprofit uses, but an article reprinted for educational purposes could still be in violation if the reprint was thought to encroach on the market for the original. The reproduction of an entire ten-line poem would be more likely to be viewed as an infringement than ten lines from a full-length novel. Ultimately, only a court can decide, and many millions of dollars in legal fees have been spent on disputes over what constitutes fair use.

One key difference, however, was the scope of protection. The Statute of Anne pertained to books. The Copyright Act of 1790 pertained not only to books but also to maps and charts. This broadening of scope reflected the needs of the strong and growing map-making industry in the newly formed and yet-to-be-charted United States. The extension of scope also illustrates the flexibility of United States copyright law to respond to the needs of changing trends in technology and publishing.

PRIVATE RIGHTS AND PUBLIC GOOD

A key similarity between the Statute of Anne and the Copyright Act of 1790 is the tension between private and public. Both acts were designed to encourage learning, a broad, public-minded goal. However, both seek to reach this goal by protecting the rights of individual authors. This combination of means based on private rights (for the good of the author) with public-minded ends (for the good of the public) has long been a source of debate. For some, copyright law is primarily about the rights of authors. For others, copyright law is about promoting learning and knowledge among the public. Copyright law is about both private rights and public values, even though in many important copyright disputes these two often come into tension.

Copyright law is about both private rights and public values, even though in many important copyright disputes these two often come into tension.

THREE IMPORTANT CASES

Three copyright cases illustrate this tension. The first one is *Wheaton v. Peters,* (1834), also the first Supreme Court decision on the question of copyright. At issue was a claim of copyright infringement brought by Henry Wheaton against Richard Peters. Wheaton claimed that Peters had copied without permission his report of the judicial opinions of the United States Supreme Court. At the time, court reporters wrote down the opinions of the Supreme Court as they were read, annotated the opinions, and distributed them to the public. Wheaton claimed that Peters had copied cases that were decided during Wheaton's term as court reporter. The Supreme Court ruled that there was no copyright infringement because there could not be a copyright in judicial opinions, which were laws that needed to be accessible to the public. The Court rejected Wheaton's argument that he was the author of the report and as author needed the protection of copyright. Instead the Court held for the rights of the public as opposed to the rights of the author.

The second case, from 1841, also involved documents of potentially public interest. At issue in *Folsom v. Marsh* was copyright in the collected letters of George Washington. Upon Washington's death the task of collecting his letters fell to a Mr. Sparks, who as editor published a multivolume collection. Mr. Upham published a two-volume work entitled *The Letters of George Washington,* large portions of which were lifted from Mr. Sparks's volumes. Supreme Court Justice Joseph Story in the opinion he wrote laid out a framework for what has come to be called "fair use" of copyrighted materials. Under the rule of fair use, a user is allowed under certain circumstances to copy from the copyright owner's work without his or her permission. Unfortunately for Mr. Upham, Justice Story also ruled that this case was not one to which fair use was applicable. Mr. Upham had simply copied too much and had produced a work that competed too closely with Mr. Sparks's work.

Finally, in *Stowe v. Thompson,* (1853), Judge Robert Grier ruled against Harriet Beecher Stowe, who was suing a publisher for selling an unauthorized German translation of her book *Uncle Tom's Cabin.* The judge reasoned that the copyright statute as written by Congress in the 1850s gave the author the exclusive right to copy and sell her books, but not the exclusive right to translate them into a foreign language. Consequently, Stowe's copyright in *Uncle Tom's Cabin* had not been infringed by an unauthorized translation. After this important decision, Congress quickly amended the Copyright Act to give authors the exclusive right to translate their works as well as create other works derived from the original.

Each of these cases illustrates the tension between the rights of the author and the rights of the public that is at the heart of copyright law. Nowhere is this tension between private rights and public needs more evident than in the international treatment of copyright.

INTERNATIONAL TREATMENT OF COPYRIGHT

The treatment of non-United States authors under United States copyright law was a hot issue in the nineteenth century. To obtain copyright protection in a specific country, an author must comply with the copyright laws of that country. More important, the country must recognize foreign authors. In the nineteenth century the United States did not recognize copyrights in works of foreign authors published overseas. This treatment greatly benefited United States publishers, who were able to sell cheap pirated copies of British bestsellers. The reading public in the United States also liked getting cheap copies of the latest works of British authors. The English novelist Charles Dickens was a vigorous critic of the United States treatment of foreign authors. During his tour of the United States in the 1840s, he spoke out against United States copyright law and urged that the law grant protections to authors like him, whose books were sold without his permission in American bookstores. Later in the century, Mark Twain took up the cause in defense of foreign authors. Twain was unhappy that the books of non-United States authors sold more cheaply than those of United States authors. In Twain's view this price difference gave foreign authors an unfair advantage.

This problem was not unique to the United States. The major European nations met and entered into the Berne Convention in 1891. Under this treaty, a country was required to treat foreign and native authors equally with respect to copyright. The United States, however, did not sign this treaty until 1989, although Congress did amend the Copyright Act in 1909 and 1976 to level the playing field for foreign and domestic authors.

The international treatment of copyright provides a good example of the tension between the rights of the author, who seeks recognition of and profit from his work, and the rights of the public, who would like cheap and plentiful supply of the work for consumption.

The international treatment of copyright provides a good example of the tension between the rights of the author, who seeks recognition of and profit from his work, and the rights of the public, who would like cheap and plentiful supply of the work for consumption. With roots deep in copyright's treatment of books under the Statute of Anne, the conflict continues into the twenty-first century not only with books, but also with access to movies, software, and music.

See also: COPYRIGHT ACT OF 1976; PATENT ACTS.

BIBLIOGRAPHY

Blackstone, William. *Commentaries on the Laws of England,* vol. 2. Chicago: University of Chicago Press, 1979.

Boyle, James. *Shamans, Software, & Spleens: Law and the Construction of the Information Society.* Cambridge: Harvard University Press, 1996.

The Debate on the Constitution, vol 1. New York: Library of America, 1993.

Maskus, Keith E. *Intellectual Property Rights in the Global Economy.* Washington, DC: Institute for International Economics, 2000.

Rose, Mark. *Authors and Owners: The Invention of Copyright.* Cambridge, MA: Harvard University Press, 1993.

Samuels, Edward. *The Illustrated History of Copyright.* New York: St. Martin's, 2000.

Story, Joseph. *Commentaries on the Constitution of the United States.* Durham, NC: Carolina Academic Press, 1987.

Vaidhyanathan, Siva. *Copyrights and Copywrongs: The Rise of Intellectual Property and How It Threatens Creativity.* New York: New York University Press, 2001.

INTERNET RESOURCES

The History of Copyright. <http://www.copyrighthistory.com>.

Timeline: A History of Copyright in the United States. <http://alr.cni.org/info/frn/copy/timeline.html>.

COPYRIGHT ACT OF 1976

Shubha Ghosh

In the 1990s John Perry Barlow, former songwriter for The Grateful Dead and contemporary social commentator, announced that copyright law was dying. What prompted this prognosis was the birth and fast growth of the Internet. In a world where information could be readily produced and copied and distributed, Barlow reasoned, copyright law could not limit the ability of people to copy songs, books, and movies. Barlow's famous eulogy for copyright illustrates the challenges confronting the law in the twentieth century and into the twenty-first. Our story begins with the player piano and ends with Napster.

> *Barlow's famous eulogy for copyright illustrates the challenges confronting the law in the twentieth century and into the twenty-first.*

THE PIANO ROLL

Copyright law faced its first big challenge in the twentieth century when the Apollo Company began selling piano rolls that allowed pianos to play music without the aid of a pianist. In the nineteenth century, if an author wanted to protect a musical composition he or she obtained a copyright on the sheet music, the printed form of a musical composition. The analogy between sheet music and a printed book is easy enough to see. Courts, however, were confounded by the piano roll. The Supreme Court ruled in a famous 1908 case that Apollo could not copyright its piano rolls, a ruling that caused quite a stir in the player piano industry. Without copyright protection, anyone could copy the piano rolls and piracy would be rampant. Fortunately for the player piano industry, Congress enacted the Copyright Act of 1909, in which copyright protection was extended to "mechanical reproductions" of music. The 1908 case represented one of the first brushes between copyright and technology. The case, and Congress's response, resonates today in the complex treatment of software under current copyright law.

FILM

Film posed an initial challenge under the 1909 Copyright Act in 1911, in a case involving a dispute between the copyright owner of the novel *Ben-Hur* and the producers of the early film version of the book. In an important decision by Judge Oliver Wendell Holmes (a central figure in copyright law), the Supreme Court ruled that the film was not just a separate and different work from the novel but one that incorporated many of the novel's copyright-protected elements, such as story, character, and plot. The Court found that the film was an unauthorized derivative work, thus setting the stage for the pursuit of "movie rights" for newly published books. The case also illustrated the ability of the courts to interpret copyright law to deal with new industries and technologies.

TELEVISION

The advent of television in the 1940s sent shock waves through the field of copyright. While the piano roll was clearly distinguishable from a book, at least both were tangible objects. With television, courts had to deal with disputes involving the dissemination of intangible bits and streams of images that were magically captured by a cathode ray tube miles away. Many courts were befuddled, and the budding television industry had to rely on copyrights in written scripts or taped versions of the shows to protect their works against piracy. Such strategies, however, would not work for live broadcast, which comprised much of the industry's work early on. Much of these works, unless recorded or based on a written script, had no copyright protection.

Television also raised issues about what it meant legally to perform a work. Copyright law has protected not only against the copying of works, but also their unauthorized performance. The question arose in the late 1960s as to what it meant to perform a television program. In two cases, the Supreme Court was confronted with the question of whether the retransmission of a broadcast television show by a cable company was infringement of copyright. At the time, cable was a new industry and laws and regulations governing cable were practically nonexistent. The Supreme Court in both cases ruled that such retransmission was not copyright infringement. All the cable company did was capture the signal from the air and send it to a consumer with a cable box. There was no copying of the work, and no performance of the program in the transmission. In short, there was no violation of the copyrights of the broadcast television networks.

These rulings were an enormous boon to the emerging cable industry. In the Copyright Act of 1976, Congress did respond to these decisions by changing the definition of public performance to include "transmitting" of copyrighted works. Under this definition, what the cable companies did in the

1960s cases would be copyright infringement. The Copyright Act of 1976, however, did maintain the Supreme Court's gift to the cable industry by permitting the cable companies to continue retransmission as long as they paid money under a "compulsory license" for the retransmission. The legacy of these cases, however, continues as television broadcast becomes more sophisticated, with satellite systems, pay-per-view, and the possibility in the near future of digital downloads of television programs.

RECORDED MUSIC

Recording of music also was a source of controversy for copyright, especially as the technology of cassette tape recording improved in the 1950s and 1960s. Copyright protected music largely through protection of sheet music and mechanical reproduction, such as piano rolls or tapes. Performers of music, however, were not protected under copyright. This discrepancy created a quandary for copyright law and for the music industry. Traditionally, a songwriter who created a musical work would obtain copyright protection in the work when it was created and written down as sheet music.

A performer, however, received no copyright in the performance of the song. Anyone who could make an unauthorized copy of the song would be violating the rights of the songwriter but not of the performer. The Grateful Dead allowed audiences to tape their concerts because they liked to share their music, but other performers were not so generous and wanted to put an end to "bootleg" tapes. They lobbied Congress for copyright protection for the recordings of their performances. Congress responded in 1972 by amending the Copyright Act of 1909 to permit copyright protection for sound recordings. The consequence is that performers were given certain rights in the reproduction and distribution of their recorded performances. In 1994 Congress extended protection to live performances of musical works by making it a crime to record live performances without the permission of the performing musicians.

Copyright on the Internet
Shubha Ghosh

Copyright law balances the interests of authors, publishers, and users. The Internet challenges this balance by turning every author into a publisher and every user into an author.

For example, peer-to-peer networks (P2P) allow every creator of music to cut out the middlemen of recording studios and distributors. Copyright law has been used by these middlemen to combat P2P. Napster, a centralized P2P network, was successfully shut down while Morpheus and Grockster, decentralized P2P networks, have been found not to violate copyright law.

The future of Internet radio is affected by Congress's grant in 1996 of a digital audio transmittal right of sound recordings to performers. While radio stations historically could broadcast songs without having to pay performers, this new right will require stations to compensate performers for certain Internet broadcasts, including simulcast.

Finally, Internet search engines have also come under scrutiny. A recent court ruling found that certain types of search engines would be fair use while others would violate the public display rights of copyright owners.

It seems that while the Internet is blurring the distinctions among authors, publishers, and users, copyright law's balance is slowly being reconfigured in the digital world.

Sonny Bono Copyright Term Extension Act

The Sonny Bono Copyright Term Extension Act, passed in 1998, extended the copyright on works created by individuals from the life of the author plus fifty years to the life of the author plus seventy years. Copyright on works of corporate authorship was extended from seventy-five to ninety-five years. Copyright on works published before January 1, 1978, had their protection extended to ninety-five years. As a result, no additional works will enter the public domain due to copyright expiration until 2019, when protection will expire for works created in 1923. Proponents of the act argued that some works would never be created unless extended protection was guaranteed, and that an extension would bring U.S. law more into line with European law. Detractors, on the other hand, argued that keeping works out of the public domain long after the creator can no longer benefit from copyright protection serves merely to enrich corporate interests and puts a damper on creative re-use of material. The act was named for the singer Sonny Bono, who had lobbied for the extension of copyright protection, and was passed shortly after his death.

Legal disputes about fair use have been a common feature of copyright disputes since the passage of the 1976 act.

THE PHOTOCOPIER

The invention of the photocopier, which allowed everyone to make copies of pages from books and other printed materials at the push of a button, further challenged copyright law. Legal battles ensued both in the courts and in Congress. Libraries were often at the center of the legal controversies. An important case involving copying by the National Library of Medicine went all the way to the Supreme Court in the mid-1970s. The case, however, resulted in a 4–4 decision by the Court that essentially upheld the lower court's ruling that the copying by the library was not infringement. Needless to say, the courts provided little clarity about the law.

Into this quagmire stepped Congress. In fact, the development of the photocopier caused Congress to rethink copyright law in the 1950s and spearheaded the movement to reform copyright law that resulted in the Copyright Act of 1976. Congress at one point toyed with the idea of levying a surcharge on the sale of photocopiers, the proceeds from which would be used to reimburse copyright owners. That scheme proved unworkable. The 1976 Act established some guidelines (not always clear ones) on permissible copying in libraries. These guidelines gave birth to the signs often posted next to photocopiers in libraries reminding the machine's user of copyright law.

FAIR USE

More important, Congress codified guidelines for fair use of copyrighted materials. Although fair use had been an important feature of copyright law since 1841, the 1976 act marked the first time that Congress set up rules to aid users in understanding when a particular use of copyrighted material was fair. The famous provision reads as follows:

> The fair use of a copyrighted work, including such use by reproduction in copies or phonorecords or by any other means specified by that section, for purposes such as criticism, comment, news reporting, teaching (including multiple copies for classroom use), scholarship, or research, is not an infringement of copyright. In determining whether the use made of a work in any particular case is a fair use the factors to be considered shall include—(1) the purpose and character of the use, including whether such use is of a commercial nature or is for nonprofit educational purposes; (2) the nature of the copyrighted work; (3) the amount and substantiality of the portion used in relation to the copyrighted work as a whole; and (4) the effect of the use upon the potential market for or value of the copyrighted work. The fact that a work is unpublished shall not itself bar a finding of fair use if such finding is made upon consideration of all the above factors.

Legal disputes about fair use have been a common feature of copyright disputes since the passage of the 1976 act.

The first major case involving fair use also raised questions about technology. In 1984 the United States Supreme Court ruled that home use of the video-recorder for the purposes of "time shifting"—in other words, watching a program at a time different from the broadcast time—was fair use. The Court, in a 5–4 vote, found that such use had little impact on the market for broadcast television programs and served an important noncommercial purpose. The closeness of the decision indicates the continuing controversy over technological developments in copying and copyright law.

DIGITIZATION

As should be evident, John Perry Barlow's statements about the death of copyright are not new. They echo throughout copyright in the twentieth century. The latest technological shift being brought about by digitization is further changing the field of copyright law. If digitization allows perfect replication and immediate distribution of a whole range of works from printed materials to films to songs and even to three-dimensional objects, does that mean copyright is dead or just morphing once again?

> *The latest technological shift being brought about by digitization is further changing the field of copyright law.*

The 2001 decision in the case for Internet website Napster possibly provides an answer. The Court of Appeals for the Ninth Circuit was confronted with the issue of whether a file-sharing system that permitted the copying and distribution of songs was copyright infringement or fair use. The court said that it was copyright infringement when copyrighted songs were being shared but not if uncopyrighted songs were being shared. In other words, if Napster users were sharing music in the public domain (i.e., works whose copyright has expired, such as music from the nineteenth century), then copyright law had not been violated. The court ruled that it was Napster's job to channel its technology to filter out copyright infringement from legal uses of the new computer technology. Under this heavy burden, Napster eventually shut down, with some talk that major recording companies would move into the file-sharing business.

Meanwhile, litigation against more sophisticated peer-to-peer systems continues. Many, like Barlow, feel that such useful technology cannot be limited. Others feel that stronger copyright enforcement is needed. Rumors of the death of copyright are perhaps greatly exaggerated. But at this point in time, the wounds are apparent. The hard question to answer is how the healing is going to occur.

See also: COPYRIGHT ACT OF 1790; PATENT ACTS.

BIBLIOGRAPHY

Barlow, John Perry. "The Economy of Ideas." *Wired* (March 1994): 84–97.

Bettig, Ronald V. *Copyrighting Culture: The Political Economy of Intellectual Property.* Boulder, CO: Westview Press, 1996.

Boyle, James. *Shamans, Software, and Spleens: Law and the Construction of the Information Society.* Cambridge, MA: Harvard University Press, 1996.

Goldstein, Paul. *Copyright's Highway: The Law and Lore of Copyright from Gutenberg to the Celestial Jukebox.* New York: Hill and Wang, 1994.

Krasilovsky, M. William, and Sidney Shemel. *This Business of Music.* New York: Billboard Books, 2000.

Lessig, Lawrence. *The Future of Ideas: The Fate of the Commons in a Connected World.* New York: Random House, 2001.

Lieberstein, Stanley H. *Who Owns What Is in Your Head?* Hartford, CT: Wildcat Publishing, 1979.

Litman, Jessica. *Digital Copyright.* Amherst, NY: Prometheus Books, 2001.

Samuels, Edward. *The Illustrated History of Copyright.* New York: St. Martin's, 2000.

"Two Cultures United." *The Economist* (November 9, 2002): 83–85.

Vaidhyanathan, Siva. *Copyrights and Copywrongs: The Rise of Intellectual Property and How It Threatens Creativity.* New York: New York University Press, 2001.

Wilhelm, Anthony G. *Democracy in the Digital Age: Challenges to Political Life in Cyberspace.* New York: Routledge, 2000.

CORPORATE INCOME TAX ACT OF 1909

Reuven S. Avi-Yonah

Excerpt from the Corporate Income Tax Act of 1909

That every corporation, joint stock company or association, organized for profit and having a capital stock represented by shares ... now or hereafter organized under the laws of the United State or of any State ... shall be subject to pay annually a special excise tax with respect to carrying on or doing business by such corporation ... equivalent to one per centum on the entire net income over and above five thousand dollars received by it from all sources during such year....

excise tax: a tax levied on the manufacture or sale of specific—usually non-essential—commodities such as tobacco or liquor

The Corporate Tax Act of 1909 (36 Stat. 11, 112) imposed an **excise tax** on corporations for the privilege of doing business in corporate form. However, the excise tax was measured by corporate income. Thus the act was the origin of the current corporate income tax, which has been part of our federal tax system ever since and is currently the source of about 10 percent of federal revenues.

In 1895 the Supreme Court decided that Congress could not impose an income tax directly on individuals, because that would violate the constitutional requirement that all "direct" taxes be apportioned (that is, divided in a proportionate way) among the states on the basis of their population. The 1909 act defined the corporate tax as an excise tax and therefore as an "indirect" tax that was not subject to apportionment. The constitutional problem of imposing an income tax without apportionment was resolved with the passage of the Sixteenth Amendment in 1913, so that from that point on the tax could be redefined as a direct income tax.

CIRCUMSTANCES LEADING TO ADOPTION OF THE ACT

consumption tax: tax imposed on outlay for goods and services

In the nineteenth century, federal revenues were derived primarily from tariffs, which were a form of **consumption tax** on imported goods. Like all consumption taxes, the tariffs were regressive (that is, imposed a heavier burden on the poor, because the poor consume a higher proportion of their income than the rich). State revenues depended primarily on property taxes, which because of enforcement difficulties were collected almost exclusively from real property. In the late nineteenth century there was a significant increase in wealth held in intangible forms, such as stocks and bonds. This wealth escaped both the federal tariff (because it was not consumed) and the state property tax (because it was intangible rather than "real").

The first income tax was imposed during the Civil War and raised significant revenues, but it was allowed to expire at the end of **Reconstruction** in 1872. Proponents of the income tax believed that this tax was fairer than the tariffs because it was progressive (that is, taxed the rich more than the poor) and was able to reach intangible wealth. The first post–Civil War income tax (imposed both on individuals and on corporations) was enacted in 1894 following the financial panic and recession of 1893, which was widely blamed on over-concentration of wealth (too few people holding too much wealth) and financial speculation (transactions that involve high risk). The Supreme Court struck down the 1894 tax in 1895, but proponents continued to push for an income tax. (The issue featured prominently in the election campaigns of 1896 and 1900.)

Support for the income tax grew with the rise of the progressive movement in the early years of the twentieth century. In 1907 President Theodore Roosevelt expressed support for the idea of a graduated income tax, but pro-tariff Republicans were able to delay its consideration until after the 1908 election. The newly elected president William H. Taft was less of a supporter of the income tax than his predecessor and was worried about enacting another tax that might be found unconstitutional. However, he was also faced with increased support for the income tax in Congress and a possible split within his own party between Northeastern opponents of the tax and Midwestern supporters. Eventually, Taft proposed a compromise: Enact a corporate excise tax measured by income, which could withstand judicial scrutiny, and simultaneously submit an amendment to the Constitution to permit enactment of an income tax.

President Taft's message to Congress not only solved the constitutional impasse, it also suggested that a corporate tax had two additional advantages. First, it was an indirect way of taxing shareholders, which were the kind of wealthy individuals that the progressives sought to tax with the 1894 income tax. The Civil War income tax already included the idea of collecting the tax on shareholders at the corporate level because such a tax would be easier to administer. This idea was given full force in the aborted 1894 tax. Second, Taft and the progressives viewed the tax as a way to regulate corporations and their management, resembling the antitrust actions begun by Roosevelt and also the regulatory efforts of the newly established Department of Commerce. They saw the corporate tax as both a way to collect information on corporations and make it public (since returns were to be published) and a way to restrain the accumulation of power in corporations that benefited from monopoly or near-monopoly status.

LEGISLATIVE DEBATE

The legislative debate on the 1909 act took place in the broader context of the debate on tariff reduction. Opponents of tariff reduction, mostly from Northeastern states, viewed high tariffs as essential to protecting American industry. They argued that the benefits of such tariffs extend to ordinary workers as well as to captains of industry. Proponents of tariff reduction, mostly from the West and the South, argued that high tariffs raised the price of goods consumed by ordinary Americans to benefit the rich. They argued that an income tax was more progressive and was also better suited to fluctu-

Reconstruction: the political and economic reorganization and reestablishment of the South after the Civil War

Support for the income tax grew with the rise of the progressive movement in the early years of the twentieth century.

Department of Commerce

The Department of Commerce was established in 1903 by Theodore Roosevelt as the Department of Commerce and Labor. Its original mission was to regulate both domestic and international commerce and oversee mining, manufacturing, shipping, and transportation. The agency expanded dramatically under Herbert Hoover, who served as commerce secretary from 1920 to 1928 and president from 1928 to 1933. However, Hoover's successor as president, Franklin Delano Roosevelt, held the agency in low regard and severely reduced its responsibilities. Over the next fifty years many of the agency's original functions were handed off or came to be shared with other agencies, but the Department of Commerce remains a strong voice for U.S. business both at home and abroad, with 40,000 workers and a budget of $5 billion. The agency collects economic data, issues patents, helps to set industrial standards, and lobbies other governments on behalf of U.S. business.

recession: a period of reduced economic activity, but less severe than a depression

ations in economic conditions (because income is more responsive to economic **recessions** than is consumption).

Initially, it seemed likely that the Republican majority in both houses of Congress would enact the tariff bill (named the Payne-Aldrich Tariff after its co-sponsors). In the House, income tax proponents like Cordell Hull, a Democrat from Tennessee, were unable to attach an income tax amendment to the tariff bill. In the Senate, however, progressive Republicans like Robert La Follette of Wisconsin and Democrats like Joseph Bailey of Texas were more effective in arguing for the income tax. La Follette and Bailey argued that because the rich benefited more than the poor from government protection, they should pay more for it, and that enacting the income tax would silence the "envious voice of anarchy" (by which they meant **socialism**).

socialism: any of various economic and political theories advocating collective or governmental ownership and administration of the means of production and distribution of goods

Ultimately, Republican Senator Nelson Aldrich of Rhode Island, the main opponent of the income tax, realized that with nineteen Republicans threatening to join the Democrats and vote for the income tax, he might lose. In a crucial meeting at the White House, Aldrich and Taft agreed to support instead a corporate tax plus a constitutional amendment empowering Congress to levy the income tax, while maintaining high tariffs. Aldrich stated, "I shall vote for a corporation tax as a means to defeat the income tax." This compromise ultimately passed the Senate by a vote of 45 to 34 and the House by a vote of 195 to 183. The act was signed into law by the president on August 5, 1909.

In a crucial meeting at the White House, Aldrich and Taft agreed to support a corporate tax plus a constitutional amendment empowering Congress to levy the income tax, while maintaining high tariffs.

POLITICAL ISSUES

The split within the governing Republicans, who had the majority in both houses of Congress and the White House, formed the political context for the enactment. The wing of the party from Northeastern states advocated high tariffs to protect American industry from European competitors, whereas progressives from the Midwest, West, and South favored reducing tariffs and replacing the revenue with an income tax. The corporate tax (and the proposed constitutional amendment), plus the high tariffs being maintained, represented a compromise between the two factions.

MAJOR COURT REVIEW AND INTERPRETATION

In 1911 the Supreme Court held that the corporate tax was an excise tax and not a "direct" tax, and therefore not unconstitutional under the 1895 precedent. This argument was made obsolete in 1913 when the Sixteenth Amendment was ratified, enabling Congress to adopt an income tax on individuals. However, the corporate tax was maintained and added to the individual income tax. It has been part of the Internal Revenue Code ever since.

dividend: a payment made by a company, based on its earnings, to its shareholders

The Supreme Court issued an important precedent interpreting the corporate tax in 1920. In the case of *Eisner v. Macomber,* the Court held that Congress did not have the power to tax **dividends** of corporate stock. In that context, the Court pointed out that corporations are separate taxpayers from shareholders and that shareholders could not be taxed on the undistributed income of corporations (as was done under the Civil War income tax).

AMENDMENTS

The corporate tax has now become Subchapter C of Chapter I of the Internal Revenue Code, containing over 100 sections. The most important changes from its original enactment are the following:

(1) The rate structure: The initial rate was 1 percent on income above $5,000. The current rate is graduated from 15 percent to 35 percent, but most large corporations pay a flat 35 percent. Over the years the rate had been higher, although not as high as the individual income tax rates (which reached 94 percent during World War II).

(2) Scope: Originally the tax applied to all corporations. Currently, it mostly applies to corporations whose shares are publicly traded on stock exchanges, because closely held corporations can usually qualify for special plans that tax their income directly to the shareholders. This is in line with Taft's original regulatory purpose, since only publicly traded corporations operate with the separation of management and control that justifies separate regulation.

(3) Integration: Originally, the corporate tax applied to corporations, and there was no tax on shareholders. When the income tax was introduced for shareholders in 1913, an exemption for dividends was included to prevent double taxation. This exemption was repealed in 1936, so since then corporate income has been taxed at the corporate level and dividends taxed at the shareholder level. In 2003, the tax rate on dividends was reduced from 35 percent to 15 percent, but the United States still separately taxes corporations and shareholders.

(4) Reorganizations: When capital gain taxation (taxing shareholders on their gain from the sale of corporate stock) was introduced in 1913, it applied to corporations and resulted in the taxation of business reorganizations (transactions in which shareholders exchange shares in one company for shares in another). Starting in the 1920s, a very elaborate system of tax-free reorganizations has been added that exempts some of these transactions from taxation. Thus, for example, setting up a new corporation and contributing property to it in exchange for the stock is generally a tax-free transaction.

ENFORCEMENT

One of the advantages of the corporate tax is that it is relatively easy to enforce because of the relatively small number of taxpayers. Currently, the medium- and large-size business division of the IRS is in charge of enforcement. However, the complexity of corporate transactions has actually made the tax difficult to enforce. The number of corporate **tax shelters**, increasing since the 1980s, has made enforcement especially difficult.

tax shelter: a strategy or method that allows one to legally reduce or avoid tax liabilities

IMPACT ON SOCIETY

The corporate tax has been a significant generator of federal revenues, accounting for about 25 percent of all revenues in the 1960s. Since then, however, the importance of the tax has declined, so that it accounts for only about 10 percent of revenues. The effective rate faced by corporations (the tax rate they actually pay as a percentage of the income they report to shareholders) varies tremendously. Figures indicate average effective rate of about

Since the 1960s the importance of the tax has declined, so that it accounts for only about 10 percent of revenues.

30 percent of book income reported to shareholders for large corporations.

It is hard to assess the impact of the tax on society. Economists are unsure as to who bears the economic burden of the tax: shareholders (through reduced profits), employees (through reduced wages), or consumers (through increased prices). Most likely the economic burdens of the tax have varied over time. As a regulatory device the tax provides the government with significant information about corporations, although the value of that information may have declined as returns became more complex and divorced from financial reporting to shareholders. Nevertheless, the fact that corporations pay about a third of their income to the government does provide some limit on corporate power and some limit on corporate monopoly profits. In addition, corporate tax payments can be used by the government to achieve social goals that corporations may not be best positioned to strive for. Thus the tax has contributed to the debate over corporate social responsibility.

See also: THE 1894 INCOME TAX AND THE WILSON-GARMAN TARIFF ACT; FEDERAL INCOME TAX ACT OF 1913; INTERNAL REVENUE ACT OF 1954.

BIBLIOGRAPHY

Bank, Steven A. "Entity Theory as Myth in the Origins of the Corporate Income Tax." 43 *William and Mary Law Review* 447 (2001).

Kornhauser, Marjorie E. "Corporate Regulation and the Origin of the Corporate Income Tax," 66 *Indiana Law Journal* 53 (1990).

Weisman, Steven R. *The Great Tax Wars: Lincoln to Wilson, the Fierce Battles Over Money and Power that Transformed the Nation.* New York: Simon and Schuster, 2002.

COUNTERFEIT ACCESS DEVICE AND COMPUTER FRAUD AND ABUSE ACT OF 1984

Ellen S. Podgor

The Counterfeit Access Device and Computer Fraud and Abuse Act (1984, P.L. 98-473, 98 Stat. 2190) was the first piece of federal legislation to focus directly on computer abuses. Enacted on October 12, 1984, it provides federal prosecutors with a specific crime titled, "Fraud and related activity in connection with computers" to prosecute criminal computer activity. The act, which can be found in title 18, section 1030 of the United States Code, initially focused on improper computer access. Because it was extremely limited in the conduct it made criminal, amendments to the statute were forthcoming, including a significant amendment in 1986 that broadened its scope to include other forms of computer abuses, and a 1990 amendment that allowed **civil actions** to be brought under the statute. Section 1030 now criminalizes seven different types of computer activity. Although Congress has enacted other criminal statutes related to computers since 1984, section 1030 remains the key basis for prosecuting federal computer crimes.

civil action: a lawsuit brought to protect an individual right or redress a wrong, as distinct from criminal proceedings

INITIAL LEGISLATION

Prior to the act's passage in 1984, federal prosecutors had no specific legislation to prosecute computer crimes. They typically used federal statutes such as the wire fraud statute to reach criminal activity. Congress passed the Counterfeit Access Device and Computer Fraud and Abuse Act to provide a "clearer statement of proscribed activity." In advocating for the passage of this act, the U.S. Department of Justice provided two computer abuse cases that demonstrated the need for legislation in this area. Had these cases not involved telephone calls that crossed state lines, the government maintained that the wire fraud statute could not have been applied, and prosecution of criminal conduct could not have occured. To rectify this problem, the new legislation allowed for prosecution absent an interstate telephone call.

Advocates for the passage of this legislation stressed the significant increase in computer activity. Although the extent of computer crime could not be quantified, a 1984 house report noted that "there is every indication that presently it is a substantial problem and the potential in the future is immense." Specific reference was made to increased activity by "hackers," individuals who could "trespass into both private and public computer systems, sometimes with potentially serious results."

When initially passed in 1984, the Counterfeit Access Device and Computer Fraud and Abuse Act permitted prosecution of three forms of computer activity. It focused primarily on computer use related to:

(1) Improper accessing of government information protected for national defense or foreign relations,
(2) improper accessing of certain financial information from financial institutions, and
(3) improper accessing of information on a government computer.

The legislation required that the criminal conduct affect interstate commerce, and as such, the constitutional basis for this act was found in the U.S. Constitution, Article I, section 8, the Commerce Clause.

Amendments Many commentators criticized the 1984 act for its vague language and limited coverage, and Congress adopted the Computer Fraud and Abuse Act of 1986 to correct these problems. Congress made changes to the statutory language, such as substituting "exceeds authorized access" for "having accessed a computer without authorization ... for purposes to which such authorization does not extend," replacing the term "knowingly" with "intentionally," and removing a specific conspiracy provision from the original 1984 act. The 1986 act also added new forms of criminality, including a criminal provision to punish "thefts of property via computer trespass that occur as part of an intent to defraud." As stated by Representative William J. Hughes, the need for this legislation was based upon expanded technology which allowed improper conduct by "the technologically sophisticated criminal who breaks into computerized data files."

Congress adopted additional amendments in 1988, 1989, and 1990, but all were mostly technical in nature, such as grammatical corrections and additions. The 1994 amendments,

Although Congress has enacted other criminal statutes related to computers since 1984, section 1030 of the Counterfeit Access Device and Computer Fraud and Abuse Act remains the key basis for prosecuting federal computer crimes.

Although the extent of computer crime could not be quantified, a 1984 house report noted that "there is every indication that presently it is a substantial problem and the potential in the future is immense."

however, were more significant, adding a civil provision allowing private individuals to sue for damages and injunctive relief.

There were also amendments made to section 1030 in 1996, 2001, and 2002. For example, in 1996 Congress substituted the words "protected computer" for "Federal interest computer." The definition of these terms was extended in the "Uniting and Strengthening America by Providing Appropriate Tools Required to Intercept and Obstruct Terrorism (USA Patriot Act) Act of 2001" to include protected computers located outside the United States. Also in 1996, as part of the National Information Infrastructure Protection Act of 1996 (which, in turn, is Title II of the Economic Espionage Act of 1996), a subsection was added to section 1030 to cover extortion conduct threatening damage to a protected computer.

Section 1030 Congress has significantly expanded section 1030 since the initial passage of the Counterfeit Access Device and Computer Fraud and Abuse Act in 1984. It now includes seven different types of computer related conduct. Where the initial act focused on computer accessing, the modern statute includes other forms of computer crime.

Where the initial act focused on computer accessing, the modern statute includes other forms of computer crime.

Among the section's seven provisions are electronic espionage and intentional accessing without authorization or exceeding authorization of certain financial information. Section 1030 also prohibits conduct related to browsing in a government computer, theft from protected computers, and causing damage by an improper transmission, trafficking in passwords, and extortion conduct related to a protected computer.

Each of the seven variants of conduct include specific legal terminology setting forth the requirements for a prosecution premised on that section of the statute. Subsection (a)(5) is further divided to include three different levels of intent that can accompany the specified conduct. The penalty provisions vary depending upon the specific act committed and the level of intent.

Court Interpretation Although only a few federal cases interpret the Counterfeit Access Device and Computer Fraud and Abuse Act, three of the decisions are significant and have been important in helping to define the contours of the legislation.

The first federal appellate decision to interpret section 1030, *United States v. Morris* (1991), resulted from the conduct of a graduate student who placed a "worm" into the Internet not realizing the extent of the damage it might cause. The court was faced with deciding whether the word "intentionally" in the statute referred only to "intentionally accessing" or also required that the defendant "intentionally caused" the damage. Looking to the changes made in the Computer Fraud and Abuse Act from its inception in 1984 to its modifications in 1986, the court concluded it was not necessary for the government to prove the defendant intended to cause the damage.

The court found that the word "intentionally" in the statute only applied to accessing, not damages. Therefore the defendant's conviction for violating the computer statute was upheld. The court also found the defendant had violated the accessing portion of the statute, rejecting the defendant's argument that, at most, he had merely exceeded authorized access. Referring back to the legislative history of the statute, the court stated, "Congress contemplated that individuals with access to some federal interest computers would be subject to liability under the computer fraud provisions for gaining unauthorized access to other federal interest computers."

The court held that the civil provision was not limited to situations where the accessing involved the "national economy."

Another court decision involved an Internal Revenue Service employee who the government charged with wire and computer fraud for allegedly browsing in a government computer. He was accused of using a government computer to obtain personal information on individuals, such as the "tax returns of two individuals involved in the David Duke presidential campaign." In *United States v. Czubinski* (1997) the court found that the employee had not obtained "anything of value," and there was no violation of the Computer Fraud and Abuse Act. The court stated that "[t]he government failed" to prove the accused "intended anything more than to satisfy idle curiosity."

A third case that provided significant interpretation involves the civil provisions of section 1030. In *Shurgard Storage Centers, Inc. v. Safeguard Self Storage, Inc.*, an employee allegedly used the company computer to transmit secret trade information to a future employer. In a motion seeking the dismissal of this civil action, the defendants argued that the case was not within the computer fraud statute. In rejecting these arguments, the court held that the statute was not limited to "outsiders" and could apply to "insiders" or employees of a company who might be improperly accessing information on a computer. The court also held that the civil provision was not limited to situations where the accessing involved the "national economy." The court stated that the statute "prohibits the obtaining of information from *any* protected computer if the conduct involved an interstate or foreign communication."

With technological advances and increased computer use, this area is clearly still developing. Future modifications and court interpretations will likely play a crucial role in the advancement of the provisions in the Computer Fraud and Abuse Act.

See also: COMPUTER SECURITY ACT OF 1987; ELECTRONIC COMMUNICATIONS PRIVACY ACT OF 1986; USA PATRIOT ACT.

BIBLIOGRAPHY

Baker, Glen D. "Trespassers Will Be Prosecuted: Computer Crime in the 1990s." *Computer Law Journal* 12, no. 61 (1993).

Best, Reba A. and D. Cheryn Picquet. *Computer Law and Software Protection: A Bibliography of Crime, Liability, Abuse and Security, 1984–1992.* London: McFarland, 1993.

Buckman, Deborah F. "Validity, Construction, and Application of Computer Fraud and Abuse Act." *American Law Reports* 174, no. 101 (2001).

Podgor, Ellen S. and Jerold H. Israel. *White Collar Crime in a Nutshell,* 2nd ed. St. Paul, MN: West, 1997.

INTERNET RESOURCE

Computer Crime and Intellectual Property Section (CCIPS) of the Criminal Division of the Department of Justice. <http://www.usdoj.gov/criminal/cybercrime/index. html>.

D

DAWES ACT

See INDIAN GENERAL ALLOTMENT ACT.

DEFENSE OF MARRIAGE ACT (1996)

Andrew Koppelman

Excerpt from the Defense of Marriage Act

In determining the meaning of any Act of Congress, or of any ruling, regulation, or interpretation of the various administrative bureaus and agencies of the United States, the word "marriage" means only a legal union between one man and one woman as husband and wife and the word "spouse" refers only to a person of the opposite sex who is a husband or wife.

The choice of law provision

No state, territory, or possession of the United States, or Indian tribe, shall be required to give effect to any public act, record, or judicial proceeding of any other State, territory, possession, or tribe respecting a relationship between persons of the same sex that is treated as a marriage under the laws of such other State, territory, possession, or tribe, or a right or claim arising from such relationship.

The Defense of Marriage Act (DOMA) (P.L. 104-199; 110 Stat. 2419) denies federal recognition to same-sex marriages and authorizes the states to deny such recognition as well. The act has two provisions. One of these defines marriage, for federal purposes, as exclusively heterosexual, thereby depriving same-sex couples of all the federal benefits to which other married couples are entitled. The other provision authorizes individual states to ignore same-sex marriages when they are performed in other states.

The constitutional basis for the provision that defines marriage is simply Congress's power to define the terms of a federal statute. The second provision relies on the "full faith and credit clause" of Article IV, sec. 1, of the U.S. Constitution. This clause, after requiring states to give "full faith and credit" to one another's acts and judicial proceedings, provides that "Congress may by General Laws prescribe the Manner in which such Acts, Records and Proceedings shall be proved, and the Effect thereof."

DOMA was enacted after a 1993 decision by the Hawaii Supreme Court strongly suggested that the state would make same-sex marriage legal. (After DOMA was enacted, the state court's decision was overturned by an amendment to the state constitution.) States usually recognize marriages celebrated in other states, and the federal government usually defers to each state's definition of marriage. But neither of these rules has been understood to be a constitutional requirement. Opponents of same-sex marriage feared that recognition of same-sex marriage would damage the institution of marriage in the United States, and so sought, through DOMA, to create an exception to these ordinary rules. Those who opposed DOMA, noting the **unprecedented** nature of the federal legislation, thought that it was an unconstitutional abuse of the Article IV power. These opponents emphasized that Congress was responding to a "problem" that did not exist, since no state then recognized same-sex marriages.

unprecedented: not resembling something already in existence

DOMA has played an important role in state courts since Vermont recognized the legality of same-sex unions. Vermont Civil Unions, created by statute in 2000, have all the rights and responsibilities of marriage without the name. State courts have cited DOMA when denying recognition to Vermont Civil Unions. For example, *Lofton v. Kearney*, a 2001 Florida ruling, states that DOMA "precludes homosexuals who marry in other states from being recognized by Florida as a legal union."

The Defense of Marriage Act is one episode in a continuing cultural and political battle over the status of same-sex couples.

Citations such as these, however, appear to rest on an error of law. The full faith and credit clause has never been interpreted to require states to recognize marriages celebrated in other states that are contrary to the public policy of the particular state. DOMA is, in fact, irrelevant to almost any question that is likely to come before a court. The Supreme Court has interpreted the full faith and credit clause to constrain state courts only when the state would violate parties' due process rights by applying its own law to the case.

The Defense of Marriage Act is one episode in a continuing cultural and political battle over the status of same-sex couples. Republican Senator Don Nickles of Oklahoma, one of the original sponsors of DOMA, argued that, because marriage is already traditionally understood to be exclusively heterosexual, the law "merely reaffirm[s] what is already known, what is already in place" (Committee on the Judiciary, U.S. Senate, 104th Cong., 2d Sess., Hearing on Defense of Marriage Act, July 11, 1996). Opponents argue that, if the exclusive heterosexuality of marriage were that obvious, there would have been no need for the statute.

BIBLIOGRAPHY

Koppelman, Andrew. "Dumb and DOMA: Why the Defense of Marriage Act Is Unconstitutional." *Iowa Law Review* 83, no. 1 (1997): 94–140.

Koppelman, Andrew. *The Gay Rights Question in Contemporary American Law*. Chicago: University of Chicago Press, 2002.

DEPARTMENT OF ENERGY ORGANIZATION ACT (1977)

Joseph P. Tomain

P rior to the 1970s, the responsibility for energy regulation was spread among a variety of federal agencies, including such cabinet-level departments as the Department of Interior and the Department of Agriculture. Energy issues also were administered by independent regulatory agencies, such as the Federal Power Commission and the Atomic Energy Commission, which were renamed, respectively, the Federal Energy Regulatory Commission (FERC) and the Nuclear Regulatory Commission. Complicating energy regulation even further is the fact that individual states regulate the natural resources used for the production of energy through their own statutes, regulations, and case law.

The major impetus for efforts at energy planning and coordination was the "energy crisis" of the mid-1970s stimulated by the OPEC Oil Embargo of October 1973.

OPEC Oil Embargo: In October 1973, the Organization of Petroleum Exporting Countries (OPEC) banned oil exports to the United States because the United States sold arms to Israel during the Arab-Israeli War of 1973

The major impetus for efforts at energy planning and coordination was the "energy crisis" of the mid-1970s stimulated by the **OPEC Oil Embargo** of October 1973. Congressional concern focused on matters of energy reliability, environmental protection, reasonable prices, economic stability, and national security.

Presidents Nixon and Ford responded to the energy crisis with several initiatives centered predominantly on controlling oil supplies and prices. President Carter introduced his National Energy Act, consisting of five pieces of major legislation supported by the declaration that the energy crisis was the "moral equivalent of war." The National Energy Act addressed a wide range of energy regulation from traditional fossil fuels such as coal, oil, and natural gas to conservation and rate design. In an attempt to coordinate all of these activities, Congress passed the Department of Energy Organization Act in 1977 (P.L. 95-91, 91 Stat. 565). In 1980 Congress passed the Energy Security Act, which addressed alternative energy sources from solar power and geothermal to oil shale and tar sands.

The Department of Energy Organization Act was based upon Congressional findings that the United States faced an increasing shortage of nonrenewable energy resources, thus increasing its dependence on foreign energy supplies, particularly oil, and presenting a threat to national security; that a strong national energy program was needed; that energy policy was fragmented in the federal government; and that a national energy program needed to be integrated and coordinated.

The Department of Energy was established on June 3, 1977. It unified services, laboratories and personnel from other federal agencies. Besides absorbing the roles and functions of the Federal Energy Administration, the Energy Research and Development Administration, and the Atomic Energy Commission, it also took on some responsibilities from the Departments of Agriculture, Commerce, Housing and Urban Development, and Transportation. DoE had some 20,000 employees and a budget of $10.4 billion.

ESTABLISHING THE DEPARTMENT OF ENERGY

The Department of Energy (DOE) was established as a cabinet-level agency with responsibility for information collection, policy planning, coordination, and program administration. To further those goals, the Economic Research and Development Administration and the Federal Energy Administration were abolished, and their powers were transferred to DOE. Also, the Federal Power Commission was renamed the Federal Energy Regulatory Commission and came under the umbrella of DOE, while retaining its status as an independent regulatory agency. DOE also had the responsibility for various energy regulations formerly administered by the Department of the Interior, the Department of Housing and Urban Development, the Interstate Commerce Commission, and Department of the Navy, and the Department of Commerce, among others. Established within the Department of Energy were an Energy Information Administration and an Economic Regulatory Administration along with an Office of Energy Research.

The DOE was charged with assisting in the development of a coordinated national energy policy. To that end, DOE is required to submit to Congress a biannual National Policy Plan containing energy production, utilization, and conservation objectives, as well as identifying strategies and recommendations for action.

ENERGY POLICY IN THE UNITED STATES

Historically, the United States has had neither a comprehensive nor a coordinated national energy policy. Several factors contribute to a lack of a national energy plan, including the fact that energy matters are spread throughout the federal government; that the preference for social ordering is the market; and that **federalism** inhibits coordination. In oil and gas matters, for example, state, statutory, and **common law** affect exploration and production; and for natural gas and electricity, state public utility commissions affect retail rates and sales.

Moreover, the Department of the Interior retains responsibility for the management of federal lands and resources. Its agencies include the Bureau of Mines which administers surface mining and reclamation regulations; the Bureau of Reclamation, which administers hydroelectric projects; the Bureau of Land Management, which is responsible for federal lands: and Minerals Management Service, which regulates the intercontinental shelf. The Department of Labor through its Mine Health and Safety Administration regulates health and safety standards for miners. To these federal agencies can be added the Environmental Protection Agency, the Council on Environmental Quality, and the Department of Transportation. Thus, even after the passage of the Department of Energy Organization Act, energy regulation and administration remains fragmented at the federal level.

It is still the case that FERC's administration of the Federal Power Act and the Natural Gas Act involves primary federal energy regulation. FERC has been very active in deregulating the natural gas and electric industries as well as revamping the hydroelectric licensing process.

At a general policy level, the United States has had a dominant model of energy policy throughout the twentieth century and continuing into the twenty-first. That dominant model largely relies on large, capital-intensive, fossil fuel industries such as coal, oil, and natural gas, and it centers on the production and distribution of those resources as well as electricity. Over recent years, energy policies and proposed energy legislation have recognized the importance of alternative energy sources, conservation, and sustainability. Nevertheless, the mainstay of national energy policy and planning remains fossil fuels.

Perhaps the most important function played by the Department of Energy has been to gather information, particularly through the Energy Information Administration. The energy information is thorough, extensive, and updated on a

federalism: a system of political organization; a union formed of separate states or groups that are ruled by a central authority on some matters but are otherwise permitted to govern themselves independently

common law: a system of laws developed in England—and later applied in the U.S.—based on judicial precedent rather than statutory laws passed by a legislative body

Perhaps the most important function played by the Department of Energy has been to gather information, particularly through the Energy Information Administration.

Energy Reorganization Act

In 1974 Congress passed the Energy Reorganization Act, which established the Nuclear Regulatory Commission. Previously, all functions related to the production and regulation of nuclear power and nuclear weapons were managed by the Atomic Energy Commission. The Energy Reorganization Act separated these functions, assigning responsibility for developing nuclear power and nuclear weapons to the Department of Energy and responsibility for regulation of nuclear power plants to the Nuclear Regulatory Commission.

regular—in some instances daily—basis. Information on production, consumption, and pricing is readily available at the DOE Web site through its biannual National Energy Policy Plan, which provides baseline information on energy industries and provides solid data for understanding the history and direction of energy policy and planning.

See also: FEDERAL POWER ACTS; NATIONAL ENERGY CONSERVATION POLICY ACT; NATURAL GAS ACT.

BIBLIOGRAPHY

Aman, Alfred C. "Institutionalizing the Energy Prices: Some Structural and Procedural Lessons." *Cornell Law Review* 65 (1979–1980): 491–598.

Byse, Clark. "The Department of Energy Organization Act: Structure and Procedure." *Administrative Law Review* (1978): 93–36.

Clark, John. *Energy and the Federal Government: Fossil Fuel Policies, 1900–1946.* Urbana: University of Illinois Press, 1987.

Tomain, Joseph P. "Institutionalized Conflicts between Law and Policy." *Houston Law Review* 22 (1985): 661–723.

Vietor, Richard H. K. *Energy Policy in America since 1945: A Study of Business-Government Relations.* Cambridge: Cambridge University Press, 1984.

INTERNET RESOURCE

U.S. Department of Energy. <http://www.energy.gov/engine/content.do>.

DEPARTMENT OF HOMELAND SECURITY ACT (2002)

Lynne K. Zusman and Neil S. Helfand

After the terrorist attacks of September 11, 2001, the George W. Bush administration, along with congressional lawmakers, decided that the U.S. government must overhaul the current governmental structure responsible for defending the domestic security of the United States. Without such an overhaul, it was believed, the United States would remain vulnerable to the omnipresent threat of global terrorism.

The agencies responsible for maintaining the security of the United States and gathering and analyzing intelligence information were charged for their failure to detect and prevent the terrorist attacks of September 11th. In particular, agencies such as the FBI and the CIA received the brunt of criticism. Critics alleged that the terrorist attacks could have been prevented if a more coordinated and streamlined domestic security system had been in place.

On June 18, 2002, the president sent a proposal to Congress for a Department of Homeland Security (P. L. 107-296). After considerable debate and further amendments, Congress approved the bill on November 22, 2002. The president signed the amended bill on November 25, 2002.

Fear of attack on U.S. soil is something new to Americans. Jerome Johnson of Virginia heeds a Department of Homeland Security warning to buy duct tape and plastic sheeting to defend against possible attacks involving chemical or biological weapons.
(© AP/WIDE WORLD PHOTOS)

The act establishes the new Department of Homeland Security and consolidates the operations of twenty-two existing federal government agencies. The act is responsible for the largest revamping of government operations since the creation of the Department of Defense following World War II. The creation of the department reflects a desire to streamline and to consolidate

The act establishes the new Department of Homeland Security and consolidates the operations of twenty-two existing federal government agencies.

domestic security functions to respond to and prevent further terrorist attacks on American soil. The department serves not only to provide effective response to a terrorist attack, but more importantly endeavors to form a more proactive defense of American soil.

THE DEPARTMENT'S MISSION

The primary mission of the Department of Homeland Security, according to Section 101(b)(l) of the Homeland Security Act, is to:

- Prevent terrorist attacks within the United States.
- Reduce the vulnerability of the United States to terrorism.
- Minimize the damage, and assist in the recovery, from terrorist attacks that do occur within the United States.
- Carry out all functions of entities transferred to the department, including acting as a focal point regarding natural and manmade crises and emergency planning.
- Ensure that the functions of the agencies and subdivision within the department that are not related directly to securing the homeland are not diminished or neglected except by a specific explicit act of Congress.
- Ensure that the overall economic security of the United States is not diminished by efforts, activities, and programs aimed at securing the homeland.
- Monitor connections between illegal drug trafficking and terrorism, coordinate efforts to sever such connections, and otherwise contribute to efforts to interdict illegal drug trafficking.

REORGANIZATION PLAN

Pursuant to Section 1502 of the act, President Bush submitted a reorganization plan on November 25, 2002 that provided a schematic of the new department's composition. The reorganization plan provided for the transfer of agencies, personnel, assets, and obligations to the new department and the consolidation, reorganization, or streamlining of the agencies transferred to the department. Thus, the reorganization plan called not only for the transfer of twenty-two existing federal agencies but also set the stage for fundamental changes in the manner in which these agencies conduct their operations.

THE DEPARTMENT'S STRUCTURE

The Department of Homeland Security officially took form on January 24, 2003, with Tom Ridge serving as the first secretary of the department. However, the department only had a skeletal structure until March 1, 2003, when the majority of agencies that would constitute the bulk of the new department were formally transferred into it. On March 1, 2003, the following federal agencies were transferred to the department: the Coast Guard; the Secret Service; the Customs Service; the Federal Emergency Management Agency; the Transportation Security Agency; the Commerce Department's Critical Infrastructure Assurance Office, the Defense Department's National

The Department of Homeland Security officially took form on January 24, 2003.

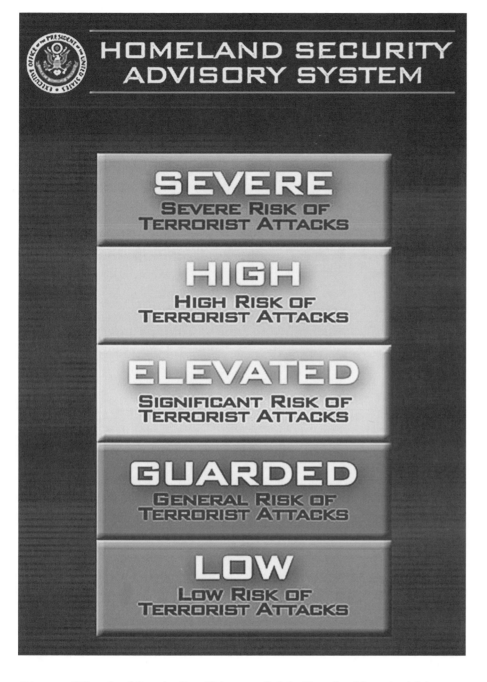

Director of Homeland Security Tom Ridge unveiled the Homeland Security Advisory System on March 12, 2002. Among the factors in assessing the threat of a terrorist attack are: (1) the credibility of the threat; (2) whether or not the threat has been corroborated; (3) how specific and imminent the threat appears to be; and (4) how grave the threat appears to be. (©AFP/CORBIS)

Communication System; the FBI's National Infrastructure Protection Center, and the functions of the former Immigration and Naturalization Service.

In addition to the transfer of these federal agencies a number of additional federal government responsibilities were transferred, including nuclear, biological and chemical defense efforts, as well as certain medical response efforts, including the Metropolitan Medical Response System and nationwide pharmaceutical and medical supply distribution efforts.

The core divisions of the department, each headed by an undersecretary, are Information Analysis and Infrastructure Protection; Science and Technology; Border and Transportation Security; and Emergency Preparedness and Response. The department is also responsible for coordinating with non-federal entities, such as state and local governments.

In addition to the consolidation of federal government functions, the act calls for federal government support in fostering the development of effective technologies necessary in combating terrorism, and it provides new powers to government officials in declaring national health emergencies, including quarantines and forced vaccination. The act also aims to facilitate homeland security information sharing procedures in an effort to maximize intelligence data analysis and utilization capabilities.

REACTION TO THE NEW DEPARTMENT

Critics of the newly formed department charged that the government reorganization did little more than create a huge new bureaucracy with its own unique challenges and areas of incompetence in mobilizing effective government operations in defense of the homeland. Early critics noted that the new department did not include the two agencies chiefly responsible for the gathering and analysis of intelligence data, the FBI and CIA. Opponents argued that the department could not effectively fulfill its mission in preventing and responding to future terrorist attacks without the expertise of these agencies and noted that the department would be dependent upon the FBI and CIA's effectiveness and willingness to share information with the department.

In addition, as the FBI and CIA were widely blamed as the source of intelligence lapses leading up to the September 11th attacks, opponents of the act also reasoned that it failed to address the weaknesses of these two agencies and the nation's vulnerability to a terrorist attack, since the FBI and CIA are beyond the purview of the department.

POLITICAL CLIMATE

Civil Liberties In an age of uncertainty, the department assumes profound responsibility in securing the homeland. Mobilizing the department's efforts is further complicated by the political difficulties of forming a cohesive and tight security mechanism while maintaining cherished civil liberties. The department must perform a careful balancing act in preserving fundamental civil liberties while maintaining national security.

Critics accuse the federal government of over-stretching the constitutional bounds of its authority and unduly curtailing the civil liberties of U.S. citizens.

Critics accuse the federal government of over-stretching the constitutional bounds of its authority and unduly curtailing the civil liberties of U.S. citizens. Those with concerns about the curtailment of civil liberties point out that the Homeland Security Act comes on the heels of the USA Patriot Act, enacted in October 26, 2001, that gave sweeping new powers to both domestic law enforcement and international intelligence agencies and severely reduced the oversight powers previously provided to the courts in reviewing government surveillance powers. They fear that the combined effect of the two acts is to contort the **checks and balances** provided by the Constitution.

The Homeland Security Act, in the interest of national security, gives companies **immunity** from damage suits brought against them regarding "anti-terrorism technology," limits the information that can be received under the Freedom of Information Act, and allows more latitude for government supervisory committees to meet in secret, among other auspices. Critics are concerned that the rights of U.S. citizens will be unnecessarily weakened, all in the name of national security.

Information Sharing The terms of the Homeland Security Act are vague, and many key provisions are open to interpretation. One of the most significant areas of ambiguity is in the area of information sharing.

The issue of intelligence information sharing is charged with political implications concerning the specific duties of various federal agencies. The FBI and CIA prefer to preserve strict limitations on the distribution of their intelligence data and analysis. Meanwhile the department is charged with the responsibility of preventing terrorist threats from harming our nation, a job in large part reliant upon the information gathered from agencies such as the CIA and the FBI. Furthermore, the department, in its infancy, lacks the capabilities to match the expertise of the established agencies in the analysis of intelligence data. The issue of information sharing will present one of the greatest political and technical challenges to the department.

COORDINATION WITH STATE AND LOCAL GOVERNMENTS

Another area in which the act failed to provide direction was the way in which the department will coordinate with state and local governments who are on the front lines in the battle against terrorism. State and local governments complain that they lack the money, equipment, and personnel to carry out the mandates of the department.

Congress has conducted hearings on these challenges. Bills have been aimed at increasing the flexibility and coordination of money going to state and local governments. The call for more flexibility recognizes the unique and varying challenges faced by different localities in enhancing their ability to respond to terrorist threats. In addition, the department announced it would allocate $700 million from the 2003 supplemental budget to help protect urban areas and critical infrastructure.

OVERHAUL OF THE ACT

Vague in its details and hastily written at a time when swift action was deemed necessary, the act will presumably undergo further evaluation and amendment as lawmakers more closely examine its effectiveness. Substantive changes are possible, as Congress examines issues such as the need to clarify the roles of federal departments related to homeland security, in particular the Defense Department.

checks and balances: the limiting powers that each branch of government has over the other two. (The government is divided into three branches: legislative, executive, and judicial, each with distinct powers.)

immunity: protection from legal action

Given the mammoth task of undertaking a reorganization of the federal government, it is expected that the complete formation of the department and the full delineation of its responsibilities will take years.

Given the mammoth task of undertaking a reorganization of the federal government, it is expected that the complete formation of the department and the full delineation of its responsibilities will in all probability take years. In the meantime, the work of defending the United States against terrorist attacks is already well under way.

See also: USA PATRIOT ACT.

BIBLIOGRAPHY

New, William. "House Chairman Plans Overhaul of Homeland Security Act." *Technology Daily,* May 2, 2003. http://www.govexec.com/dailyfed/0503/050203dl.htm.

McCarthy, Bill. "New Bureaucracy." *Mobile Radio Technology,* January 1, 2003.

Peckenpaugh, Jason, "Ridge Announces Reorganization of Border Agencies." *Congress Daily,* January 30, 2003. http://www.govexec.com/dailyrfed/0103/013003p2.htm.

Serivo, Karen Kee. "Senator Seeks Flexibility for First Responder." *Congress Daily,* April 28, 2003. http://www.govexec.com/dailyfed/0403/042803cdam1.htm.

DOMESTIC VOLUNTEER SERVICE ACT OF 1973 (VISTA)

Lawrence Schlam

The idea of VISTA (Volunteers in Service to America) arose in 1963, when President John F. Kennedy expressed the desire to create a domestic volunteer program modeled after the Peace Corps, created in 1961.

In 1964, President Lyndon B. Johnson granted Kennedy's wish when he signed the Economic Opportunity Act of 1964, an act that created the Volunteers in Service to America. Congress founded VISTA under the belief that it had solved the biggest problems of the nation with the help of citizen volunteers, and that by providing the people of impoverished communities with volunteers from across the country, it would help empower the poor to raise their standards of living.

By the end of 1965, VISTA had volunteers working to build homes in the Appalachian Mountains, supporting migrant workers in California, and helping the poor in Connecticut. By the end of the 1960s, VISTA had helped begin the first Head Start programs to provide early preparation for preschoolers, and Job Corps camps to engage in vocational training.

VISTA also began to recruit trained professionals to serve in low-income neighborhoods. Doctors set up free clinics in areas with little or no access to health care. Architects were asked to donate time to design new low-income housing or help renovate existing housing. Lawyers assisted the poor in obtaining benefits to which they were entitled and lobbied courts and legislators for expansion of existing protections for low-income people. These lawyers also

The idea of VISTA (Volunteers in Service to America) arose in 1963, when President John F. Kennedy expressed the desire to create a domestic volunteer program modeled after the Peace Corps, created in 1961.

helped start agricultural cooperatives, community groups, and small businesses.

In 1973 Congress merged VISTA with the Peace Corps under a new federal "ACTION" agency, which would run all domestic volunteer programs. Depending on the type of service the individual supplied, terms of service ran from as little as a summer, to as long as five years. Congress established the Domestic Volunteer Service Act of 1973 (P.L. 93-113), in part, to provide funding and regulations for the operation of VISTA. Senator Alan Cranston introduced the act on March 9, 1973, with the support of several other prominent senators and President Richard M. Nixon.

In 1973 Congress merged VISTA with the Peace Corp under a new federal "ACTION" agency, which would run all domestic volunteer programs.

Proponents of the act cited the long-standing importance of volunteerism throughout American history, and sought greater involvement on the part of both young and older citizens in this tradition. In the words of the enacting legislation:

> The purpose of this [Act] is to foster and expand voluntary citizen service in communities throughout the Nation in activities designed to help poor, disadvantaged, the vulnerable, and the elderly. In carrying out this purpose, the Corporation for National and Community Service shall utilize to the fullest extent the programs authorized under this chapter, coordinate with other Federal, State, and local agencies and utilize the energy, innovative spirit, experience, and skills of all Americans.

The statute detailed the requirements, goals and funding for VISTA, expanded testing and development of innovations in volunteer activities, and specified that health services, housing, the environment, educational development, manpower, and community planning would be the main areas of focus of VISTA activities.

Among the innovative provisions in the act were those addressing the University Year for VISTA, which provided academic credits for full-time volunteer services in anti-poverty projects, and new voluntary activities and demonstration programs providing alternatives to incarceration for youthful offenders, services and opportunities for returning veterans, and community-based peer counseling for the drug and alcohol addicted.

In addition, the act created a Retired Senior Volunteer Program (RSVP) and a Foster Grandparents (FGP), both geared towards providing services to the elderly and to use retired citizens as volunteers. Title III of the Act restated the divisions of responsibility between ACTION and the SCORE/ACE volunteers. SCORE is the Service Corps of Retired Executives, and ACE is the Active Corps of Executives, comprised of both businesspersons and volunteer organizations.

SUBSEQUENT LEGISLATION AND COURT RULINGS

The Domestic Volunteer Services Act has under gone many amendments since 1973. In the 1980s, VISTA began to encourage less outside volunteerism, and instead emphasized community self-help. In 1986, amendments established the VISTA Literacy Corps and "literacy councils" intended to expand adult education. A large majority of VISTA's work was then focused on trying to raise the literacy rates throughout the nation. In 1990, VISTA

In 1993 President Bill Clinton created AmeriCorps and merged it with VISTA, creating AmeriCorpsVISTA to develop new programs to meet the changing needs of the impoverished.

plaintiff: one who brings legal action against another

returned to its roots of national volunteerism for all of the needs of the poor when President George H.W. Bush formed the Commission on National and Community Service as part of his "Thousand Points of Light" program.

In 1993 President Bill Clinton created AmeriCorps and merged it with VISTA, creating AmeriCorpsVISTA to develop new programs to meet the changing needs of the impoverished. The new agency developed tenant-owned, cooperative low-income housing, and expanded Individual Development Accounts to assist poor individuals in saving money to help adjust to the transition from welfare to work.

The most significant case interpreting the act has been *Cook County Legal Assistance Foundation v. Pauken* (1983). This case dealt with the rights, responsibilities, and ability of agencies sponsoring volunteers to recover reimbursement for actions done on behalf of VISTA. VISTA failed to renew a legal aid corporation as a VISTA sponsor because, although VISTA's objective was to have sponsors direct community organizations toward self-help, the **plaintiff** legal agency was providing "direct services." The court ruled that sponsors were not constitutionally entitled to refunding once the term of funding had expired, and that neither the Administrative Procedure Act nor Domestic Volunteer Service Act conferred any right to money damages against the United States. Other court decisions have dealt with whether VISTA volunteers should claim their VISTA stipends as income, whether states could include VISTA workers as part of their worker's compensation schemes.

On October 30, 2000, VISTA's thirty-fifth anniversary, Senator Jay Rockefeller of West Virginia entered in the congressional record a written statement by a prominent former VISTA volunteer, John Gherty, CEO of Land-o-Lakes, who described the impact VISTA has had on society and the important learning experience that VISTA can offer volunteers. The statement included comments concerning the value of taking responsibility and creating opportunities, the essential role of teamwork and team building, the importance of building effective alliances, strength in diversity, and the need to identify leaders and build leadership skills in America.

See also: ECONOMIC OPPORTUNITY ACT OF 1964; PEACE CORPS ACT OF 1961.

BIBLIOGRAPHY

Committee on Education and Labor. *Domestic Volunteer Service Act of 1973: Report (to Accompany H.R. 7265).* Washington, D.C.: GPO, 1973.

Committee on Labor and Public Welfare. *Domestic Volunteer Service Act of 1973: Report (to Accompany S. 1148).* Washington, D.C.: GPO, 1973.

Robinson, Dale H. *Domestic Volunteer Service Act Programs.* Washington, D.C.: GPO, 1994.

DRUG ABUSE PREVENTION, TREATMENT, AND REHABILITATION ACT (1980)

Steven Harmon Wilson

Excerpt of the Drug Abuse Prevention, Treatment, and Rehabilitation

Shifts in the usage of various drugs and in the Nation's demographic composition require a Federal strategy to adjust the focus of drug abuse programs to meet new needs and priorities on a cost-effective basis…. The growing extent of drug abuse indicates an urgent need for prevention and intervention programs designed to reach the general population and members of high-risk populations such as youth, women, and the elderly…. Effective control of drug abuse requires high-level coordination of Federal international and domestic activities relating to both supply of, and demand for, commonly abused drugs…. Local governments with high concentrations of drug abuse should be actively involved in the planning and coordination of efforts to combat drug abuse.

The Drug Abuse Prevention, Treatment, and Rehabilitation Act (P.L.96-181, 93 Stat. 1309) is an amendment to the Drug Abuse Office and Treatment Act. These statutes together provide federal funding to various programs for the prevention of drug abuse and for the treatment and rehabilitation of drug abusers. In adopting these acts Congress aimed to coordinate a national strategy and establish a framework of federal, state, and local partnerships to combat drug abuse. The various amendments have extended programs to account for demographic shifts in the country and to respond to changing patterns of drug abuse.

Narcotics Anonymous

Narcotics Anonymous (NA) was founded in the 1950s as a small nonprofit group inspired by Alcoholics Anonymous. The principles of NA included the following: "seeking help; engaging in a thorough self-examination; confidential self-disclosure; making amends for harm done; and helping other drug addicts who want to recover." The group stresses spiritual principles and mutual support, and in weekly meetings, members share their experiences and encourage one another to abstain completely from all drugs, including alcohol. The organization has spread throughout the world: In 2002 there were approximately 20,000 registered groups holding more than 31,000 weekly meetings in more than 100 countries.

A HISTORY OF FEDERAL LEGISLATION ADDRESSING ADDICTION

Federal legislation leading to the adoption of the federal Drug Abuse Prevention, Treatment, and Rehabilitation Act reflects a varied approach to addiction. Proponents of a medical response to addiction have often competed with proponents of a punitive, or punishment, model. During the 1920s, thousands of private doctors were arrested for treating addiction by prescribing regulated "maintenance" doses of narcotics. Yet congressional interest in rehabilitating addicts emerged even as federal penalties for narcotics trafficking were being increased. With the Porter Act (1929), Congress established two "narcotic farms" for the confinement and treatment of addicts serving time in the federal prison system. These were built at Lexington, Kentucky (1935), and Fort Worth, Texas (1938). They continued to operate until the early 1970s.

The view that addiction was a treatable illness gained renewed popularity with lawmakers in the 1960s.

The view that addiction was a treatable illness gained renewed popularity with lawmakers in the 1960s. This led Congress to pass the Narcotic Addict Rehabilitation Act in 1966, which diverted some addicts charged with federal crimes into a civil process of treatment and rehabilitation. Two years later, in 1968, Congress passed the Alcoholic and Narcotic Addict Rehabilitation Amendments. Both laws authorized federal grants to assist the states and private organizations in the development of rehabilitation and treatment services. In order to clarify federal drug policy, Congress later combined various disparate enforcement laws into a single statute, the Comprehensive Drug Abuse Prevention and Control Act adopted in 1970. This legislation dealt with prevention and treatment of drug abuse as well as with the interdiction of drug traffic. The same year, Congress allocated $3.5 million to the Office of Education and $1 million to the National Institutes of Health for drug abuse research, education, and training.

The Congress, seeking to establish a diverse national network of drug abuse treatment programs, passed the Drug Abuse Office and Treatment Act (DAOTA) on March 21, 1972. The law created a Special Action Office for Drug Abuse Prevention and established the National Institute on Drug Abuse (NIDA) under the auspices of the National Institute of Mental Health. The

Inmates take part in an intensive substance abuse program at the Henrico Regional Jail East in Richmond, Virginia. The Drug Abuse Prevention, Treatment, and Rehabilitation Act of 1980 recognized the need for prevention and intervention programs designed to reach the general population and members of high-risk populations such as youth, women, and the elderly. The act provides federal funding to various programs for the prevention of drug abuse and for the treatment and rehabilitation of drug abusers. (© AP/WIDE WORLD PHOTOS)

federal role was to provide coordination, training, and **seed money** to assist state drug abuse prevention activities. Although in the years subsequent to the DAOTA the nation saw a marked reduction in the rate of increase of drug abuse, the apparent continuing spread of drug abuse indicated to Congress that the need for more effective and visible federal leadership was ongoing. This leadership has come through periodic amendments to the 1972 statute that extended prevention education and treatment programs.

The Drug Abuse Prevention, Treatment and Rehabilitation Act of 1979, which was actually enacted January 2, 1980, mandated that at least seven percent in 1980 and ten percent in 1981 of the community programs portion of NIDA's budget be spent on prevention. This act also recognized the emerging need for prevention and intervention programs designed to reach not only the general population but also members of such high -risk populations as youth, women, and the elderly. The Congress also sought to target federal support for planning and coordination efforts to communities with high concentrations of drug abuse.

seed money: money needed or provided to start a new project

SUBSEQUENT LEGISLATION

During the 1980s the federal war on drugs gathered strength and brought a renewal in the punitive approach to drug abuse. Nevertheless, when Congress passed the Anti-Drug Abuse Act of 1986, it enhanced the federal **block grant** program for substance abuse treatment and increased funds for research of AIDS, the spread of which seemed to be aggravated by drug use. In 1988 Congress passed the Omnibus Anti-Drug Abuse Act, which authorized funds for school-based drug prevention efforts and drug abuse treatment with special emphasis on injection drug abusers at high risk for AIDS. Although the 1986 and 1988 acts increased federal funding for treatment and rehabilitation, these statutes also reintroduced to federal law a system of mandatory minimum prison sentences. Disproportionate impact of these laws on racial minority defendants has been the source of much critical analysis and debate.

block grant: an unrestricted grant of federal money to state and local governments to support social welfare programs

See also: ALCOHOLIC AND NARCOTIC REHABILITATION ACT; ANTI-DRUG ABUSE ACT.

BIBLIOGRAPHY

Inciardi, James A. *The War on Drugs II: The Continuing Epic of Heroin, Cocaine, Crack, Crime, AIDS, and Public Policy.* Mountainview, CA: Mayfield Publishing, 1992.

Jonnes, Jill. *Hep-Cats, Narcs, and Pipe Dreams: A History of America's Romance with Illegal Drugs.* New York: Scribner, 1996.

Marion, Nancy E. *A History of Federal Crime Control Initiatives, 1960–1993.* Westport, CT: Praeger, 1994.

Musto, David F. *The American Disease: Origins of Narcotic Control,* 3rd ed. New York: Oxford University Press, 1999.

Rachal, Patricia. *Federal Narcotics Enforcement: Reorganization and Reform.* Boston, MA: Auburn House, 1982.

Sharp, Elaine B. *The Dilemma of Drug Policy in the United States.* New York: Harper-Collins, 1994.

Walker, William O. *Drug Control in the Americas.* Albuquerque: University of New Mexico Press, 1981.

Narcotic Addict Rehabilitation Act of 1966

Adopted in 1966, the Narcotic Addict Rehabilitation Act provided the option of sending addicts to rehabilitation programs as an alternative to jail. Addicts who were interested in treatment could be granted a civil commitment to Public Health Service hospitals; if they had been convicted of crimes, they could be treated at a Bureau of Prisons facility. If the patient was unsuccessful in the rehabilitation program, the original prosecution could be resumed.

E

ECONOMIC COOPERATION ACT OF 1948 (MARSHALL PLAN)

Charles M. Dobbs

On June 5, 1947, Secretary of State George C. Marshall spoke after lunch to graduates on commencement day for Harvard College. Speaking outdoors in the famed Harvard Yard, to an audience of privileged young men and their equally privileged families, this distinguished American soldier and statesman—who President Harry S. Truman called "the greatest living American"—discussed the dire situation in Europe and its consequences for the American people.

Marshall stated, "I need not tell you gentlemen that the world situation is very serious." After reminding them of the destruction that the fighting in the Second World War had caused, Marshall noted, "the truth of the matter is that Europe's requirements for the next three or four years of foreign food and other essential products—principally from America—are so much greater than her present ability to pay that she must have substantial additional help, or face economic, social and political deterioration of a very grave character." He warned that action was needed "to end poverty, desperation, and chaos" and to "permit the emergence of political and social conditions in which free institutions can exist." He concluded by calling upon the nations of Europe to review their needs and capacities, draw up a series of plans and he urged the American people to provide the resources to help meet the challenge.

The situation in Europe was, indeed, desperate. World War II not only took more than 50 million lives, it also destroyed factories, mines, transportation systems, water control systems, communication systems, and power grids. The suffering continued into the postwar era, for the 1946 European harvest was weak, and the winter of 1946–47 was one of the harshest in memory.

It appeared that this human suffering provided great opportunities for a Soviet-controlled, communist takeover in

George C. Marshall, at Harvard College commencement: "the truth of the matter is that Europe's requirements for the next three or four years of foreign food and other essential products—principally from America—are so much greater than her present ability to pay that she must have substantial additional help, or face economic, social and political deterioration of a very grave character."

The sign above the speaker in this November 1948 photograph, taken in Furth In Wald, Germany, reads "America helps to rebuild Europe. These freight cars were delivered through the Marshall Plan." A ceremony is being held for the delivery of seventy-five freight cars purchased for Germany from Czechoslovakia under the Marshall Plan. From 1948 to 1952 the United States provided $13.3 billion in aid to participating European countries through the Marshall Plan. (©BETTMAN/CORBIS)

Europe and perhaps elsewhere. The Cold War was beginning, and Soviet leader Josef Stalin and his advisors may have feared the overwhelming economic power of the United States (which emerged from the war with some 45 percent of the world's industrial capacity). Western leaders watched the Soviets establish friendly regimes in Poland, the Baltic States, Rumania, Hungary, and Bulgaria. It also appeared that the Soviets were setting up a separate regime in eastern Germany. Communist parties in Italy and France were large, well-supported, and seemed on the verge of coming to power, perhaps thereby surrounding the western occupation zones in Germany and handing the entire continent to the Soviet Union.

As a reflection of a long-standing humanitarian and charitable impulse in American life, the United States had provided billions of dollars in postwar relief to help the peoples of Europe through the United Nations and other newly formed international organizations, but it was not enough. That is, providing food, clothing, medical and heating supplies, especially during the difficult winter and early spring months could not restore the economies and rebuild the societies so that Europe could return once again to a viable system of nations and states. Moreover, the ongoing relief costs were significant, and many in and out of government questioned this continuing expense to American taxpayers. By spring, 1947, the troubled British economy might force America to bear the entire cost of relief for Europe.

Marshall at Harvard had called for European nations to meet for the purpose of determining needs and plans for recovery. The British and French foreign ministers, Ernest Bevin and Georges Bidault, issued a call on June 19, only two weeks later, inviting twenty-two European nations to send representatives to a meeting in Paris. The Soviet Union did not participate (although Soviet Foreign Minister Vyacheslav Molotov did briefly stay in Paris) and pressured its Eastern European satellites to stay away. Two months after that initial meeting, in September, 1947, the Committee of European Economic Cooperation submitted a plan to the U.S. government.

The Truman Administration had followed a script of a sort. It began with Marshall's earlier trip to Moscow. A proposal by William Clayton became the genesis of the plan, and staff work coordinated by George Kennan, head of the newly established Policy Planning Staff created support for an ambitious aid program while providing few details of that program.

It began with Marshall's earlier trip to Moscow. A proposal by William Clayton became the genesis of the plan, and staff work coordinated by George Kennan, head of the newly established Policy Planning Staff created support for an ambitious aid program while providing few details of that program.

As the majority of European nations embraced Marshall's call to action, the drama moved to the halls of the Congress, where the outcome was not certain. In the 1946 Congressional elections, the Republicans gained control of both houses of Congress, and already many people were predicting with an unwarranted certainty that Truman, who came to the presidency after Franklin Roosevelt died in April 1945, would lose the presidential election in 1948.

One prominent Democrat, Henry A. Wallace, who had been Roosevelt's vice president and then served as secretary of commerce, opposed the Marshall Plan because it threatened the Soviet Union and seemed to divide the world into hostile camps. Wallace called it a "martial plan" and believed it would end any chance for postwar cooperation between the former wartime allies. He also feared the plan would provide for greater business influence in American life, and would exacerbate economic inequalities at home. Wallace would resign from the Truman administration and ultimately run for president in 1948, polling more than one million votes.

The more serious opposition came from the right wing of the Republican Party. Republican senator Robert Taft of Ohio, who thought he would head his party's ticket in 1948, opposed this expanded aid program for many reasons, including a dislike of nationalized industries and centralized planning in many European countries, concern about spending so many American tax dollars, fear of expanding presidential power, and the longstanding doubts about foreign entanglements. Taft and former president Herbert Hoover, who had strongly opposed most of the New Deal agencies his successor, Roosevelt, had established, also feared, as Hoover noted in testimony, that such great economic aid would bring about "serious taxation on our own people" and would create "scarcity and high prices and economic unrest at home." Henry Hazlitt, a conservative media commentator, told Congress to insist that European countries first dismantle programs for nationalization of industry, government con-

The first cargo of Caribbean sugar under the Marshall Plan arrived at Royal Victoria Docks in London, February 3, 1949. (© Hulton-Deutsch Collection/Corbis)

trol of trade, and social-welfare as a condition of receiving Marshall Plan aid. Others, including Republican senator James Kem of Missouri and Democratic senator Walter George of Georgia, feared the amount of government involvement and wanted a return to a more **laissez-faire** system in Europe.

There were also concerns from the broad middle of the political spectrum. Such legislative leaders as Sam Rayburn, Democratic House minority leader, and Charles Halleck, Republican House majority leader, noted that the American people were tired of the billions of dollars in never-ending relief. There were many in Congress who wondered about the impact on the U.S. economy of such large spending on assistance to Europe, and business people questioned the wisdom of strengthening European industries to compete with American ones. Indeed, President Truman was in such a weak position politically that he asked Secretary Marshall to be the administration's point

laissez-faire: a doctrine opposing governmental interference in economic affairs beyond the minimum necessary for the maintenance of peace and property rights.

There were many in Congress who wondered about the impact on the U.S. economy of such large spending on assistance to Europe, and business people questioned the wisdom of strengthening European industries to compete with American ones.

person in hearings before Congress and in the resulting debate, which the great soldier agreed to do. The ensuing success in Congress also owed a great deal to the advice and assistance of Republican senator Arthur Vandenberg, chair of the powerful Senate Foreign Relations Committee. Marshall was the leadoff witness in hearings before the Senate Foreign Relations Committee on January 8, 1948, insisting that the European Recovery Program would reduce the expansion of Soviet power. He also made the opening statement on January 12, 1948, before the House Foreign Affairs Committee. Marshall then followed up with speeches to the Pittsburgh Chamber of Commerce, the National Cotton Council in Atlanta, the National Farm Institute in Des Moines (by long distance call since poor weather grounded his flight), to the Federal Council of Churches in Washington, D.C., and the General Federation of Women's Clubs in Portland, Oregon.

Senator Vandenberg helped shape the Truman Administration's proposal into something his fellow Republicans could support. Vandenberg came to Washington as an isolationist, but over the years he had become his party's leading internationalist and advocate for a bipartisan foreign policy. He helped to tighten the proposal, reducing the amount of the aid request, insisting that, after four years of aid, the participating European countries should be back on their feet. Vandenberg also helped to write the act's preamble calling for more inter-European cooperation than the State Department proposed and thus ultimately leading to the European Common Market. Lastly, he made the administration set up a separate agency, later called the Economic Cooperation Agency, headed by a non-State Department official, Studebaker Corporation CEO Paul Hoffman, to oversee the vast recovery program.

Vandenberg helped defend the administration's request. In a famous exchange, Senator Taft proposed reducing the first year request from $4 billion to $3 billion. Senator Vandenberg responded, "when a man is drowning 20 feet away, it's a mistake to throw him a 15-foot rope." Taft's motion to cut the first twelve-month authorization lost 56 to 31, and the final Senate vote would be 69 to 17 in favor of the plan. There were other issues, including discussions how to establish the values, in terms of aid dollars, of commodities provided and sold.

Other members of Congress supported the administration's proposal given the gravity of the situation. Representative Everett Dirksen posed three options for Congress: to withdraw from Europe, to give minimal aid, or, "the choice we must make ... Do it—do it now—and do it right." A committee led by Representative Christian Herter returned from a trip to Europe and, as a consequence of what they found, most members returned as committed supporters of the Marshall Plan.

Soviet actions in Eastern Europe certainly assisted the administration's effort to secure passage of the legislation. In February 1948, Soviet agents killed the leader of democratic Czechoslovakia, Jan Masaryk, and that little country soon passed into the Soviet orbit. Combined with Soviet intransigence in occupied Germany (and Austria), the establishment of the Cominform, the continuing division of Korea into Soviet and America zones, and the likelihood of a great communist military victory in Manchuria in the Chinese civil war, Stalin's seemingly aggressive expansionism helped convince doubtful Republicans to support the legislation. Resisting the spread of international communism was far more acceptable than supporting the spending of American funds for economic assistance to Europe.

The administration worked hard to build public support for its plan and to press Congress to approve it. To help garner business support, and thus to mitigate Republican opposition, Truman created the Committee on Foreign Aid, chaired by Averell Harriman, with heavy business membership, to study the Marshall Plan's impact on business. Attorney General Tom Clark and FBI Director J. Edgar Hoover helped lead a campaign for patriotic sentiment that would indirectly help. Along with reports from the newly formed Council of Economic Advisors and a Committee for the Marshall Plan to aid European Recovery, this propaganda offensive made the case that the plan would protect America's "vital interests—humanitarian, economic, strategic, and political."

The lobbying and public relations effort proved successful. The Truman administration agreed to include China in the plan, and that won over some conservative Republicans who also were staunch members of the China lobby for Jiang Jieshr's (failing) nationalist regime. Congress approved the European Recovery Plan by a vote of 69 to 17 in the Senate and 329 to 74 in the House in March, 1948, President Harry Truman held a White House signing ceremony on April 3, 1948, and the Economic Cooperation Act became law.

Over the next four years, the United States provided $13.3 billion (more than $120 billion in current dollars) and the European economy revived. Britain, France, and Italy avoided collapse; the western zones of Germany, known as the Federal Republic of Germany, recovered from wartime devastation and postwar troubles. Although historians have debated and will continue to debate the measurable effectiveness of the Marshall Plan, most observers agreed it was needed and it helped achieve the revival of the western European economy and consequently of western European society.

"Our policy is not directed against any country or doctrine, but is directed against hunger, poverty, desperation and chaos. Its purpose should be the revival of a working economy in the world so as to permit the emergence of political and economic conditions in which free institutions can exist." —George C. Marshall (1880–1959), General, U.S. Army, U.S. Secretary of State and U.S. Secretary of Defense. Commencement Speech, Harvard University, June 5, 1947.

BIBLIOGRAPHY

Briggs, Philip J. *Making American Foreign Policy: President-Congress Relations from the Second World War to the Post-Cold War Era.* Lanham, MD: Rowman & Littlefield, 1994.

Donovan, Robert J. *The Second Victory: The Marshall Plan and the Postwar Revival of Europe.* New York: Madison Books, 1987.

Fossedal, Gregory A. *Our Finest Hour: Will Clayton, the Marshall Plan, and the Triumph of Democracy.* Stanford, CA: Hoover Institution Press, 1993.

Hogan, Michael J. *The Marshall Plan: America, Britain, and the Reconstruction of Western Europe, 1947–1952.* New York: Cambridge University Press, 1987.

Levering, Ralph B. *The Cold War: A Post-Cold War History.* Arlington Heights, IL: Harland Davidson, 1994.

McCormick, Thomas J. *America's Half-Century: United States Foreign Policy in the Cold War and After.* Baltimore, MD: Johns Hopkins University Press, 1995.

Mee, Charles L. *The Marshall Plan: The Launching of the Pax Americana.* New York: Simon & Schuster, 1984.

Paterson, Thomas G. *On Every Front: The Making and Unmaking of the Cold War.* New York: W.W. Norton, 1992.

ECONOMIC OPPORTUNITY ACT OF 1964

Stephen J. Pollak

Excerpt from the of Economic Opportunity Act of 1964

Findings and Declaration of Purpose:

Although the economic well-being and prosperity of the United States have progressed to a level surpassing any achieved in world history, and although these benefits are widely shared throughout the Nation, poverty continues to be the lot of a substantial number of our people. The United States can achieve its full economic and social potential as a nation only if every individual has the opportunity to contribute to the full extent of his capabilities and to participate in the workings of our society. It is, therefore, the policy of the United States to eliminate the paradox of poverty in the midst of plenty in this Nation by opening to everyone the opportunity for education and training, the opportunity to work, and the opportunity to live in decency and dignity. It is the purpose of this Act to strengthen, supplement, and coordinate efforts in furtherance of that policy.

Congress adopted the Economic Opportunity Act of 1964 (EOA) (P.L. 88-452, 78 Stat. 508) when President Lyndon Johnson was in office. In his first State of the Union message, President Johnson declared the EOA would launch the "war on poverty." At the signing ceremony, the president said the American people were making history:

> For so long as man has lived on this earth poverty has been his curse. On every continent in every age men have sought escape from poverty's oppression. Today for the first time in all history of the human race, a great nation is able to make and is willing to make a commitment to eradicate poverty among its people.

The philosophy behind the statute was not wealth distribution, but the belief that government can and must provide poor people with opportunities to earn a decent living and maintain their families in a comfortable living standard. President Johnson identified the constitutional basis for the legislation, stating, "The Congress is charged by the Constitution 'to provide ... for the general welfare of the United States.'"

"This administrations today, here and now, declares unconditional war on poverty."
—Lyndon Baines Johnson in his first annual message to Congress, January 8, 1964.

The act employed two mechanisms to reach its lofty goal. First, it established eleven new programs that the Office of Economic Opportunity (OEO) would operate or supervise. The new programs included:

(1) The Job Corps, which provides work, basic education, and training in separate residential centers for young men and young women, ages sixteen to twenty-one;

(2) Neighborhood Youth Corps, which provides work and training for young men and women, ages sixteen to twenty-one, from impoverished families and neighborhoods;

(3) Work Study, which provides grants to colleges and universities for part-time employment of students from low-income families who need to earn money to pursue their education;

(4) Urban and Rural Community Action, which provides financial and technical assistance to public and private **nonprofit** agencies for community action programs developed with "maximum feasible participation" of the poor and giving "promise of progress toward elimination of poverty";

(5) Adult Basic Education, which provides grants to state educational agencies for programs of instruction for persons eighteen years and older whose inability to read and write English is an impediment to employment;

(6) Voluntary Assistance for Needy Children, which establishes an information and coordination center to encourage voluntary assistance for deserving and needy children;

(7) Loans to Rural Families, which provides loans not exceeding $2,500 that will assist low income rural families in permanently increasing their income;

(8) Assistance for Migrant Agricultural Employees, which provides assistance to state and local governments, public and private nonprofit agencies or individuals in operating programs to assist migratory workers and their families with housing, sanitation, education, and day care of children;

(9) Employment and Investment Incentives, which provides loans and guarantees, not in excess of $25,000 to a single borrower, for the benefit of very small businesses;

(10) Work Experience, which provides payments for experimental, pilot, and demonstration projects to expand opportunities for work experience and needed training of persons who are unable to support or care for themselves or their families, including persons receiving public assistance; and

(11) Volunteers in Service to America (VISTA), which recruits, selects, trains, and refers volunteers to state or local agencies or private nonprofit organizations to perform duties in combating poverty.

Second, recognizing that there were already many federal programs addressing problems of the poor, the statute empowered the OEO Director to coordinate the anti-poverty efforts of all federal agencies. It directed those agencies to cooperate with the director and established an Economic Opportunity Council, chaired by the director and composed of the members of the president's Cabinet, to consult with the director in carrying out his functions.

nonprofit: an organization that's business is not conducted or maintained for the purpose of making a profit usually aimed at providing services deemed for the public good

CIRCUMSTANCES LEADING TO THE ADOPTION OF THE EOA

The 1960s were a period of reform, sometimes referred to as the "Second Reconstruction." Michael Harrington, a prominent writer on social issues, graphically described the plight of the poor in 1962 in *The Other America: Poverty in the United States,* a book said to have made a significant impression on both President Kennedy and President Johnson. President Kennedy's brother, Attorney General Robert F. Kennedy, visited pockets of poverty in Appalachia, in urban slums, and on Native American reservations, and spoke out for remedial action. The President's Council of Economic Advisers' Annual Report published in January 1964 focused on the "Problem of Poverty in America," pulling together compelling statistics and showing that in a period of unprecedented prosperity, one-fifth of all families and nearly one-fifth of the total U.S. population—33 to 35 million people—were poor, having incomes below the **poverty line** (then $3,000 for a family of four), and that nearly one-half of all non-whites were living in poverty. It also revealed that,

poverty line: level of personal or family income below which a person or family is classified as poor. The standard is set by the government despite the decline from generation to generation in the proportion of the poor in the adult population, there were groups (for example, farm families and families headed by women) where the poverty rate was stubbornly stable and "the cruel legacy of poverty is passed from parents to children."

In January 1964 the president asked R. Sargent Shriver, the head of the successful Peace Corps, which provided volunteers to assist poor people outside the United States, to head a Cabinet-level task force charged with developing a bill to carry on the war against poverty here at home. In March the president transmitted to the Congress the administration's bill, which was introduced in the House by Representative Phil M. Landrum, Democrat of Georgia, a southern conservative, and in the Senate by Senator Pat McNamara, Democrat of Michigan, a northern liberal. Subcommittees of the House Education and Labor Committee and a subcommittee of the Senate Labor and Public Welfare Committee held hearings, and each committee reported the bill favorably, with some amendments, but substantially intact. After debating the bill for two days, the full Senate passed it, with limited amendments, on July 23, 1964, by a vote of sixty-one to thirty-four, with ten of thirty-two Republicans voting for it and the southern Democrats split eleven to eleven. The House debated the Senate-passed bill over four days in August, and by a vote of 226 to 185 adopted that bill, with a few amendments, on August 8, 1964. Twenty-two Republicans, 144 northern Democrats, sixty southern Democrats voted for the bill, while 145 Republicans and forty southern Democrats opposed it. On the same day, the Senate, by a voice vote, adopted the House-passed bill. The president signed the bill on August 20, 1964.

"Poverty is not an individual affair. It is also a condition, a relationship to society, and to all the institutions which comprise society."— R. Sargent Shriver, Testimony, House Education and Labor Committee, April 12, 1965.

Floor debate in the House, where the outcome of the final vote was in doubt, was highly partisan, according to the *Congressional Quarterly*. There was fierce competition for the votes of southern Democrats. The powerful Democratic chairman of the House Rules Committee, Howard W. Smith of Virginia, had delayed granting a rule for floor action, saying that the legislation was "too vague and indefinite." He questioned Representative Landrum, manager of the bill, about racial integration at Job Corps centers. With Republican Representative Peter H. B. Frelinghuysen, Jr. of New Jersey, ranking member of the House Education and Labor Committee, taking the lead, Republicans in the House accused the administration of putting "unprecedented pressure" on members to vote, and of being locked out in developing a **bipartisan** bill. They emphasized the far-reaching authority given the OEO Director over other federal programs and in funding of projects within states and local jurisdictions without the approval of governors, mayors, and county executives. Opponents attacked the job training and work experience provisions of the bill for focusing on low-skilled jobs or makework, when the economy needed highly skilled workers.

bipartisan: involving members of two parties, especially the two major political parties

States' rights were a driving force behind opponents' arguments in both the Senate and the House. Two similar states' rights amendments were accepted during floor debate in the Senate. One gave the governors veto power over establishment of Job Corps centers in their states, provided they acted within thirty days of notice. The second gave the governors veto power over any Job Corps center or National Youth Corps or Community Action project contracted between the federal government and private agencies within their states. The House extended the governors' veto to Community

Action projects contracted with public agencies. Reflecting the opponents' views was a Republican-sponsored alternative to the administration's bill, which would have authorized $1.5 billion in grants to be expended over a three-year period (1965–67) through existing governmental agencies. Consistent with the Republicans' opposition to expansion of the federal bureaucracy, their alternative did not provide for creation of any new anti-poverty operating or coordinating agency.

The fact that the bill did not preclude aid to poverty projects sponsored by **sectarian** schools or institutions was also debated. An amendment to bar grants to sectarian schools was defeated in the Senate.

sectarian: characteristic of a group following a specific doctrine or leader

During the time the bill was being debated, President Johnson was running for re-election, and the Republicans were selecting their candidate, Sen. Barry Goldwater of Arizona, to run against him. The anti-poverty program was frequently discussed during the presidential primaries and in the fall campaign. Senator Goldwater was a leader in opposing the bill and its reliance upon the federal government to address the problems of the poor. He accused the president of "playing politics with poverty."

EXPERIENCE UNDER THE ECONOMIC OPPORTUNITY ACT

Congress funded the programs authorized by the EOA on the last day of the 1964 congressional session, October 8, with $800 million for fiscal year 1965, 15 percent less than the $947.5 million authorized. On November 25, 1964, OEO Director Shriver announced the first 119 projects, budgeted at $35 million, including thirty-two Job Corps camps and an urban training center; fourteen Neighborhood Youth Corps projects serving 10,500 youths in thirteen states; community action grants in twelve cities, six rural areas and one Native American reservation; work experience programs for unemployed parents in two cities and two counties; and work-study programs for needy college students at thirty-one colleges. Using the flexibility afforded by the statute for community action projects, OEO in 1965 inaugurated four innovative programs: Head Start, to assist preschool children from deprived families to enter kindergarten and first grade; Upward Bound, to prepare talented poverty-stricken youths for college; Neighborhood Legal Services, to provide free legal counsel for the poor in civil matters; and Foster Grandparents, to train unemployed elderly poor to care for neglected children and bedridden sick persons.

"One thousand dollars invested in salvaging an unemployable youth can return $40,000 or more in his lifetime." —Lyndon Baines Johnson in his first annual message to Congress, January 8, 1964.

From the beginning, Republicans, often with the support of southern Democrats, attempted to dismantle the OEO and transfer its operating programs to "old-line" departments and agencies. While Congress ultimately repealed the Economic Opportunity Act in 1981, the first year of the presidency of Ronald Reagan, many of the programs established by the 1964 act or created by OEO have survived, often with enhanced budgets and changes in name and configuration. Examples include Head Start and Work-Study which are administered by the Department of Education; and Legal Services which is now a federally funded corporation under a presidentially appointed board.

Neither the act nor OEO ever had the profound impact on society envisioned by President Johnson and the proponents of the legislation—bringing

"If we can spend money to put a man on the moon, we ought to be able to find the funds to put a man on his feet." —Hubert H. Humphrey, address to Job Corps awards ceremony, 1966.

about the elimination of poverty. Commentators have strongly debated the reasons for this result. According to Michael Harrington in *The New American Poverty,* the act failed to achieve its purpose "to eliminate the paradox of poverty in the midst of plenty" because of the Vietnam War and the lack of funding. For the first five fiscal years (1965–69), Congress appropriated a total of $7.634 billion to fund all EOA programs. The Council of Economic Advisers, in its January 1964 report, had stated that "about $11 billion a year would bring all poor families up to the $3,000 income level we have taken to be the minimum for a decent life." Other commentators say the anti-poverty program was misdirected. Daniel Patrick Moynihan, a member of the poverty task force (later Senator representing New York), has pointed to the lack of any provision for the employment of adult men as a crucial decision. Another critic, James L. Sundquist, also a task force member, says that Sargent Shriver mistakenly opted for OEO to be an operating agency, focusing on administering programs such as Job Corps and VISTA, rather than coordinating the many programs of the federal government impacting poverty.

On balance, while the label "war against poverty" reflected the hyperbole of politics, the Economic Opportunity Act focused the attention of the nation and the agencies of the federal government on poverty and the need for coordinated, multidimensional approaches to reduce, if not to eliminate, its root causes. The statute launched several effective programs that demonstrated what could be accomplished and challenged the citizenry and government not to accept the adage that the "poor will always be with us."

BIBLIOGRAPHY

Douglas, Paul H. *In Our Time.* New York: Harcourt, Brace & World, Inc., 1968.

"Economic Opportunity Act of 1964, S. Rep. No 1458 (1964)." *United States Code Congressional and Administrative News,* 88th Cong., 2d Sess. (1964): 2900–89.

Ferman, Louis A. "Evaluating the War on Poverty." *Annals of the American Academy of Political and Social Science* (September 1969).

Galbraith, John K. *The Affluent Society.* Boston: Houghton Mifflin, 1958.

Harrington, Michael. *The Other America.* New York: The Macmillan Company, 1963.

Harrington, Michael. *The New American Poverty.* New York: Viking Penguin, 1984.

Kershaw, Joseph A. *Government against Poverty.* Washington, DC: Brookings Institution, 1970.

Levitan, Sar A. *The Great Society's Poor Law.* Baltimore: Johns Hopkins Press, 1969.

Moynihan, Daniel P. *On Understanding Poverty.* New York: Basic Books, 1968.

Moynihan, Daniel P. *Maximum Feasible Misunderstanding.* New York: The Free Press, 1969.

Moynihan, Daniel P. "The Professors and the Poor." *Commentary* (August 1968): 19.

Plotnick, Robert D., and Skidmore, Felicity. *Progress against Poverty: A Review of the 1964–1974 Decade.* New York: Academic Press, 1975.

"President's 'War on Poverty' Approved." *Congressional Quarterly* 4 (1964): 208.

Sundquist, James L. *Making Federalism Work.* Washington, DC: Brookings Institution, 1969.

Sundquist, James L. *On Fighting Poverty.* New York: Basic Books, 1969.

EDUCATION AMENDMENTS

See TITLE IX EDUCATION AMENDMENTS.

1894 INCOME TAX AND THE WILSON-GORMAN TARIFF ACT

Norman Stein

Prior to the Civil War (1861–1865), America's revenue needs were met primarily through tariffs, duties, and other consumption taxes. In 1861, however, Congress adopted an income tax aimed at the nation's most affluent to finance the Civil War. The U.S. Supreme Court upheld the constitutionality of the income tax in *Springer v. U.S.* (1864). And in 1871, when the need for government revenue declined, Congress repealed the income tax, thereby placing the burden of financing government again almost entirely on tariffs and duties, increasing the cost of goods paid by workers. Thus, the repeal of the income tax shifted a portion of the tax burden away from the affluent to consumers generally.

Many Americans and populist politicians saw the tariff-based tax system as protecting capitalists by immunizing their products from competition from imports. Some also resented the wealthy, who were sometimes seen as shirking their responsibility to help pay for government services. Thus, the idea and appeal of an income tax—reducing tariffs and increasing the tax burden on the affluent—never fully retreated from the American political landscape. There was, in fact, constant political pressure on Congress to restore the income tax; Congress introduced more than sixty bills between 1871 and 1894 to restore the income tax, culminating in passage of an income tax as part of the Wilson-Gorman Tariff Act of 1894. Less than a year after its passage, however, the U.S. Supreme Court held that portions of the income tax levied by the Wilson-Gorman Tariff Act of 1894 were unconstitutional.

> *At the time the 1894 law was passed, financier J.P. Morgan exclaimed, "the public be damned," reflecting the thinking of his own social circle.*

THE SOCIAL, ECONOMIC, AND POLITICAL CONTEXT OF THE INCOME TAX DEBATE

An understanding of the controversy and public policy debate surrounding the income tax at the close of the nineteenth century requires an exploration of that era's social, economic and political context. After the Civil War, the Republican Party dominated national politics and local politics in states that had aligned with the Union in the Civil War. The interests of those states—or rather the interests of the powerful political actors within those states—dictated much of the Republican Party's platform during that era.

The former Union states were centers of finance and industry and contained areas of concentrated wealth. This era, sometimes called the "Gilded Age," was noted for its robber barons, industrialists and financiers who amassed great wealth often at the expense of the working class. The most important issues to Republicans were relatively high tariffs to support Ameri-

"As we view the achievements of aggregated capital, we discover the existence of trusts, combinations, and monopolies, while the citizen is struggling far in the rear or is trampled to death beneath an iron heel. Corporations, which should be the restrained creatures of the law and the servants of the people, are fast becoming the nation's masters." —President Grover Cleveland, fourth annual message to Congress, December 1888.

can industry and limit foreign competition with domestic products; maintaining a gold standard for currency to check inflation; and governmental regulation of the work force (both in limiting relief networks for the unemployed and in preventing workers from organizing unions). The Republican Party of the Gilded Age tended to incorporate the positions of the great industrialists and financiers on these issues into its platform.

This was not, however, an era of universal prosperity or stability; rather, it was an era of extremes—great poverty for many amidst great wealth for a few. The average family income was less than $400 and fewer than 90 percent of American families had income in excess of $12,000. It was a hard time, especially for wage earners in cities and family farmers in the rural West and South. Many farmers and wage earners viewed government policy as favoring the interests of the financiers and capitalists, with high tariffs serving as an example of this preference. Such tariffs raised the price of domestic goods, imposing a steep tax burden on consumers. It was from this environment that populism emerged as a national political force at the end of the nineteenth century.

Populists, along with farm and labor political groups, sought lower tariffs. To replace the lost tariff revenue, some populist leaders favored reintroducing an income tax, which would also addressing the problem of the concentration of vast wealth in the hands of a few citizens.

The Democratic Party began to adopt some of these populist ideas. In 1892 Democrat Grover Cleveland won back the White House on a platform that favored lower tariffs and duties. Some Democratic members of Congress also sought to reinstitute an income tax.

THE WILSON-GORMAN TARIFF ACT

In 1894, Cleveland supported the Wilson-Gorman Tariff Act, whose original purpose was to lower tariffs substantially. In the House, however, Benton McMillan, a Tennessee representative, amended the Wilson-Gorman Tariff Act to include an income tax. The amendment began:

> That from and after the 1st day of January, 1895, there shall be levied, collected, and paid annually upon the gains, profits, and income of every person residing in the United States, or any citizen of the United States residing abroad, derived in each preceding calendar year, whether derived from any kind of property, rents, interest, dividends, or salaries, or from any profession, trade, employment, or vocation carried on in the United States or elsewhere, a tax of 2 per cent on the amount so derived over and above $4,000.

Thus, a flat 2 percent tax would be imposed on income in excess of $4,000. Fewer than 5 percent of Americans earned sufficient income to have to pay the tax. The amendment also imposed a 2 percent tax on the income of corporations and certain associations, although there were exceptions for charitable organizations, mutual banks, and insurance companies.

The income-tax amendment was bitterly opposed by all Republicans and many northern Democrats, as the tax would disproportionately affect citizens of northern states. The amendment, however, found a fiery and gifted advocate in Nebraska Congressman William Jennings Bryan. Responding to those

VOL. XXXVII. No. 949.   PUCK BUILDING, New York, May 15th, 1895.   PRICE 10 CENTS.
Copyright, 1895, by Keppler & Schwarzmann.

WITHOUT A FRIEND.

Cover illustration from Puck, *May 15, 1895. A mongrel dog representing income tax cowers in front of the Treasury Department. The can tied to the dog's tail illustrates the Supreme Court decision in* Pollack v. Farmers' Loan and Trust Co. *The dog is bombarded by bricks representing public disapproval and the press.* (©CORBIS)

who argued that subjecting only the wealthy to the tax was socialism, Bryant retorted that "they weep more because fifteen millions are to be collected from the rich than they do at the collection of three hundred millions upon the goods which the poor consume."

The Wilson-Gorman Tariff Act, with the income-tax amendment, passed in the House. Its fate in the Senate was a different story. Republicans and northern Democrats, oriented toward protecting manufacturing and financial interests, generally opposed the lowered tariffs contained in the House bill. They were joined by senators from Louisiana (interested in protective tariffs on sugar), and West Virginia and Maryland (interested in protective tariffs on coal and iron). Ultimately, the Senate gutted the provisions that lowered tariffs. But the income tax amendment—despite fierce opposition from Republicans and northern Democrats, who labeled it "class legislation" and a communistic idea foreign to American ideals—passed. It passed, perhaps in large part, because America was in the midst of a depression and its revenue needs might not be met by tariffs and duties alone. President Cleveland, furious that many Democratic senators had deserted his call for lower tariffs, allowed the bill to become law without his signature.

Just before the Pollack *decision came down, Justice Stephen Field (1816–1899) wrote: "The capital is but the beginning; it will be the stepping-stone to others larger and more sweeping, till our political contests will become a war of the poor against the rich, a war constantly growing in intensity and bitterness."*

POLLOCK V. FARMERS' LOAN AND TRUST CO.

Litigation on the constitutionality of the income tax commenced almost immediately after the tax became law. Opponents of the tax argued principally that the tax was a direct tax, which Article I, Section 2, of the Constitution requires be "apportioned among the several states" according to their populations. The classic direct tax would have been a tax on property. The income tax, on the other hand, taxed wages and earnings derived from property. Supporters of the tax argued that a tax on earnings was not a direct tax on the property itself, thus constitutional as an indirect tax.

The U.S. Supreme Court consolidated several separate cases challenging the tax in *Pollock v. Farmers' Loan and Trust Co.* (1865). The Supreme Court, with one justice not participating because of illness, held, in a 5–3 vote, that the income tax as applied to rents earned on real property was an unconstitutional direct tax on that property. The Court also held, on federalism grounds, that the federal government lacked constitutional authority to tax income from state government bonds. The *Pollock* Court, however, split 4–4 on the constitutionality of an income tax to income produced by personal property, such as stocks and bonds. The Supreme Court granted a rehearing on the case, allowing all nine judges to participate. On rehearing, the *Pollock* Court, by a 5-4 vote, held that a tax on income from personal property was also constitutionally infirm as an unapportioned direct tax. The decision declared the entire statute unconstitutional, as the court determined that enforcing the remaining portions of the law was inconsistent with the intent of Congress.

In finding the income tax unconstitutional, the court distinguished a case that affirmed the constitutionality of an income tax during the Civil War. The *Pollock* Court held that the earlier case had only considered the constitutionality of a tax on wages, not a tax on income from property. Some commentators, then and now, have argued that the *Pollock* Court's distinction of *Springer* was disingenuous.

Justice Harlan issued a stinging and memorable dissent in *Pollock,* considered by some as one of the great dissents in U.S. Supreme Court history. The dissent traced Supreme Court jurisprudence on the federal taxing power, concluding that *Pollock* was a radical and unfortunate break from the legal precedent. Justice Harlan also criticized the decision as one intended to favor the wealthy, who derive their wealth from capital rather than labor:

> [B]y its present construction of the Constitution the court, for the first time in all its history, declares that our government has been so framed that, in matters of taxation for its support and maintenance those who have incomes derived from the renting of real estate or from the leasing or using

of tangible personal property, or who own invested personal property, bonds, stocks and investments of whatever kind, have privileges that cannot be accorded to those having incomes derived from the labor of their hands, or the exercise of their skill, or the use of their brains.

Ultimately, the nation enacted the 16th Amendment, which made the income tax a part of the nation's Constitutional scheme, rendering *Pollock* void.

See also: INCOME TAX ACT OF 1954; INTERNAL REVENUE CODE OF 1986; PERSONAL INCOME TAX ACT OF 1913; TAX REFORM ACT OF 1986.

BIBLIOGRAPHY

Grossfeld, Bernhard, and James D. Bryce. "A Brief Comparative History of the Origins of the Income Tax in Great Britain, Germany and the United States." *American Journal of Tax Policy* 211 (1983).

Seligman, Edwin R.A. *The Income Tax: A Study of the History, Theory and Practice of Income Taxation at Home and Abroad.* New York: Macmillan, 1914.

Weisman, Steven R. *The Great Tax Wars.* New York: Simon & Schuster, 2002.

ELECTRONIC COMMUNICATIONS PRIVACY ACT OF 1986

Jennifer Byram

The Electronic Communications Privacy Act of 1986 (ECPA) (P. L. 99-508, 100 Stat.1848) was enacted to extend federal wiretap laws to new forms of communication. The prior law, the Omnibus Crime Control and Safe Streets Act of 1968, protected only those communications that could be heard and understood by the human ear, such as telephone calls made over a public, wire-based system and private *in person* conversations overheard with a microphone from interception or disclosure by law enforcement or private individuals. It did not address new communication technologies such as email, computer data transmissions, faxes, pagers and cellular or cordless telephones.

These new technologies created significant uncertainty about their privacy protections, and about any limits on law enforcement's right to gather and use these communications as evidence in a criminal prosecution. Congress also feared that, without clear privacy protections, the public would not use or accept these new technologies.

In addition to extending current protections against interception and disclosure to new communication technologies, the ECPA also expanded the list of crimes that justified law enforcement interceptions of communications; limited access to stored communications and data including email without a person's consent; prohibited interference with the operation of a satellite; and regulated the use of pen registers to record the telephone numbers received, as well as tap and trace devices to record the telephone numbers dialed, on a particular telephone line.

Congress held extensive hearings and negotiations, beginning in 1975, leading up to the introduction and passage of the ECPA. Representatives of many groups testified at the hearings, including law enforcement, prosecutors, tele-

ECPA protects electronic communications (i.e., faxes, email, and cordless and cellular phones) but not as fully as the 1968 law protects "wire" and "oral" communications. Penalties for illegally intercepting a cell-phone conversation are much less than for a hard-wire telephone.

warrant: a document issued by a judge granting authority to do something

phone and computer companies, the American Civil Liberties Union, and amateur radio enthusiasts. Thus, the final bill had broad support from interested parties.

The ECPA is based on the privacy rights derived from the protection against unreasonable searches and seizures found in the Fourth Amendment and Congress's power to regulate interstate commerce granted in Article I of the U.S. Constitution. In *Bartnicki v. Vopper, aka Williams* (2001), the U.S. Supreme Court ruled on the constitutionality of the ECPA. In that case, an unknown person illegally intercepted and recorded a cellular telephone conversation. The recording was delivered subsequently to a radio station that broadcast it. The individual who made the call sued the radio station for disclosing the call, claiming an ECPA violation. The Supreme Court held that, in this case, enforcing the ECPA's ban on disclosing the contents of illegally intercepted communications would violate the radio station's First Amendment right to free speech. The ECPA was unconstitutional as applied in this case, because the radio station was not involved in the illegal interception of the call, and the callers discussed an important matter of public concern. The ECPA is still constitutional and can be enforced under other circumstances.

In 2001, Congress passed the Uniting and Strengthening America by Providing Appropriate Tools Required to Intercept and Obstruct Terrorism Act (USA Patriot Act) and amended the ECPA to make it more effective in the fight against terrorism. It added terrorist activities to the list of crimes that justify a wiretap. It allows law enforcement to seize voice-mail messages when they have a **warrant**, and have electronic communications providers record the email addresses from messages coming in to or going out from *tapped* email accounts. Law enforcement can also intercept and use any information or communications left by a trespasser on someone else's computer, if the computer owner agrees.

The USA Patriot Act amended the disclosure provisions of the ECPA to increase the situations in which someone can legally make a voluntary disclosure of the contents of an intercepted communication. After 2001, people could disclose information about emergencies "involving immediate danger of death or serious physical harm" to another person. Therefore, if a person intercepts a message that appears to threaten a murder or terrorist attack, that information can legally be given to the police.

Finally, the USA Patriot Act makes it more difficult to sue the government for its violations of the ECPA's privacy protections. Any civil suits against the government must comply with provisions of the Federal Tort Claims Act, which mandates specific, more complex, procedures for the lawsuit.

The ECPA has had a significant impact on the administration of justice in the United States. It regulates when and how law enforcement can intercept and use electronic communications. It also protects electronic and telephone communications from non-government eavesdroppers so that people can feel secure using new technologies for private communications. This increased consumer confidence in privacy protections has helped people decide to buy and use new technologies, which promotes innovation and helps the U.S. economy.

See also: COMPUTER SECURITY ACT OF 1987; COUNTERFEIT ACCESS DEVICE AND COMPUTER FRAUD AND ABUSE ACT OF 1984; FEDERAL TORT CLAIMS ACT; USA PATRIOT ACT.

BIBLIOGRAPHY

Decew, Judith Wagner. *In Pursuit of Privacy: Law, Ethics, and the Rise of Technology.* Ithaca, N.Y.: Cornell university press, 1997.

Diffie, Whitfield, and Susan Landau. *Privacy on the Line: The Politics of Wiretapping and Encryption.* Cambridge: MIT Press, 1998.

Stevens, Gina, and Charles Doyle. *Privacy: Wiretapping and Electronic Eavesdropping.* Huntington, N.Y.: Nova Science, 2002.

ELECTRONIC SIGNATURES IN GLOBAL AND NATIONAL COMMERCE ACT (2000)

Steven Puro

Congress enacted the Electronic Signatures in Global and National Commerce Act (P.L. 106-229; also known as E-SIGN) on June 30, 2000, and the law became effective on October 1, 2000. The main purpose of this statute is to create an equivalent legal status for electronic signatures and documents with the legal status of handwritten documents. This act enhances possibilities of e-commerce especially in legal transactions and the financial services industry. The act's purpose is "to facilitate the use of electronic records and signatures in interstate and foreign commerce by ensuring the validity and legal effect of contracts entered into electronically."

An electronic signature is information or data in electronic form connected to an electronic record. The person, or an electronic agent of the person, authorizes the signature as part of the intent to sign a contract, agreement, or record. Both consumers and businesses can now enter into contracts through electronic transactions. This law also allows transfer and use of electronic records and documents, and it grants legal status and legitimacy to these transactions, records, and documents. The electronic record-keeping provisions of this legislation became effective on March 1, 2001.

The key element of the act is presented in Title I:

(a) In General. Notwithstanding any statute, regulation, or other rule of law (other than this title and title II), with respect to any transaction in or affecting interstate or foreign commerce—

(1) a signature, contract, or other record relating to such transaction may not be denied legal effect, validity, or enforceability solely because it is in electronic form; and

(2) a contract relating to such transaction may not be denied legal effect, validity, or enforceability solely because an electronic signature or electronic record was used in its formation.

An important part of national government responsibility through the Federal Trade Commission and the U.S. Department of Commerce is to prevent fraud and deception in the operation of the electronic transactions. Congress sought to protect consumers by requiring that they consent to receive electronic records. Prior to this law, many transactions—especially financial or credit matters—required consumers to receive such items as disclosures, statement of rights, obligations, or other notices in writing, and the law required the consumer to provide a written acceptance. This legislation allows this process to occur electronically.

The Uniform Electronic Transactions Act

The Uniform Electronic Transactions Act (UETA) is a law proposed by the National Conference of Commissioners on Uniform State Laws. Adopted by twenty states by mid-2003, UETA, like the federal Electronic Signatures Act, was designed to remove barriers to electronic trade by providing a set of legal principles to govern electronic signatures and records. Some states adopted the uniform version proposed by the conference, while others incorporated additional consumer protections. States were not required to adopt legislation on this topic and could rely on the Electronic Signatures Act alone to govern their electronic transactions.

A key question and an ongoing debate about this legislation centers on how to demonstrate consumer consent. The legislation addressed this concern and provides that the consumer must "consent(s) electronically or confirm(s) his or her consent electronically, in a manner that reasonably demonstrates that the consumer can access information that is the subject of the consent." For example, if a consumer has access only to Microsoft Word, the law would require businesses to format documents in that language. Another key issue is whether the federal legislation controls state consumer protection laws. In this legislation Congress protected state interests by allowing the federal law to be displaced by state action. States have the option of adopting either the Uniform Electronic Transactions Act (UETA) or another set of rules that effectively adhere to the electronic signatures legislation. The legislation takes into consideration that states could enact both the UETA and their own consumer protection provisions.

The societal importance of this legislation is that it legitimizes and expands the electronic marketplace. The law provides a basis for both consumers and business to ensure that electronic signatures and electronic records are valid legal documents with an assurance for the security of the signatures. The rapid extension of electronic resources combined with an accurate and acceptable form of electronic signatures allows for quick and effective operation of both global and national marketplaces. The Electronic Signatures in Global and National Commerce Act encompasses legal standards to create economic decisions in a technological era.

See also: ELECTRONIC COMMUNICATIONS PRIVACY ACT OF 1986.

BIBLIOGRAPHY

Federal Trade Commission. "Federal Trade Commission and National Telecommunications Information Administration, Department of Commerce, ESIGN Public Workshop," April 13, 2001. <http://www.ftc.gov/bcp/workshop/esign>.

Menna, M. "From Jamestown to the Silicon Valley, Pioneering a Lawless Frontier: The Electronic Signatures In Global and National Commerce Act." *Virginia Jornal of Law & Technology* 12 (2001).

ELEMENTARY AND SECONDARY EDUCATION ACT OF 1965

Tomiko Brown-Nagin

Congress enacted the Elementary and Secondary Education Act of 1965 (ESEA) (P.L. 89-10), the most expansive federal education bill ever passed to date, on April 9, 1965, as a part of President Lyndon B. Johnson's "War on Poverty." A former teacher who had witnessed poverty's impact on his students, Johnson believed that equal access to education was vital to a child's ability to lead a productive life.

Prior presidents' commitments to improving the educational system also inspired the law's passage. American leaders began discussing the need for a competitive technology industry during President Harry S. Truman's administration, at the beginning of the **Cold War**. As the Cold War progressed during the Eisenhower and Kennedy administrations, improving the educational system

Cold War: a conflict over ideological differences carried on by methods short of military action and usually without breaking off diplomatic relations; usually refers to the ideological conflict between the U.S. and the former U.S.S.R.

came to be understood as an imperative. The Soviet Union's successful launching of the Sputnik spacecraft on October 4, 1957, raised concerns that the Soviet school system was superior to America's and could produce superior scientists.

President Kennedy developed a number of proposals to ensure that American students were competitive with those in other countries and that every American received a good education, regardless of religious, racial, or class background. After Kennedy's assassination in November 1963, President Johnson reviewed and revised Kennedy's proposed legislative agenda. Congress derived the bill that became the ESEA from Kennedy's proposals. President Johnson orchestrated the introduction of the ESEA bill in Congress and its rapid passage into law; the ESEA passed in only eighty-seven days, with little debate and no amendments. The law became the educational centerpiece of Johnson's legislative agenda, the "Great Society," and in particular, his "War on Poverty" programs. The ESEA was designed to address the problem of inequality in education that had been laid bare by civil rights activists who lobbied for passage of the landmark anti-discrimination statute, the Civil Rights Act of 1964.

Congress has reauthorized the ESEA several times since its initial passage, most recently in 2002. The law consists of five titles, pursuant to which the federal government provides funding to 90 percent of the nation's public *and* parochial schools. The first and most important is Title I, which provides funding and guidelines for educating "educationally disadvantaged" children. Congress budgeted more than 80 percent of the monies originally appropriated under the ESEA for Title I programs; in 2002, the federal government allocated over $8 billion to fund Title I programs. These programs are intended to meet the special educational needs of "educationally deprived" children and school districts with high concentrations of such students, who typically are from poor families. Title II provides money to purchase library materials and audio/visual equipment. Title II includes a provision stating that the government can have no say in what specific materials libraries purchase; Congress incorporated this provision into the original law in response to concerns that the federal government would regulate the content of materials purchased with Title II funds. Title III provides funding for programs designed to meet the educational needs of students "at risk" of school failure, including after-school, radio and television, counseling, and foreign language programs. Title IV provides funding for college and university research on education, and Title V provides funding to individual state departments of education. The ESEA's final title, Title VI, lays out the law's general provisions.

The enactment of the ESEA revolutionized the federal government's role in education. Prior to the law's passage, educational policy-making had been the near exclusive domain of state and local governments. However, part of the ESEA's legacy is a fierce debate over whether the federal government has become overly involved in regulating local school districts' affairs through programs like the ESEA. Moreover, some question whether Title I's costly programs actually raise student performance. Nevertheless, cash-strapped school districts continue to seek and accept ESEA funding.

"We just must not, we just cannot afford the waste that comes from the neglect of a single child!" —President Lyndon Baines Johnson, March 1, 1965.

BIBLIOGRAPHY

Bailey, Stephen K., and Edith K. Mosher. *ESEA: The Office of Education Administers a Law.* Syracuse, NY: Syracuse University Press, 1968.

Jeffrey, Julie R. *Education for the Children of the Poor: A Study of the Origins and Implementation of the Elementary and Secondary Education Act of 1965.* Columbus: Ohio State University Press, 1978.

Jennings, John F., ed. *National Issues in Education: Elementary and Secondary Education Act.* Bloomington, IN: Phi Delta Kappa International, 1995.

McLaughlin, Milbery W. *Evaluation and Reform: The Elementary and Secondary Education Act of 1965, Title I.* Cambridge, MA: Ballinger, 1975.

INTERNET RESOURCE

U.S. Department of Education. *Index of Legislation Directory.* <http:www.ed.gov/legislation/>.

EMERGENCY PLANNING AND COMMUNITY RIGHT-TO-KNOW ACT (1986)

John Cary Sims

Excerpt from the Emergency Planning and Community Right-To-Know Act

Not later than six months after October 17, 1986, the Governor of each State shall appoint a State emergency response commission.... Not later than nine months after October 17, 1986, the State emergency response commission shall designate emergency planning districts in order to facilitate preparation and implementation of emergency plans.... Not later than 30 days after designation of emergency planning districts or 10 months after October 17, 1986, whichever is earlier, the State emergency response commission shall appoint members of a local emergency planning committee for each emergency planning district.

The Emergency Planning and Community Right-To-Know Act of 1986 (EPCRA) (88 Stat. 2156) establishes a framework of state, regional, and local agencies that can inform the public about the presence of hazardous and toxic chemicals and provide for emergency response if accidental release of such chemicals threatens public health.

Congress passed EPCRA in response to the tragedy in Bhopal, India, in December 1984, in which many thousands were killed by an accidental release of a toxic chemical from a Union Carbide facility. Within the year, a similar but less serious accident occurred in Institute, West Virginia. The disorganized response of local authorities prompted further calls for systematic planning in anticipation of such incidents. Those in support of such planning also argued for improved disclosure to the public about the use, storage, and release of dangerous chemicals.

The act requires systematic planning at the state and local level to prepare responses to emergencies created by chemical releases. Under the act, facilities that exceed specified thresh-

EPCRA is a free-standing law included under Title III of the Superfund Amendments and Reauthorization Act (SARA). SARA was signed into law on October 17, 1986 by President Ronald Reagan.

old amounts of hazardous chemicals must make recurrent reports to authorities. EPCRA limits the use of the "trade secret" protection, which allows facilities to withhold the specific chemical identity of the substances they use.

LEGISLATIVE DEBATE

The legislative debate that led to the passage of EPCRA involved a much broader range of issues than those addressed in the act itself. EPCRA was closely related to the "Superfund" legislation, formally known as the Comprehensive Environmental Response, Compensation, and Liability Act (CERCLA). Congress enacted EPCRA as part of the Superfund Amendments and Reauthorization Act of 1986. Intense controversy developed over the cost of the Superfund legislation. President Ronald Reagan threatened to veto the bill, and the bill's supporters planned to mount an effort to **override** that veto. However, Reagan signed the statute on October 17, 1986, as he had been urged to do by the head of the Environmental Protection Agency (EPA).

override: if the president vetoes a bill passed by Congress, the bill can still become law if two-thirds of each house of Congress votes to override the veto

ENFORCEMENT

EPCRA is enforced in a variety of ways. The EPA may use a broad range of enforcement mechanisms, and those violating the act may be subject to criminal, civil, or administrative penalties. State and local governments may also seek civil penalties or ask courts to issue injunctions to stop a particular action at a facility. Private individuals and other entities can also take action against alleged violators. The EPA must be notified sixty days before an enforcement action is filed by others against the owner or operator of a chemical facility. If the agency is "diligently" seeking enforcement then no other enforcement action is permitted against the owner.

EFFECTIVENESS

EPCRA has improved governmental planning to deal with releases of dangerous chemicals that may harm the public, and the reports required by the act have greatly expanded the amount of information available to the public about risks relating to such substances.

The Internet has made this information easy to obtain for those interested in receiving it. EPCRA's system of community notification uses the material safety data sheets (MSDS) prepared under the requirements of the Occupational Safety and Health Act of 1970 (OSHA). Over the years that EPCRA has been in force, the reported releases of toxic chemicals into the environment have decreased significantly, suggesting that the statute has been effective in reducing the risks to communities. However, some have suggested that EPCRA is less effective than it seems. This is because the chemicals industry has to some extent shifted from using chemicals subject to EPCRA reporting to alternative dangerous chemicals that are beyond the reach of the statute.

EPCRA has improved governmental planning to deal with releases of dangerous chemicals that may harm the public, and the reports required by the act have greatly expanded the amount of information available to the public about risks relating to such substances.

See also: COMPREHENSIVE ENVIRONMENTAL RESPONSE, COMPENSATION, AND LIABILITY ACT; NATIONAL ENVIRONMENTAL POLICY ACT; OCCUPATIONAL SAFETY AND HEALTH ACT OF 1970.

EMPLOYEE RETIREMENT INCOME SECURITY ACT OF 1974

James A. Wooten

Excerpt from the Employee Retirement Income Security Act of 1974

It is hereby ... declared to be the policy of this Act to protect interstate commerce, the Federal taxing power, and the interests of participants in private pension plans and their beneficiaries by improving the equitable character and the soundness of such plans by requiring them to vest the accrued benefits of employees with significant periods of service, to meet minimum standards of funding, and by requiring plan termination insurance.

---

private sector: the part of the economy that is not controlled by the government

The Employee Retirement Income Security Act of 1974 (P.L. 93-406, 88 Stat. 829), commonly known as ERISA, is the principal federal law regulating employee-benefit plans in the **private sector**. There are two general types of employee-benefit plans: 1) *pension plans* are arrangements for providing retirement income; 2) *welfare plans* include arrangements for providing benefits such as health, life, and disability insurance and severance pay. Because the legislators who drafted ERISA were primarily concerned with protecting employees who lost retirement benefits, they established detailed regulations for pension plans. They paid much less attention to welfare plans.

HISTORY OF PENSION AND HEALTH PLANS

Although some employers provided pensions or medical benefits as early as the 1880s, only a small minority of private-sector workers was covered by a pension or health plan in 1940. During World War II the number of pension and health plans rose dramatically. One reason was federal tax policy. The income tax gave (and continues to give) more favorable treatment to employer-financed retirement and health benefits than to wages. Rates of taxation were high during the war, so employees could significantly reduce their income tax by substituting a pension or health plan for cash compensation. Also, the federal government froze wages during the war but exempted employer-financed pensions and medical insurance from the freeze. Many businesses adopted a pension or health plan as a means of increasing employee compensation. Shortly after the war, labor unions began demanding pensions and health insurance for their members. By 1965 almost half of private-sector employees were covered by a pension plan and more than 70 percent of government and private-sector employees were covered by a health-insurance plan.

By 1965 almost half of private-sector employees were covered by a pension plan and more than 70 percent of government and private-sector employees were covered by a health-insurance plan.

Government oversight of employee-benefit plans was relatively limited in the 1940s and 1950s. Federal law aimed to prevent the use of pension plans for tax avoidance and to ensure that funds held by pension and welfare plans were used to benefit employees, rather than the firm or union that managed the plan. Otherwise, there was little federal or state regulation of employee-benefit plans. In the mid-1950s, government investigations exposed lurid cases in which union officials, sometimes in league with insurance agents or brokers, misused or stole funds from welfare plans. Congress responded by passing the first federal law exclusively concerned with employee-benefit plans, the Welfare and Pension Plans Disclosure Act of 1958. The Disclosure Act required plan managers to publish information so that employees, unions, and the press could monitor employee-benefit plans.

Although the press and public paid the most attention to cases in which funds were wasted or stolen, employees were also threatened by less sensational risks. Many plans did not give employees a legal right to a pension until they had worked for a firm for many years or attained a specific age. Workers who quit or were laid off before they *vested* (that is, by satisfying service or age requirements) would not receive a pension. Another danger was that a pension plan would not have enough money to pay the benefits it promised. The most famous case of this sort occurred when the Studebaker Corporation closed a plant in South Bend, Indiana, in 1963. Older employees and retirees received their full pension, but workers under age 60 received payments worth only a fraction of the pension they expected or nothing at all.

LEGISLATIVE DEBATES AND THE ADOPTION OF ERISA

By the early 1960s pension experts were debating whether Congress should pass additional regulations to protect employees. In March 1962 John F. Kennedy established the President's Committee on Corporate Pension Funds to study private-pension plans and recommend reforms. The committee's report, which appeared in January 1965, called for a major expansion of federal oversight of private-pension plans.

Titled *Public Policy and Private Pension Programs,* the report argued that the federal government should regulate pension plans to ensure that employees actually received the benefits their plan promised. The committee urged Congress to pass 1) minimum vesting standards, which would prevent plans from making the requirements for receiving benefits too strict, and 2) minimum funding standards, which would require firms to set aside resources so that pension plans would be more likely to meet their obligations. Several months before the committee's report appeared, Democratic Senator Vance Hartke of Indiana proposed another major reform. In August 1964 Hartke, whose constituents included workers at Studebaker, introduced legislation to create a government-run insurance program that would pay retirement benefits if a plan could not do so.

The reforms proposed by the committee and Hartke were very controversial. Business groups and most labor unions opposed minimum vesting and funding standards. If Congress created uniform federal standards, they claimed, managers and union officials would not be able to adapt pension plans to the needs of particular firms. This might lead employers to abandon their pension plan or to not create a plan in the first place. Most labor unions favored an insurance program for private pensions, but the business community vehemently rejected the idea. Business

Insuring Pension Plans

The income tax structure in the United States makes employer-financed retirement and health plans attractive options for employees from a tax viewpoint. This is because, unlike wages, employees do not have to pay taxes on money that an employer contributes to a retirement fund until many years (or even decades) after that money was contributed. Health benefits are even more favorable, as the employee never pays taxes on those benefits.

Insurance programs are a controversial part of pension plans. Labor unions and workers prefer that plans have an insurance program, while business leaders tend to oppose insurance. Insurance programs work this way: when a program is put in place, the pension plan is required to pay a tax. If at some point the plan is shut down without sufficient funds to pay the retirement benefits it promised to pay to vested employees, the insurance program would use the funds generated by the tax to pay those employees the pension they were expecting.

By the early 1960s pension experts were debating whether Congress should pass additional regulations to protect employees.

Despite opposition from business and organized labor, reform initiatives advanced during the presidency of Lyndon Johnson.

representatives said there was little need for such insurance because most firms set aside enough funds to pay future pension obligations.

Despite opposition from business and organized labor, reform initiatives advanced during the presidency of Lyndon Johnson. In February 1967 Johnson proposed legislation that aimed to prevent theft or misuse of plan funds by creating standards of conduct for officials who managed employee-benefit plans. Later that month, Senator Jacob Javits, a Republican from New York, introduced a much broader bill that included vesting and funding standards and an insurance program as well as rules of conduct for plan managers.

In May 1968 the Department of Labor proposed a bill with vesting and funding standards and an insurance scheme. In light of the strong opposition of business groups and many labor unions, it seemed unlikely that Congress would approve the vesting, funding, and insurance proposals. What is more, Richard Nixon's election in November 1968 brought to power an administration that was not sympathetic to sweeping new regulation of pension plans. Recognizing these political realities, Senator Javits set out to bring the press and public opinion into the campaign for pension reform.

In spring 1970 Javits persuaded New Jersey's Senator Harrison Williams, a Democrat and chair of the Senate Committee on Labor and Public Welfare, to conduct a survey of pension plans. The survey was designed to present a bleak picture. In March 1971 Javits and Williams released figures that did just that. In Javits's words, the study revealed that "only a relative handful" of employees would receive benefits from their pension plan. Pension experts denounced Javits and Williams's data, but the statistics received wide coverage in the press.

The Senate Labor Committee followed up on the survey with hearings highlighting "horror stories" of workers who failed to receive a pension because they changed or lost their job or because their plan could not pay.

In the spring of 1973, the business community abruptly reversed course and endorsed federal regulation when several state legislatures began considering pension reform.

Although the hearings were successful in creating broad support for pension reform, interest groups and the president continued to oppose key reforms. When the Labor Committee reported a bill for consideration by the full Senate in September 1972, Russell Long, a Democrat from Louisiana who chaired the Senate Committee on Finance, killed the bill, reportedly at the urging of the president and the business community.

In the spring of 1973, the business community abruptly reversed course and endorsed federal regulation when several state legislatures began considering pension reform. If the states regulated pension plans, then plans that operated in more than one state might have to comply with different laws in different states. Employers and labor unions preferred federal regulation because Congress could establish uniform national rules. In September 1973 the Senate passed a comprehensive pension-reform bill. The House of Representatives followed suit in February 1974. President Gerald Ford signed ERISA on September 2, Labor Day. The law created a comprehensive regulatory program, including disclosure requirements, rules of conduct for plan managers, vesting and funding standards, and a pension-insurance program, to protect workers who depended on private-pension plans. ERISA created few rules or standards for welfare plans but greatly limited the authority of state governments to regulate these plans.

ERISA was a long and complex law, and Congress has passed numerous amendments to it.

A COMPLICATED REGULATORY PROGRAM

ERISA was a long and complex law, and Congress has passed numerous amendments to it. Some revisions aim to help ERISA better perform its protective function. For example, when it became clear that the insurance program had serious flaws, Congress required employers to make larger pension contributions and limited the circumstances in which an employer could shut down a pension plan. Lawmakers also revised ERISA's vesting standards to protect spouses of employees and to require plans to vest employees more rapidly.

The 1980s and 1990s also brought a major shift in the makeup of the private-pension system. Broadly speaking, there are two types of pension plans: 1) In a *defined-benefit* plan, employees generally receive regular pension payments after they retire. The payments are calculated according to a benefit formula in the plan. 2) In a *defined-contribution plan,* each employee has an account much like an account in a savings bank. The employee's retirement benefit is the balance of the account.

For most of the twentieth century, defined-benefit plans dominated the private-pension system. In the 1980s and 1990s, defined-contribution plans assumed an increasingly important role. By the mid-1990s, the number of employees in defined-contribution plans exceeded the number of employees in defined-benefit plans. This shift raises new regulatory issues because ERISA does not deal as extensively with risks that threaten employees in defined-contribution plans. For example, in a defined-contribution plan, an employee's retirement benefit depends on the performance of the investments in his or her account. If the investments do badly, the employee will have less money to spend in retirement. (In a defined-benefit plan, by contrast, an employee's pension depends on the benefit formula, rather than the performance of the plan's investments.) The Enron collapse in 2001 vividly demonstrated that employees may suffer ruinous losses if they invest defined-contribution plan funds in their employer's stock.

See also: CIVIL WAR PENSIONS.

BIBLIOGRAPHY

Gordon, Michael S. "Overview: Why ERISA was Enacted?" in U.S. Senate Committee on Aging, *An Information Paper on The Employee Retirement Income Security Act of 1974: The First Decade,* 98th Cong., 2nd sess., 1984, Committee Print.

Hacker, Jacob S. *The Divided Welfare State: The Battle over Public and Private Social Benefits in the United States.* Cambridge: Cambridge University Press, 2002.

President's Committee on Corporate Pension Funds and Other Private Retirement and Welfare Programs. *Public Policy and Private Pension Programs: A Report to the President on Private Employee Retirement Plans.* Washington, DC: U.S. Government Printing Office, 1965.

Sass, Steven A. *The Promise of Private Pensions.* Cambridge: Harvard University Press, 1997.

Scofea, Laura A. "The Development and Growth of Employer-Provided Health Insurance." *Monthly Labor Review* 117, no. 3 (1994): 3–10.

EMPLOYMENT ACT OF 1946

Louis Fisher

Excerpt from the Employment Act of 1946

The Congress hereby declares that it is the continuing policy and responsibility of the Federal Government to use all practicable means consistent with its needs and obligations and other essential considerations of national policy, with the assistance and cooperation of industry, agriculture, labor, and State and local governments, ... for the purpose of creating and maintaining, in a manner calculated to foster and promote free competitive enterprise and the general welfare, conditions under which there will be afforded useful employment opportunities, including self-employment, for those able, willing, and seeking to work, and to promote maximum employment, production, and purchasing power.

During the last year of World War II (1939–1945), Congress worked on legislation to avert what many feared would be a post-war depression. It was widely believed that heavy military spending had been the main cure for the economic collapse of the 1930s, and that without stimulus from the federal government millions of American soldiers would be returning home to a country without jobs or opportunities. The Employment Act of 1946 (P.L. 79-304) declared it to be the continuing policy and responsibility of the federal government to use all practicable means "to promote maximum employment, production, and purchasing power." The statute required the president to submit an annual economic report, created the Council of Economic Advisers to assist the president with that task, and established the Joint Economic Committee in Congress to study the means needed to further the policy of the statute.

It was widely believed that heavy military spending had been the main cure for the economic collapse of the 1930s, and that without stimulus from the federal government millions of American soldiers would be returning home to a country without jobs or opportunities.

Historians credit Senator James E. Murray (D-Mont.) for supplying the "spark of will" that transformed an idea into the Employment Act. Yet the statute reflected leadership and initiative at many levels, public and private. In his annual message to Congress in January 1944, President Franklin D. Roosevelt spoke of a new Economic Bill of Rights, including the "right to a useful and remunerative job." Economists such as John Maynard Keynes and William H. Beveridge influenced Roosevelt. Keynes, rejecting the traditional assumption that the capitalist system was self-adjusting, advocated government intervention to preserve existing economic forms and individual initiative. Beveridge, in his 1945 book, *Full Employment in a Free Society,* regarded the greatest evil of unemployment as "not physical but moral, not the want which it may bring but the hatred and fear which it breeds." He urged that public spending be directed toward social priorities and the satisfaction of human needs. Also key to passage of the statute were private organizations such as the National Planning Association and the legislative staff who worked in concert with executive agencies, interest groups, and individuals.

HOUSE AND SENATE DEBATES

As introduced in the Senate, the Full Employment Bill of 1945 reiterated Roosevelt's principle by declaring that "all Americans able to work and seeking work have the right to useful, remunerative, regular, and full-time employment." The bill centered major powers and responsibilities in the presidency. In cases where the private sector failed to provide full employment, the bill directed the president to prepare a program of federal investment and expenditures to close the gap. The president would review federal programs on a quarterly basis and alter their rate as he considered necessary to assure full employment. The Senate passed this bill in September 1945 by an overwhelming vote of 71 to 10.

> *In cases where the private sector failed to provide full employment, the bill directed the president to prepare a program of federal investment and expenditures to close the gap.*

Critics in the House charged that the bill contained within it the seeds of **paternalism**, **socialism**, and even **communism**. They claimed that the bill jeopardized the existence of free enterprise, individual initiative, and business confidence by vesting of power in the federal government and the president. It was predicted that the Full Employment Act would lead to excessive government spending, a dangerous concentration of power in the presidency, and crippling inflation.

This criticism led the House to remove or dilute several substantive and forceful passages in the Senate bill. For example, the basic commitment to employment as a human right was taken out, two sections on presidential discretionary powers were deleted, the original goal of full employment was whittled down to "maximum employment," and, instead of the federal government *assuring* government, it would only "promote" it. Moreover, the specific reliance on public works and federal loans as instruments of economic recovery was replaced by the noncommittal phrase "all practicable means."

The resulting declaration of policy in the Employment Act of 1946 stated that the federal government, assisted by industry, labor, and state and local governments, was responsible for coordinating plans, functions, and resources for the purpose of creating and maintaining conditions—consistent with the free enterprise system—that would offer "useful employment opportunities, including self-employment, for those able, willing, and seeking to work, and to promote maximum employment, production, and purchasing power."

paternalism: a policy or practice of treating or governing people in a fatherly manner especially by providing for their needs without giving them responsibility

socialism: any of various economic and political theories advocating collective or governmental ownership and administration of the means of production and distribution of goods

communism: an economic and social system characterized by the absence of classes and by common ownership of the means of production and subsistence

SUBSEQUENT LEGISLATION

During the latter half of the 1970s, the U.S. economy encountered sluggish growth, heavy unemployment, and high inflation. Responding to those problems, Senator Hubert Humphrey and Rep. Augustus Hawkins called for a massive federal jobs and economic planning bill, placing the federal government in the position as the "last resort" for the unemployed. Instead, Congress enacted the Full Employment and Balanced Growth Act of 1978, known as the Humphrey-Hawkins Act, to redefine national goals and targets without providing explicit federal assistance. The statute determined that the nation had suffered from substantial unemployment and underemployment, idleness of productive resources, high rates of **inflation**, and inadequate economic growth.

> *Congress established as a national goal "the fulfillment of the right to full opportunities for useful paid employment at fair rates of compensation of all individuals able, willing, and seeking to work."*

Congress established as a national goal "the fulfillment of the right to full opportunities for useful paid employment at fair rates of compensation of all individuals able, willing, and seeking to work." That statute required the

inflation: an increase in the volume of money and credit relative to available goods and services resulting in a continuing rise in the general price level

real income: income of an individual, organization, or country, after taking into consideration the effects of inflation on purchasing power

president to establish and to submit to Congress five-year numerical goals for employment, unemployment, production, **real income**, productivity, and prices in each economic report. The statute also set a goal of reducing unemployment to 4 percent by 1983 (compared to the 6.1 percent rate in 1978). Congress specified that the inflation rate be reduced to a level of no more than 3 percent by 1983 (in contrast to the 9 percent level in 1978). Finally, the Humphrey-Hawkins Act required the Federal Reserve Board to report to Congress twice a year on its monetary policies and to relate them to the goals of the act. Setting statutory goals, of course, is not the same as achieving them. There are no penalties, sanctions or remedies in the statute if the nation fails to meet the identified goals and targets.

BIBLIOGRAPHY

Bailey, Stephen Kemp. *Congress Makes a Law: The Story Behind the Employment Act of 1946.* New York: Columbia University Press, 1950.

Beveridge, William H. *Full Employment in a Free Society.* New York: W.W. Norton, 1945.

Norton, Hugh S. *The Employment Act and the Council of Economic Advisers, 1946-76.* Columbia: University of South Carolina Press, 1977.

Stein, Herbert. *The Fiscal Revolution in America.* Chicago: University of Chicago Press, 1969.

ENDANGERED SPECIES ACT (1973)

Federico Cheever

The Endangered Species Act (ESA) represents two important legal traditions: environmental law and wildlife law. Congress passed the ESA as part of the explosion of federal legislation enacted between 1970 and 1980 to protect the environment. As a wildlife law, the ESA is part of a thousand-year **common law** tradition of government regulation of the taking of wildlife.

common law: a system of laws developed in England—and later applied in the U.S.—based on judicial precedent rather than statutory laws passed by a legislative body

commerce clause: the provision of the U.S. Constitution (Article I, section 8, clause 3) that gives Congress exclusive powers over interstate commerce—the buying, selling or exchanging of goods or products between states

The United States Constitution grants the federal government no specific authority over wildlife. Congress protects endangered species under the **commerce clause** authority the Constitution grants it to regulate interstate and foreign commerce. Wildlife is generally a matter of state concern, as it has been since the American Revolution, when the power once invested in the British crown to protect and regulate the taking of wildlife passed to the states. States grant hunting and fishing licenses and monitor and manage wildlife populations.

During the twentieth century, the federal government became increasingly involved in wildlife protection. The Lacey Act of 1900 allowed federal officials to assist in enforcement of state laws against unauthorized takings of wildlife by making interstate transportation of wildlife taken in violation of state law a federal crime. The Migratory Bird Treaty Act of 1918 authorized federal protection of migratory birds, which habitually cross both state and national borders.

In the 1960s the federal government began specifically to protect species in danger of extinction. Congress passed early

Congress passed the ESA as part of the explosion of federal legislation enacted between 1970 and 1980 to protect the environment.

forms of endangered species protection legislation in 1966 and 1969. Dissatisfaction with this early legislation, coupled with the increased concern for the environment expressed in the demonstrations on the first Earth Day in April 1970, led to the passage of the broader, more powerful, Endangered Species Act of 1973.

NEED FOR THE ESA

Over the course of the twentieth century, scientists became increasingly concerned about the disappearance of once common species of animals and plants. Scientific organizations began to keep lists of extinct and endangered species as an indicator of the health of the environment. By the late twentieth century, most recognized that human activities were driving species to extinction at many times the natural rate. If unchecked, these human activities would result in the annihilation of a significant share of the species inhabiting the planet. The legislative history of the Endangered Species Act of 1973 demonstrates concern about this extinction crisis and a commitment to "the conservation of species and of the ecosystems on which they depend." Many statements in Congress supporting enactment of the law contained references to the extinction crisis. Legislative documents recognized the limited scientific understanding of the crisis and recommended both a "certain humility and sense of urgency" in our efforts to protect the "incalculable" value of biological diversity.

> By the late twentieth century, most recognized that human activities were driving species to extinction at many times the natural rate.

ENFORCEMENT AND CORE PROVISIONS

Two federal agencies administer and enforce the ESA. The United States Fish and Wildlife Service (FWS), in the Department of the Interior, administers the act for all terrestrial and fresh water species. The National Marine Fisheries Service (NMFS), in the Department of Commerce, administers the act for marine and anadromous species (animals, such as shad, that ascend rivers from the sea for breeding).

Four provisions form the core of the ESA. Section 4 requires the federal designation or "listing" of both *endangered* and *threatened* species of both plants and animals. Species must be listed as endangered if they are "in danger of extinction throughout all or a significant portion of their range." Species must be listed as threatened if they are "likely to become ... endangered ... within the foreseeable future throughout all or a significant portion of its range." Since 1978, section 4 has also explicitly required the designation of *critical habitat* for protected species. It also authorizes individuals and groups to petition for the listing of species and notifies the public when a species is subject to the protections of the 1973 act.

Section 7 requires all federal agencies to insure that activities they "authorize, fund or carry out" will not jeopardize the continued existence of any species listed under section 4 or any critical habitat designated under section 4. This obligation must be fulfilled in consultation with the FWS or NMFS. Section 9 forbids any person in the United States or on the high seas from taking any endangered species of fish or wildlife. *Take* is broadly defined in this section "as to harass, harm, pursue, hunt, shoot, wound, kill, trap, capture, or collect, or to attempt to engage in any such conduct."

After recuperating from wing surgery, an endangered bald eagle is released by the Sierra Club of South Carolina. Historically, states possessed the power to grant hunting and fishing licenses and to monitor and manage wildlife populations. As the environmental movement grew in the 1970s and 1980s, the federal government stepped in to protect animals that were either "endangered species" like the bald eagle or "threatened species" (© AP/WIDE WORLD PHOTOS)

The protections offered by section 7 and section 9 differ in three significant ways. First, section 7 protects all listed threatened and endangered species of plants and animals and all designated critical habitat, whereas section 9 protects only endangered species of fish and wildlife. Second, section 7 protects species as a whole, while section 9 protects every member of every species of endangered fish or wildlife. Third, section 7 applies only to actions authorized, funded, or carried out by federal agencies, while section 9 prohibits takings by any person.

Finally, section 10 provides exceptions to the prohibitions of section 9. First, the federal government may grant an exception for scientific purposes or to enhance the propagation or survival of the affected species. Second, since 1982 the federal government may authorize takings of protected species that do not jeopardize the continued existence of the species if (1) the takings occur as part of an otherwise legal action, and (2) the taking results from an activity subject to an approved habitat conservation plan (HCP).

EXPERIENCE UNDER THE ACT

The ESA emerged as a powerful wildlife preservation law in 1978 when the United States Supreme Court in *Tennessee Valley Authority v. Hill,* affirmed an order stopping construction of the Tellico Dam to protect an endangered fish, the snail darter. A majority of the Court found that "the language, history, and structure of the legislation under review ... indicates beyond doubt that Congress intended endangered species to be afforded the highest of priorities." Despite the opinion and other controversy surrounding the project, Congress subsequently passed a law authorizing completion of the Tellico Dam, which resulted in destruction of the snail darters' habitat.

Later in 1978, Congress amended the Endangered Species Act, creating a narrow exception to section 7's prohibition against jeopardizing species or habitats. The exception applies to actions of "regional or national significance" when "the benefits of the action clearly outweigh the benefits of alternative

Why Save Endangered Species?

Beyond the ethical reasons for preserving plant and other animal species, there are many self-interested reasons that humans should protect other forms of life. Plants and animals are the source of chemical compounds used for at least 25 percent of medications. These include, for example, foxglove, which is used to treat heart disease, and the Pacific yew, whose bark contains a substance that may be effective in treating breast and ovarian cancer. In agriculture, only twenty species of the world's plants provide 90 percent of food crops; however, an additional 80,000 edible plants provide options for food sources that are disease-resistant, drought tolerant, more nutritious, or otherwise suitable for reducing hunger in the world. In industry, wild plants are used to produce oil, rubber, and many other products. The richness of plant and animal life also contributes to the health of ecosystems, which humans depend on for food, clean air, and clean water. According to the U.S. Fish and Wildlife Service, the loss of a single plant species can trigger the loss of thirty more in an ecosystem. This chain reaction is evident in the Florida Keys, where pollution is killing off the coral reefs that provide a habitat for hundreds of species of fish, and both commercial fishing and the tourism industry have begun to suffer. Many local and regional economies—and thus people's livelihoods—are based on flora and fauna; in the Pacific Northwest, for example, salmon fishing is responsible for 60,000 jobs and $1 billion in personal income. Finally, the natural world is a mainstay of the American tourism industry, with more than 100 million people taking part in wildlife-related activities annually.

courses of action" and "there is no reasonable and prudent alternative" to the proposed action. Under the amendment, this exception could be invoked by decision of the Endangered Species Committee, which the amendment created. This committee is often called the "God Committee" or "God Squad" because it has the power to sentence an entire species to extinction. The Endangered Species Committee exception has rarely been invoked.

The Supreme Court revisited the Endangered Species Act in 1995 in *Sweet Home Communities for Greater Oregon v. Babbitt*. In that case, the Court upheld an FWS regulation defining *harm* in the statutory definition of *take* to include destruction of habitat essential for species breeding, feeding, or sheltering. This regulation can make destruction of essential habitat a violation of the section 9 taking prohibition.

See also: PLANT VARIETY PROTECTION ACT.

BIBLIOGRAPHY

Bean, Michael J., and Melanie J. Rowland. *The Evolution of National Wildlife Law,* 3d ed. Westport, CT: Praeger, 1997.

Cheever, Federico. "The Road to Recovery: A New Way of Thinking about the Endangered Species Act." 23 *Ecology L.Q.* 1 (1996).

Hood, Laura C. *Frayed Safety: Conservation Planning Under The Endangered Species Act.* Washington, DC: Defenders of Wildlife, 1998.

Mann, Charles, and Mark Plummer. *Noah's Choice: The Future of Endangered Species.* New York: Knopf, 1995.

National Research Council. *Science and the Endangered Species Act.* Washington DC: National Academy Press, 1995.

Stein, Bruce A., Lynn S. Kutner, and Jonathan S. Adams. *Precious Heritage: The Status of Biodiversity in the United States.* New York: Oxford University Press, 2000.

Wilson, Edward O. *The Diversity of Life.* Cambridge, MA: Belknap Press, 1992.

INTERNET RESOURCE

United States Fish and Wildlife Service, Endangered Species Program. <http://www.fws.gov/>.

ENFORCEMENT ACT OF 1871

See KU KLUX KLAN ACT.

ENROLLMENT ACT (1863) (THE CONSCRIPTION ACT)

Daniel W. Hamilton

The Union and the Confederacy armies instituted the first federal military draft in American history during the Civil War. In the wake of military losses and a shortage of soldiers, the Union resorted to a federal draft in

March 1863, almost a year after the Confederacy. President Lincoln signed The Enrollment Act on March 3, 1863, requiring the enrollment of every male citizen and those immigrants who had filed for citizenship between ages twenty and forty-five. Federal agents established a quota of new troops due from each congressional district.

The Union and the Confederacy armies instituted the first federal military draft in American history during the Civil War.

Once set, states were responsible to fill the enrollment quota through the enlistment of volunteers and draftees. States worked not to draft soldiers, instead offering volunteers a considerable amount of money to enlist. Volunteers received a bounty of $100 from the federal government, plus state and local bounties. Combined bounties in some locations exceeded $500. This gave way to the practice of bounty jumping—men enlisted, took the bounty, deserted, and then enlisted elsewhere to receive another set of bounties.

Even those that were drafted often successfully avoided military service. Many simply failed to report, and those with disabilities or who were the sole supporters of dependent family members were excused. Any draftee not excused could hire a substitute, guaranteeing exemption from any future draft, or pay a fee of $300, providing exemption for one draft. The $300 commutation fee soon became the most controversial part of the act, leading to the widespread charge in newspapers and political meetings that the Civil War was "a rich man's war and a poor man's fight" (Mcpherson 1989). Ironically, the $300 fee was fashioned by Republicans who "saw this as a way of bringing exemption within reach of the working class instead of discriminating against them." Paying for substitutes had a long tradition in European and American warfare and was employed during the American Revolution. In setting a $300 fee, the drafters of the act hoped to cap the price of substitutes, who at time received over $1,000 in the Confederacy, where the use of substitutes was abandoned in late 1863. In the Union, Congress ultimately repealed the use of a commutation fee in July 1864.

Because of the widespread use of bounties to spur enlistment, only a relatively small amount of men fought in the war as draftees. Conscription was most important for its social impact—in particular, the class and racial divisions it revealed and provoked. Whatever the intent of its framers, the practice of substitution and commutation fees provoked violent opposition to the law's enforcement. The most serious reaction to the Conscription Act took place in New York, a city with significant southern sympathy. The Irish population of New York, many living in cramped, disease-ridden tenements, feared competition from black workers. It was largely opposed to abolition and hostile to a conscription law that exempted the rich. In the wake of the Emancipation Proclamation and the Enrollment Act, both in 1863, New York's Irish opposed both the practice of substitution and commutation at the expense of the working class and participation in a war to free the slaves. In a July 4 speech New York's Democratic governor, Horatio Seymour, openly condemned the conscription law, declared the bill unconstitutional and suggested that conscription was enforced along partisan lines, claiming that Democrats were being drafted at a greater rate than Republicans.

Conscription was most important for its social impact—in particular, the class and racial divisions it revealed and provoked.

On July 11, 1863 the first names for induction into the army were called. The next day, New York erupted into some the most violent riots in American history. The office of the provost marshal—charged with enforcing the draft—was burned, railroad lines were destroyed, and telegraph lines cut. Signaled out for attacks were the rich and African Americans, together the chief targets of the mob violence. Mobs attacked those who appeared rich as "$300 men." Rioters burned the Colored Orphanage Asylum and businesses that employed blacks. Some blacks were lynched and scores were beaten. For nearly a week the city raged, overpowering local police. Ultimately five Union regiments, along with police, **militia,** and even cadets from West Point, subdued the rioters. Over one hundred people died in the rioting, thousands were wounded, and thousands of African Americans fled New York.

militia: a part-time army made up of ordinary citizens

While New York saw the most violent draft riot, it was far from an isolated event. Draft riots took place, among other places, in Newark and Albany, as well as in rural counties in Indiana and Illinois. Still, there was, overall, a remarkable degree of compliance with draft legislation, if only because the legislation was structured so that a draft was a measure of last resort. The lack of resistance to the conscription legislation is important to the extent that it shows the widespread participation in the Civil War by nearly a million white soldiers and nearly 180,000 black soldiers. While bounties were expensive, they did result in a nearly all-volunteer Union army during the Civil War. Resistance to conscription is also important historically, in part for what it revealed about the legal and popular opposition to federal conscription legislation; but even more so for exposing the smoldering tensions within communities brought to the surface by conscription legislation. The Enrollment Act was a national law enforced locally, and the resistance to the law offers insight into divisions within communities in the North in the midst of the Civil War.

The Enrollment Act was a national law enforced locally, and the resistance it met offers insight into divisions splitting communities in the North in the midst of the Civil War.

BIBLIOGRAPHY

Bernstein, Iver. *The New York City Draft Riots.* New York: Oxford University Press USA, 2001.

Donald, David H., et al. *The Civil War and Reconstruction.* New York: Norton, 2001.

McPherson, James M. *Battle Cry of Freedom.* New York: Ballantine Books, 1989.

EQUAL PAY ACT OF 1963

Lawrence Schlam

The Equal Pay Act of 1963 (EPA) (P.L. No. 88-38, 77 Stat. 56, 59) prohibits employers from discriminating on the basis of gender by compensating workers differently for jobs that require equal skill, effort and responsibility. In adopting the EPA, an amendment to the Fair Labor Standards Act of 1938, Congress hoped to eliminate wage differentials because they were thought to depress wages and the standard of living, prevent maximum utilization of available labor resources, lead to labor disputes, and constitute an unfair method of competition. Congress also strove to eliminate stereotypes and misconceptions regarding the value of work performed by women.

Attempts to curb gender-based pay disparities in American industry were not new in 1963. In fact, during World War II (1939–1945), the War Labor Board declared and administered a policy of "equal pay for women." Prior to the passage of the EPA, several presidential administrations had proposed legislation to eliminate gender-based wage discrimination. They argued that employees doing equal work should be paid equal wages regardless of their gender.

Success finally came on February 14, 1963, when, in a letter to the Speaker of the House of Representatives, the Secretary of Labor Willard Wirtz recommended enactment of "equal pay" legislation and submitted a draft bill. In its deliberations over the act, however, Congress purposely rejected the concept of "equal pay for comparable work" promoted by some advocates of this law, opting instead to adopt an "equal pay for equal work" formula. "Equal work" means jobs the performance of which requires equal skill, effort and responsibility and which workers perform under similar working conditions.

In adopting the EPA, an amendment to the Fair Labor Standards Act of 1938, Congress hoped to eliminate wage differentials which were thought to depress wages and the standard of living, prevent maximum utilization of available labor resources, lead to labor disputes, and constitute an unfair method of competition.

DETAILS OF THE EQUAL PAY ACT

Congress made this legislative choice because it worried that the adoption of a doctrine of comparable worth would ignore the economic realities of supply and demand. It would also burden government agencies and courts with the "impossible task of ascertaining the worth of comparable work, an area in which they have little expertise." Congress concluded, therefore, that government intervention to equalize wage differentials would only succeed where men's and women's jobs were identical or nearly so, thus unarguably of equal worth.

Section One of the act provided that those employers covered by the Fair Labor Standards Acts (FLSA) must provide equal pay for equal work regardless of gender, and Section Two of the bill amends the FLSA to state that wage differentials based solely on the gender of the employee are an unfair labor standard. Section Three lists special circumstances and exemptions to the act. Section Four, among other things, gives employers bound by **collective bargaining** agreements a one-year **moratorium** on enforcement, or until the collective bargaining agreement expired, whichever came first, before compliance was required.

Congress exempted several forms of discrimination from the operation of the EPA. These exceptions include shift differentials, restrictions on or differences based on the time of day worked, hours of work, and the lifting or moving of heavy objects. The EPA also excluded differences based on experience, training or ability, as well as unusual or higher than normal wage rates which employers maintained for valid reasons.

In addition the law exempts wage payments if made pursuant to a seniority system, a merit system, a system which measures earnings by quantity or quality of production, or one which creates a differential based on any factor other than sex. For example, differences in the employer's economic benefit received from the work performed can justify a wage differential. All of the occupational exemptions originally allowed for in the FLSA as a matter of political compromise

collective bargaining: negotiation between an employer and a representative of organized employees concerning wages, hours, and other conditions of employment

moratorium: a legally required suspension of activity

Congress concluded, therefore, that government intervention to equalize wage differentials would only succeed where men's and women's jobs were identical or nearly so, thus unarguably of equal worth.

also apply to the EPA, so workers in agriculture, hotels, motels, restaurants, and laundries, are excluded from the EPA, as are workers in professional, managerial and administrative occupations.

LITIGATION AND SUBSEQUENT LEGISLATION

In establishing the EPA, Congress provided employees with remedies for employer violations of the law, such as private enforcement in certain carefully defined situations. The legislation includes a comprehensive remedial scheme. The Equal Employment Opportunity Commission (EEOC) currently enforces the EPA so that compliance with all employment-related laws prohibiting discrimination, such as Title VII of the Civil Rights Act of 1964, may be coordinated.

Actions involving wage discrimination based on sex can be brought under both the EPA and Title VII. The standards for evaluation of claims under the two statutes, however, are not the same.

Congress eventually broadened the EPA's coverage by the passage of the Civil Rights Act of 1964. Title VII of the Civil Rights Act, which prohibits discrimination in employment on the basis of race, color, religion, national origin, and sex, is broader than the EPA. Title VII is, in other words, a general anti-discrimination law covering more than just gender discrimination in pay.

Nevertheless, actions involving wage discrimination based on sex can be brought under both the EPA and Title VII. The standards for evaluation of claims under the two statutes, however, are not the same. There is, for example, no "equal work" requirement necessary to bring Title VII gender discrimination claims. Under the EPA, courts determine whether jobs are to be considered "equal work" on a case by case basis.

In sum, courts use many factors to determine similarities and differences between jobs which might establish a valid difference in pay regardless of gender. Generally, job classification systems make allowances for these fac-

Equal Pay Today

In 1963 women were paid fifty-nine cents on average for every dollar paid to men. Forty years later that figure has grown, but only to an average of seventy-six cents. The statistics are sobering:

There are more than a million women in the United States earning less than the federally established minimum wage.

Women with college educations earn only seventy-two cents for every dollar paid men. African-American women earn sixty-six cents; Hispanic women fifty-four cents.

A 2002 Government Accounting Office study found that full-time female managers earned less than men in each of the ten industries examined in the study. Furthermore, between 1995 and 2000, the wage gap between male and female managers had actually increased in seven of the ten industries.

According to the Institute for Women's Policy Research, the average 25-year-old woman who works full time, year-round for 40 years will earn $523,000 less than the average 25-year-old man who does the same.

Two pieces of legislation have been proposed in recent years in attempt to redress the inequity. The Paycheck Fairness Act, sponsored by Senator Tom Daschle (D-S.D.) and Representative Rosa DeLauro (D-Conn.), would increase penalties for equal pay violations and prohibit retaliation against whistleblowers. The Fair Pay Act, sponsored in past years by Senator Tom Harkin (D-Iowa) and Representative Eleanor Holmes Norton (D-D.C.), would prohibit wage discrimination based on sex, race, or national origin and require employers to provide equal pay for work of equal value, whether or not jobs are the same.

tors. A job classification system that does not discriminate on the basis of gender will serve as a valid defense to a charge of discrimination.

See also: CIVIL RIGHTS ACTS OF 1964; FAIR LABOR STANDARDS ACT; PREGNANCY DISCRIMINATION ACT.

BIBLIOGRAPHY

Fogel, Walter A. *The Equal Pay Act.* New York: Praeger Publishers, 1984

Hewitt, Patricia. *Rights for Women: A Guide to the Sex Discrimination Act, the Equal Pay Act, Paid Maternity Leave, Pension Schemed and Unfair Dismissal.* London: National Council for Civil Liberties, 1975

ESPIONAGE ACT (1917) AND SEDITION ACT (1918)

Robert N. Strassfeld

On the evening of April 2, 1917, President Woodrow Wilson addressed a joint session of Congress seeking a declaration of war against Germany and its allies. Later that night, Representative Edwin Webb, of North Carolina, and Senator Charles Culberson, of Texas, introduced bills in the House of Representatives and the Senate to deal with **espionage** and **treason**. On June 15, 1917, after much debate and some alteration, Congress enacted these bills into law as the Espionage Act (40 Stat. 217).

Even before America's entry into war, the Wilson administration had sought such legislation. Despite official neutrality, beginning in July 1915, the United States embarked on a program of military preparedness and financial and material support of Great Britain and its allies. As U.S. foreign policy shifted toward support of Great Britain, the administration became increasingly concerned about criticism of its policies and about pro-German propaganda. Democrats and Republicans both appealed to popular anxiety about the loyalty of so-called "hyphenate Americans," especially German-American and Irish-American immigrants. On December 7, 1915, congressmen and senators reacted enthusiastically when Wilson proclaimed in his Third Annual Message to Congress: "There are citizens of the United States ... born under other flags but welcomed by our generous naturalization laws to the full freedom and opportunity of America, who have poured the poison of disloyalty into the very arteries of our national life" (Shaw 1924, p. 151). Wilson added that such advocates of "disloyalty, and anarchy must be crushed out."

Twice before April 1917, Attorney General Thomas W. Gregory had proposed legislation on behalf of the Wilson administration that would punish espionage and curtail disloyal speech. Congress declined to enact these bills in June 1916 and during the winter of 1917. The Webb-Culberson legislation closely resembled these failed bills.

espionage: the act of spying on the government to obtain secret information

treason: the offense of attempting to overthrow the government of one's own state or country

Democrats and Republicans both appealed to popular anxiety about the loyalty of so-called "hyphenate Americans," especially German-American and Irish-American immigrants.

FEATURES OF THE ACT

The Espionage Act dealt with a wide range of issues, from criminalizing various acts of espionage to protecting shipping. Mostly it was uncontroversial.

The Espionage Act dealt with a wide range of issues, from criminalizing various acts of espionage to protecting shipping.

insurrection: a rebellion against a government or civil authority

The act is remembered, however, for those provisions that affected civil liberties.

First, Title 1, section 3, of the act made it a crime, punishable by up to twenty years' imprisonment and a $10,000 fine, to "make or convey false reports or false statements with intent to interfere with the operation or success of the military or naval forces of the United States" and to "cause or attempt to cause insubordination, disloyalty, mutiny, or refusal of duty in the military or naval forces ... or ... willfully obstruct the recruiting or enlistment service of the United States."

Second, title 12 empowered the postmaster general to declare any material that violated any provision of the Espionage Act or that urged "treason, **insurrection**, or forcible resistance to any law of the United States" unmailable. Use of the mails to transmit such materials was punishable by imprisonment and a fine.

Finally, as originally introduced, the bill gave the president the power to censor publication of material that he deemed potentially useful to the enemy. The censorship provision faced stiff opposition from the press and from across the political spectrum. Opponents included Republicans from the progressive wing of the party, such as Senators William Borah and Hiram Johnson, as well as Wilson's constant critic from the party's conservative wing, Senator Henry Cabot Lodge. Despite a direct appeal by Wilson to Congress to enact this provision, Congress removed it from the bill.

THE SEDITION ACT

At the urging of Attorney General Gregory, Congress enacted the Sedition Act (40 Stat. 553), which amended the Espionage Act, on May 16, 1918. Most notably, it added a variety of prohibited acts to Title 1, section 3, including writing or uttering:

> any disloyal, profane, scurrilous, or abusive language about the form of government of the United States, or the Constitution of the United States, or the military or naval forces of the United States, or the flag of the United States, or the uniform of the Army or Navy of the United States, or any language intended to bring [any of the above] into contempt, scorn, contumely, or disrepute.

The Sedition Act also amended the Espionage Act to enhance the postmaster general's powers.

PROSECUTIONS UNDER THE ACT

During the war not a single person was convicted of spying or sabotage under the Espionage Act. However, federal prosecutors used the act to bring over 2,000 cases, mostly under section 3, and at least 1,055 convictions resulted. Representatives of the American political Left were especially targeted. The government prosecuted leaders and members of the American Socialist Party, including its leader and perennial presidential candidate, Eugene V. Debs. They also targeted the leadership of the militant left-wing Industrial Workers of the World (IWW), then the largest industrial union in the United States. Both groups had publicly opposed U.S. entry into the war.

During the war not a single person was convicted of spying or sabotage under the Espionage Act.

Some prosecutions involved antiwar or anti-conscription speech that was at least partly directed at soldiers or potential conscripts. But much more innocuous speech that had little chance of causing disloyalty among the troops also prompted prosecution. In *United States v. Nagler* (1918), the defendant was convicted of publicly stating that the YMCA and the Red Cross are a "bunch of grafters." In another case, *Stokes v. United States* (1920), Rose Pastor Stokes, even though she rejected the Socialist Party's stand against the war, was sentenced to ten years' imprisonment for writing in a newspaper, "I am for the people, while the government is for the profiteers." And in a case resplendent with irony, *United States v. Motion Picture Film "The Spirit of '76"* (1917), a federal court upheld government seizure of a film about the Revolutionary War because it depicted atrocities committed by British soldiers and might therefore undermine support for an ally. The producer received a ten-year sentence.

The wreckage of the Chicago Federal Building, as seen in this 1918 photograph, was allegedly the result of a bomb planted by members of the Industrial Workers of the World (IWW). One of the leaders of the IWW, William D. "Big Bill" Haywood, was arrested for sedition in 1918. This bombing was thought to be in reprisal for the arrest of Haywood and ninety-four other members of the union. (©CORBIS)

Attorney General Gregory sent mixed messages about aggressive use of the Espionage Act.

Attorney General Gregory sent mixed messages about aggressive use of the Espionage Act. Although he cautioned against interference with civil liberties, he also directed the prosecution of Debs and orchestrated raids on IWW offices. He gave federal prosecutors broad discretion, which resulted in a varied pattern of prosecution. Nearly half of the prosecutions occurred in just thirteen of eighty-seven federal districts, mostly those located in Western states where the IWW was most active. For instance, there were five prosecutions in Massachusetts, whose population was over 3 million people. At the same time, in North Dakota, which had less than one-sixth of Massachusetts' population, 103 people were prosecuted.

Unlike Attorney General Gregory, the next postmaster general, Albert S. Burleson, had few reservations about using the Espionage Act to its fullest repressive potential. Within a month of its enactment, Burleson had censored fifteen publications. In addition to the radical press, he censored journals that criticized the administration's method of financing the war or British policy in Ireland. Burleson also revoked the second-class mailing privileges of such journals as *The Masses,* a radical literary and political journal, and the *Milwaukee Leader,* a socialist newspaper. Burleson reasoned that the interruption of their circulation caused by his seizure of a particular issue meant they were no longer *periodicals* entitled to the mailing privilege and the low postal rates.

JUDICIAL INTERPRETATION OF THE ACT

Most judges and juries applied the act expansively. Judges routinely instructed juries that they could infer unlawful intent from the likely effects of the defendant's words. These judges often instructed juries that they could convict on the basis of the "bad tendency" of the defendant's language, whether or not prosecutors had shown actual bad effects, or that any soldiers or possible recruits had been exposed to the defendant's words. So instructed, juries usually convicted. A handful of judges construed the act narrowly in an effort to reconcile the act with First Amendment free-speech values. For example, the Eighth Circuit Court of Appeals ordered a new trial for Rose Pastor Stokes.

Judges often instructed juries that they could convict on the "bad tendency" of the defendant's language.

Most notably, in *Masses Publishing Co. v. Patten* (1917), the publisher of the journal *The Masses* sought an injunction to prevent the seizure of the August issue as nonmailable because of its antiwar articles and cartoons. Judge Learned Hand granted that the material might undermine obedience in the military and, through its praise of jailed conscription opponents, might tend to obstruct recruitment. Nevertheless, he granted the injunction, because he concluded that Congress must have intended to prohibit only speech that advocated insubordination or resistance to enlistment. By construing the statute this way, he avoided deciding whether the statute unconstitutionally infringed on free speech. The United States Court of Appeals for the Second Circuit rejected Judge Hand's narrow interpretation of the act and reversed his decision.

Like the Second Circuit, the United States Supreme Court rejected a narrow reading of the act. In three cases decided in 1919, *Debs v. United States,*

MUST LIBERTY'S LIGHT GO OUT?

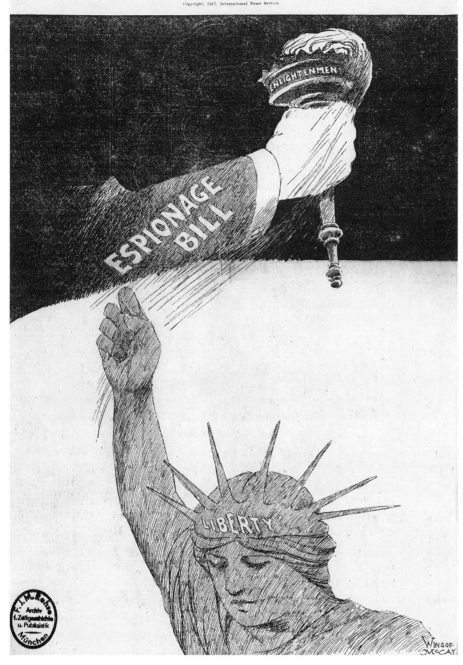

This 1917 wood engraving was published just over a month before the enactment of the Espionage Act, and represents clear commentary on the proposed legislation. The Espionage Act is viewed here as taking away fundamental freedoms that are guaranteed to each individual under the Bill of Rights. (LIBRARY OF CONGRESS, PRINTS AND PHOTOGRAPHS DIVISION)

Frohwerk v. United States, and *Schenck v. United States,* the Court upheld expansive application of the act and rejected a First Amendment challenge. Writing for a unanimous Court in each case, Justice Oliver Wendell Holmes, Jr., adopted the lower courts' approach of looking to the bad tendency of the language under the circumstances and of inferring intent from that bad ten-

In Schenck v. United States *(1919), Justice Oliver Wendell Holmes, Jr., stated: "The question in every case is whether the words used are used in such circumstances and are of such a nature as to create a clear and present danger that they will bring about the substantive evils that Congress has a right to prevent."*

dency. *Schenck* contains Holmes's famous statement that the First Amendment "would not protect a man in falsely shouting fire in a theatre and causing a panic." Rejecting the First Amendment argument, Holmes continued:

> The question ... is whether the words used are used in such circumstances and are of such a nature as to create a clear and present danger that they will bring about the substantive evils that Congress has a right to prevent....When a nation is at war many things that might be said in time of peace are such a hindrance to its effort that their utterance will not be endured.

In a series of famous dissents in cases involving the prosecution of political radicals that arose mostly in the 1920s, Justice Holmes and Justice Louis D. Brandeis invoked the "clear and present danger" test, but they interpreted it in a fashion that was far more protective of free speech, than to Holmes's use of the concept intent in the *Schenck* ruling. While Holmes asserted that these dissents with the earlier Espionage Act rulings, both in tone and application they were more protective of free speech. Importantly, Holmes and Brandeis required a much closer and immediate link between the speech in question and the danger that the government sought to avert than the Court had in the Espionage Act cases and in the subsequent prosecutions that prompted their dissents. With time, their dissenting approach prevailed, triumphing finally under the Warren Court.

CIVIL LIBERTIES

Although Congress rejected Wilson's request for a peacetime Sedition Act, the repression of the Left continued in the postwar years in a series of raids, prosecutions (sometimes under state acts directed against the IWW), and deportations. This period in American history, when repressive actions were taken against allegedly disloyal citizens, is known as the "Red Scare" (red being the color associated with communism). The excessive response to supposed sedition during the war and postwar years also prompted increased concern about civil liberties. Both the American Civil Liberties Union, founded in 1920, and the Holmes and Brandeis dissents, which led eventually to a broader understanding of First Amendment rights, were reactions to this experience. Nonetheless, the Espionage Act, in somewhat amended form, remains a part of federal law.

The excessive response to supposed sedition during the war and postwar years also prompted increased concern about civil liberties.

See also: ALIEN AND SEDITION ACTS OF 1798; COMMUNIST CONTROL ACT OF 1954; USA PATRIOT ACT.

BIBLIOGRAPHY

Chafee, Zechariah. *Free Speech in the United States*. Cambridge: Harvard University Press, 1941.

Kennedy, David. *Over Here: The First World War and American Society*. New York: Oxford University Press, 1980.

Murphy, Paul L. *World War I and the Origin of Civil Liberties in the United States*. New York: Norton, 1979.

Peterson, H. C., and Gilbert C. Fite. *Opponents of War, 1917–1918*. Madison: University of Wisconsin Press, 1957.

Preston, William. *Aliens and Dissenters: Federal Suppression of Radicals, 1903–1933.* Cambridge, MA: Harvard University Press, 1963.

Rabban, David M. *Free Speech in the Forgotten Years.* New York: Cambridge University Press, 1997.

Scheiber, Harry N. *The Wilson Administration and Civil Liberties, 1917–21.* Ithaca, NY: Cornell University Press, 1960.

ESTATE AND GIFT TAXATION

Richard Gershon

Congress generally imposes an estate and gift tax on large transfers of wealth between individuals. In essence, they are tolls imposed on the transfer of wealth. The Federal Gift Tax (26 USC 2501) is imposed on transfers made during an individual's lifetime, and The Federal Estate Tax (26 USC 2001) is imposed on transfers made at the time of death. Gift taxes and estate taxes are paid separately, but they are subject to a single **graduated rate schedule** that applies to the cumulative total of taxable transfers made through gifts and estates.

Each year, the taxpayer must report the amount of taxable gifts he or she made during that year. Upon death, an estate tax return is filed on behalf of the **decedent's** estate. The tax is determined by adding the total lifetime taxable gifts to the taxable estate, and then applying the applicable tax rate. Like the federal income tax, the rates for the estate and gift taxes are graduated. Accordingly, the **marginal rates** of tax increase as the amount of wealth transferred increases. The maximum rate for estate and gift taxes since 1986 has been 55 percent. Congress, however, amended the law so that this maximum rate will decrease gradually until it is fully phased out in 2010.

For purposes of imposing the estate tax, the law requires that the decedent's property be valued. The taxable estate includes the value of all property controlled by the decedent at the time of death, including such items as life insurance, retained interests in trusts, and **powers of appointment**. However, the value of debts, funeral expenses, and costs of administering and settling the estate can reduce the estate's residual value. Furthermore, any portion of a decedent's estate that is given to a spouse or to charity is not taxed.

Generation–Skipping Transfer Tax. Closely related to the estate and gift tax provisions is the Generation–Skipping Transfer Tax. Congress created the Generation–Skipping Transfer Tax to prevent taxpayers from skipping several generations of tax on wealth transfers through a succession of **life estates**. Since the federal estate tax is only applicable where the decedent retained control over property at the time of death, it would not apply to an inherited life estate, which, by definition, terminates on death. The Generation– Skipping Transfer Tax imposes the highest tax rate on transfers deemed to be generation skips. In other words, Congress wants to insure that the value of wealth is taxed anytime it is passed from one generation to the next. The "toll" on wealth is collected, even if the decedent did not have property sub-

> Congress generally imposes an estate and gift tax on large transfers of wealth between individuals.

graduated rate schedule: tax structured so that the rate increases as the amount of income of taxpayer increases

decedent: one who has died; the deceased

marginal rates: the total percentage of tax one pays on one's income, taking into account all the separate taxes levied on one's wages or salary

powers of appointment: the right to appoint or give away property

life estate: an estate that lasts for the duration of the life of the person holding it

The taxable estate includes the value of all property controlled by the decedent at the time of death, including such items as life insurance, retained interests in trusts, and powers of appointment.

ject to the estate tax. To understand the law, consider a situation in which a grandfather passes a life interest in a trust worth $25 million to his son, with the remainder going to his grandson. The son gets the use of the $25 million for life, but owns nothing of the trust on death, since his life interest will have terminated. Accordingly, there will be no federal estate tax collected on the transfer of the property to the grandson, because the son did not have the right to control the property. The son's rights disappeared upon his death. The Generation-Skipping Transfer Tax, however, will apply to insure that the wealth transmitted from the son's generation to the grandson's generation does not escape taxation.

MAJOR PROVISIONS OF THE ESTATE AND GIFT TAX

Each taxpayer is allowed to transfer $11,000 in present interest gifts to any single individual in the course of a year, tax-free.

The Annual Gift Exclusion. Each taxpayer is allowed to transfer $11,000 in present interest gifts to any single individual in the course of a year, tax-free. This means that the taxpayer will not be subject to the estate, gift, or generation–skipping taxes just described. The exemption, however, does not apply to transfers of future interests. The exemption is available for as many recipients as the donor chooses. For example, a taxpayer wishing to give away $99,000 to his nine grandchildren could do so tax-free (if the gifts were split evenly) in 2003. This means that the only way gifts can be taxed is if a single taxpayer gives more than $11,000 to each individual or to any one person.

Major Estate and Gift Tax Deductions: The Marital Deduction. A taxpayer can transfer any amount of money or property to a spouse without incurring either estate or gift tax, provided that the transfer to the spouse qualifies for the marital deduction. In order to qualify for the marital deduction, the property must be of a kind that can be included in the surviving spouse's estate upon his or her death. The idea behind the marital deduction is that each couple's property should only be taxed once.

The Charitable Deduction. The Internal Revenue Code provides for a deduction for all amounts transferred to charity during the decedent's lifetime, or at death. A charitable contribution is defined as a bequest, legacy, devise, or transfer:

- To or for the use of the United States, any State, any political subdivision thereof, or the District of Columbia, for exclusively public purposes
- To or for the use of any corporation organized and operated exclusively for religious, charitable, scientific, literary, or educational purposes, including the encouragement of art, or to foster national or international amateur sports competition (but only if no part of its activities involve the provision of athletic facilities or equipment), and the prevention of cruelty to children or animals, no part of the net earnings of which inures to the benefit of any private stockholder or individual, which is not disqualified for tax exemption under section 501(c)(3) by reason of attempting to influence legislation, and which does not participate in, or intervene in

The estate tax is a progressive tax measure—the vast majority of Americans are exempted from it. In the early twenty-first century, only those with estates worth over $1 million had to pay an estate tax (that number is gradually to increase to $3.5 million by 2009). However, during debates in 2002 over whether or not to permanently repeal the estate tax, the tax was portrayed as affecting family farmers and small business owners by those lobbying in favor of its repeal. (©IMAGES.COM/CORBIS)

(including the publishing or distributing of statements), any political campaign on behalf of (or in opposition to) any candidate for public office

- To a trustee or trustees, or a fraternal society, order, or association operating under the lodge system, but only if such contributions or gifts are to be used by such trustee or trustees, or by such fraternal society, order, or association, exclusively for religious, charitable, scientific, literary, or educational purposes, or for the prevention of cruelty to children or animals, such trust, fraternal society, order, or association would not be disqualified for tax exemption under section 501(c)(3) by reason of attempting to influence legislation, and such trustee or trustees, or such fraternal society, order, or association, does not participate in, or intervene in (including the publishing or distributing of statements), any political campaign on behalf of (or in opposition to) any candidate for public office

- To or for the use of any veterans' organization incorporated by act of Congress, or of its departments or local chapters or posts, no part of the net earnings of which inures to the benefit of any private shareholder or individual. For purposes of this subsection, the complete termination before the date prescribed for the filing of the estate tax return of a power to consume, invade, or appropriate property for the benefit of an individual before such power has been exercised by reason of the death of such individual or for any other reason shall be considered and deemed to be a qualified disclaimer with the same full force and effect as though he had filed such qualified disclaimer.

ESTATE TAX CHANGES

In June, 2001, Congress passed legislation that significantly increased the amount that is tax exempt, and significantly reduced the maximum tax rate on taxable property. While this law contained many details, the most notable feature is that the estate tax is scheduled to be phased out by 2010. The law will continue to tax gifts. After 2011, the estate tax provisions revert back to their 2001 rates, with the first million dollars of taxable transfers remaining exempt. Technically, therefore, the estate tax repeal will only last one year.

In 2002 Congress came close to repealing the estate tax permanently.

The 2001 changes also affect individuals who receive property from an estate. Currently, a person acquiring property from a decedent takes a "basis" in that property equal to the fair market value at the date of the decedent's death. Beginning in 2010, however, the transferee will take the decedent's basis, rather than a basis equal to the fair market value. This new basis provision is important because generally an individual can only be taxed on the value of property that exceeds basis.

In 2002 Congress came close to repealing the estate tax permanently. The Senate rejected the repeal, 54-44, six votes shy of the necessary 60 required for passage. The House voted 256-171 in favor of repeal. Thus the estate law, with its phase out in 2010 and return in 2011, continues to exist.

BIBLIOGRAPHY

McDaniel, Paul R., Paul L. Caron and James R. Repetti. *Federal Wealth Transfer Taxation: Cases and Materials.* 5th ed. New York: Foundation Press, 2003.

Stephens, Richard B., et. al. *Federal Estate and Gift Taxation.* 8th ed. Valhalla, N.Y.: Warren, Gorham and Lamont, 2002.

ETHICS IN GOVERNMENT ACT (1978)

Robert G. Vaughn

The Ethics in Government Act of 1978 (P.L. 95-521, 92 Stat. 1824) addressed the constitutional crisis surrounding the **Watergate** break-in and the resignation of President Richard M. Nixon. These events prompted calls for ethics and openness in government. In response, the act established certain rules of conduct for former federal employees. These rules were designed to

Watergate: the scandal following the break-in at the Democratic National Committee headquarters located in the Watergate apartment and office complex in Washington, D.C. in 1972

reduce corruption and prevent the improper use of knowledge gained while in the government's employ. The two most significant provisions of the law (1) require public officials and higher-ranking civil servants to make public financial disclosures and (2) prohibit certain activities by federal employees after their government employment ends. In addition, the act imposed limits on gifts and honoraria (payments at a set price for speeches or other services) and created new administrative procedures for enforcing ethics provisions.

The act imposed limits on gifts and honoraria that federal employees could accept.

FINANCIAL DISCLOSURE

At the time of enactment, several states already had public financial disclosure laws, and the act drew in part on these laws. In the name of ethics and openness, it also sought to correct the existing disclosure system for federal officials, which relied only on internal reporting within each agency. In 1974 the General Accounting Office, an investigative arm of Congress, had cast doubt on the effectiveness of that disclosure system, and Congress was responding to these criticisms.

Who Must Report? Within the executive branch, the act requires reporting by the president and vice president, all employees whose positions are classified at GS-16 (a classification for a federal civil service pay rate) or above, higher-ranking military officers, and administrative law judges. The reporting requirement also applies to members of Congress, federal judges, certain employees of the judiciary, and certain officers and employees of Congress.

What Must They Report? People covered by the act must report income derived from various sources, gifts, assets and liabilities, including some transactions, and certain positions held in businesses and in nonprofit organizations. Gifts of food, lodging, transportation, and entertainment are to be reported if gifts from any individual in a calendar year total $250 or more. Other gifts must be reported if gifts from any individual in a calendar year total $100 or more.

Income derived from dividends, interest, rent, and capital gains exceeding $100 must be reported but only in nine broad categories of value, from not more that $1,000 to greater than $5 million. As to other forms of income, the employee must report the source, type, amount, and value of income exceeding $200.

Assets and liabilities are reported within broad categories of value and include both real and personal property. The act does not require the reporting of the value of a personal residence not used for the production of income, provides a $1,000 exception, and excludes savings accounts and certificates of deposit totaling $5,000 or less. The employee must report all transactions, including a description, date, and value involving the purchase, sale, or exchange of real property, stocks, bonds, or commodity futures. Excluded is any transaction between the employee and the employee's spouse or children as well as the transfer, purchase, or sale of a personal residence.

An employee covered by the act must report the names of anyone who paid the employee compensation in excess of $5,000 in any of the two calendar years before a report is first filed. The employee must also include a brief

The act seeks to ensure that reporting requirements will not compromise personal privacy or create opportunities for abuse of the financial information.

description of the services performed. An employee must also disclose all positions held as an officer, trustee, director, partner, employee, representative, proprietor, or consultant of any corporation, firm, or business, including nonprofit organizations.

Protection of Privacy. The act seeks to ensure that reporting requirements will not compromise personal privacy or create opportunities for abuse of the financial information. Although the interests of spouses must be reported, the act creates several exemptions that reduce the effect of the reporting requirements on spouses. In addition, an agency must evaluate an employee's report before disclosure and indicate if no conflicts of interest were found. The custodian of the reports must destroy them after six years, and penalties are imposed for use of the reports for unlawful purposes or for commercial purposes, such as solicitation.

POSTEMPLOYMENT RESTRICTIONS

Before passage of the act, the federal criminal code placed limitations on the postemployment activities of federal employees. One such restriction barred appearances by former employees of an agency in certain proceedings conducted by that agency. The act added prohibitions on communications by former employees with their agencies.

Communications. Today, these restrictions create a lifetime bar against communications, including submission of memoranda, letters, and telephone calls, to an employee of the United States "in connection with a particular matter involving a specific party or parties, in which [the former employee] participated personally and substantially as an employee." The matter must be one in which the United States is "a party or has a direct and substantial interest." This prohibition seeks to prevent a former employee from "switching sides" by representing a party in a matter in which the former employee had previously worked as a government employee. For example, an employee representing the U.S. government in a particular matter should not be allowed to leave government service and soon after begin to represent in the same matter a private party whose interests may be antagonistic to those of the government. The appearance of impropriety is simply too great. It applies to appearances before the agency and communications with it but not to "behind the scenes" assistance given to others representing a party in the same matter. An employee might also be able to avoid this prohibition by disqualifying herself from the particular matter while still a government employee. A disqualification would have to remove the employee from all involvement in the matter.

A two-year prohibition applies in similar circumstances to communications by former employees regarding matters that they know or should know were actually pending under their official responsibility within a one-year period prior to leaving government employment. This prohibition addresses the improper use after leaving a job of knowledge that was gained while on the job. Employees have official responsibility for many matters in which they do not participate personally or substantially. Because the prohibition covers more matters with which employees have a more limited connection, it is of shorter duration. Because the prohibition applies to every particular matter

Effects of Nixon's Resignation

In the aftermath of the Watergate scandal, in which President Richard Nixon resigned rather than face impeachment for crimes committed by his administration, numerous reforms were instituted to protect the public interest from official malfeasance. These included campaign finance regulations, conflict-of-interest guidelines, safeguards on the freedom of information, and improved privacy laws. Candidates for public office came under increased scrutiny for both their public and private lives, and public interest groups such as Common Cause greatly increased their membership rolls. While Watergate was neither the first nor the last presidential scandal of shocking proportions, it did mark a milestone in the growth of public cynicism about elected officials.

that an employee oversees or reviews as part of their official responsibilities, an employee can not disqualify themselves without significantly impairing their performance as a government employee. Therefore disqualification will not remove the matter from those official responsibilities and will not affect the application of the prohibition. Like the other restrictions on communication, this prohibition seeks to prevent a former employee from "switching sides" by representing a party in a matter for which the former employee had official responsibility as a government employee, and does not apply to "behind the scenes" assistance given to others representing a party in the matter.

> *Like the other restrictions on communication, this prohibition seeks to prevent a former employee from "switching sides" by representing a party in a matter for which the former employee had official responsibility as a government employee; it does not apply to "behind the scenes" assistance given to others representing a party in the matter.*

Modifications. The act originally prohibited a broader range of communications, including the prohibition of some "behind the scenes" communications, but concerns about the breadth of the prohibitions led to modifications. As a result, these restrictions now apply only to actions in which former employees communicate with an agency on behalf of a third party. The prohibition seeks to prevent an appearance that government decisions have been unduly influenced by former employees.

Senior Personnel. A prohibition on the postemployment activities of senior and very senior government personnel extends to other activities involving representing a third party. Senior employees, paid at the highest executive levels, may not, on behalf of any person, attempt to influence, through communication to or appearance before, the employee's former agency. This prohibition does not require that the matter on which official action is sought is one in which the former senior employee participated personally or substantially or was within the former employee's official responsibilities. It prohibits any representation of another person regarding any matter, including rule making or policy matters pending before the former senior employee's agency. The matter need not have been pending before the agency while the senior employee worked for the federal government. The Office of Government Ethics may **waive** these restrictions in certain limited circumstances, and some exceptions apply.

waive: to give up voluntarily

A similar prohibition regarding cabinet-level officials and a few employees paid at the level of deputy secretaries of cabinet departments extends beyond the agency for which the former employee worked and includes representation before the highest-ranking government officials in other agencies. The Office of Government Ethics may not waive this prohibition, although some limited exceptions apply.

Honoraria. Under the act, federal employees may not receive honoraria for speeches and writings directly related to official duties or paid because of the status of the recipient as a government employee. The act also restricts certain types of outside employment by government employees.

ENFORCEMENT

The Office of Government Ethics, established by the act, has responsibility for interpreting the act's provisions. The Office is treated as a separate agency

> *The act permits civil as well as criminal enforcement of its prohibitions.*

within the executive branch. It has issued both regulations and advisory opinions that further define the prohibitions contained in the statute, and it has played an important role in clarifying them. The director of the Office of Government Ethics may seek to discipline an employee, and individual government agencies may take administrative action in some situations. The act permits civil as well as criminal enforcement of its prohibitions. The attorney general may seek civil penalties and injunctions against violation of these restrictions.

As part of a system of regulations including presidential executive orders, the Ethics in Government Act remains an important part of the legal regulation of public service ethics in the federal government. In Congress and the courts as well, it is a component of other ethical provisions imposed by rule and by statute.

BIBLIOGRAPHY

Roberts, Robert. "Regulatory Bias and Conflict of Interest Regulation." In *Handbook of Regulation and Administrative Law*. Ed. David H. Rosenbloom and Richard D. Schwartz. New York: Marcel Dekker, 1994.

Vaughn, Robert G. *Conflict of Interest Regulation in the Federal Executive Branch*. Lexington, MA: Lexington Books, 1979.

EXPORT-IMPORT BANK ACT OF 1945

Lynda D. Vargha

The Export-Import Bank Act of 1945 (P.L. 79-173, 59 Stat. 526) made the Export-Import Bank of Washington an independent government agency operating under a renewable charter. President Franklin D. Roosevelt initially established the bank by an executive order in 1934 and funded it with $1 billion from the U.S. Treasury. President Roosevelt originally intended to fund U.S. trade with the Soviet Union, but within the decade, the mission of the bank expanded to include the provision of loans and grants to U.S. companies seeking to export their products. By executive order, jurisdiction over the bank was transferred between government agencies four times between 1939 and 1943 before Congress established it as an independent agency with the enactment of the Export-Import Bank Act of 1945.

> *President Roosevelt originally intended to fund U.S. trade with the Soviet Union, but within the decade, the mission of the bank expanded to include the provision of loans and grants to U.S. companies seeking to export their products.*

The creation of the bank in 1934 was part of a larger economic policy promoting government spending as a means for economic growth. At the time, the U.S. economy of the Great Depression was characterized by high unemployment, low income, low demand for goods and services, and slowed industrial production. Meanwhile, the communist Soviet Union experienced high industrial production from state-owned firms and zero unemployment. Under these economic conditions the Soviet Union was seen as a market for U.S.-produced goods and the export of U.S. goods to the Soviet Union was a reasonable strategy for promoting U.S. economic growth and lowering U.S. unemployment.

Although the original mission of the Export-Import Bank of Washington was to subsidize U.S. industrial production for export to the Soviet Union, within a decade, its mission quickly expanded to include other foreign countries. By the end of World War II (1939–1945), the Export-Import Bank played a vital role in helping U.S. companies participate in the expansion of U.S. industry to Europe and Asia as part of the post-war reconstruction effort. Because of the expanding post-war role of the bank and its growing importance, Congress formally designated it an independent government agency when it adopted the Export-Import Bank Act of 1945.

A 1968 amendment to the Export-Import Bank Act of 1945 renamed the bank the Export-Import Bank of the United States, and this continues to be its name today. Before 1980, the main avenue of export promotion through the

The Export-Import Bank Act of 1945 made the Export-Import Bank of Washington an independent government agency operating under a renewable charter. The bank was originally created to fund U.S. trade with the Soviet Union, but within the decade, the mission of the bank expanded to the provision of loans and grants to U.S. companies exporting their products abroad. The act has been renewed through 2006. Above, in 1945, U.S. secretary of state James F. Byrnes signs the agreement for a $4,400,000,000 loan to Great Britain. (© AP/WIDE WORLD PHOTOS)

A 1968 amendment to the Export-Import Bank Act of 1945 renamed the bank the Export-Import Bank of the United States, and this continues to be its name today.

The global environment in which the Export-Import Bank of the United States must operate today is very different from that of 1945 when the Export-Import Bank Act made it an independent government agency.

bank was by way of direct loans to producers seeking to sell goods abroad. This program provided fixed interest rate loans and were most often given to producers to fund high capital (plant and equipment) expenditures in industries such as aircraft manufacture and nuclear power. Perhaps the most well-known case of such government funding is that provided to aircraft manufacturer Boeing. The government has supported Boeing though the Export-Import Bank for decades as a response to the European Union's subsidy of Boeing's major European competitor, Airbus. In 1980, when Congress limited the amount of direct lending, the bank decreased its direct lending and increased its use of loan guarantees and insurance coverage as a means of facilitating the export of American goods.

Despite all of these changes, the underlying goal of the Export-Import Bank of the United States has not changed, it continues to promote the sale of U.S. goods abroad. The bank provides loans and insurance to privately-owned companies to reduce the risk of selling in countries experiencing political or economic instability. In addition, the bank attempts to level the playing field of global markets for U.S. companies by subsidizing U.S. industries in competition with foreign firms subsidized by their governments.

President George W. Bush signed the Export-Import Reauthorization Act of 2002 on July 14, 2002. This act renewed the bank's charter through September 30, 2006 and included new rules for the provision of loans and insurance. The law now requires the bank to make a human rights assessment of any project over $10 million and to focus on projects that will promote U.S. job growth. Most importantly, the law draws attention to compliance with U.S. responsibilities as a nation member of the World Trade Organization (WTO). The Export-Import Reauthorization Act of 2002 prohibits subsidization to any industry subject to a retaliatory countervailing duty through the WTO agreements.

The global environment in which the Export-Import Bank of the United States must operate today is very different from that of 1945 when the Export-Import Bank Act made it an independent government agency. At that time, the bank was a mechanism for economic growth, as well as a means to promote the involvement of U.S. companies in the post-war reconstruction of Europe and Asia. At the time Congress intended these government subsidies to promote U.S exports abroad, thus increasing industrial production and lowering unemployment in the U.S. Today, the role of government subsidization to achieve economic growth is a source of debate among politicians and economists—some continuing to support the mechanism, while others argue that it undermines growth and productivity. However, the Export-Import Bank of the United States still enables U.S. companies to compete with foreign competitors that are subsidized by their own governments.

BIBLIOGRAPHY

Jackson, James "Export-Import Bank Background and Legislative Issues." Report for Congress. Congressional Research Service (March 10, 2003).

INTERNET RESOURCES

Export-Import Bank of the United States. <http://www.exim.gov>

"Records of the Export-Import Bank of the United States." U.S. National Archives and
   Records Administration. <http://www.archives.gov>

Appendices

CONSTITUTION OF
THE UNITES STATES
OF AMERICA

We the People of the United States, in Order to form a more perfect Union, establish Justice, insure domestic Tranquility, provide for the common defense, promote the general Welfare, and secure the Blessings of Liberty to ourselves and our Posterity, do ordain and establish this Constitution for the United States of America.

ARTICLE I

Items in italic have since been amended or superseded. A portion of Article I, Section 2, was modified by Section 2 of the Fourteenth Amendment; Article I, Section 3, was modified by the Seventeenth Amendment; Article I, Section 4, was modified by Section 2 of the Twentieth Amendment; and Article I, Section 9, was modified by the Sixteenth Amendment.

Section 1: All legislative Powers herein granted shall be vested in a Congress of the United States, which shall consist of a Senate and House of Representatives.

Section 2: The House of Representatives shall be composed of Members chosen every second Year by the People of the several States, and the Electors in each State shall have the Qualifications requisite for Electors of the most numerous Branch of the State Legislature.

No Person shall be a Representative who shall not have attained to the Age of twenty five Years, and been seven Years a Citizen of the United States, and who shall not, when elected, be an Inhabitant of that State in which he shall be chosen.

Representatives and direct Taxes shall be apportioned among the several States which may be included within this Union, according to their respective Numbers, which shall be determined by adding to the whole Number of free Persons, including those bound to Service for a Term of Years, and excluding Indians not taxed, three fifths of all other Persons. The actual Enumeration shall be made within three Years after the first Meeting of the Congress of the United States, and within every subsequent Term of ten Years, in such Manner as they shall by Law direct. The Number of Representatives shall not exceed one for every thirty Thousand, but each State shall have at Least one Representative; and until such enumeration shall be made, the State of New Hampshire shall be entitled to chuse three, Massachusetts eight, Rhode-Island

and Providence Plantations one, Connecticut five, New-York six, New Jersey four, Pennsylvania eight, Delaware one, Maryland six, Virginia ten, North Carolina five, South Carolina five, and Georgia three.

When vacancies happen in the Representation from any State, the Executive Authority thereof shall issue Writs of Election to fill such Vacancies.

The House of Representatives shall chuse their Speaker and other Officers; and shall have the sole Power of Impeachment.

Section 3: The Senate of the United States shall be composed of two Senators from each State, *chosen by the Legislature thereof* for six Years; and each Senator shall have one Vote.

Immediately after they shall be assembled in Consequence of the first Election, they shall be divided as equally as may be into three Classes. The Seats of the Senators of the first Class shall be vacated at the Expiration of the second Year, of the second Class at the Expiration of the fourth Year, and of the third Class at the Expiration of the sixth Year, so that one third may be chosen every second Year; *and if Vacancies happen by Resignation, or otherwise, during the Recess of the Legislature of any State, the Executive thereof may make temporary Appointments until the next Meeting of the Legislature, which shall then fill such Vacancies.*

No Person shall be a Senator who shall not have attained to the Age of thirty Years, and been nine Years a Citizen of the United States, and who shall not, when elected, be an Inhabitant of that State for which he shall be chosen.

The Vice President of the United States shall be President of the Senate, but shall have no Vote, unless they be equally divided.

The Senate shall chuse their other Officers, and also a President pro tempore, in the Absence of the Vice President, or when he shall exercise the Office of President of the United States.

The Senate shall have the sole Power to try all Impeachments. When sitting for that Purpose, they shall be on Oath or Affirmation. When the President of the United States is tried, the Chief Justice shall preside: And no Person shall be convicted without the Concurrence of two thirds of the Members present.

Judgment in Cases of Impeachment shall not extend further than to removal from Office, and disqualification to hold and enjoy any Office of honor, Trust or Profit under the United States: but the Party convicted shall nevertheless be liable and subject to Indictment, Trial, Judgment and Punishment, according to Law.

Section 4: The Times, Places and Manner of holding Elections for Senators and Representatives, shall be prescribed in each State by the Legislature thereof; but the Congress may at any time by Law make or alter such Regulations, except as to the Places of chusing Senators.

The Congress shall assemble at least once in every Year, and such Meeting shall *be on the first Monday in December,* unless they shall by Law appoint a different Day.

Section 5: Each House shall be the Judge of the Elections, Returns and Qualifications of its own Members, and a Majority of each shall constitute a Quorum to do Business; but a smaller Number may adjourn from day to day, and may be authorized to compel the Attendance of absent Members, in such Manner, and under such Penalties as each House may provide.

Each House may determine the Rules of its Proceedings, punish its Members for disorderly Behaviour, and, with the Concurrence of two thirds, expel a Member.

Each House shall keep a Journal of its Proceedings, and from time to time publish the same, excepting such Parts as may in their Judgment require Secrecy; and the Yeas and Nays of the Members of either House on any question shall, at the Desire of one fifth of those Present, be entered on the Journal.

Neither House, during the Session of Congress, shall, without the Consent of the other, adjourn for more than three days, nor to any other Place than that in which the two Houses shall be sitting.

Section 6: The Senators and Representatives shall receive a Compensation for their Services, to be ascertained by Law, and paid out of the Treasury of the United States. They shall in all Cases, except Treason, Felony and Breach of the Peace, be privileged from Arrest during their Attendance at the Session of their respective Houses, and in going to and returning from the same; and for any Speech or Debate in either House, they shall not be questioned in any other Place.

No Senator or Representative shall, during the Time for which he was elected, be appointed to any civil Office under the Authority of the United States, which shall have been created, or the Emoluments whereof shall have been encreased during such time; and no Person holding any Office under the United States, shall be a Member of either House during his Continuance in Office.

Section 7: All Bills for raising Revenue shall originate in the House of Representatives; but the Senate may propose or concur with Amendments as on other Bills.

Every Bill which shall have passed the House of Representatives and the Senate, shall, before it become a Law, be presented to the President of the United States: If he approve he shall sign it, but if not he shall return it, with his Objections to that House in which it shall have originated, who shall enter the Objections at large on their Journal, and proceed to reconsider it. If after such Reconsideration two thirds of that House shall agree to pass the Bill, it shall be sent, together with the Objections, to the other House, by which it shall likewise be reconsidered, and if approved by two thirds of that House, it shall become a Law. But in all such Cases the Votes of both Houses shall be determined by yeas and Nays, and the Names of the Persons voting for and against the Bill shall be entered on the Journal of each House respectively. If any Bill shall not be returned by the President within ten Days (Sundays excepted) after it shall have been presented to him, the Same shall be a Law, in like Manner as if he had signed it, unless the Congress by their Adjournment prevent its Return, in which Case it shall not be a Law.

Every Order, Resolution, or Vote to which the Concurrence of the Senate and House of Representatives may be necessary (except on a question of

Adjournment) shall be presented to the President of the United States; and before the Same shall take Effect, shall be approved by him, or being disapproved by him, shall be repassed by two thirds of the Senate and House of Representatives, according to the Rules and Limitations prescribed in the Case of a Bill.

Section 8: The Congress shall have Power To lay and collect Taxes, Duties, Imposts and Excises, to pay the Debts and provide for the common Defence and general Welfare of the United States; but all Duties, Imposts and Excises shall be uniform throughout the United States;

To borrow Money on the credit of the United States;

To regulate Commerce with foreign Nations, and among the several States, and with the Indian Tribes;

To establish an uniform Rule of Naturalization, and uniform Laws on the subject of Bankruptcies throughout the United States;

To coin Money, regulate the Value thereof, and of foreign Coin, and fix the Standard of Weights and Measures;

To provide for the Punishment of counterfeiting the Securities and current Coin of the United States;

To establish Post Offices and post Roads;

To promote the Progress of Science and useful Arts, by securing for limited Times to Authors and Inventors the exclusive Right to their respective Writings and Discoveries;

To constitute Tribunals inferior to the supreme Court;

To define and punish Piracies and Felonies committed on the high Seas, and Offences against the Law of Nations;

To declare War, grant Letters of Marque and Reprisal, and make Rules concerning Captures on Land and Water;

To raise and support Armies, but no Appropriation of Money to that Use shall be for a longer Term than two Years;

To provide and maintain a Navy;

To make Rules for the Government and Regulation of the land and naval Forces;

To provide for calling forth the Militia to execute the Laws of the Union, suppress Insurrections and repel Invasions;

To provide for organizing, arming, and disciplining, the Militia, and for governing such Part of them as may be employed in the Service of the United States, reserving to the States respectively, the Appointment of the Officers, and the Authority of training the Militia according to the discipline prescribed by Congress;

To exercise exclusive Legislation in all Cases whatsoever, over such District (not exceeding ten Miles square) as may, by Cession of particular States, and the Acceptance of Congress, become the Seat of the Government of the United States, and to exercise like Authority over all Places purchased by the

Consent of the Legislature of the State in which the Same shall be, for the Erection of Forts, Magazines, Arsenals, dock-Yards, and other needful Buildings;—And

To make all Laws which shall be necessary and proper for carrying into Execution the foregoing Powers, and all other Powers vested by this Constitution in the Government of the United States, or in any Department or Officer thereof.

Section 9: The Migration or Importation of such Persons as any of the States now existing shall think proper to admit, shall not be prohibited by the Congress prior to the Year one thousand eight hundred and eight, but a Tax or duty may be imposed on such Importation, not exceeding ten dollars for each Person.

The Privilege of the Writ of Habeas Corpus shall not be suspended, unless when in Cases of Rebellion or Invasion the public Safety may require it.

No Bill of Attainder or ex post facto Law shall be passed.

No Capitation, or other direct, Tax shall be laid, *unless in Proportion to the Census or enumeration herein before directed to be taken.*

No Tax or Duty shall be laid on Articles exported from any State.

No Preference shall be given by any Regulation of Commerce or Revenue to the Ports of one State over those of another; nor shall Vessels bound to, or from, one State, be obliged to enter, clear, or pay Duties in another.

No Money shall be drawn from the Treasury, but in Consequence of Appropriations made by Law; and a regular Statement and Account of the Receipts and Expenditures of all public Money shall be published from time to time.

No Title of Nobility shall be granted by the United States: And no Person holding any Office of Profit or Trust under them, shall, without the Consent of the Congress, accept of any present, Emolument, Office, or Title, of any kind whatever, from any King, Prince, or foreign State.

Section 10: No State shall enter into any Treaty, Alliance, or Confederation; grant Letters of Marque and Reprisal; coin Money; emit Bills of Credit; make any Thing but gold and silver Coin a Tender in Payment of Debts; pass any Bill of Attainder, ex post facto Law, or Law impairing the Obligation of Contracts, or grant any Title of Nobility.

No State shall, without the Consent of the Congress, lay any Imposts or Duties on Imports or Exports, except what may be absolutely necessary for executing it's inspection Laws: and the net Produce of all Duties and Imposts, laid by any State on Imports or Exports, shall be for the Use of the Treasury of the United States; and all such Laws shall be subject to the Revision and Controul of the Congress.

No State shall, without the Consent of Congress, lay any Duty of Tonnage, keep Troops, or Ships of War in time of Peace, enter into any Agreement or Compact with another State, or with a foreign Power, or engage in War, unless actually invaded, or in such imminent Danger as will not admit of delay.

ARTICLE II

Article II, Section 1, was superseded by the Twelfth Amendment; Article II, Section 1, was modified by the Twenty-fifth Amendment.

Section 1: The executive Power shall be vested in a President of the United States of America. He shall hold his Office during the Term of four Years, and, together with the Vice President, chosen for the same Term, be elected, as follows:

Each State shall appoint, in such Manner as the Legislature thereof may direct, a Number of Electors, equal to the whole Number of Senators and Representatives to which the State may be entitled in the Congress: but no Senator or Representative, or Person holding an Office of Trust or Profit under the United States, shall be appointed an Elector.

The Electors shall meet in their respective States, and vote by Ballot for two Persons, of whom one at least shall not be an Inhabitant of the same State with themselves. And they shall make a List of all the Persons voted for, and of the Number of Votes for each; which List they shall sign and certify, and transmit sealed to the Seat of the Government of the United States, directed to the President of the Senate. The President of the Senate shall, in the Presence of the Senate and House of Representatives, open all the Certificates, and the Votes shall then be counted. The Person having the greatest Number of Votes shall be the President, if such Number be a Majority of the whole Number of Electors appointed; and if there be more than one who have such Majority, and have an equal Number of Votes, then the House of Representatives shall immediately chuse by Ballot one of them for President; and if no Person have a Majority, then from the five highest on the List the said House shall in like Manner chuse the President. But in chusing the President, the Votes shall be taken by States, the Representation from each State having one Vote; A quorum for this purpose shall consist of a Member or Members from two thirds of the States, and a Majority of all the States shall be necessary to a Choice. In every Case, after the Choice of the President, the Person having the greatest Number of Votes of the Electors shall be the Vice President. But if there should remain two or more who have equal Votes, the Senate shall chuse from them by Ballot the Vice President.

The Congress may determine the Time of chusing the Electors, and the Day on which they shall give their Votes; which Day shall be the same throughout the United States.

No Person except a natural born Citizen, or a Citizen of the United States, at the time of the Adoption of this Constitution, shall be eligible to the Office of President; neither shall any Person be eligible to that Office who shall not have attained to the Age of thirty five Years, and been fourteen Years a Resident within the United States.

In Case of the Removal of the President from Office, or of his Death, Resignation, or Inability to discharge the Powers and Duties of the said Office, the Same shall devolve on the Vice President, and the Congress may by Law provide for the Case of Removal, Death, Resignation or Inability, both of the President and Vice President, declaring what Officer shall then act as President, and such Officer shall act accordingly, until the Disability be removed, or a President shall be elected.

The President shall, at stated Times, receive for his Services, a Compensation, which shall neither be increased nor diminished during the Period for which he shall have been elected, and he shall not receive within that Period any other Emolument from the United States, or any of them.

Before he enter on the Execution of his Office, he shall take the following Oath or Affirmation:—"I do solemnly swear (or affirm) that I will faithfully execute the Office of President of the United States, and will to the best of my Ability, preserve, protect and defend the Constitution of the United States."

Section 2: The President shall be Commander in Chief of the Army and Navy of the United States, and of the Militia of the several States, when called into the actual Service of the United States; he may require the Opinion, in writing, of the principal Officer in each of the executive Departments, upon any Subject relating to the Duties of their respective Offices, and he shall have Power to grant Reprieves and Pardons for Offences against the United States, except in Cases of Impeachment. He shall have Power, by and with the Advice and Consent of the Senate, to make Treaties, provided two thirds of the Senators present concur; and he shall nominate, and by and with the Advice and Consent of the Senate, shall appoint Ambassadors, other public Ministers and Consuls, Judges of the supreme Court, and all other Officers of the United States, whose Appointments are not herein otherwise provided for, and which shall be established by Law: but the Congress may by Law vest the Appointment of such inferior Officers, as they think proper, in the President alone, in the Courts of Law, or in the Heads of Departments.

The President shall have Power to fill up all Vacancies that may happen during the Recess of the Senate, by granting Commissions which shall expire at the End of their next Session.

Section 3: He shall from time to time give to the Congress Information of the State of the Union, and recommend to their Consideration such Measures as he shall judge necessary and expedient; he may, on extraordinary Occasions, convene both Houses, or either of them, and in Case of Disagreement between them, with Respect to the Time of Adjournment, he may adjourn them to such Time as he shall think proper; he shall receive Ambassadors and other public Ministers; he shall take Care that the Laws be faithfully executed, and shall Commission all the Officers of the United States.

Section 4. The President, Vice President and all civil Officers of the United States, shall be removed from Office on Impeachment for, and Conviction of, Treason, Bribery, or other high Crimes and Misdemeanors.

ARTICLE III
A portion of Section 2 was modified by the Eleventh Amendment

Section 1: The judicial Power of the United States shall be vested in one supreme Court, and in such inferior Courts as the Congress may from time to time ordain and establish. The Judges, both of the supreme and inferior Courts, shall hold their Offices during good Behaviour, and shall, at stated Times, receive for their Services a Compensation, which shall not be diminished during their Continuance in Office.

Section 2: The judicial Power shall extend to all Cases, in Law and Equity, arising under this Constitution, the Laws of the United States, and Treaties made, or which shall be made, under their Authority;—to all Cases affecting Ambassadors, other public Ministers and Consuls;—to all Cases of admiralty and maritime Jurisdiction;—to Controversies to which the United States shall be a Party; to Controversies between two or more States;—*between a State and Citizens of another State;*—between Citizens of different States; between Citizens of the same State claiming Lands under Grants of different States, and between a State, or the Citizens thereof, and foreign States, Citizens or Subjects.

In all Cases affecting Ambassadors, other public Ministers and Consuls, and those in which a State shall be Party, the supreme Court shall have original Jurisdiction. In all the other Cases before mentioned, the supreme Court shall have appellate Jurisdiction, both as to Law and Fact, with such Exceptions, and under such Regulations as the Congress shall make.

The Trial of all Crimes, except in Cases of Impeachment, shall be by Jury; and such Trial shall be held in the State where the said Crimes shall have been committed; but when not committed within any State, the Trial shall be at such Place or Places as the Congress may by Law have directed.

Section 3: Treason against the United States, shall consist only in levying War against them, or in adhering to their Enemies, giving them Aid and Comfort. No Person shall be convicted of Treason unless on the Testimony of two Witnesses to the same overt Act, or on Confession in open Court.

The Congress shall have Power to declare the Punishment of Treason, but no Attainder of Treason shall work Corruption of Blood, or Forfeiture except during the Life of the Person attainted.

ARTICLE IV
A portion of Section 2 was superseded by the Thirteenth Amendment.

Section 1: Full Faith and Credit shall be given in each State to the public Acts, Records, and judicial Proceedings of every other State. And the Congress may by general Laws prescribe the Manner in which such Acts, Records and Proceedings shall be proved, and the Effect thereof.

Section 2: The Citizens of each State shall be entitled to all Privileges and Immunities of Citizens in the several States.

A Person charged in any State with Treason, Felony, or other Crime, who shall flee from Justice, and be found in another State, shall on Demand of the executive Authority of the State from which he fled, be delivered up, to be removed to the State having Jurisdiction of the Crime.

No Person held to Service or Labour in one State, under the Laws thereof, escaping into another, shall, in Consequence of any Law or Regulation therein, be discharged from such Service or Labour, but shall be delivered up on Claim of the Party to whom such Service or Labour may be due.

Section 3: New States may be admitted by the Congress into this Union; but no new State shall be formed or erected within the Jurisdiction of any other State; nor any State be formed by the Junction of two or more States, or Parts of States, without the Consent of the Legislatures of the States concerned as well as of the Congress.

The Congress shall have Power to dispose of and make all needful Rules and Regulations respecting the Territory or other Property belonging to the United States; and nothing in this Constitution shall be so construed as to Prejudice any Claims of the United States, or of any particular State.

Section 4: The United States shall guarantee to every State in this Union a Republican Form of Government, and shall protect each of them against Invasion; and on Application of the Legislature, or of the Executive (when the Legislature cannot be convened), against domestic Violence.

ARTICLE V

The Congress, whenever two thirds of both Houses shall deem it necessary, shall propose Amendments to this Constitution, or, on the Application of the Legislatures of two thirds of the several States, shall call a Convention for proposing Amendments, which, in either Case, shall be valid to all Intents and Purposes, as Part of this Constitution, when ratified by the Legislatures of three fourths of the several States, or by Conventions in three fourths thereof, as the one or the other Mode of Ratification may be proposed by the Congress; Provided that no Amendment which may be made prior to the Year One thousand eight hundred and eight shall in any Manner affect the first and fourth Clauses in the Ninth Section of the first Article; and that no State, without its Consent, shall be deprived of its equal Suffrage in the Senate.

ARTICLE VI

All Debts contracted and Engagements entered into, before the Adoption of this Constitution, shall be as valid against the United States under this Constitution, as under the Confederation.

This Constitution, and the Laws of the United States which shall be made in Pursuance thereof; and all Treaties made, or which shall be made, under the Authority of the United States, shall be the supreme Law of the Land; and the Judges in every State shall be bound thereby, any Thing in the Constitution or Laws of any State to the Contrary notwithstanding.

The Senators and Representatives before mentioned, and the Members of the several State Legislatures, and all executive and judicial Officers, both of the United States and of the several States, shall be bound by Oath or Affirmation, to support this Constitution; but no religious Test shall ever be required as a Qualification to any Office or public Trust under the United States.

ARTICLE VII

The Ratification of the Conventions of nine States, shall be sufficient for the Establishment of this Constitution between the States so ratifying the Same.

Attest William Jackson Secretary

Done in Convention by the Unanimous Consent of the States present the Seventeenth Day of September in the Year of our Lord one thousand seven hundred and Eighty seven and of the Independence of the United States of America the Twelfth In witness whereof We have hereunto subscribed our Names,

Go. Washington Presidt and deputy from Virginia
Delaware: Geo: Read, Gunning Bedford jun, John Dickinson, Richard Bassett, Jaco: Broom
Maryland: James McHenry, Dan of St Thos. Jenifer, Danl. Carroll
Virginia: John Blair—, James Madison Jr.
North Carolina: Wm. Blount, Richd. Dobbs Spaight, Hu Williamson
South Carolina: J. Rutledge, Charles Cotesworth Pinckney, Charles Pinckney, Pierce Butler
Georgia: William Few, Abr Baldwin
New Hampshire: John Langdon, Nicholas Gilman
Massachusetts: Nathaniel Gorham, Rufus King
Connecticut: Wm. Saml. Johnson Roger Sherman
New York: Alexander Hamilton
New Jersey: Wil: Livingston, David Brearley, Wm. Paterson, Jona: Dayton
Pennsylvania: B Franklin, Thomas Mifflin, Robt. Morris, Geo. Clymer, Thos. FitzSimons, Jared Ingersoll, James Wilson, Gouv Morris

AMENDMENTS TO THE CONSTITUTION

The first 10 amendments to the Constitution were ratified December 15, 1791, and form what is known as the "Bill of Rights."

AMENDMENT I

Congress shall make no law respecting an establishment of religion, or prohibiting the free exercise thereof; or abridging the freedom of speech, or of the press; or the right of the people peaceably to assemble, and to petition the Government for a redress of grievances.

AMENDMENT II

A well regulated Militia, being necessary to the security of a free State, the right of the people to keep and bear Arms, shall not be infringed.

AMENDMENT III

No Soldier shall, in time of peace be quartered in any house, without the consent of the Owner, nor in time of war, but in a manner to be prescribed by law.

AMENDMENT IV

The right of the people to be secure in their persons, houses, papers, and effects, against unreasonable searches and seizures, shall not be violated, and no Warrants shall issue, but upon probable cause, supported by Oath or affirmation, and particularly describing the place to be searched, and the persons or things to be seized.

AMENDMENT V

No person shall be held to answer for a capital, or otherwise infamous crime, unless on a presentment or indictment of a Grand Jury, except in cases arising in the land or naval forces, or in the Militia, when in actual service in time of War or public danger; nor shall any person be subject for the same offence to be twice put in jeopardy of life or limb; nor shall be compelled in any criminal case to be a witness against himself, nor be deprived of life, liberty, or property, without due process of law; nor shall private property be taken for public use, without just compensation.

AMENDMENT VI

In all criminal prosecutions, the accused shall enjoy the right to a speedy and public trial, by an impartial jury of the State and district wherein the crime shall have been committed, which district shall have been previously ascertained by law, and to be informed of the nature and cause of the accusation; to be confronted with the witnesses against him; to have compulsory process for obtaining witnesses in his favor, and to have the Assistance of Counsel for his defence.

AMENDMENT VII

In suits at common law, where the value in controversy shall exceed twenty dollars, the right of trial by jury shall be preserved, and no fact tried by a jury, shall be otherwise reexamined in any Court of the United States, than according to the rules of the common law.

AMENDMENT VIII

Excessive bail shall not be required, nor excessive fines imposed, nor cruel and unusual punishments inflicted.

AMENDMENT IX

The enumeration in the Constitution, of certain rights, shall not be construed to deny or disparage others retained by the people.

AMENDMENT X

The powers not delegated to the United States by the Constitution, nor prohibited by it to the States, are reserved to the States respectively, or to the people.

AMENDMENT XI

Passed by Congress March 4, 1794. Ratified February 7, 1795. A portion of Article III, Section 2, was modified by the Eleventh Amendment.

The Judicial power of the United States shall not be construed to extend to any suit in law or equity, commenced or prosecuted against one of the United States by Citizens of another State, or by Citizens or Subjects of any Foreign State.

AMENDMENT XII

Passed by Congress December 9, 1803. Ratified June 15, 1804. A portion of Article II, Section 1, was superseded by the Twelfth Amendment. A portion of the Twelfth Amendment was superseded by Section 3 of the Twentieth Amendment.

The Electors shall meet in their respective states and vote by ballot for President and Vice-President, one of whom, at least, shall not be an inhabitant of the same state with themselves; they shall name in their ballots the person voted for as President, and in distinct ballots the person voted for as Vice-President, and they shall make distinct lists of all persons voted for as President, and of all persons voted for as Vice-President, and of the number of votes for each, which lists they shall sign and certify, and transmit sealed to the seat of the government of the United States, directed to the President of the Senate;—the President of the Senate shall, in the presence of the Senate and House of Representatives, open all the certificates and the votes shall then be counted;—The person having the greatest number of votes for President, shall be the President, if such number be a majority of the whole number of Electors appointed; and if no person have such majority, then from the persons having the highest numbers not exceeding three on the list of those voted for as President, the House of Representatives shall choose immediately, by ballot, the President. But in choosing the President, the votes shall be taken by states, the representation from each state having one vote; a quorum for this purpose shall consist of a member or members from two-thirds of the states, and a majority of all the states shall be necessary to a choice. *And if the House of Representatives shall not choose a President whenever the right of choice shall devolve upon them, before the fourth day of March next following, then the Vice-President shall act as President, as in case of the death or other constitutional disability of the President.*—The person having the greatest number of votes as Vice-President, shall be the Vice-President, if such number be a majority of the whole number of Electors appointed, and if no person have a majority, then from the two highest numbers on the list, the Senate shall choose the Vice-President; a quorum for the purpose shall consist of two-thirds of the whole number of Senators, and a majority of the whole number shall be necessary to a choice. But no person constitutionally ineligible to the office of President shall be eligible to that of Vice-President of the United States.

AMENDMENT XIII

Passed by Congress January 31, 1865. Ratified December 6, 1865. A portion of Article IV, Section 2, was superseded by the Thirteenth Amendment.

Section 1: Neither slavery nor involuntary servitude, except as a punishment for crime whereof the party shall have been duly convicted, shall exist within the United States, or any place subject to their jurisdiction.

Section 2: Congress shall have power to enforce this article by appropriate legislation.

AMENDMENT XIV

Passed by Congress June 13, 1866. Ratified July 9, 1868. A portion of Article I, Section 2, was modified by Section 2 of the Fourteenth Amendment. A portion of the Fourteenth Amendment was modified by Section 1 of the Twenty-sixth Amendment.

Section 1: All persons born or naturalized in the United States, and subject to the jurisdiction thereof, are citizens of the United States and of the State wherein they reside. No State shall make or enforce any law which shall abridge the privileges or immunities of citizens of the United States; nor shall any State deprive any person of life, liberty, or property, without due process of law; nor deny to any person within its jurisdiction the equal protection of the laws.

Section 2: Representatives shall be apportioned among the several States according to their respective numbers, counting the whole number of persons in each State, excluding Indians not taxed. But when the right to vote at any election for the choice of electors for President and Vice-President of the United States, Representatives in Congress, the Executive and Judicial officers of a State, or the members of the Legislature thereof, is denied to any of the male inhabitants of such State, *being twenty-one years of age,* and citizens of the United States, or in any way abridged, except for participation in rebellion, or other crime, the basis of representation therein shall be reduced in the proportion which the number of such male citizens shall bear to the whole number of male citizens twenty-one years of age in such State.

Section 3: No person shall be a Senator or Representative in Congress, or elector of President and Vice-President, or hold any office, civil or military, under the United States, or under any State, who, having previously taken an oath, as a member of Congress, or as an officer of the United States, or as a member of any State legislature, or as an executive or judicial officer of any State, to support the Constitution of the United States, shall have engaged in insurrection or rebellion against the same, or given aid or comfort to the enemies thereof. But Congress may by a vote of two-thirds of each House, remove such disability.

Section 4: The validity of the public debt of the United States, authorized by law, including debts incurred for payment of pensions and bounties for services in suppressing insurrection or rebellion, shall not be questioned. But neither the United States nor any State shall assume or pay any debt or obligation incurred in aid of insurrection or rebellion against the United States, or any claim for the loss or emancipation of any slave; but all such debts, obligations and claims shall be held illegal and void.

Section 5: The Congress shall have the power to enforce, by appropriate legislation, the provisions of this article.

AMENDMENT XV
Passed by Congress February 26, 1869. Ratified February 3, 1870.

Section 1: The right of citizens of the United States to vote shall not be denied or abridged by the United States or by any State on account of race, color, or previous condition of servitude—

Section 2: The Congress shall have the power to enforce this article by appropriate legislation.

AMENDMENT XVI

Passed by Congress July 12, 1909. Ratified February 3, 1913. A portion of Article I, Section 9, was modified by the Sixteenth Amendment.

The Congress shall have power to lay and collect taxes on incomes, from whatever source derived, without apportionment among the several States, and without regard to any census or enumeration.

AMENDMENT XVII

Passed by Congress May 13, 1912. Ratified April 8, 1913. Portions of Article I, Section 3, were modified by the Seventeenth Amendment.

The Senate of the United States shall be composed of two Senators from each State, elected by the people thereof, for six years; and each Senator shall have one vote. The electors in each State shall have the qualifications requisite for electors of the most numerous branch of the State legislatures.

When vacancies happen in the representation of any State in the Senate, the executive authority of such State shall issue writs of election to fill such vacancies: Provided, That the legislature of any State may empower the executive thereof to make temporary appointments until the people fill the vacancies by election as the legislature may direct.

This amendment shall not be so construed as to affect the election or term of any Senator chosen before it becomes valid as part of the Constitution.

AMENDMENT XVIII

Passed by Congress December 18, 1917. Ratified January 16, 1919. Repealed by the Twenty-first Amendment.

Section 1: After one year from the ratification of this article the manufacture, sale, or transportation of intoxicating liquors within, the importation thereof into, or the exportation thereof from the United States and all territory subject to the jurisdiction thereof for beverage purposes is hereby prohibited.

Section 2: The Congress and the several States shall have concurrent power to enforce this article by appropriate legislation.

Section 3: This article shall be inoperative unless it shall have been ratified as an amendment to the Constitution by the legislatures of the several States, as provided in the Constitution, within seven years from the date of the submission hereof to the States by the Congress.

AMENDMENT XIX

Passed by Congress June 4, 1919. Ratified August 18, 1920.

The right of citizens of the United States to vote shall not be denied or abridged by the United States or by any State on account of sex.

Congress shall have power to enforce this article by appropriate legislation.

AMENDMENT XX

Passed by Congress March 2, 1932. Ratified January 23, 1933. A portion of Article I, Section 4, was modified by Section 2 of the Twentieth Amendment. In addition, a portion of the Twelfth Amendment was superseded by Section 3 of the Twentieth Amendment.

Section 1: The terms of the President and the Vice President shall end at noon on the 20th day of January, and the terms of Senators and Representatives at noon on the 3d day of January, of the years in which such terms would have ended if this article had not been ratified; and the terms of their successors shall then begin.

Section 2: The Congress shall assemble at least once in every year, and such meeting shall begin at noon on the 3d day of January, unless they shall by law appoint a different day.

Section 3: If, at the time fixed for the beginning of the term of the President, the President elect shall have died, the Vice President elect shall become President. If a President shall not have been chosen before the time fixed for the beginning of his term, or if the President elect shall have failed to qualify, then the Vice President elect shall act as President until a President shall have qualified; and the Congress may by law provide for the case wherein neither a President elect nor a Vice President shall have qualified, declaring who shall then act as President, or the manner in which one who is to act shall be selected, and such person shall act accordingly until a President or Vice President shall have qualified.

Section 4: The Congress may by law provide for the case of the death of any of the persons from whom the House of Representatives may choose a President whenever the right of choice shall have devolved upon them, and for the case of the death of any of the persons from whom the Senate may choose a Vice President whenever the right of choice shall have devolved upon them.

Section 5: Sections 1 and 2 shall take effect on the 15th day of October following the ratification of this article.

Section 6: This article shall be inoperative unless it shall have been ratified as an amendment to the Constitution by the legislatures of three-fourths of the several States within seven years from the date of its submission.

AMENDMENT XXI

Passed by Congress February 20, 1933. Ratified December 5, 1933.
Repealed the Eighteenth Amendment.

Section 1: The eighteenth article of amendment to the Constitution of the United States is hereby repealed.

Section 2: The transportation or importation into any State, Territory, or Possession of the United States for delivery or use therein of intoxicating liquors, in violation of the laws thereof, is hereby prohibited.

Section 3: This article shall be inoperative unless it shall have

been ratified as an amendment to the Constitution by conventions in the several States, as provided in the Constitution, within seven years from the date of the submission hereof to the States by the Congress.

AMENDMENT XXII

Passed by Congress March 21, 1947. Ratified February 27, 1951.

Section 1: No person shall be elected to the office of the President more than twice, and no person who has held the office of President, or acted as President, for more than two years of a term to which some other person was elected President shall be elected to the office of President more than once. But this Article shall not apply to any person holding the office of President when this Article was proposed by Congress, and shall not prevent any person who may be holding the office of President, or acting as President, during the term within which this Article becomes operative from holding the office of President or acting as President during the remainder of such term.

Section 2: This article shall be inoperative unless it shall have been ratified as an amendment to the Constitution by the legislatures of three-fourths of the several States within seven years from the date of its submission to the States by the Congress.

AMENDMENT XXIII

Passed by Congress June 16, 1960. Ratified March 29, 1961.

Section 1: The District constituting the seat of Government of the United States shall appoint in such manner as Congress may direct:

A number of electors of President and Vice President equal to the whole number of Senators and Representatives in Congress to which the District would be entitled if it were a State, but in no event more than the least populous State; they shall be in addition to those appointed by the States, but they shall be considered, for the purposes of the election of President and Vice President, to be electors appointed by a State; and they shall meet in the District and perform such duties as provided by the twelfth article of amendment.

Section 2: The Congress shall have power to enforce this article by appropriate legislation.

AMENDMENT XXIV

Passed by Congress August 27, 1962. Ratified January 23, 1964.

Section 1: The right of citizens of the United States to vote in any primary or other election for President or Vice President, for electors for President or Vice President, or for Senator or Representative in Congress, shall not be denied or abridged by the United States or any State by reason of failure to pay poll tax or other tax.

Section 2: The Congress shall have power to enforce this article by appropriate legislation.

AMENDMENT XXV

Passed by Congress July 6, 1965. Ratified February 10, 1967. A portion of Article II, Section 1, was modified by the Twenty-fifth Amendment.

Section 1: In case of the removal of the President from office or of his death or resignation, the Vice President shall become President.

Section 2: Whenever there is a vacancy in the office of the Vice President, the President shall nominate a Vice President who shall take office upon confirmation by a majority vote of both Houses of Congress.

Section 3: Whenever the President transmits to the President pro tempore of the Senate and the Speaker of the House of Representatives his written declaration that he is unable to discharge the powers and duties of his office, and until he transmits to them a written declaration to the contrary, such powers and duties shall be discharged by the Vice President as Acting President.

Section 4: Whenever the Vice President and a majority of either the principal officers of the executive departments or of such other body as Congress may by law provide, transmit to the President pro tempore of the Senate and the Speaker of the House of Representatives their written declaration that the President is unable to discharge the powers and duties of his office, the Vice President shall immediately assume the powers and duties of the office as Acting President.

Thereafter, when the President transmits to the President pro tempore of the Senate and the Speaker of the House of Representatives his written declaration that no inability exists, he shall resume the powers and duties of his office unless the Vice President and a majority of either the principal officers of the executive department or of such other body as Congress may by law provide, transmit within four days to the President pro tempore of the Senate and the Speaker of the House of Representatives their written declaration that the President is unable to discharge the powers and duties of his office. Thereupon Congress shall decide the issue, assembling within forty-eight hours for that purpose if not in session. If the Congress, within twenty-one days after receipt of the latter written declaration, or, if Congress is not in session, within twenty-one days after Congress is required to assemble, determines by two-thirds vote of both Houses that the President is unable to discharge the powers and duties of his office, the Vice President shall continue to discharge the same as Acting President; otherwise, the President shall resume the powers and duties of his office.

AMENDMENT XXVI

Passed by Congress March 23, 1971. Ratified July 1, 1971. A portion of the Fourteenth Amendment, Section 2, was modified by Section 1 of the Twenty-sixth Amendment.

Section 1: The right of citizens of the United States, who are eighteen years of age or older, to vote shall not be denied or abridged by the United States or by any State on account of age.

Section 2: The Congress shall have power to enforce this article by appropriate legislation.

AMENDMENT XXVII

Originally proposed Sept. 25, 1789. Ratified May 7, 1992.

No law, varying the compensation for the services of the Senators and Representatives, shall take effect, until an election of representatives shall have intervened.

TIMELINE

YEAR	PRESIDENT	CONGRESS	US HISTORY	LEGISLATION
1787			Constitutional Convention, Independence Hall, Philadelphia	Northwest Ordinance
1788			Congress picks New York City as site of government	
1789	George Washington: 1789–1797 (Nonpartisan)	1st 1789–1791 Senate: 17 F; 9 Opp. House: 38 F; 26 Opp.	House of Representatives, Senate, executive branch organized, Supreme Court is established George Washington inaugurated in New York City Pres. Washington signs first act of Congress	Judiciary Act Tariff Act of 1789
1790			1st census: U.S. population 3,929,214 Congress meets in Philadelphia, new temporary capital Congress submits Bill of Rights to states for ratification Supreme Court meets for the first time	Copyright Act of 1790 Naturalization Act Patent Act Southwest Ordinance
1791		2d 1791–1793 Senate: 16 F; 13 DR House: 37 F; 33 DR	Bill of Rights ratified	Bank of the United States
1792			U.S. Mint established through Coinage Act New York Stock Exchange organized Cornerstone to White House laid	Coinage Act of 1792
1793		3d 1793–1795 Senate: 17 F; 13 DR House: 57 DR; 48 F	Cotton gin invented by Eli Whitney	Anti-Injunction Act Fugitive Slave Act of 1793

YEAR	PRESIDENT	CONGRESS	US HISTORY	LEGISLATION
1794			Excise tax on distilled liquor causes Whiskey Rebellion Creation of U.S. Navy authorized by Congress	
1795		4th 1795–1797 Senate: 19 F; 13 DR House: 54 F; 52 DR	Eleventh Amendment goes into effect (limits judicial powers) First state university, University of North Carolina, opens	
1796			*Hylton v. United States* is first Supreme Court case that upholds an act of Congress George Washington's farewell address is published, but never delivered as speech	
1797	John Adams: 1797–1801 (Federalist)	5th 1797–1799 Senate: 20 F; 12 DR House: 58 F; 48 DR	Congress creates 80,000 member militia	
1798			Undeclared war with France begins (conflict ends 1800) Rebellion in Haiti ends slavery there; many white Haitians flee to U.S., increasing fears among whites of slave rebellion and French revolution	Alien and Sedition Acts
1799		6th 1799–1801 Senate: 19 F; 13 DR House: 64 F; 42 DR		
1800			2d census: U.S. population 5,308,483 Library of Congress established Site of government moves to Washington, DC	
1801	Thomas Jefferson: 1801–1809 (Democratic-Republican)	7th 1801–1803 Senate: 18 DR; 13 F House: 69 DR; 36 F		Judiciary Act of 1801
1802				
1803		8th 1803–1805 Senate: 25 DR; 9 F House: 102 DR; 39 F	*Marbury v. Madison* is first Supreme Court case that declares an act of Congress unconstitutional Lewis and Clark expedition begins Louisiana Purchase (U.S. purchased about 828,000 square miles between the Mississippi River and Rocky Mountains from France, for $15 million)	
1804			Twelfth amendment ratified (separate ballots for president and vice president)	

YEAR	PRESIDENT	CONGRESS	US HISTORY	LEGISLATION
1805		9th 1805–1807 Senate: 27 DR; 7F House: 116 DR; 25 F		
1806				
1807		10th 1807–1809 Senate: 28 DR; 6 F House: 118 DR; 24 F	Steamboat (Robert Fulton's *Clermont*) completes round trip from New York to Albany in 62 hours, first practical steamboat trip Importation of slaves into the U.S. prohibited	Prohibition of the Slave Trade
1808			Anthracite coal first used as stove fuel in Pennsylvania	
1809	James Madison: 1809–1817 (Democratic-Republican)	11th 1809–1811 Senate: 28 DR; 6 F House: 94 DR; 48 F	Supreme Court case *United States v. Peters* affirms federal government power over states	Nonintercourse Act
1810			3d census: U.S. population 7,239,881 Revolt against Spanish by southern expansionists results in the U.S. gaining territory in the south	
1811		12th 1811–1813 Senate: 30 DR; 6 F House: 108 DR; 36 F	Non-intercourse policy against Great Britain renewed Senate declines to renew charter of Bank of the United States Construction of Cumberland Road begins (completed 1818; Cumberland, MD, to Wheeling, WV)	
1812			First war-bond issue; first interest-bearing U.S. Treasury notes are authorized War is declared on Great Britain (War of 1812, 1812–1814)	
1813		13th 1813–1815 Senate: 27 DR; 9 F House: 112 DR; 68 F	Creek War with Indian nations in southern United States	
1814			Peace treaty signed ending Creek War; Americans led to victory over Native Americans by Gen. Andrew Jackson Treaty of Ghent (Belgium) signed ending war with Britain	
1815		14th 1815–1817 Senate: 25 DR; 11 F House: 117 DR; 65 F	Treaties signed with Algiers, Tunis, and Tripoli ending piracy on U.S. ships	

YEAR	PRESIDENT	CONGRESS	US HISTORY	LEGISLATION
1816			Second Bank of United States is created	
1817	James Monroe: 1817–1825 (Democratic-Republican)	15th 1817–1819 Senate: 34 DR; 10 F House: 141 DR; 42 F	First Seminole War begins; Andrew Jackson named as commander of U.S. forces	
1818			Seminole War ends after American capture of St. Marks and Pensacola, FL	
1819		16th 1819–1821 Senate: 35 DR; 7 F House: 156 DR; 27 F	Adams-Onis treaty signed with Spain; Spain cedes East Florida to U.S., ends claim on West Florida Financial panic of 1819, economic recession begins First American savings banks open and begin paying interest on deposits	
1820			4th census: U.S. population 9,638,453	Missouri Compromise
1821		17th 1821–1823 Senate: 44 DR; 4 F House: 158 DR; 25 F	Republic of Liberia founded by American Colonization Society as haven for freed African-American slaves Sante Fe trail opened (Independence, MO, to Sante Fe, NM)	
1822			Planned slave revolt in Charleston, SC, blocked	
1823		18th 1823–1825 Senate: 44 DR; 4 F House: 187 DR; 26 F	In annual message to Congress, Pres. Monroe lays out what will become known as the Monroe Doctrine Treaties signed with Osage and Kansa Indian nations that cede lands in present-day Kansas, Oklahoma, and Missouri to the U.S. Great Britain abolishes slavery in its territories	
1824			Supreme Court case *Gibbons v. Ogden* upholds Congress's power to regulate interstate commerce	
1825	John Quincy Adams: 1825–1829 (Democratic-Republican)	19th 1825–1827 Senate: 26 A; 20 J House: 105 A; 97 J	Erie canal opens between Buffalo, NY, and New York City	
1826			John Stevens demonstrates use of first steam locomotive in Hoboken, NJ	

YEAR	PRESIDENT	CONGRESS	US HISTORY	LEGISLATION
1827		20th 1827–1829 Senate: 28 J; 20 A House: 119 J; 94 A	Mechanics Union of Trades Association, first central labor union, is created in Philadelphia	
1828			Treaty signed by United States and Mexico establishes Sabine River as common boundary	
1829	Andrew Jackson: 1829–1837 (Democratic)	21st 1829–1831 Senate: 26 D; 22 NR House: 139 D; 74 NR		
1830			5th census: U.S. population 12,860,702 Various Native American tribes sign treaties ceding western lands of present-day Iowa, Missouri, and Minnesota Mexico prohibits further settlement of Texas by Americans Baltimore & Ohio Railroad begins operation (first U.S. passenger railroad)	Indian Removal Act
1831		22d 1831–1833 Senate: 25 D; 21 NR; 2 O House: 141 D; 58 NR; 14 O	Nat Turner leads a slave rebellion in Virginia, is captured and executed along with 19 other blacks First U.S. built locomotive goes into service	
1832			Black Hawk War with Sac and Fox Indians; Creek nation cedes all its lands east of the Mississippi River to the United States; Seminoles cede lands in Florida Virginia legislature considers, but rejects, gradual termination of slavery	
1833		23d 1833–1835 Senate: 20 D; 20 NR; 8 O House: 147 D; 53 AM; 60 O	Oberlin College (Ohio) is first college in U.S. to adopt coeducation	
1834				
1835		24th 1835–1837 Senate: 27 D; 25 W House: 145 D; 98 W	Texas declares independence from Mexico; Mexico establishes military state in Texas Second Seminole War begins in response to attempts to remove Seminoles by force Cherokee nation cedes lands east of the Mississippi River	

293

YEAR	PRESIDENT	CONGRESS	US HISTORY	LEGISLATION
1836			Siege of the Alamo in San Antonio, TX, by Mexicans; entire garrison killed Mexican general Santa Anna captured at Battle of San Jacinto; Sam Houston installed as president of Republic of Texas	
1837	Martin Van Buren: 1837–1841 (Democratic)	25th 1837–1839 Senate: 30 D; 18 W; 4 O House: 108 D; 107 W; 24 O	Financial panic of 1837 leads to economic depression that lasts until 1842	
1838			Underground railroad becomes force in assisting slaves to reach the North and Canada Forced removal of Cherokee Indians from their native land in Georgia to Oklahoma begins (Trail of Tears)	
1839		26th 1839–1841 Senate: 28 D; 22 W House: 124 D; 118 W		
1840			6th census: U.S. population 17,063,353 Great National Pike completed (Cumberland, MD, to Vandalia, IL; formerly known as the Cumberland Road)	
1841	William Henry Harrison: 1841 (Whig) John Tyler: 1841–1845 (Whig)	27th 1841–1843 Senate: 28 W; 22 D; 2 O House: 133 W; 102 D; 6 O	First wagon train leaves for California from Independence, MO (47 people)	Bankruptcy Act of 1841
1842			Dorr's Rebellion in Rhode Island (demanded new state constitution guaranteeing equal voting rights) Settlement of Oregon begins via Oregon Trail Webster-Ashburton Treaty fixes northern border of U.S. in Maine and Minnesota	
1843		28th 1843–1845 Senate: 28 W; 25 D; 1 O House: 142 D; 79 W; 1 O		
1844			Treaty of Wanghia signed with China; opens five Chinese ports to American commerce Commercial telegraph service begins	
1845	James K. Polk: 1845–1849 (Democratic)	29th 1845–1847 Senate: 31 D; 25 W House: 143 D; 77 W; 6 O	Texas annexed by U.S.; Mexico breaks off relations with U.S.	

YEAR	PRESIDENT	CONGRESS	US HISTORY	LEGISLATION
1846			Mexican-American War begins (1846–1848) Treaty with Great Britain setting northern boundary of Oregon Territory at 49th parallel	
1847		30th 1847–1849 Senate: 36 D; 21 W; 1 O House: 115 W; 108 D; 4 O	Establishment of new government in California begins after treaty ends Mexican-American War hostilities there	
1848			Treaty of Guadelupe Hidalgo ends Mexican-American War California gold rush begins First women's rights convention in Seneca Falls, NY	
1849	Zachary Taylor: 1849–1850 (Whig)	31st 1849–1851 Senate: 35 D; 25 W; 2 O House: 112 D; 109 W; 9 O	Mormons establish state of Deseret after migration to Utah from Illinois (1846); Deseret becomes Territory of Utah in 1850	
1850	Millard Fillmore: 1850–1853 (Whig)		7th census: U.S. population 23,191,876	Compromise of 1850 Fugitive Slave Act of 1850
1851		32d 1851–1853 Senate: 35 D; 24 W; 3 O House: 140 D; 88 W; 5 O		
1852			Harriet Beecher Stowe publishes *Uncle Tom's Cabin*	
1853	Franklin Pierce: 1853–1857 (Democratic)	33d 1853–1855 Senate: 38 D; 22 W; 2 O House: 159 D; 71 W; 4 O	Commodore Matthew Perry arrives in Japan to deliver letter from the president, who wants to open trade Gadsden Purchase (southern areas of present-day Arizona and New Mexico)	
1854			Treaty of Kanagawa opens Japanese ports to the U.S. Large-scale immigration of Chinese begins First American oil company incorporated (Pennsylvania Rock Oil Co.)	Kansas Nebraska Act
1855		34th 1855–1857 Senate: 40 D; 15 R; 5 O House: 108 R; 83 D; 43 O	U.S. Court of Claims established Congress authorizes construction of telegraph line from Mississippi River to Pacific Ocean	

YEAR	PRESIDENT	CONGRESS	US HISTORY	LEGISLATION
1856			Violence in Kansas breaks out between pro- and anti-slavery factions over question of slavery; federal troops keep temporary peace	
1857	James Buchanan: 1857–1861 (Democratic)	35th 1857–1859 Senate: 36 D; 20 R; 8 O House: 118 D; 92 R; 26 O	Dred Scott case decided by Supreme Court (decision says Scott is not a citizen, therefore cannot sue in federal court; his residence in a free state does not make him free; Missouri Compromise is unconstitutional) Financial panic results from speculation in railroad securities and real estate	
1858				
1859		36th 1859–1861 Senate: 36 D; 26 R; 4 O House: 114 R; 92 D; 31 O	Kansas approves constitution making it a free state Harper's Ferry incident (abolitionist John Brown and 21 other men seize a U.S. Armory, are captured, Brown is hanged) First trip of a Pullman sleeping car on a railroad is completed	
1860			8th census: U.S. population 31,443,321 South Carolina is first state to secede from Union	
1861	Abraham Lincoln: 1861–1865 (Republican)	37th 1861–1863 Senate: 31 R; 10 D; 8 O House: 105 R; 43 D; 30 O	Confederate government created; Jefferson Davis elected president of the Confederacy Civil War begins (1861–1865) First transcontinental telegraph line is completed	Civil War Pensions First Confiscation Act
1862				Homestead Act Militia Act Morrill Land Grant Act Second Confiscation Act
1863		38th 1863–1865 Senate: 36 R; 9 D; 5 O House: 102 R; 75 D; 9 O	Pres. Lincoln issues Emancipation Proclamation Draft riots in New York City, about 1000 killed, some blacks lynched	Enrollment Act (Conscription Act)
1864			J. P. Morgan & Co. established	National Bank Act

YEAR	PRESIDENT	CONGRESS	US HISTORY	LEGISLATION
1865	Andrew Johnson: 1865–1869 (Democratic)	39th 1865–1867 Senate: 42 U; 10 D House: 149 U; 42 D	Gen. Robert E. Lee surrenders to Gen. U. S. Grant at Appomattox Court House Pres. Abraham Lincoln assassinated in Ford's Theater, Washington, DC Thirteenth Amendment is ratified (abolished slavery)	Freedmen's Bureau Act
1866			Reconstruction of the South begins Ku Klux Klan founded Fourteenth Amendment enacted by Congress (guarantees that no person is to be denied life, liberty, or pursuit of happiness by a state without due process of law) First refrigerated rail car built	Civil Rights Act of 1866
1867		40th 1867–1869 Senate: 42 R; 11 D House: 143 R; 49 D	U.S. purchases Alaska from Russia for $7.2 million National Grange is formed to protect farmer's interests	Reconstruction Acts (1867–1868)
1868			House of Representatives votes to impeach Andrew Johnson for violating the Tenure of Office Act after he tries to remove the secretary of war from office; Senate one vote short of two-thirds required for conviction	
1869	Ulysses S. Grant: 1869–1877 (Republican)	41st 1869–1871 Senate: 56 R; 11 D House: 149 R; 63 D	Congress enacts Fifteenth Amendment (makes it illegal to deprive a citizen of the right to vote based on race, color, or previous condition of servitude) National Woman Suffrage Association organized Freedmen's Bureau goes out of operation First transcontinental railroad completed with the joining of Union Pacific and Central Pacific railroads at Promontory, UT Knights of Labor (national labor union) formed	
1870			9th census: U.S. population 38,558,371 Justice Department is created Standard Oil Co. is incorporated	

YEAR	PRESIDENT	CONGRESS	US HISTORY	LEGISLATION
1871		42d 1871–1873 Senate: 52 R; 17 D 5 O House: 134 R; 104 D; 5 O	The Tweed Ring in New York City (led by Boss William Tweed of Tammany Hall) is broken up Race riots against Chinese in Los Angeles; 15 lynched Disastrous fire in Chicago destroys over 17,000 buildings, leaves 100,000 homeless	Ku Klux Klan Act Force Act
1872				Mail Fraud Statute Yellowstone National Park Act
1873		43d 1873–1875 Senate: 49 R; 19 D; 5 O House: 194 R; 92 D; 14 O	U.S. monetary policy shifts from bimetallic standard to gold standard Financial panic of 1873 results in New York Stock Exchange closing for ten days, substantial unemployment, and drastic fall in security prices Bethlehem Steel Co. begins operating	Coinage Act Comstock Act
1874				
1875		44th 1875–1877 Senate: 45 R; 29 D; 2 O House: 169 D; 109 R; 14 O		Civil Rights Act of 1875
1876			Battle of Little Bighorn in Montana; Col. George Custer and 266 are surrounded and killed in "Custer's last stand" Alexander Graham Bell receives patent for telephone, makes first telephone call	
1877	Rutherford B. Hayes: 1877–1881 (Republican)	45th 1877–1879 Senate: 39 R; 36 D; 1 O House: 153 D; 140 R	Federal troops withdraw from South in return for allowing Rutherford B. Hayes to become president in disputed election (Compromise of 1877) Strike on Baltimore & Ohio Railroad in protest of wage cuts leads to strikes on other railroads; 100,000 workers eventually involved	

YEAR	PRESIDENT	CONGRESS	US HISTORY	LEGISLATION
1878			First commercial telephone exchange opened, New Haven, CT	Bland-Allison Act Posse Comitatus Act
1879		46th 1879–1881 Senate: 42 D; 33 R; 1 O House: 149 D; 130 R; 14 O	First Woolworth five-and-dime store opens Incandescent electric lamp invented by Thomas Edison	
1880			10th census: U.S. population 50,155,783	
1881	James A. Garfield: 1881 (Republican) Chester A. Arthur: 1881–1885 (Republican)	47th 1881–1883 Senate: 37 R; 37 D; 1 O House: 147 R; 135 D; 11 O	Pres. Garfield shot and killed in Washington, DC, by disappointed office seeker Sitting Bull and Sioux surrender to U.S. Army Southern Pacific Railroad completed (New Orleans to Pacific) Tuskegee Institute founded by Booker T. Washington Western Union Telegraph Co. formed	
1882			First trust formed by Standard Oil Co. Severe strikes in iron and steel industry	Chinese Exclusion Act
1883		48th 1883–1885 Senate: 38 R; 36 D; 2 O House: 197 D; 118 R; 10 O	Brooklyn Bridge in New York City completed Northern Pacific Railroad completed	Civil Services Act (Pendleton Act)
1884			Statue of Liberty presented to U.S. by France (arrives in U.S. 1885, dedicated 1886) First tall building to use steel beams is erected (Home Insurance Building, Chicago) First large-scale electric street car system established in Richmond, VA First long-distance telephone service established between New York and Boston	
1885	Grover Cleveland: 1885–1889 (Democratic)	49th 1885–1887 Senate: 43 R; 34 D House: 183 D; 140 R; 2 O		
1886			Apache Indians (Southwest) surrender to U.S. Haymarket Massacre in Chicago American Federation of Labor (AFL) organized by 25 labor groups	

YEAR	PRESIDENT	CONGRESS	US HISTORY	LEGISLATION
1887		50th 1887–1889 Senate: 39 R; 37 D House: 169 D; 152 R; 4 O	Free mail delivery begins in cities of 10,000 or more The Interstate Commerce Commission, first U.S. regulatory commission, is created to regulate railroads	Indian General Allotment Act (Dawes Act) Interstate Commerce Act
1888			Department of Labor established	
1889	Benjamin Harrison: 1889–1893 (Republican)	51st 1889–1891 Senate: 39 R; 37 D House: 166 R; 159 D	Carnegie Steel Co. organized by Andrew Carnegie	
1890			11th census: U.S. population 62,979,766 Sioux Indians are defeated at Wounded Knee; last major battle of Indian wars	Sherman Antitrust Act
1891		52d 1891–1893 Senate: 47 R; 39 D; 2 O House: 235 D; 88 R; 9 O	Immigration and Naturalization Service is established	
1892			Ellis Island opens as an immigration receiving station	
1893	Grover Cleveland:1893–1897 (Democratic)	53d 1893–1895 Senate: 44 D; 38 R; 3 O House: 218 D; 127 R; 11 O	Free mail delivery extended to rural communities Stock market crash, financial panic of 1893 begins, 491 banks and 15,000 commercial institutions fail; economy in severe depression until 1897	
1894			American Railway Union strikes at Pullman plant in Chicago; federal injunction breaks strike	1894 Income Tax and the Wilson-Gorman Tariff Act
1895		54th 1895–1897 Senate: 43 R; 39 D; 6 O House: 244 R; 105 D; 7 O	Internal combustion engine patented; first automobile company started	
1896			Supreme Court upholds Louisiana law calling for "separate but equal" accommodations on public transportation in *Plessy v. Ferguson*	
1897	William McKinley: 1897–1901 (Republican)	55th 1897–1899 Senate: 47 R; 34 D; 7 O House: 204 R; 113 D; 40 O	Thomas Edison patents a movie camera First section of a U.S. subway opens, in Boston	

YEAR	PRESIDENT	CONGRESS	US HISTORY	LEGISLATION
1898			Spanish-American War begins and ends; Spain cedes Puerto Rico, Philippines, and Guam to U.S. and relinquishes all claims to Cuba	
1899		56th 1899–1901 Senate: 53 R; 26 D; 8 O House: 197 R; 151 D; 9 O	Filipino nationalists revolt against U.S. First Hague Conference held; 26 nations participate	
1900			12th census: U.S. population 76,212,168 U.S. announces Open Door Policy in China (opens Chinese markets to all nations)	Gold Standard Act
1901	Theodore Roosevelt: 1901–1909 (Republican)	57th 1901–1903 Senate: 55 R; 31 D; 4 O House: 197 R; 151 D; 9 O	Pres. McKinley assassinated in Buffalo, NY, by an anarchist	
1902			Pres. Roosevelt asks attorney general to bring first antitrust suit to dissolve a railroad holding company	National Reclamation Act Panama Canal Purchase Act
1903		58th 1903–1905 Senate: 57 R; 33 D House: 208 R; 178 D	Hay-Herran Treaty with Colombia provides for 100-year lease of 10-mile-wide strip across isthmus of Panama for canal Wright brothers demonstrate first motor-driven airplane	
1904			Muckraker Ida Tarbell publishes *The History of the Standard Oil Company* First section of New York City subway opens	
1905		59th 1905–1907 Senate: 57 R; 33 D House: 250 R; 136 D		
1906			Upton Sinclair publishes *The Jungle*, muckraking account of the meat-packing industry Dow Jones Industrial Average closes over 100 for the first time	Antiquities Act Pure Food and Drug Act
1907		60th 1907–1909 Senate: 61 R; 31 D House: 222 R; 164 D	Food and Drug Administration begins operation Financial panic of 1907 Indiana passes world's first compulsory sterilization law for "all confirmed criminals, idiots, rapists, and imbeciles" held in state institutions; 32 states eventually adopt such laws	

YEAR	PRESIDENT	CONGRESS	US HISTORY	LEGISLATION
1908			Bureau of Investigation formed (later to become FBI) Model T automobile introduced by Henry Ford, sells for $850	Federal Employers' Liability Act
1909	William Howard Taft:1909–1913 (Republican)	61st 1909–1911 Senate: 61 R; 32 D House: 219 R; 172 D	Congress passes Sixteenth Amendment (allows federal income tax; ratified 1913) NAACP created	Corporate Income Tax Act
1910			13th Census: U.S. population 92,228,496	Mann Act
1911		62d 1911–1913 Senate: 51 R; 41 D House: 228 D; 161 R; 1 O	Supreme Court orders dissolution of Standard Oil Co. as a monopoly; same goes for the American Tobacco Co. and the DuPont Co.	
1912				
1913	Woodrow Wilson: 1913–1921 (Democratic)	63d 1913–1915 Senate: 51 D; 44 R; 1 O House: 291 D; 127 R; 17 O	Seventeenth Amendment ratified (calls for popular election of senators) First drive-in gasoline station opens in Pittsburgh, PA Ford Motor Co. introduces conveyor-belt assembly-line production of cars	Federal Income Tax Act of 1913 Federal Reserve Act
1914			War breaks out in Europe; Woodrow Wilson issues neutrality proclamation Federal Trade Commission established Commercial traffic begins on Panama Canal Margaret Sanger launches *The Woman Rebel*, feminist magazine dedicated to birth control; is indicted for "inciting violence and promoting obscenity" (goes on to found first family planning clinic, 1916; American Birth Control League, precursor to planned parenthood, 1921)	Clayton Act Federal Trade Commission Act Narcotics Act
1915		64th 1915–1917 Senate: 56 D; 40 R House: 230 D; 196 R; 9 O	First transcontinental telephone call Film *Birth of a Nation* debuts and increases support for the new Ku Klux Klan	

YEAR	PRESIDENT	CONGRESS	US HISTORY	LEGISLATION
1916			Congress votes to increase size of army; authorizes 450,000 person national guard	Keating-Owen Act
				National Park Service Act
			U.S. buys Danish West Indies	
			In first half of year, nearly 2,100 strikes and lockouts occur	
			First woman elected to House of Representatives (Jeanette Rankin, R-MT)	
1917		65th 1917–1919	U.S. declares war on Germany and on Austria-Hungary; first U.S. troops arrive in Europe	Espionage Act
		Senate: 53 D; 42 R		Selective Service Act
		House: 216 D; 210 R; 6 O		Trading With the Enemy Act
			Puerto Rico becomes U.S. territory	Vocational Education Act
1918			Woodrow Wilson outlines "Fourteen Points" for a peace program	Sedition Act
			Armistice signed with Germany and Austria-Hungary	
			Regular airmail service established (between Washington, DC, and New York City)	
			Influenza epidemic kills around 20 million people worldwide; 548,000 die in U.S.	
1919		66th 1919–1921	Treaty of Versailles signed by Germany and Allies (excluding Russia)	National Prohibition Act
		Senate: 49 R; 47 D		
		House: 240 R; 190 D; 3 O	In *Schenck v. United States*, Supreme Court finds that free speech can be restricted in wartime, upholding Espionage and Sedition Acts	
			Riots in Chicago, Washington, and many other cities	
1920			14th Census: U.S. population 106,021,537	Merchant Marine Act
			Eighteenth Amendment goes into effect (Prohibition)	Mineral Leasing Act
			Nineteenth Amendment goes into effect (women's suffrage)	
			American Civil Liberties Union founded	
			First commercial radio broadcasts	

YEAR	PRESIDENT	CONGRESS	US HISTORY	LEGISLATION
1921	Warren G. Harding: 1921–1923 (Republican)	67th 1921–1923 Senate: 59 R; 37 D House: 301 R; 131 D; 1 O	Congress limits the number of immigrants from each country to 3 percent of the number of that foreign-born nationality living in U.S. First state sales tax levied (West Virginia)	
1922				
1923	Calvin Coolidge: 1923–1929 (Republican)	68th 1923–1925 Senate: 51 R; 43 D; 2 O House: 225 R; 205 D; 5 O	Pres. Harding dies in San Francisco during return trip from Alaska First transcontinental nonstop plane flight First sound-on-film motion picture (*Phonofilm*) shown in New York City	
1924			Regular transcontinental air service begins Annual immigration quota reduced to 2 percent of number of that foreign-born nationality living in U.S. Congress passes law making all Indians U.S. citizens First woman elected state governor (Nellie Tayloe Ross, D-WY)	Bonus Bill (Adjusted Compensation Act)
1925		69th 1925–1927 Senate: 56 R; 39 D; 1 O House: 247 R; 183 D; 4 O	National Aircraft Board created to investigate government's role in aviation	
1926			First liquid-fuel rocket demonstrated by Robert H. Goddard, Auburn, MA	
1927		70th 1927–1929 Senate: 49 R; 46 D; 1 O House: 237 R; 195 D; 3 O	Charles Lindbergh makes first New York–Paris nonstop flight	
1928				
1929	Herbert Hoover: 1929–1933 (Republican)	71st 1929–1931 Senate: 56 R; 39 D; 1 O House: 267 R; 167 D;1 O	Teapot Dome scandal (former secretary of state is found guilty of leasing government land for bribes) Stock market crash sets off Great Depression (1929–1939)	Migratory Bird Conservation Act
1930			15th census: U.S. population 123,202,624 Bank of the United States in New York closes; over 2,100 banks close between late 1929 and end of 1930	Smoot-Hawley Tariff Act

YEAR	PRESIDENT	CONGRESS	US HISTORY	LEGISLATION
1931		72d 1931–1933 Senate: 48 R; 47 D; 1 O House: 220 R; 214 D; 1 O		
1932			Bonus March on Washington, DC (WWI veterans demand early payment of their bonus) First woman elected to U.S. Senate (Hattie W. Caraway, D-AR)	Federal Home Loan Bank Act Norris-LaGuardia Act
1933	Franklin D. Roosevelt: 1933–1945 (Democratic)	73d 1933–1935 Senate: 60 D; 35 R; 1 O House: 310 D; 117 R; 5 O	An estimated 25 percent of the workforce is unemployed First 100 days of Roosevelt administration marked by passage of much New Deal social and economic legislation U.S. officially goes off gold standard Congress passes legislation providing for independence of the Philippine Islands after 12 years U.S. recognizes U.S.S.R. Twentieth Amendment ratified (moves presidential inauguration and beginning of congressional term to January; were previously in March) Twenty-first Amendment goes into effect (repeals Eighteenth Amendment)	Agricultural Adjustment Act Farm Credit Act Federal Deposit Insurance Act Glass-Steagall Act National Industrial Recovery Act Securities Act of 1933 Tennessee Valley Authority Act
1934			Dust storms in Midwest blow thousands of tons of topsoil away (Dust Bowl) Longshoremen strike in San Francisco leads to first general strike in the U.S.	Communications Act Gold Reserve Act Indian Reorganization Act Securities Exchange Act
1935		74th 1935–1937 Senate: 69 D; 25 R; 2 O House: 319 D; 103 R; 10 O	George H. Gallup founds Institute of Public Opinion, which holds Gallup polls First U.S. Savings Bonds issued Committee of Industrial Organization, precursor to Congress of Industrial Organizations (CIO), created	Aid to Dependent Children Motor Carrier Act National Labor Relations Act Neutrality Acts (1935–1939) Public Utility Holding Company Act Social Security Act Soil Conservation and Domestic Allotment Act
1936				Commodity Exchange Act Rural Electrification Act Walsh-Healey Public Contracts Act

YEAR	PRESIDENT	CONGRESS	US HISTORY	LEGISLATION
1937		75th 1937–1939 Senate: 76 D; 16 R; 4 O House: 331 D; 89 R; 13 O	First African-American federal judge (William H. Hastie) Pres. Roosevelt's plan to increase number of Supreme Court justices from 9 to 16 is defeated	United States Housing Act
1938			House Committee on Un-American Activities created to investigate subversive activities Federal minimum wage established	Civil Aeronautics Act Fair Labor Standards Act Federal Food, Drug, and Cosmetic Act Natural Gas Act
1939		76th 1939–1941 Senate: 69 D; 23 R; 4 O House: 261 D; 164 R; 4 O	U.S. declares neutrality in World War II Scientists, including Albert Einstein, warn Pres. Roosevelt of possibility of atomic bomb	Federal Unemployment Tax Act Hatch Act
1940			16th census: U.S. population 132,164,569 Congress approves first peace-time draft	
1941		77th 1941–1943 Senate: 66 D; 28 R; 2 O House: 268 D; 162 R; 5 O	First commercial television license issued to NBC Japanese attack on Pearl Harbor U.S. enters World War II	Lend-Lease Act Public Debt Act
1942			Manhattan Project organized for production of atomic bomb 10,000 Japanese-Americans on West Coast are relocated to camps in the interior	
1943		78th 1943–1945 Senate: 58 D; 37 R; 1 O House: 218 D; 208 R; 4 O	Building of Pentagon (to house Department of Defense) completed	
1944			Conference at Dumbarton Oaks, Washington, DC, lays groundwork for United Nations First large scale digital computer completed by IBM, given to Harvard University	Veterans' Preference Act

YEAR	PRESIDENT	CONGRESS	US HISTORY	LEGISLATION
1945	Harry S. Truman: 1945–1953 (Democratic)	79th 1945–1947 Senate: 56 D; 38 R; 1 O House: 242 D; 190 R; 2 O	Pres. Roosevelt dies suddenly while on vacation First atomic bomb detonated successfully in New Mexico Germany agrees to unconditional surrender; German occupational zones established Pres. Truman orders dropping of two atomic bombs on Japanese cities of Hiroshima and Nagasaki; Japan quickly surrenders; U.S. begins occupation United Nations is formed as representatives of 50 nations meet in San Francisco Nuremberg War Crimes Trials begin Lend-Lease program ends	Export-Import Bank Act United Nations Participation Act
1946			U.S. gives Philippine Islands independence U.N. General Assembly holds first session World Bank organizes	Administrative Procedure Act Atomic Energy Act Employment Act of 1946 Farmers Home Administration Act Federal Tort Claims Act Foreign Service Act Hill-Burton Act Hobbs Anti-Racketeering Act Richard B. Russell National School Lunch Act
1947		80th 1947–1949 Senate: 51 R; 45 D House: 245 R; 188 D; 1 O	The president pledges aid to Greece and Turkey (to prevent the spread of communism), known as the "Truman Doctrine" U.S. Army, Navy, and Air Force combined into Defense Department; Joint Chiefs of Staff and National Security Council created (National Security Act)	National Security Act Taft-Hartley Act
1948			U.S.S.R. blockades Allied sectors of Berlin; U.S. and British airlift food and coal into city (blockade ends in 1949) Universal Declaration on Human Rights adopted by U.N. General Assembly Israel declared an independent state Executive order issued by Pres. Truman outlawing racial segregation in armed forces Organization of American States formed by 21 Western Hemisphere nations	Economic Cooperation Act (Marshall Plan) United States Information and Educational Exchange Act Federal Water Pollution Control Act

YEAR	PRESIDENT	CONGRESS	US HISTORY	LEGISLATION
1949		81st 1949–1951 Senate: 54 D; 42 R House: 263 D; 171 R; 1 O	North Atlantic Treaty signed; NATO created	Central Intelligence Agency Act
1950			17th census: U.S. population 151,325,798 Korean War begins when North Korea invades South Korea; U.S. leads U.N. troops Thirty-five military advisers, along with arms and supplies, sent to South Vietnam to aid anti- Communist government Army seizes railroads to prevent general strike (ordered by Pres. Truman)	Federal Civil Defense Act
1951		82d 1951–1953 Senate: 49 D; 47 R House: 234 D; 199 R; 1 O	Twenty-second Amendment ratified (sets a maximum of two terms for the presidency) Credit card is introduced by Franklin National Bank of New York	Mutual Security Act
1952			First hydrogen bomb tested Pres. Truman orders seizure of steel mills to prevent strike; Supreme Court rules seizure is unconstitutional Ralph Ellison's novel *Invisible Man* published	Immigration and Nationality Act
1953	Dwight D. Eisenhower: 1953–1961 (Republican)	83d 1953–1955 Senate: 48 R; 47 D; 1 O House: 221 R; 211 D; 1 O	Armistice signed in Korea	Outer Continental Shelf Lands Act Small Business Act
1954			Supreme Court rules that racial segregation in public schools violates the Fourteenth Amendment (*Brown v. Board of Education of Topeka, Kansas*) Senator Joseph McCarthy conducts televised hearings concerning Communists in the U.S. government and Democratic Party Southeast Treaty Organization created First atomic-powered submarine is launched	Communist Control Act Federal National Mortgage Association Charter Act Internal Revenue Act of 1954

YEAR	PRESIDENT	CONGRESS	US HISTORY	LEGISLATION
1955		84th 1955–1957 Senate: 48 D; 47 R; 1 O House: 232 D; 203 r	American occupation of Germany ends U.S. agrees to help train South Vietnamese Army Rosa Parks refuses to give up her seat to a white man on a bus in Montgomery, AL; this leads to a boycott of buses and to Supreme Court decision that outlaws segregation in public transportation AFL and CIO, two largest labor organizations in U.S., merge McDonald's fast-food chain founded	National Housing Act (Capehart Act)
1956			Commercial telephone service over transatlantic cable begins Minimum wage raised to $1 per hour Dow Jones Industrial Average closes over 500 for the first time	Highway Act of 1956
1957		85th 1957–1959 Senate: 49 D; 47 R House: 233 D; 200 R	Southern Christian Leadership Conference founded, Martin Luther King, Jr., president	Civil Rights Act of 1957
1958			National Aeronautics and Space Administration (NASA) created	Federal Aviation Act National Aeronautics and Space Act
1959		86th 1959–1961 Senate: 64 D; 34 R House: 283 D; 153 R	Nikita Khrushchev, Soviet premier, visits U.S.	
1960			18th Census: U.S. population 179,323,175 Russia announces it shot down an American U-2 spy plane; President Eisenhower says he authorized the flight Sit-ins begin when 4 black college students refuse to move from a Woolworth lunch counter in Greensboro, NC Student Non-Violent Coordinating Committee established	

YEAR	PRESIDENT	CONGRESS	US HISTORY	LEGISLATION
1961	John F. Kennedy: 1961–1963 (Democratic)	87th 1961–1963 Senate: 65 D; 35 R House: 263 D; 174 R	Bay of Pigs invasion by Cuban exiles is crushed Peace Corps created by executive order; legislation follows Twenty-third Amendment ratified (allows residents of District of Columbia to vote for president) Minimum wage raised to $1.25 per hour	Arms Control and Disarmament Act Foreign Assistance Act Peace Corps Act
1962			Cuban missile crisis (Soviet missile buildup in Cuba) Cesar Chavez organizes National Farm Workers Association John Glenn becomes first U.S. astronaut to orbit the Earth	Bribery Act
1963	Lyndon B. Johnson: 1963–1969 (Democratic)	88th 1963–1965 Senate: 67 D; 33 R House: 258 D; 177 R	Pres. Kennedy is assassinated in Dallas, TX Dr. Martin Luther King gives "I have a dream" speech during March on Washington for equal rights, Washington, DC Ninety-nine nations, including U.S., U.S.S.R., and Great Britain agree to limited Nuclear Test Ban Treaty	Clean Air Act Equal Pay Act
1964			Pres. Johnson announces air attacks on Vietnam; Gulf of Tonkin Resolution passed by Congress gives the president broad authority for military action in Vietnam Three civil rights workers murdered in Philadelphia, MS; 21 white men arrested, 7 convicted of conspiracy in killings Twenty-fourth Amendment ratified (bars poll tax in federal elections)	Civil Rights Act of 1964 Economic Opportunity Act Food Stamp Act Urban Mass Transportation Act

YEAR	PRESIDENT	CONGRESS	US HISTORY	LEGISLATION
1965		89th 1965–1967 Senate: 68 D; 32 R House: 295 D; 140 R	First combat troops land in South Vietnam (125,000 total troops in Vietnam by year's end) Malcolm X assassinated in New York City Civil rights activists march 54 miles from Selma to Montgomery, AL	Elementary and Secondary Education Act Federal Cigarette Labeling and Advertising Act Higher Education Act Highway Beautification Act Housing and Urban Development Act Medicaid Act Medicare Act National Emissions Standard Act Solid Waste Disposal Act Voting Rights Act
1966			More than 10,000 protest Vietnam War in front of White House National Organization for Women (NOW) established	Freedom of Information Act Highway Safety Act National Historic Preservation Act National Traffic and Motor Vehicle Safety Act National Wildlife Refuge System Administration Act
1967		90th 1967–1969 Senate: 64 D; 36 R House: 246 D; 187 R	First African-American Supreme Court justice (Thurgood Marshall) Blacks riot in Newark, NJ, and Detroit, MI Twenty-fifth Amendment ratified (sets up presidential succession scheme)	Age Discrimination in Employment Act Public Broadcasting Act
1968			Martin Luther King, Jr., and Robert Kennedy are assassinated Lyndon B. Johnson announces that he will not seek reelection	Alcoholic and Narcotic Rehabilitation Act Fair Housing Act Gun Control Act Indian Civil Rights Act Omnibus Crime Control and Safe Streets Act
1969	Richard M. Nixon: 1969–1974 (Republican)	91st 1969–1971 Senate: 57 D; 43 R House: 245 D; 189 R	Peace talks to end Vietnam War begin; 250,000 protest war in Washington, DC U.S. astronauts land on moon	Consumer Credit Protection Act National Environmental Policy Act Truth in Lending Act
1970			19th Census: U.S. population 203,302,031 Four students at Kent State College in Ohio are killed during an antiwar demonstration First draft lottery since WWII is held Intel introduces its first computer memory chip	Controlled Substances Act Occupational Safety and Health Act Organized Crime Control Act Plant Variety Protection Act Rail Passenger Service Act

YEAR	PRESIDENT	CONGRESS	US HISTORY	LEGISLATION
1971		92d 1971–1973 Senate: 54 D; 44 R; 2 O House: 254 D; 180 R	Pentagon Papers, classified documents on Vietnam War leaked to the press, published in newspapers Amtrak begins operation Twenty-sixth Amendment ratified (lowers voting age to 18)	Alaska Native Claims Settlement Act Federal Election Campaign Act
1972			Pres. Nixon makes historic visits to China and U.S.S.R. Peace talks on Vietnam War begin and then stall Strategic Arms Limitation Treaty I signed with U.S.S.R. Five men are arrested for breaking into Democratic National Headquarters at the Watergate building in Washington, DC, beginning a series of events that would lead to Richard Nixon's resignation Dow Jones Industrial Average closes over 1,000 for the first time	Federal Advisory Committee Act Marine Mammal Protection Act Title IX, Education Amendments
1973		93d 1973–1975 Senate: 56 D; 42 R; 2 O House: 239 D; 192 R; 1 O	Cease fire signed between U.S., South Vietnam, and North Vietnam OPEC oil embargo (Arab countries ban oil exports to U.S. because of U.S. support to Israel in Arab-Israeli War) In *Roe v. Wade* Supreme Court rules that a state cannot prevent a woman from having an abortion in the first six months of pregnancy	Domestic Volunteer Service Act (VISTA) Endangered Species Act War Powers Resolution
1974	Gerald R. Ford: 1974–1977 (Republican)		House of Representatives authorizes an impeachment investigation of Pres. Nixon, votes and approves three impeachment articles; Nixon resigns Work begins on Alaskan oil pipeline Minimum wage raised to $2.00 per hour	Congressional Budget and Impoundment Control Act Employee Retirement Income Security Act Juvenile Justice and Delinquency Prevention Act Legal Services Corporation Act Privacy Act Safe Drinking Water Act Trade Act of 1974

YEAR	PRESIDENT	CONGRESS	US HISTORY	LEGISLATION
1975		94th 1975–1977 Senate: 61 D; 37 R; 2 O House: 291 D; 144 R	Remaining U.S. military evacuated from Vietnam after the shelling of Saigon by Communist forces; South Vietnam surrenders unconditionally to the Viet Cong U.S. military academies open to women Minimum wage raised to $2.10 per hour	Individuals with Disabilities Education Act Hazardous Materials Transportation Act
1976			Homestead Act of 1862 repealed for all states except Alaska Apple I desktop computer introduced Minimum wage raised to $2.30 per hour	Copyright Act of 1976 Federal Land Policy and Management Act Government in the Sunshine Act National Forest Management Act Toxic Substances Control Act
1977	James E. Carter: 1977–1981 (Democratic)	95th 1977–1979 Senate: 61 D; 38 R; 1 O House: 292 D; 143 R	Agreement between U.S. and Canada for oil pipeline from Alaska to continental U.S. Pres. Carter pardons most Vietnam War draft evaders Microsoft corporation is formed	Community Reinvestment Act Department of Energy Organization Act Foreign Corrupt Practices Act International Emergency Economic Powers Act Surface Mining Control and Reclamation Act
1978			Deregulation of the airline industry Minimum wage raised to $2.65 per hour	Bankruptcy Act of 1978 Civil Service Reform Act Contract Disputes Act Ethics in Government Act Foreign Intelligence Surveillance Act National Energy Conservation Policy Act Nuclear Non-Proliferation Act Pregnancy Discrimination Act Whistleblower Protection Laws
1979		96th 1979–1981 Senate: 58 D; 41 R; 1 O House: 276 D; 157 R	Sixty-three U.S. citizens taken hostage when Iranian militants seize U.S. embassy in Tehran; black and women hostages released in just over two weeks Nuclear accident (partial meltdown) at Three Mile Island, Middletown, PA Minimum wage raised to $2.90 per hour	

YEAR	PRESIDENT	CONGRESS	US HISTORY	LEGISLATION
1980			20th Census: U.S. population 226,542,203 Military mission to rescue U.S. hostages in Iran fails Residents are evacuated from homes in Love Canal, Niagara Falls, NY, a former toxic waste dump Minimum wage raised to $3.10 per hour	Comprehensive Environmental Response, Compensation, and Liability Act Drug Abuse Prevention, Treatment, and Rehabilitation Act Fish and Wildlife Conservation Act Paperwork Reduction Act Regulatory Flexibility Act Staggers Rail Act
1981	Ronald W. Reagan: 1981–1989 (Republican)	97th 1981–1983 Senate: 53 R; 46 D; 1 O House: 242 D; 189 R	Iran releases remaining 52 U.S. hostages First manned space shuttle (*Columbia*) launched into space Nationwide strike by Professional Air Traffic Controllers Association; most controllers are fired Sandra Day O'Connor becomes first woman Supreme Court justice Minimum wage raised to $3.35 per hour	
1982			Equal Rights Amendment to Constitution defeated (would assure equal rights regardless of sex) Unemployment reaches 10.8 percent of the labor force, highest since 1940 U.S. and Soviet Union hold arms control talks in Geneva, Switzerland	Nuclear Waste Policy Act
1983		98th 1983–1985 Senate: 54 R; 46 D House: 268 D; 167 R	Soviet Union shoots down a Korean Airlines plane, killing all 269 passengers, including 52 Americans U.S. Embassy in Beirut is bombed, killing 17 U.S. citizens; a truck bomb kills 241 Americans at a U.S. Marine compound in Beirut	
1984			Truck filled with explosives strikes U.S. Embassy annex in Beirut; U.S. Marines are withdrawn from Beirut As a result of an antitrust settlement, AT&T gives up 22 local Bell System telephone companies	Counterfeit Access Device and Computer Fraud and Abuse Act Hazardous and Solid Waste Amendments Sentencing Reform Act

YEAR	PRESIDENT	CONGRESS	US HISTORY	LEGISLATION
1985		99th 1985–1987 Senate: 53 R; 47 D House: 253 D; 182 R	U.S. and Soviet Union hold arms control talks in Geneva	Balanced Budget and Emergency Deficit Control Act (Gramm-Rudman-Hollings Act)
1986			Pres. Reagan signs secret order authorizing sale of arms to Iran; Lt. Col. Oliver North is dismissed when it is learned that some proceeds from the arms sales helped finance Nicaraguan Contras Space shuttle *Challenger* explodes in air after liftoff, killing entire crew	Anti-Drug Abuse Act Electronic Communications Privacy Act Emergency Planning and Community Right-To-Know Act Immigration Reform and Control Act Tax Reform Act
1987		100th 1987–1989 Senate: 55 D; 45 R House: 258 D; 177 R	Iran-Contra hearings in Congress last about three months U.S. and U.S.S.R. sign treaty banning medium- and short-range missiles Dow Jones Industrial Average closes over 2,000 for the first time	Computer Security Act McKinney-Vento Act
1988			Senate approves free trade agreement made with Canada (1987), all tariffs between the two countries will be eliminated by 1999	Civil Liberties Act Indian Gaming Regulatory Act
1989	George H. W. Bush: 1989–1993 (Republican)	101st 1989–1991 Senate: 55 D; 45 R House: 260 D; 175 R	Oil tanker, *Exxon Valdez*, runs aground on a reef in Prince William Sound, off the coast of Alaska, creating largest oil spill in American history Failing savings and loan industry receives $159 million bailout legislated by Congress 20,000 U.S. troops invade Panama, overthrow regime of Manuel Noriega Minimum wage raised to $4.25 per hour	Flag Protection Act
1990			21st census: U.S. population 249,632,692 U.N. forces begin air attacks on Iraq, after Iraq invades Kuwait	Administrative Dispute Resolution Act Americans with Disabilities Act Negotiated Rulemaking Act Oil Pollution Act

YEAR	PRESIDENT	CONGRESS	US HISTORY	LEGISLATION
1991		102d 1991–1993 Senate: 56 D; 44 R House: 267 D; 167 R; 1 O	First Persian Gulf War begins and ends, freeing Kuwait from Iraqi occupation U.S.S.R. is formally dissolved, effectively ending the Cold War Dow Jones Industrial Average closes over 3,000 for the first time	
1992			Representatives from Canada, Mexico, and U.S. approve draft agreement establishing free trade among the three nations in 15 years Riots in south-central Los Angeles after a jury acquits four white police officers on charges of brutality against a black man, Rodney King Twenty-seventh Amendment is ratified (legislated pay raises for congress don't take effect until a new Congress is convened)	Weapons of Mass Destruction Control Act
1993	William J. Clinton: 1993–2001 (Democratic)	103d 1993–1995 Senate: 56 D; 44 R House: 258 D; 176 R; 1 O	Bomb explodes in parking garage beneath World Trade Center, killing 6 people Twenty U.S. soldiers are killed in Mogadishu, Somalia, in an effort to protect food shipment and distribution to the population Second Strategic Arms Reduction Treaty signed with Russia U.S. and 117 other countries agree to GATT (General Agreement on Tariffs and Trade), to be signed in 1995, will remove export barriers and tariffs on thousands of products	Brady Handgun Violence Protection Act Family and Medical Leave Act NAFTA Implementation Act Religious Freedom Restoration Act
1994			U.S. and North Korea sign agreement that allows for U.N. inspection of North Korea nuclear facilities Republicans win control of Congress for the first time since 1952; Newt Gingrich to become Speaker of the House (1995–1999)	Community Development Banking and Financial Institutions Act Federal Blackmail Statute Freedom of Access to Clinic Entrances Act Violence Against Women Act Violent Crime Control and Law Enforcement Act

YEAR	PRESIDENT	CONGRESS	US HISTORY	LEGISLATION
1995		104th 1995–1997 Senate: 52 R; 48 D House: 230 R; 204 D; 1 O	U.S. troops arrive in Balkans as part of U.N. force, mission is to halt years of fighting in Bosnia Bombing of Oklahoma City Federal Building, killing 160 people Dow Jones Industrial Average closes over 4,000 (Feb.) and 5,000 (Nov.) for the first time	Lobbying Disclosure Act
1996			Nineteen U.S. military personnel die, several hundred wounded, in bombing of military complex near Dhahran, Saudi Arabia Minimum wage raised to $4.75 per hour Dow Jones Industrial Average closes over 6,000 for the first time	Antiterrorism and Effective Death Penalty Act Communications Decency Act Defense of Marriage Act Food Quality Protection Act Personal Responsibility and Work Opportunity Reconciliation Act
1997		105th 1997–1999 Senate: 55 R; 45 D House: 226 R; 208 D; 1 O	Settlement for $368.5 billion reached between four major tobacco companies and several state attorneys general (a $200 billion settlement with 46 states would happen in 1998) Minimum wage raised to $5.15 Dow Jones Industrial Average closes over 7,000 (Feb.) and 8,000 (July) for the first time	
1998			House of Representatives approves two articles of impeachment against Pres. Clinton for perjury and obstruction of justice; he is accused of lying under oath about his relationship with a White House intern Newt Gingrich steps down as Speaker of the House and leaves Congress amid ethics charges and poor results in the midterm congressional elections Dow Jones Industrial Average closes over 9,000 for the first time	Children's Online Privacy Protection Act Taxpayer Bill of Rights III

YEAR	PRESIDENT	CONGRESS	US HISTORY	LEGISLATION
1999		106th 1999–2001 Senate: 54 R; 46 D House: 222 R; 208 D; 1 O	Two students of Columbine High School in Littleton, CO, open fire and kill 12 students and a teacher, then commit suicide; at least 4 other school shootings occur during the year Pres. Clinton impeached but not convicted; investigation led by independent council Kenneth Starr reveals much about Clinton's sexual indiscretions Dow Jones Industrial Average closes over 10,000 (Mar.) and 11,000 (May) for the first time	
2000			Disputed results in the presidential election, centering around election results and ballot irregularities in Florida, lead to a Supreme Court decision that does not allow a vote recount to proceed in that state; George W. Bush declared winner over Al Gore, who won the popular vote U.S.S. *Cole*, an American ship, is bombed by terrorists while refueling in Yemen; 17 sailors killed, 39 injured in the blast "Dot com" boom experienced throughout the late 1990s begins to go bust, starting with the bursting of the stock market "bubble" in March; 4 of the 10 greatest point losses on the Dow Jones Industrial Average occur this year (3 of the 10 greatest point increases occur as well)	Electronic Signatures in Global and National Commerce Act

YEAR	PRESIDENT	CONGRESS	US HISTORY	LEGISLATION
2001	George W. Bush: 2001– (Republican)	107th 2001–2003 Senate: 50 D; 49 R; 1 O House: 222 R; 211 D; 1 O	On September 11, the U.S. comes under terrorist attack when two hijacked planes fly into the towers of the World Trade Center in New York, another plane flies into the Pentagon, and a fourth crashes in Pennsylvania Letters containing Anthrax spores, sent to congressmen and journalists, contaminate the U.S. mail system U.S. begins bombing of Afghanistan to oust the Taliban (Islamic fundamentalist party in power) and capture Osama Bin Laden (leader of Al-Qaeda, the group thought responsible for the September 11 attacks); Taliban removed from power, Bin Laden not captured	No Child Left Behind Act USA Patriot Act
2002			The Enron Corporation collapses as a scandal regarding the company's accounting practices emerges, its share prices plummet and the company declares bankruptcy; other similar corporate scandals follow Bush administration begins to announce an aggressive policy toward Iraq, including the possibility of a "preemptive" strike with the aim of "regime change"; U.N. passes resolution sending weapons inspectors to Iraq; Congress passes resolution authorizing the president to use military force in Iraq	Born-Alive Infants Protection Act Department of Homeland Security Act

YEAR	PRESIDENT	CONGRESS	US HISTORY	LEGISLATION
2003		108th 2003-2005 Senate: 51 R; 48 D; 1 O House: 229 R; 205 D; 1 O	Although U.N. weapons inspectors are still at work, U.S., Britain, and allies declare that Iraq has not disarmed and is in violation of a U.N. resolution passed in November 2002; U.S. is unable to get U.N. approval for the use of force against Iraq because of international opposition; U.S. and a "coalition of the willing" attack Iraq without U.N. approval and win war easily; after Pres. Bush declares an end to major combat a guerilla war ensues; reconstruction of Iraq's infrastructure proves to be more costly than thought; as of five months after Bush's declaration of victory, banned weapons—the major rationale for the war—had not been found Space shuttle *Columbia* breaks apart during reentry killing all seven crew members; independent investigation of accident lasts nearly seven months and concludes that flaws in NASA's management and culture were underlying causes of the disaster In California, a petition gathers enough signatures to force a recall election for governor (incumbent is Gray Davis [D]); 135 candidates to appear on ballot, including actor Arnold Schwarzenegger (R) Massive, rolling blackout across northern Midwest, Canada, and northeastern U.S. results in 50 million people losing power	

GLOSSARY

abate:
to reduce in amount; put an end to; make void or annul

abet: to actively, knowingly, and intentionally assist another in the committing (or attempt) of a crime

abolitionist: one favoring principles or measures fostering the end of slavery

absolute: complete, pure, free from restriction or limitation

adherent: a follower of a leader or party, or a believer in a cause

adjournment: the closing, or end, of a session

adjudicate: to settle something judicially

adjudicated: a matter or controversy that has already been decided through judicial procedure

adjudication: the act of settling something judicially

adjudicatory: having to do with the process of settling something judicially

adverse: contrary to one's interests; harmful or unfavorable

aggrieved: suffering physical injury or a loss of one's property interest, monetary interest, or personal rights

agrarian: having to do with farming or farming communities and their interests

alien: a citizen of another country

alternative dispute resolution: any means of settling disputes outside of the courtroom, typically including arbitration, mediation, early neutral evaluation, and conciliation

amend: to alter or change

antitrust: laws protecting commerce and trade from monopolistic restraints on competition

appellate: a court having jurisdiction to review the findings of lower courts

appoint: to select someone to fill an office or position

apportion: to divide and assign according to a plan

appropriate: to set aside for or assign to a particular purpose or group

arbitrate: to resolve disagreements whereby parties choose a person or group of people familiar with the issues in question to hear and settle their dispute

arbitration the settling of a dispute by a neutral third party

Articles of Confederation: first constitution of the United States (in effect 1781–1789); it established a union between the thirteen states, but with a weak central government

bipartisan: involving members of two parties, especially the two major political parties

blacklist: a list of persons who are to be denied employment

block grant: an unrestricted grant of federal money to state and local governments to support social welfare programs

bondage: a state of being involuntarily bound or subjugated to someone or something

boycott: to refuse to purchase goods or services from a specific company

capitulate: to surrender under specific conditions; to give up resistance

carcinogenic: cancer-causing

cause of action: reason or ground for initiating a proceeding in court

censor: to restrict the expression of something considered objectionable

charter: document that creates a public or private corporation and outlines the principles, functions, and organization of the corporate body

checks and balances: the limiting powers that each branch of government has over the other two. (The government is divided into three branches: legislative, executive, and judicial, each with distinct powers.)

civil action: a lawsuit brought to protect an individual right or redress a wrong, as distinct from criminal proceedings

civil disobedience: nonviolent protest

civil libertarian: one who is actively concerned with the protection of the fundamental freedoms guaranteed to the individual in the Bill of Rights

civil penalties: fines or money damages imposed as punishment

Civil Rights movement: the movement to win political, economic, and social equality for African Americans

class action: a lawsuit brought by a representative member of a large group of people who have suffered the same injury or damages

Cold War: a conflict over ideological differences carried on by methods short of military action and usually without breaking off diplomatic relations; usually refers to the ideological conflict between the U.S. and former U.S.S.R.

collateral: property put up by a borrower to secure a loan that could be seized if the borrower fails to pay back the debt

collective bargaining: a method of negotiations, usually between employees and an employer, in which a representative negotiates on behalf of an organized group of people

commerce: the large-scale exchange of goods, involving transportation from one place to another

commerce clause: the provision of the U.S. Constitution (Article I, section 8, clause 3) that gives Congress exclusive powers over interstate commerce—the buying, selling, or exchanging of goods between states

commodity: an article of trade or commerce that can be transported; especially an agricultural or mining product

common law: a system of laws developed in England—and later applied in the U.S.—based on judicial precedent rather than statutory laws passed by a legislative body

communism: an economic and social system characterized by the absence of classes and by common ownership of the means of production and subsistence

comply: to act in accordance with a wish, request, demand, rule, order, or statute

constraint: a restriction

consumer credit information: credit experiences, such as your bill-paying history, the number and type of accounts you have, late payments, collection actions, outstanding debt, and the age of your accounts

consumption tax: tax imposed on outlay for goods and services

contempt: disobedience of a court's order; interference with the court's operation

Continental Congress: the first central governing body of the United States (1774–1789)

contract: a formal agreement, usually in writing, between two or more parties that can be legally enforced

conventional mortgage: a home mortgage loan that is not federally insured

de novo: (Latin) anew, a second time; the same as if it had not been heard before

debtor: one who owes payment or other performance on an obligation; anyone liable on a claim

decedent: one who has died; the deceased

deduction: an amount subtracted from the amount of income that is used to calculate income tax due

default: the failure by the borrower to comply with the terms of the loan, usually the failure to make payments

defaulter: one who fails to comply with the terms of a loan or contract, usually by failing to make payments on a debt

defendant: one against whom a legal action is brought

deflation: a general decline in the prices of goods and services

demagogue: a leader who obtains power by means of impassioned appeals to the emotions and prejudices of the populace

dependency: a territory under the jurisdiction of a sovereign nation

detain: to keep in custody or temporary confinement

directors: those who establish the policies of the corporation

discharge petition: a method for moving a bill from a committee to the floor of the House when a committee refuses to do so itself. The bill must have been held by a committee for at least thirty legislative days, and half of the House membership must sign the petition for release that is filed

disclosure: obligation of parties to reveal material facts deemed necessary for one to make an informed decision

discount window: a lending facility available to member banks of the Federal Reserve System

dividend: a payment made by a company, based on its earnings, to its shareholders

dogma: an established opinion expressed as an authoritative statement

draconian: severe, harsh

Dust Bowl: a semiarid region in the south-central United States where the topsoil was lost by wind erosion in the mid-1930s

egalitarian: marked by a belief in human equality

electorate: the body of people qualified to vote

emancipate: to free from another's control, restraint, or bondage

embargo: a prohibition on commerce with a particular country for political or economic reasons

encroach: to infringe upon or violate

equal protection: Constitutional guarantee that prevents states from denying a person or class of persons from the same protection under the law as those enjoyed by other persons or classes of persons

espionage: the act of spying on the government to obtain secret information

ex officio: (Latin) from office, by virtue of office; powers may be exercised by an officer which are not specifically conferred upon him, but are necessarily implied in his office

excise tax: a tax levied on the manufacture or sale of specific—usually non-essential—commodities such as tobacco or liquor

executive order: an order issued by the president that has the force of law

exorbitant: an amount that far exceeds what is fair or customary

extortion: the obtaining of money (or other concessions) by force or intimidation

F

faction: a party or group united by a common cause

Federal Register: a newspaper published daily by the National Archives and Records Administration to notify the public of federal agency regulations, proposed rules and notices, executive orders, and other executive branch documents

federal securities laws: federal securities laws include the Securities Act of 1933, the Securities Exchange Act of 1934, and various rules and regulations under these acts. These acts regulate the offer and sales of securities as well as secondary markets for securities. They require numerous disclosures and prohibit deceptive practices

federalism: a system of political organization; a union formed of separate states or groups that are ruled by a central authority on some matters but are otherwise permitted to govern themselves independently

felony: a crime punished with a lengthy prison sentence (more than one year) or the death penalty

filibuster: a tactic involving unlimited debate on the floor of the Senate designed to delay or prevent legislative action

fiscal year: the term used for a business's accounting year; the period is usually twelve months which can begin during any month of the calendar year

foreclosure: when a person defaults on (fails to pay) a mortgage debt, the owner's legal right to the property is terminated. The real estate may be sold at an auction by the creditor; the money raised is then put toward the mortgage debt

forfeiture: the loss of something (property, assets) as a result of breaking the law

free expression: the right to state opinions without interference or censorship

freedman: one freed from slavery

G

garnish: process whereby one's property or money that is in the possession of a third party is paid to another to satisfy one's debt

gold standard: a monetary standard under which the basic unit of currency is equal in value to and can be exchanged for a specified amount of gold

graduated rate schedule: tax structured so that the rate increases as the amount of taxpayer income increases

grassroots: originating or operating at the basic level of society

Great Depression: the longest and most severe economic depression in American history (1929–1939); its effects were felt throughout the world

Great Society: broad term for the domestic programs of President Lyndon B. Johnson, in which he called for "an end to poverty and racial injustice

gross domestic product: the total market value of goods and services produced within a nation in a given time period (usually one year)

habeas corpus: (Latin, "you should have the body") a written order to bring a prisoner in front of a judge, to determine whether his or her detention is lawful

high-rate mortgages: a mortgage with a high interest rate because it is perceived to be a higher risk based on the purchaser's credit history

illiquid: incapable of being readily converted to cash

immigrant: one who comes to a country to take up permanent residence

immunity: protection from legal action

impair: to lessen or reduce

impeach: to set up a formal hearing on charges of high crimes and misdemeanors which could result in removal from office

imperial presidency: a powerful president who is being belligerent internationally, being intrusive domestically, and running roughshod over another branch of government

import: to bring in merchandise from another country as part of a commercial business

individual retirement account (IRA): an account into which a person can deposit up to a certain amount of money annually without being taxed until either retirement or early withdrawal (withdrawal when the person is under a certain age)

inflation: a general rise in the prices of goods and services

infringe: to exceed the limits of; to violate

ingress: a means or place for entering

injunctive relief: a court order that requires a person to refrain from doing something; the order guards against future damages rather than remedies past damages

insurgent: one who revolts against authority; especially a member of a political party who rebels against its leadership

insurrection: a rebellion against a government or civil authority

interest expense: the money a corporation or individual pays out in interest on loans

interest rate: the fee for borrowing money, expressed as a percentage of the amount borrowed

interstate commerce: trade involving the transportation of goods from one state to another, or the transfer of property between a person in one state and a person in another

interventionism: a policy of getting involved in international affairs through membership in international organizations and multinational alliances

invidious: tending to arouse ill will or animosity; an offensive or discriminatory action

involuntary servitude: forced service to a master

isolationism: a policy of not getting involved in international affairs

Jim Crow: the systematic practice of segregating and suppressing African Americans; the name is from a character in a nineteenth-century minstrel show

judgment debtor: one who owes money as a result of a judgment in favor of a creditor

judicial: having to do with judgments in courts of law or with the administration of justice

judicial decree: the ruling of a court

jurisdiction: the territory or area within which authority may be exercised

labor union: an organization of workers whose main purpose is to collectively bargain with employers about the terms and conditions of employment

laissez-faire: a doctrine opposing governmental interference in economic affairs beyond the minimum necessary for the maintenance of peace and property rights

lame-duck: an elected officer holder who is to be succeeded by another; in the case of Congress, the time it is in session between the November elections and the convening of the new Congress the following year

legal tender: an offer of money in the form of coin, paper money, or another circulating medium that the law compels a creditor to accept in payment of a debt

liability: an obligation, responsibility, or duty that one is bound by law to perform

libel: the publication of statements that wrongfully damage another's reputation

libertarian: one who upholds the principles of absolute and unrestricted liberty and strongly opposes any government-imposed restrictions

licentious: lacking moral discipline or sexual restraint

lien: legal claim to property by a creditor (one who makes a loan) as a condition of a contract

life estate: an estate that lasts for the duration of the life of the person holding it

litigation: a lawsuit

lobby: to try to persuade the legislature to pass laws and regulations that are favorable to one's interests and to defeat laws that are unfavorable to those interests

lockout: the withholding of work from employees by management, to get them to agree to certain terms and conditions

long-term capital gains: profit made on the sale or exchange of a capital asset (usually stock or real estate) that has been owned for more than twelve months

loophole: a means of evading or escaping an obligation or enforcement of a law or contract

mandate: an order or requirement

marginal rates: the total percentage of tax one pays on one's income, taking into account all the separate taxes levied on one's wages or salary

Mason-Dixon line: the boundary line between Pennsylvania on the north and Maryland on the south which, before the end of slavery, was the line between the slave and the free states

median: the middle value in a distribution, above and below which lie an equal number of values

migrate: to move from one place to another

militia: a part-time army made up of ordinary citizens

mirabile dictu "wonderful to relate"

monopoly: exclusive control of a market by one company, often marked by the controlling of prices and exclusion of competition

moratorium: a legally required suspension of activity

mortgage loan: a loan to purchase real estate; the real estate purchased with the loan usually serves as collateral against default

muckraker: one who tries to find and expose real or alleged evidence of corruption

multilateral: undertaken by multiple persons, parties, or entities, in conjunction with one another

N

nadir: lowest point

naturalize: to grant the privileges and rights of citizenship

necessary and proper clause: provision in the U.S. Constitution (Article I, section 8, clause 18) that authorizes Congress to pass laws needed in order to exercise its constitutional powers

negotiate: to deal or bargain with another as in the preparation of a treaty or contract

New Deal: the legislative and administrative program of President Franklin D. Roosevelt designed to promote economic recovery and social reform (1933–1939)

nominate: to propose one for appointment to office

nonprofit: an organization whose business is not conducted or maintained for the purpose of making a profit but is usually aimed at providing services for the public good

nonpunitive: not having the character of punishment or penalty

notice and disclosure requirements: in contracts and other transactions, the law requires that key provisions and penalties be disclosed in plain English so a consumer can make an informed decision

null and void: having no legal force; invalid

O

obscene: morally offensive; designed to degrade or corrupt

offender: one who breaks a rule or law

omnibus: including many things at once

OPEC oil embargo: in October 1973, the Organization of Petroleum Exporting Countries (OPEC) banned oil exports to the United States because the United States sold arms to Israel during the Arab-Israeli War of 1973

open market operations: purchases and sales of government securities by the Federal Reserve Bank, designed to control the money supply and short-term interest rates

opining: to hold or state as an opinion

ordinance: a law

originate: a loan is originated when the loan is first made by the lender to a borrower. The origination function includes taking the borrower's loan application, checking the borrower's credit history and employment, obtaining an appraisal of valuation of the home, and funding the loan

override: if the President vetoes a bill passed by Congress, the bill can still become law if two-thirds of each house of Congress votes to override the veto

P

partisan: someone loyal to a particular party, cause, or person

paternalism: a policy or practice of treating or governing people in a fatherly manner especially by providing for their needs without giving them responsibility

penal: having to do with punishments or penalties

perjury: lying under oath or otherwise breaking an oath by not doing what was promised

personal consumption goods: goods purchased for personal use

photovoltaic: relating to the technology used to capture radiation (light) from the sun and turn it into electricity

plaintiff: one who brings legal action against another

populist: someone who identifies with and believes in the rights and virtues of the common people (often as the foundation of a political philosophy)

poverty line: level of personal or family income below which a person or family is classified as poor. The standard is set by the government

powers of appointment: the right to appoint or give away property

preemption when a conflict of authority arises between the federal and state governments, the federal government prevails

president-elect: one who has been elected president but has not yet begun his term of office

preventive relief: relief granted to prevent a foreseen harm

private litigation: a civil lawsuit (one brought to protect an individual right or redress a wrong), as distinct from criminal proceedings

private sector: the part of the economy that is not controlled by the government

Prohibition: period from 1919 to 1933, during which the making, transport, and sale of alcoholic beverages was illegal in the United States

promulgate: to make the terms of a law known by formal public announcement

proponent: an advocate

prosecute: to begin and carry on a lawsuit; to bring legal action against

protectionism: the use of tariffs to protect domestic industries from foreign competition

protectionist: advocating the use of tariffs to protect domestic industries from foreign competition

public held company: a corporation whose stock anyone can buy on a stock exchange

public offering: the making available of corporate stocks or bonds to the general public

pursuant: to execute or carry out in accordance with or by reason of something

quid pro quo: (Latin, "something for something") an equal exchange or substitution

quorum: the number of members required to be present for a vote to take place

ratify: to formally approve; three-fourths of all states in the Union must approve an amendment for it becomes part of the Constitution

real income: income of an individual, organization, or country, after taking into consideration the effects of inflation on purchasing power

recession: a period of reduced economic activity, but less severe than a depression

Reconstruction: the political and economic reorganization and reestablishment of the South after the Civil War

redress: to make right what is wrong

refinance: to pay off existing loans with funds secured from new loans

Regulation Q: a banking regulation that prohibits paying interest on short-term deposits; the scope of this regulation has narrowed over time, so that most non-commercial deposits are unaffected

remedy: the means to compensate a person whose rights have been violated, which usually takes the form of money damages

repatriate: to return to the country of one's birth or citizenship

repeal: to revoke or cancel

rescind: to declare a contract void in its inception and to put an end to it as though it never existed

rescission provisions: provisions in a contract that, if they occur or fail to occur, allow the contract to be rescinded

resolution: a formal statement of opinion, intent, or will voted by an official body

reverse mortgage: a type of home mortgage under which an elderly homeowner is allowed a long-term loan in the form of monthly payments against his or her paid-off equity as collateral, repayable when the home is eventually sold

sabotage: the destruction of property or obstruction of an action intended to hinder the normal operations of a company or government

secede: to depart or withdraw from an organization

secondary market: the market that exists for an issue of stock after large blocks of shares have been publicly distributed, or items not obtained directly from the manufacturer

sectarian characteristic of a group following a specific doctrine or leader

securities: stocks, bonds, and certain other instruments of investment

security interest: a form of interest in property which provides that the property may be sold on default in order to satisfy the obligation for which the security interest is given; a mortgage

is used to grant a security interest in real property

seditious: urging resistance to or overthrow of the government

seed money: money needed or provided to start a new project

self-incrimination: the giving of testimony that will likely subject one to criminal prosecution

separation of powers: the division of the government into three branches: legislative, executive, and judicial, each with distinct powers. This separation supports a system of checks and balances

Sexual Revolution: the liberalization of social and moral attitudes toward sex and sexual relations

slander: to make a false statement that defames and damages another's reputation

socialism: any of various economic and political theories advocating collective or governmental ownership and administration of the means of production and distribution of goods

sovereign: self-governing and independent

sovereign immunity: the doctrine that prevents bringing a lawsuit against the government without the government's consent

special session: an extraordinary or special session of Congress is called to meet in the interval between regular sessions

specie: money in the form of coins, usually in a metal with intrinsic value, such as gold or silver

speculate: to engage in the buying or selling of a commodity with the expectation (or hope) of making a profit

statute: a law enacted by the legislative branch of government

stipend: a fixed or regular payment, such as a salary for services rendered or an allowance

stipulate: to specify as a condition of an agreement

strike: to stop work in protest, usually so as to make an employer comply with demands

subpoena: a writ issued under authority of a court to compel the appearance of a witness at a judicial hearing

superannuated: retired or discharged because of age; obsolete; out of date

surveillance: the close observation of a person, place, or process

T

tariff: a tax imposed on goods when imported into a country

tax credit: a reduction in the amount an individual or corporation owes in taxes

tax shelter: a strategy or method that allows one to legally reduce or avoid tax liabilities

temperance: moderation in or abstinence from the consumption of alcohol

tender offer: a public offer to purchase shares of a specific corporation, usually at a price above what the market offers, in an attempt to accumulate enough shares to take control of the company

terminology: the vocabulary of technical terms and usages appropriate to a particular trade, science, or art

tort: any wrongdoing other than a breach of contract for which a civil lawsuit can be brought. Examples include physical injury, damage to property, and damage to one's reputation

tortuous: unlawful conduct that subjects a person to tort liability

totalitarian: the political concept that the citizen should be totally subject to an absolute state authority

treason: the offense of attempting to overthrow the government of one's own state or country

treaty: a binding international agreement

treaty clause: provision of the U.S. Constitution (Article II, section 2, clause 2) that grants the power to make treaties with foreign nations to the president, which are subject to approval by the Senate

truancy: skipping out of school

U

underwrite: to assume financial responsibility and risk for something

unilateral: undertaken by one person, party, or entity

United States Trade Representative (USTR): a cabinet-level official appointed by the president who has primary responsibility for directing U.S. trade policy and trade negotiations

unprecedented: not resembling something already in existence

unsolicited: not wanted or requested

V

veto: when the president returns a bill to Congress with a statement of objections

vigilante: a member of a self-appointed group of citizens who undertake law enforcement within their community without legal authority

W

waive: to give up voluntarily

waivers of immunity: legal statement that gives up the government's right to sovereign immunity (the doctrine that the government cannot be sued without its consent)

warrant: a document issued by a judge granting authority to do something

Watergate: the scandal following the break-in at the Democratic National Committee headquarters located in the Watergate apartment and office complex in Washington, D.C., in 1972

COURT CASE INDEX

Each entry has (in order): the case name and the year the act became law (in parenthesis). The numbers after the date denote the volume and page number(s) where information can be found in Major Acts of Congress.

CUMULATIVE INDEX